Gower
Handbook of Internal
Communication

To Tessa Smallbone, as promised in 1968,
and also to Margaret Morley.

GOWER HANDBOOK OF INTERNAL COMMUNICATION

Edited by Eileen Scholes
The ITEM Group

Gower

Published by
Gower Publishing Limited
Gower House
Croft Road
Aldershot
Hampshire GU11 3HR
England

Gower
Old Post Road
Brookfield
Vermont 05036
USA

Reprinted 1998

British Library Cataloguing in Publication Data

Gower handbook of internal communication
   1. Business communication 2. Communication in management
   I. Scholes, Eileen II. Handbook of internal communication
   658.4'5

ISBN 0 566 07700 0

Library of Congress Cataloging-in-Publication Data

Gower handbook of internal communication / edited by Eileen Scholes,
   the ITEM Group.
      p.   cm.
   Includes index.
   ISBN 0-566-07700-0 (cloth)
   1. Communication in personnel management.   2. Communication in
  management.   I. Scholes, Eileen.
  HF5549.5.C6G69   1997
  658.4'5—dc21   96–45168
                                                    CIP

Typeset in Cheltenham and Fenice by Raven Typesetter, Chester
and printed in the United Kingdom at the University Press, Cambridge

Contents

PART VI   IC STRATEGY AT WORK

List of figures

List of contributors

Stuart Bayliss, director, Alexander Consulting Group Communication Practice

John Bishop, general manager, Communications Department, BP Chemicals

Joan Campbell, marketing project coordinator, F.I. Group

Lyn Cannings, UK Speak Up! coordinator, IBM

Chris Carey, internal communications manager, Comet Group

David Clutterbuck, chairman, The ITEM Group

Liz Cochrane, communications manager, Glaxo Operations

Kim Fernihough, formerly general manager, public relations, DO IT ALL

Susan Foreman, lead tutor in marketing, Henley Management College

Anna Foster, employee communications and quality manager, Bass Taverns

Robert Greenshields, account director, Pauffley PRL

James Harkness, head of internal communications, The Body Shop

David James, communication consultant, The ITEM Group

Roy Johnson, managing director, PACE Ltd

Mike Long, managing director,The ITEM Group

Toby Maloney, vice-president and director of internal communication and services, SmithKline Beecham

Tony Newbold, specialist business writer

Angela Newman, WOW TV/Bright Ideas coordinator, WH Smith Retail

Mike Reed, Clayton Reed Associates

Paul Samuels, formerly head of IC, Digital UK

Nick Throp, communication consultant, Sedgwick Noble Lowndes

Judith Trafford MIPR, publicity manager, Kent County Council

Richard Varey, director of the BNFL corporate communications unit at the University of Salford

Susan Walker, managing director, MORI Human Resource Research

Jon White, visiting professor, public affairs, City University Business School, London

John Williams, managing director, Fishburn Hedges

Nicholas Wright, head of employee communications, The Boots Company

Preface

'Civilisation is an enormous improvement on the lack thereof'
PJ O'Rourke, *Holidays in Hell*.

Ten years ago, if you had tried to find out about Internal Communication you would have been pulled in an assortment of directions: a management hand-book chapter here, a media production manual there, maybe an article in a public relations or personnel industry magazine.

It is less of a problem these days. The thought that IC can be a strategic tool, rather than a strictly welfare one, has begun to enter the management psyche. There are signs of its emergence as a distinct management discipline, reporting direct to the CEO or organizational head. Such developments have in turn prompted books, technical reports and surveys, and even regular newsletters and magazines, all dedicated to the subject.

Still it seemed to me and the rest of ITEM's senior consultant team that the field lacked some kind of 'central' reference work. We felt there was a need for something which aimed at being comprehensive – although we realized that IC is likely to remain fragmented for some time to come and that any such first attempt could hardly hope to meet the aspirations of the many interest groups in the specialist IC community.

Thankfully, Gower agreed with us: the *Handbook* became a project and, now a reality.

WHY YOU SHOULD CONTINUE TO READ THIS PREFACE

The *Handbook* makes numerous assumptions that you need to be aware of. It has to, because IC is still a developing area. Both theory and practice have a considerable way to go before consensus is achieved at even the most basic levels. That only makes it more important to 'define our terms'.

So what is IC?

There are still those who think of IC as media-based support for an organization's top managers in passing messages 'down' to other employees. My own view, shared by most of the *Handbook*'s contributors, is that IC can usefully take on a much expanded brief: the professional management of interactions between all those with an interest – or 'a stake' – in a particular organization.

The 'professional management' element of that definition signifies a more rigorous and performance-related approach to IC, setting it within business and financial contexts. The newer definition also expands IC's scope from one-way message-giving to facilitating profitable interchange. That in turn leads to IC's having a role in setting the cultural context for communication and ensuring that the people involved have not just the tools but the awareness and the skills they need to play their part.

And while the emphasis remains on employees, there is growing acceptance that IC's *inclusive* approaches and techniques can add considerable value to communication with such groups as suppliers, investors, neighbours and, in some circumstances, customers.

And what should the IC professional offer?

It follows that today's IC practitioner must be able to perform on a much wider range of fronts than in the past, cutting across the traditional boundaries of HR, PR and marketing expertise, for example. We assume the need to:

- be familiar with the business context (in particular the need to manage change), the role of strategic planning and of IC within it, also research methods and statistical interpretation, and budgeting
- relate to the work of other corporate functions, for example recruitment and induction, reward and recognition, community relations
- have an understanding of organizational dynamics and at least the basics of behavioural psychology
- have skills in facilitation, handling feedback mechanisms, consultancy, seminar handling and even training – at least to a sufficient level to understand their potential and how to manage their provision.

All this, of course, comes on top of having a broad, up-to-the-minute awareness of relevant media and technologies.

WHAT CAN YOU EXPECT FROM THE *HANDBOOK*?

Anyone who knows ITEM would have predicted that this *Handbook* begins and ends with the aim of being of practical use. We know from direct experience with our own clients and from IC practitioners who belong to ASPIC (Association for Strategic Planning in Internal Communication), that the great majority are still fire fighting most of the time. And that many more people are coming into communication roles with no preparation.

That's why, in addition to addressing subject areas directly, the *Handbook* does not give 'academic references' at the end of each chapter but concentrates on opening up routes to further information or help. The least the *Handbook* should do is provide you with useful information here and there. At best, it will become a regular companion, helping you to exercise much greater control over events and people around you.

Of course, what you can take from the *Handbook* largely depends on who you are and what you need to do. While casting a wide net, I have had in mind some specific needs. So here again, there are a number of assumptions, starting with the obvious one – that you have some form of professional interest.

Are you a newcomer?

You could be a complete novice to this area – a fast-track generalist manager, for example. Let's say you have been given the nebulous remit to 'improve internal communication', or to handle communication relating to a particular initiative. One of the *Handbook*'s principal aims is to provide an all-round, practical introduction to IC, bringing together in a single book what has up to now been a scattered array of knowledge, opinion, techniques and experience.

Or you may be a manager with line responsibilities – at senior, team or supervisory level. Maybe at this stage you are only vaguely conscious of what improvements in communication might do to help you bring out the best qualities in your people. You're anxious to find out more without, or before, putting yourself in the hands of a consultant, for example.

Or an old hand?

Of course you could equally well be someone who has a background in professional communication. Maybe, like most people currently in IC, you came into it via journalism, PR, events management, marketing, even training or HR. Now you see it becoming necessary to broaden your awareness of other communication disciplines, and to add to your wider strategic and planning capabilities. The *Handbook* is designed to provide you with new perspectives and good practice examples which will move you on and, with any luck, up.

One skill most IC people need today is *buying*, since few organizations now hold substantial communication resources in house. Throughout the *Handbook*, there are tips and checklists to put you in control of such situations, helping you to realize the best deal for your organization. If you are in an agency, by contrast, it should sharpen your appreciation of the standards you should be aspiring to in order to meet current client needs.

Even if you are a highly-experienced all-rounder, the *Handbook* strives in every area not to stay locked into today's thinking but to open at least one fresh door.

Finally, you may belong to the new generation of academics and students involved in this growing field. One function of the *Handbook* is to put on display *xix* the many challenges facing people and organizations as IC develops, all of which provide scope for additional research and new ideas.

If you recognize your role or aspiration among any of these, the *Handbook* has been designed to help your use IC to improve an organization's prospects – and in so doing, I hope, your own.

How does the *Handbook* work?

Broadly, my aim has been to give you the means to add value by:

- making good decisions about what needs doing
- making it happen in a quality way
- 'proving' the effect you have had
- learning from it.

Part I will help you to take part in mutually beneficial exchanges about IC, for example with senior functional or line managers.

Part II is there to help you start putting together a properly-targeted, convincing plan of action.

Part III is your passport into the domain of IC's 'black arts', from face-to-face techniques to tips on using modern technologies. Organized for quick reference, it is geared to helping you make informed decisions between, and about, the many different means by which you can elect to achieve your plan.

Part IV moves you on to thinking about the development side of communication – people and systems.

Part V is about measurement: it sets you on the road to collecting and analysing data on IC performance, both with a view to informing your decisions about future communication and as a means to attract the support you need at all levels.

Part VI is where all the elements of the picture fit together – practical examples of how managers like you have used IC to tackle challenges in 16 different organizations.

OTHER ASSUMPTIONS YOU SHOULD KNOW ABOUT

There's a growing view that IC could do itself a favour by making a distinction between communication (the result) and communications (the means). Some, I know, will see this as simply a nicety. For me, the distinction represents exactly that shift in focus needed to spread recognition of IC (that is, Internal Communication) as a strategic function and a genuine participator in business, rather than a producer of media deliverables. Most *Handbook* contributors have welcomed the switch and found it easy to follow through – though there may be a few places where old habits have proved stubborn.

Most chapter authors have tended to assume the 'organization' to be a commercial one and the bulk of case study material currently stems from private sector experience. This is an imbalance that any future edition of the *Handbook* will attempt to redress, especially as the most recent Industrial Society survey shows public sector spending on communication to be proportionately higher.

One last 'assumption' the *Handbook* makes. Some people in and around IC (particularly those locked into the HR/PR debate) tend to focus on 'face-to-face' communication and are rather dismissive of 'media' solutions. I see continuing reference to and emphasis on that particular distinction only hindering IC's progress as a strategic discipline. In the *Handbook* (as in most dictionaries) the word media covers *all* means of communication. The position taken is that, as between all other forms of media, differences arise only in the suitability of any given approach for a particular context, and in the skills and facilities needed for successful implementation. The *Handbook* adopts a strategic viewpoint, therefore, and looks at each method of communicating as a potentially manageable medium, open to the same analysis as any other in terms of benefit potential, new opportunities provided and output to be measured.

ONE FINAL WORD ON TERMINOLOGY

There's no doubt that IC needs to develop a more rigorous approach in various areas. One of the most important is thinking about how communication actually travels in and around an organization. We could do worse than start by tightening up our language. For example, many of us use words like 'channels', 'links' and 'routes', 'media', and 'vehicles' interchangeably, and to cover everything from events to print media. We can little afford to continue with such fuzzy thinking, especially when it comes to survey questions and audits, for example.

One useful option would be to follow marketing practice and restrict 'channel' to meaning a route between people: 'media' would be the word for the delivery mechanisms which fill it. A 'channel' would always exist – say between the CEO and the shopfloor – though it can be full or empty, becoming bypassed or blocked or even develop a gap: 'media' come and go, are adapted and rejuvenated, according to need. I would be grateful for comment on that and indeed for feedback and suggestions on any aspect of the *Handbook* for inclusion in any future edition.

SEXUAL REFERENCE

Handbooks are not designed to be read left to right. You could do worse than begin by turning to page 390 in the Glaxo case study, where a quote from an attendee at a change event will give you a standard to aspire to. After taking part in a successful communication event, he announced to the company at large that it had been 'better than having sex'.

Happy reading.

Eileen Scholes

Acknowledgements

I am grateful to all the chapter and case study authors, and also to a number of other people for their less visible but no less valuable contributions. They are:

Sarah Anderson
Andy Clarke
Cami Evans
Valerie Fletcher
David Glynn
Fiona Hamman
Sheila Hirst
Chrissy Kimmons
Archie Lennox
Peter Mulvany
Chris Noone
Hugh Price
Jamie Scholes
Sue Sharp
Malcolm Stern
Dr John Vorhaus
David Watson
Bernard Wynne

Marilyn Arnott
Paul Cronk
Julie Farnworth
Linda Gatley
Gwen Gober
Ian Hawkins
Paul Johnson
James King
Elizabeth Lennox
David Nicoll
Emma Norcliffe
Peter Roe
Audrey Shanks
Richard Smelt
Dianne Thompson
Simon Ward
Ian Watson

Jo Chapple
Jenny Davenport
Annie Fennimore
Hilary Gibbons
Richard Grimes
Frank Martin Hein
Caroline Khambatta
Domna Lazidou
Alison Moore
Frank Nigriello
Mike Poundsford
Tom Scholes
Solveig Gardner Servian
Vicky Staveacre
Gill Tickner
Anne Watson
Jennifer Watson

From that list, I must single out Ian Hawkins. Ian's efforts to produce a wide-ranging guide to development opportunities in internal communication were not rewarded by full chapter status. That is largely because higher education courses directly relevant to IC, though increasing, are as yet thin on the ground. A round-up of what is available appears instead as an appendix within Part IV (see pp. 256–259).

ES

Introduction

David Clutterbuck, *chairman, The ITEM Group*

As a management discipline, Internal Communication (IC) is still remarkably new. The largest survey ever of IC departments in the UK, conducted in 1995 by an ITEM team for Business Intelligence, found that more than half were five years old or under, many of them less than two. The survey also found that many IC departments were still at a very early stage of evolution – 41 per cent did not even have their own budget, for example.

The sudden emergence of IC as a significant corporate player, and its acceptance (albeit sometimes grudgingly) into the strategic framework, can be seen as the result of a combination of problems faced by the top management team.

HOW DID WE GET WHERE WE ARE?

Cost-cutting and new technology have brought chronic industrial relations problems – in both public and private sector organizations – for several years now. Early on, problems were exacerbated by the fact that trade union sources managed to reach people before management did. One response to this was the widespread adoption of team briefings, for example.

Competition has also meant that organizational inefficiencies can no longer be tolerated (including the 'bureaucracy' of layers of middle management, now blamed for diluting strategic plans out of existence). Quality circles and other problem-solving team formats required by aspirations to 'world-class standards' have become part of the regular cycle of management and of communication.

Wider share ownership and profit-related pay have followed as yet more responses to increasing external standards and competitive pressures. *xxv*

Organizations have begun looking for greater 'involvement' and 'innovation' from employees, which has also accounted for the appearance of so many mission statements and the attempt to sign people up to them. Then there has been the search for new ways to attract and motivate the right people in the post 'job-for-life' era.

IMPACT ON EXISTING MEDIA

The regular internal publication – up to now (and still largely) the core communication effort – was initially funded as an industrial relations tool (hence its traditional association with the HR function) but one which set out only to provide a social record and to make people feel part of a family. At its best, often, it was handled without management 'interference', either in the selection or the content of stories.

Today's best equivalents are very different. They are a conscious management tool, and at the same time much more genuinely reader-focused. They tend to be targeted not necessarily just at all employees but at specific groups, including other important internal audiences like suppliers, third party users and so on. And they have much clearer goals, usually centred on education, culture change, best practice exchange and helping achieve an effective alignment of personal and organization goals. Many have also shifted away from print – or spawned supplementary versions in other formats, like TV, video, audio and e-mail.

The employee annual report, pioneered by companies such as GKN, was one early side-effect: people needed more information before they would believe that the bonus to be shared was indeed fairly calculated. Since then, some companies have moved on to sharing the business plan – or at least detailed aspects of strategy and performance indicators – through conferences, briefings, videos and roadshows.

IMPACT ON SYSTEMS

Aside from media, organizations have done some analysis of patterns in day-to-day communication, and some have revised forums and networks to suit organizational or cultural changes. A few have begun systematic upgrading of awareness and skill levels among managers and others asked to participate.

Last, but far from least, organizations – and individuals within them – have been trying to cope with the current impact and future potential of new communications technologies.

Much as these changes have been happening at the same time time, however, they have been largely composed of discrete, almost unconnected activities. It was not – still is not – unusual to see them spread among several functions in the organization, most usually HR/Personnel, Corporate Relations/PR and Marketing – and to an extent, IT.

TURNING POINT

The turning point for IC may well have been when management perceived the need to articulate and communicate its 'vision' more widely. The underlying concept probably is valid: create a unifying purpose, which everyone can understand and commit to – and the organization will be much stronger. In practice, most mission statements turned out to be trite, uninspiring and rapidly forgotten.

Ironically, it was the shock of this communication failure that made many top management teams begin to think about IC in a different light. What tools were at their disposal to influence the way people thought and behaved? The old methods of creating a 'family feeling' on the one hand, and of stick and carrot on the other, operated through the discipline and reward processes, were having less and less effect on an increasingly educated workforce. The realization dawned that they would have to talk and listen to the workforce and that doing this was an important part of *their* job.

The more recent realization that communication failures between the functional silos, and between head office and the front line, are serious barriers to the effective delivery of organizational goals is also fuelling the development of an IC function with its own identity, which forms a focus for the integration of the various activities.

SO WHERE IS IC HEADED?

Predicting the future is always dangerous, even when it extrapolates from what appear to be strong current trends. For a start, different organizations and cultures will generate different solutions to the communication problems they face. However, from what we know and can guess about the future needs of organizations, the following predictions seem relatively safe.

IC will in a high proportion of organizations become a stand-alone department

The more IC carves out a distinct role for itself, the more it will need to maintain effective links – standing committees or project team structures – with other functions, especially Corporate Communications/PR and HR/Personnel. How well those links operate will determine, in large part, whether IC retains its independence. It will report to the chief executive or to a subcommittee of the board, and have a fairly wide remit in influencing the internal environment of the organization.

IC will play an advisory/consultancy role at the centre

Implementation and administration will largely rest in the field. This has substantial implications for the competence requirements of IC professionals at the centre. They will become involved in a core set of strategic activities, built around:

- helping top management define key messages
- increasing the communication competence of the organization as a whole, particularly line managers (working with HR)
- ensuring that new communication technology really does improve communication
- maximizing the efficiency and impact of new communication vehicles
- actively helping build new culture (working with HR and top management).

Audience segmentation and measurement will become integral parts of all IC activities

The focus of measurement will spread from its present emphasis on how people feel about a particular publication, for example, to direct support for organizational objectives (e.g. has it helped change attitudes and behaviours in line with desired culture change objectives?).

IC professionals will increasingly need to have spent some time in line management

This experience will be necessary to gain credibility and personal understanding of the difficulties of day-to-day communication. Conversely, a period in IC will increasingly be seen as a beneficial career move for ambitious line managers.

The breadth and depth of demands on the IC function will increase

Increased demand will occur as IC proves what it can contribute. Other functions will involve IC in helping develop and implement their own internal marketing plans and in measuring the impact of initiatives.

IC will have to help the organization establish better control over communications technology

Leaving control in the hands of the IT department is like letting the wolf guard the sheep.

Should all these trends continue, the brave new world could look something like the fictional account which follows. This may at least provide a useful image for any professionals in this field as they struggle with current barriers and limitations.

A DAY IN THE LIFE OF A FUTURE INTERNAL COMMUNICATION MANAGER

6.30 a.m.   *The IC manager wakes up to a proof of the company electronic newspaper on screen, put together daily in the small hours by a small editorial team. S/he makes a few comments, before it is sent to every employee's terminal. In some cases, the newspaper is printed off before they arrive and left at their desk or machine.*

9.30 a.m.   *On the desk when s/he arrives is a daily report of communication breakdowns from the joint IC/Quality team steering group. Employees report routinely whenever a Quality cost is incurred as a result of communication failure. . . .*

Also on the desk is a revised schedule for communication training. Real-time evaluation of each segment of the new presentation skills course for supervisors last week shows that people lost interest (and therefore didn't take in the message) in Sessions 3 and 5. The HR manager has already left an e-mail message suggesting a meeting to resolve the problem.

10.30 a.m.   *A meeting with the top management team to discuss its credibility rating. Also present is the external relations director, who has figures for credibility among key external audiences. Both show a worrying recent decline.*

The two also share responsibility (with HR) for community investment and employee volunteering. Some companies have developed a combined department – Stakeholder Communication – which co-ordinates communication between and to key internal and external audiences. Shareholders are increasingly seen as an internal audience, now that the concept of shareholder responsibility has been recognized in company law.

The meeting with the top team takes an hour and a half and results in an outline strategy that involves increasing the number and reducing the length of strategic briefings by the top team.

12.00 p.m.   *As s/he is about to leave the meeting, one of the directors brings up a complaint from managers that a high volume of customers taking advantage of the on-line facility to check on the progress of their orders was slowing down operational computers. Is there a way to manage when people call, to avoid the problem? The IC manager promises to look into it with the IT manager.*

12.30 p.m.   *This reminds the marketing director that there has been little progress in reducing the volume of order cancellations from customers – would it be worth discussing over lunch whether this might be a matter of poor communication (wrong expectations),*   xxix *rather than poor products? The IC manager promises to arrange some research and produce some recommendations.*

2.00 p.m.   *Back in the office, the IC manager finds the regular monthly report by one of his/her team on the quality of correspondence. Outgoing mail is sampled randomly across the month. An internal evaluation reviewing clarity, precision and appropriate tone is supplemented by telephone interviews with internal and external customers (people who received the letters and memos). An increase has been highlighted in the jargon count in correspondence from the property department for the third month in a row. S/he makes a note to investigate further.*

2.30 p.m.   *The six-monthly review of the company's World-Class Communication programme is due in two weeks and there is still much work to be done on the draft report. A series of experiments has been launched each year for the past five years and, as expected, there is a mixture of results from spectacular success to complete failure.*

4.30 p.m.   *The IC manager is pleased to receive an e-mailed report that suggests that the current campaign to switch team briefings from being supervisor-delivered to being delivered in rotation by other members of the work teams is going well. There had been a hesitant start, as people doubted their competence to present formally to their team mates, but training and practice have overcome most of their fears.*

Regular samplings – like this one – after each briefing are beginning to indicate a slow but steady growth in the confidence both of the presenters and of the audience in the messages they are hearing. (Persuading top managers to allow team presenters to gather the information in person, in question and answer sessions, before the official briefing papers were published, had done a great deal for credibility.)

5.00 p.m.   *S/he is puzzled to see so few sign-ups for the new training course for people willing to act as correspondents for the various internal periodicals. Everyone's willingness to contribute had appeared to be increasing thanks to universal access to computerized networks. (All periodicals now appeared both in print and in multimedia screen versions – the latter accessed via tailored 'home' pages with options for business line, site, corporate and special interest pages designed to encourage sharing of ideas and best practice.)*

A short discussion with the field internal communication manager entrusted to manage this project on behalf of the group reveals that time constraints had meant that the normal audience research had been left out of the process this time. They agree to carry out a short qualitative study and report to the monthly communication review meeting, chaired by the chief executive, under the regular agenda item 'Learning issues'.

Learning has in fact become one of the biggest areas of influence of IC. Once it had been widely recognized that learning depends heavily on communication (and vice versa), it was only a small step to develop a cross-functional steering committee, reporting direct to the board and responsible for building a Learning Organization. Remarkably, that piece of jargon was still accepted, not having been devalued by misuse. S/he takes a minute to reflect why, then puts it down as an interesting question for Internal Communication's Learning Team discussion, carried on through electronic mail and at regular best practice sharing sessions.

6.00 p.m.   *While in reflective mode, s/he looks up and notices a faded frame on the wall, reading Message–media–measurement.... How valid those fundamentals are, even now when the IC's status has evolved so much. The chime of the video-phone interrupts the cogitation. S/he checks to see who the caller is before switching on. Oh dear, this could be a long one: bang goes making it to the fitness class again. There's something else that hasn't changed either!*

Although this scenario is set in the future, most of the elements are already with us. There are IC departments that are already making ten-year plans to achieve world-class status, that already segment their audiences in detail and measure the impact of communication, that take an active role in promoting and managing complex culture change and in many of the other activities in this fictional manager's day.

All that is lacking in most organizations is the vision and the confidence to see what managed internal communication is capable of contributing to an organization. With the right leadership, both of the organization and of the IC function, this scenario isn't just possible; it is inevitable.

Part I
THE BUSINESS CONTEXT

1 IC's role in competitiveness and innovation

Jon White, *visiting professor, Public Affairs, City University Business School, London*

This chapter assesses the mounting case for a change in attitude among Britain's senior managers towards internal communication. It reviews evidence from British and international studies relating IC to competitiveness and innovation, and argues that it is to the UK's cost that our organizations have up to now largely ignored IC's potential as a source of business and operational advantage. In particular, it examines the need, currently overlooked in much management training and education, to prepare people for the communication tasks inherent in organizational roles.

There is no doubt about the importance of communication in and to organizations, even taken at the simplest and most obvious levels:

- organizations can themselves be regarded as communication structures
- the entire task of management can be reformulated in terms of communication: the primary task of management is to point to, and to communicate, the significance of aspects of organizational life
- without communication, organizations could not exist: they come into existence – moment-by-moment, day-by-day – in the interaction that takes place between organization members, and as a result of the communication between them.

Many studies have pointed to areas where communication is vital to the success of organizations. Yet it is still infrequently singled out for specific attention, and is often taken for granted. It is assumed that most people know how to communicate, that it is a skill learned in the early years of life and does not require re-examination in later life.

However, there are growing signs that the case for a more serious treatment of communication matters is mounting, along with acceptance of the need to develop the necessary skills.

In 1993, for example, senior executives from 25 leading UK businesses came together under the auspices of the RSA (Royal Society for the encouragement of Arts, Manufactures and Commerce). Led by Sir Anthony Cleaver, the then Chairman of IBM UK, they developed a shared vision of the successful company of the future, which was published in 1995 as the influential report, *Tomorrow's Company*. It concluded that tomorrow's company will be *inclusive*: it will actively communicate with, and involve a wide range of stakeholder groups, not just shareholders. High on this list of stakeholder groups will be those people who make up the organization, employees.

Three practical questions surface early in any consideration of the future development of communication in organizations.

- How can the importance of the communication be established on the business and management agenda, so that practical steps to use communication effectively can be taken?
- What are the key communication skills needed in business today, and how competent are managers in these key skills?
- How can standards for communication be set, and is it possible to evaluate the contribution that communication can make to organizational success?

PUTTING COMMUNICATION ON BRITISH MANAGEMENT'S AGENDA

In the UK, a number of reports have raised questions about current British management practice and, by implication, the extent to which managers in this country make effective use of communication.

The Sunday Times of 14 March 1993, reported on an internal study from the Department of Trade and Industry which, according to the newspaper, concluded that British industry is fundamentally weak and beset by inferior management and products. It said that managers are responsible for the 'hole in the heart' of British manufacturing. Compared to their overseas counterparts, they are poorly educated, ill-trained and failing to turn technology into products that will win out in world markets.

Research supported by Hedron, a London-based communication management consultancy, set out in the same year to find out what role communication may play in improvements to British management practice and the competitiveness of British industry. The study found that, although there is a dearth of convincing research that directly establishes the link between communication and business performance, studies from the 1970s onwards have argued for more attention to be paid to communication with employees, as a key to greater productivity, improved morale, stronger commitment to organizational goals and more job satisfaction.

The paradox revealed by the Hedron study was that while communication was much talked about, little was actually being done to improve communication practice. The study also found, in its review of international material, that failure to attend to communication is not unique to British approaches to management. What was instructive about the British situation was the number of reports concerned with attempts to improve the competitiveness of British business. In these, a number of factors – communication among them – are identified as crucial to competitive performance.

Establishing the link with competitiveness

A pessimistic view of Britain's industrial competitiveness was set in the *World Competitiveness Reports* produced by the World Economic Forum and the International Institute for Management Development. This shows that Britain has lost ground in recent years. In 1995 it was ranked 18th out of 22 leading industrialized countries, down five places from its position in 1992.

Competitiveness for a firm is defined in a memorandum from the Department of Trade and Industry to the Parliamentary Trade and Industry Committee's *Enquiry into Competitiveness of UK Manufacturing Industry* (1994) as 'selling the right product at the right price, thereby satisfying customer needs more efficiently than competitors'. The memorandum states that for a nation, competitiveness is the degree to which it can, under free and fair market conditions, produce goods and services that meet the test of international markets while simultaneously maintaining and expanding the real incomes of its citizens. It stresses that competitiveness for a firm or nation cannot be measured using a single measure. A range of measures are needed, but among determinants of competitiveness are productivity, innovation, quality of management and the skills of the workforce.

According to a recent memorandum from the Department of Trade and Industry, a country's competitiveness will be influenced by:

- the macroeconomic climate, which, through low inflation and sound public finances, provides a base for industry to prosper
- the commercial setting: the culture, environment and regulatory framework within which business has to operate
- competition within the national economy
- the education and training of the workforce
- sources of finance
- innovation
- involvement in international trade
- inward investment
- size, mobility, flexibility and skill levels of the available pool of labour
- management
- physical infrastructure
- purchasing practices, for example by public procurement agencies.

The DTI memorandum considers recent British experience in each of the areas listed above – two of which, education and training, and management, are especially relevant in considerations of the uses made of communication. For example, in education and training, the country's low skills base has been cited as one of the reasons for the productivity gap between the UK and its competitors. General standards of educational attainment are lower in Britain than in France, Germany, Japan and other countries. The best of British management is as good as the best in the world, but the quality of management is described as uneven. The country's record on innovation is below average.

Establishing the link with innovation

Innovation is an essential feature of industrial competitiveness. Akio Morita, Chairman of the Board of the Sony Corporation, said in the 1992 UK Innovation Lecture that the successful exploitation of new ideas is central to sustained wealth creation and maintaining corporate advantage. 'The innovation process begins with a mandate which must be set at the highest levels of the corporation by identifying goals and priorities – and once identified these must be communicated all the way down the line.' Moreover, the mandate can succeed only in an environment that nurtures it.

According to a study of innovation completed in early 1993 by the DTI's Innovation Unit and the Confederation of British Industry's Technology Group, innovative firms have larger market shares and higher growth rates and profits than non-innovators. A handbook on communication and innovation from the DTI's Innovation Advisory Board also stresses that the correlation between long-term sales growth and innovation is indisputable.

The DTI/CBI study found that only one in ten of the British companies surveyed could be described as truly innovative, although five in ten showed elements of good performance. Innovation, which is described as the process of taking new ideas effectively through to satisfied customers, depends on a willingness to accept change and regard it as an opportunity. It also depends on a culture that is conducive not only to managed risk taking, but also to an open communicative style of management.

Communication is one of the main factors contributing to innovation, which is seen in the DTI/CBI report as synonymous with good management. The best companies have a clear sense of mission and purpose, and have communicated it throughout the organization. The DTI memorandum referred to earlier suggests that quality of management is probably the key issue in innovation.

Establishing the link with education and training

A report from the CBI's Manufacturing Advisory Group – *Competing with the World's Best*, 1991 – addresses discrepancies in company performance. Companies, according to the report, need to accelerate improvement in their own performance, and to broaden their understanding of what constitutes good management practice. The report, unlike other recently published analyses of British industry, suggests that the state of the manufacturing nation is better than is generally recognized, but that there is a need for greater emphasis on management education and development. There is also a need to involve employees in the development and implementation of company strategies through programmes of total communication, which build commitment and draw on the full capability of company human resources.

Commentary by the Industrial Society on the Bullock Report (1977), which advocated increased industrial democracy, suggested that 'the problem of Britain as an industrial nation is not a lack of native capacity in its working population so much as a failure to draw out their energies and skill to anything like their full potential'.

Management is partly blamed for this failure in studies by the CBI as far back as 1976 of priorities for in-company communications, and by Market and Opinion Research International in 1985 of working people's attitudes.

Commentary in the *World Competitiveness Reports* points out that the country's future depends on how it ranks in terms of the education and preparation of its workforce, its skills and attitudes, and the quality of management. The country's people are described in the report as having the least energy and enthusiasm in the whole of the industrialized world, and the lack of quality in the country's workforce is compounded by lack of senior management competence.

The report suggests that competitiveness cannot be attained if people are treated like disposable assets. Drastic reductions of employment, although perhaps necessary for short-term business advantages of streamlining operating costs, have the long-term effects of destroying corporate credibility and cohesion.

The possible effects of recent developments on British employees have been noted in a finding of the International Survey Research Organisation, reported in the *Financial Times* of 14 June 1993, that British employees are the most dissatisfied of all employees surveyed, identify least with their organizations and feel most insecure in their jobs. By contrast, Swiss employees are the most satisfied, followed by the Dutch. In the World Economic Forum's 1993 survey of competitiveness, these two countries rank fourth and sixth respectively.

Reviewing the complete picture

Recent research into Britain's competitiveness and the competitiveness of its companies show it to have the following features:

- after a long period of decline, Britain's competitiveness, industrial productivity and share of world trade are showing some signs of improvement
- even so, Britain is still slipping down the list of the world's wealthiest nations
- a number of steps have been taken to address the factors that contribute to competitiveness – despite public perceptions and experience to the

7

contrary, efforts have been made by government to create an environment in which business and industry can thrive: attention has been given to improving education and training, and to management education and development; good management practice has been studied and, through the Management Charter Initiative, national efforts have been made to improve management practice

● efforts to improve the country's competitiveness will need to continue on a number of fronts, but it will be essential to guard against complacency as progress is made. For example a study of participation in technological change carried out in 1990 by the European Foundation for the Improvement of Living and Working Conditions found that British management is becoming increasingly paternalistic in style, moving away from involving employees in changes that affect them.

For a practical – if extreme – example of why companies need to get better at internal communication, we need look no further than the much-publicized Brent Spar case involving the Shell oil company in 1995.

Shell had decided to dispose of the Brent Spar, one of its large seagoing platforms, at sea. It had taken the view, on what it regarded as the best available evidence, that this was the most appropriate and safest way of making the disposal. But it ran into increasing opposition from pressure groups and consumers at large, alarmed at the precedent the company would be setting in disposing of redundant equipment at sea. After seeming at first to stick to its guns, the company eventually changed its decision.

Initial information suggests that a failure in internal communication contributed significantly to Shell's predicament. Management had clearly been taken by surprise at the strength of public reaction. As pressure built, it was experienced by different parts of the company in different ways. It is not yet clear whether internal communication links allowing for realistic assessments of pressure were in place, or, if in place, whether they were working. Such links could surely have helped the company, even after the initial problems, to make its case and win support.

Communication at a time of crisis can take place where there is a real threat to the organization and its interests, as well as, possibly, to lives and personal safety. Such situations are characterized by the element of surprise involved – key people are not in their places – and by the stress experienced by decision-makers forced to take risks in the absence of complete information.

Communication management is vital to crisis management. Information needs to flow more effectively than ever, internally and externally. Yet communication links are often the first to break at time of crisis, as systems set up to cope with routine management requirements become overloaded.

The Brent Spar case suggests that management groups need to consider how communication can be managed in non-routine circumstances as well as day-to-day operations, and that an emphasis on the former might well aid improvements in the latter.

KEY COMMUNICATION SKILLS IN BUSINESS TODAY

The 1991 report from the Price Waterhouse/Cranfield School of Management project, which looked at international human resource management, pointed out that the recent recession had brought to prominence the need for education and communication, adding another facet to change management. In all ten countries in which the study was carried out, the project team found that training in communicating with staff is widespread, reflecting the importance of the subject.

So far, however, managers continue to prove reluctant to communicate with employees on financial and strategic issues. According to the report (page 20): 'Managers seem to concentrate on feeding themselves and each other with information, neglecting the important task of taking their staff and organisations with them.'

And, according to Marchington *et al.*'s study *New Developments in Employee Involvement* (1992), communication skills are still seen as 'soft management' by practising managers, particularly in manufacturing, and they are not given sufficient attention in programmes of management education and development.

Yet the ability to communicate, and to develop an understanding of how communication can help achieve objectives, are both key management skills. Few managers ever stop to consider the real nature of the communication skills involved in their work, some examples of which follow.

- *Sense-making* – making sense of confusing and complex information under conditions of uncertainty and inadequate information so that courses of action can be developed and described to allow for action: outcomes of this process include statements setting out organizational mission, vision and values, objectives and plans.
- *Listening skills* – considered broadly, listening skills involve research, to detect and gather information on concerns felt throughout the organization and by individuals, as well as interpersonal skills in listening.
- *Presentation skills* – the skills usually thought of under this heading, but also interpersonal skills that enable individuals to explain themselves clearly to others.
- *Media skills* – skills in using different means of communication, such as electronic and print media, including such specific tools as e-mail, video, publications and other written forms of communication.
- *Self-awareness and empathy* – self-awareness involves consciousness of emotional states and of the requirements of role performance, for example as a manager or as an adviser; empathy is the skill of seeing the world as though from the perspective of another.

Communication is not simply a matter of passing information, but is more concerned with the transference of understanding. Managers have not been found particularly willing or skilful in this task.

Indeed, the gulf of distrust between managers and employees is attributed to lack of communication skills on the part of managers (Coulson-Thomas 1992). A *Fortune* magazine article (3 June 1991), on champions of communication, included the estimate that only 10 per cent of corporate senior managers are effective communicators, able to talk candidly with employees and encourage their participation and contribution of ideas.

On both sides of the Atlantic, the characteristics of effective management style rated most favourably are positive leadership allied to a warm disposition (*The Independent*, 4 July 1989).

The US management training organization Psychological Associates and People Skills International carried out a study in London, involving leading Fortune 500 companies. According to its findings, the most important leadership qualities include listening to and understanding the needs of others, and their feelings and ideas. In the USA, lack of communication was seen by 71 per cent of respondents as the most prevalent fault of poor management. In Britain, 63 per cent believed the main fault of poor management to be acquiescence and a lack of positive direction.

It is clear that any one manager, or other individual, is unlikely to have all the skills identified as key skills for communication. In larger, well-resourced organizations, the skills may be acquired as part of tailored programmes developed by in-house or external specialists. For the smaller organization, or the individual, skills can be developed through ad hoc external training or on-the-job development. Either way, skills will be developed only if they are *seen to be needed* – that is if their absence has clear organizational or personal consequences. Predictably perhaps, therefore, the place to look for changes in attitude to internal communication, is in organizations that are themselves under pressure to change.

The influence of change situations

A typical example is AEA Technology, a new creation dating from April 1994, but which until then was the trading name used by the United Kingdom Atomic Energy Authority. The name is now reserved for the authority's commercial division, privatized in March 1996, under the chairmanship of Sir Anthony Cleaver.

Over recent years, the organization has been restructured a number of times – a staff complement of over 40 000 people in the early 1960s is now down to 4000. In preparation for privatization, the division's highly qualified staff, for the most part committed to the AEA's old culture based on scientific, research and public service values, have had to come to terms with commercial practices and realities, and for many this has been hard.

Kevin Murray was then the division's director of corporate affairs. His department was created to provide a central corporate communication service to support the organization through change and in achieving its commercial and privatization objectives.

Murray's approach was to use research to help management learn to listen to its internal audiences in a structured way and to respond to what they hear. Among the techniques employed:

- *e-mail*, used to poll staff on the future direction of the organization, and its purpose and values; the findings used as a basis for workshops around the country; workshop feedback used to help shape management decisions and forward planning
- *staff surveys* following each issue of the internal newsletter
- *questionnaire surveys* following management presentations, including roadshows (much to the initial discomfort of managers involved)
- plans for *electronic newsletters*, with a built-in facility for instant feedback to questions about content.

Murray reports that people have responded well to this direct approach and management has been encouraged by that. As a result, there is now an implicit deal between managers and staff to engage in a continuous dialogue aimed at continuous improvement. Opinion research has also been conducted among important external groups, such as customers and financial analysts.

Murray lists the following benefits that can be looked for from improved listening:

- managers begin to show that they care
- employees become more involved
- planning improves
- performance improves, including the quality of work produced
- more emphasis on continuous improvement
- sharper competitive edge.

In general, Murray believes that managers and specialists alike have yet to realize the full benefits to be gained from listening to internal audiences. Next on his agenda is training managers in the skills involved in empathy, which he believes will change the nature of management itself. AEA Technology has already recognized the importance of supervisors and is investing particular effort in communicating with this group.

The role of confidence and trust

Managers need confidence in their ability to communicate, and to overcome a fear of not having all the answers (*Management Today*, April 1988). An open style of management requires strong managers, who have confidence, knowledge and skills (CBI 1979). Employees have to be able to trust and believe in their managers as sources of information. According to Seitel (1990), everyone who tracks employee opinion finds evidence of a trust gap between employer and employee. Drennan, writing in *Management Today* (1988), suggests that psychologically the company and managers are like substitute parents to the employee.

A number of studies point to discrepancies between managers' perceptions and employees' perceptions of the effectiveness of communication in UK companies. The CBI's 1991 study *Competing with the World's Best* reported on a CBI/KPMG finding that 65 per cent of companies surveyed felt that their communications were very good, good or adequate.

A study of employee opinion carried out in 1988 found that most employees were dissatisfied with current arrangements for workplace communication, and that there were discrepancies between management and employee perceptions of the effectiveness of communication (CBI/TUC/ACAS, reported in *Industrial Participation*, Summer 1988). An analysis of US data gathered by Towers Perrin found that employees felt that management was out of touch with the problems they faced in their jobs, and that management was unwilling to listen or to act on ideas (Foehrenbach and Goldfarb 1990). Similar results have been found in Britain. Employees are sceptical that ideas provided to management through responses to employee questionnaires will lead to any changes (*Financial Times*, 14 June 1993).

The influence of culture

Studies of different corporate cultures emphasize that high performance depends on open and free communication between all levels of organizations (Hampden-Turner 1990). Different national cultures have different preferences for steeper or flatter hierarchies, and stronger national economies have flatter hierarchies in their business organizations. Flatter hierarchies indicate a willingness on the part of managers to delegate authority. Of 30 countries ranked in terms of willingness of managers to delegate authority, Britain ranked 18th.

In Britain, a number of approaches to improving management communication with employees have been discussed over recent years. These discussions have reflected current social and political concerns. In the 1970s, debate centred on proposals for radical extensions of industrial democracy, which would allow employees representation on boards of directors (*The Bullock Report* 1977). The 1980s saw movement away from industrial democracy and participation by employees in management decision-making, to an emphasis on employee involvement. This approach relies on initiatives by management to improve communication with employees and enhance their contribution to the organization (Marchington *et al.*, 1992).

Employee involvement is viewed as an important component in the search for competitive advantage, but employees see the approach as of more benefit to employers than to themselves. The 1983 Institute of Directors *Guide to Boardroom Practice on Employee Involvement* describes employee involvement as an intrinsic part of management style and an active function that helps to harness the enthusiasm of employees to the achievement of better results.

How competent are UK managers in key communication skills?

British managers clearly have difficulties in preparing themselves for the communication requirements of their roles. These difficulties are cultural and attitudinal, and also stem in part from inadequacies in management education and training.

Culturally, it is a matter of concern that the country's 'brightest and best' do not go into management. As the House of Lords Select Committee on Science and Technology argued in 1991: 'The most urgent need is for a change in culture ... industry is held in low esteem and so attracts too little of the country's talent and other resources' (HMSO 1991).

Cross-cultural studies of management (Hofstede 1980, 1991) suggest that British managers prefer to take a laissez-faire approach to matters of employee relations and to work through negotiation rather than established procedures to the resolution of problems. At the same time, they are the product of what Hofstede calls a 'masculine' culture which subscribes to values of competition and assertiveness, rather than to values which allow for easier negotiation, listening and attendance to the needs of others.

The Institute of Directors *Guide to Boardroom Practice on Employee Involvement* (1983), emphasizes the need for 'powerful management' that will earn the respect necessary to secure employee commitment to success. The same document (page 6) also states that changes in employee attitudes to company success and competitiveness 'cannot occur if management policies and attitudes are based on an outdated autocracy or paternalism' that fails to recognize changed employee expectations.

The 1990 study of participation in technological change from the European Foundation for the Improvement of Living and Working Conditions suggests (page 10) that management in Britain is becoming increasingly paternalistic in style. An important question raised by Marchington *et al.* in their 1992 report on new developments in employee involvement concerns the extent to which employers believe that their employees are a long-term resource. They emphasize that the employee involvement programmes they studied were established during the upturn in economic activity in the late 1980s. Recent media commentary suggests that management is now treating staff with less consideration and less openly than before. It would appear that the recession, changes in employment patterns, and increasing use of part-time and contract staff, have all enabled management to forget the lessons of the past and believe that the fear of redundancy is all that is needed to keep people in line.

According to a 3i/Cranfield European Enterprise Centre study of managers in five European countries (*The Euro-Manager Survey* 6, 1993), British managers are likely to overestimate their performance on important aspects of the management role. In general, British managers rate themselves as the best managers in the five European countries studied, but their counterparts in France, Italy, Germany and Spain disagree and rate them as poor in terms of compassion – their chief weakness – and their ability to get on with others.

In summary, communication is a key skill in management, but it is not a skill   *13* that the majority of managers, in this country and others, have mastered. Beyond the cultural and attitudinal barriers to effective communication by British managers, there is a lack of appropriate education and training for this aspect of the managerial role.

Discussion of communication in management has occurred in the context of concerns for industrial democracy, participation and employee involvement. There is a danger that the importance of communication can be overlooked as fads in management thinking come and go. Communication with employees and employee involvement are part of a style of management, to be sustained over time.

British managers are rather more satisfied with communication within their organizations than employees, who feel that employee involvement schemes benefit employers rather than themselves. They are, on the basis of evidence reviewed, sceptical about management sincerity in communication and willingness to act on employee feedback.

British managers need to guard against complacency in their approach to communication, and to check their own attitudes to it. Their skills in communication are not highly regarded by their counterparts in other European countries, or by their employees. Their own attitudes are suspect: by some, communication is regarded as a part of 'soft management'; by others as a means to the end of improving corporate performance, carried forward without real commitment to the process of communication itself.

The general picture created by studies of management and internal communication is one in which managers, complacent of their skills in communication, fail to make adequate use of it, to be responsive to the concerns of members of their organizations and to make organizational requirements clear to them.

Traditional approaches to education and training take communication for granted, instead of ensuring first that participants have the developed communication skills that will enable them to derive maximum benefit from the remainder of their education or training experience.

The traditional management education degree syllabus provides an example. The typical master's level student studying for a degree in business administration will take required foundation courses in financial management and quantitative methods, but will be left to acquire communication skills through group work and to study communication as only one part of a course on all aspects of organization behaviour. The preparation may also include presentation skills, but these are seen as preparation for information-passing, rather than for communication. Communication, therefore, is not separated out at the beginning of the course as a key skill that will require development before full benefit can be derived from other parts of the course.

CAN NEW STANDARDS BE SET?

Management education and training came under scrutiny in the late 1980s, and reports such as the 1987 Handy Report *The Making of Managers* exposed some of the weaknesses of existing approaches to management education, including the lack of attention given to the development of communication skills.

The Management Charter Initiative, introduced in 1988, was intended to deal comprehensively with the standards of performance to be met by British managers. The initiative is aimed at improving the performance of British organizations by improving the quality of British managers. Standards for levels of performance for supervisory, first-line and middle managers have now been developed, but these do not deal specifically with required communication skills. The middle management standards, for example, refer to aspects of communication found throughout the standards, but communication is not dealt with separately and explicitly.

The Management Charter Initiative has the support of 1400 employers, employing more than 25 per cent of the country's workforce. 'Ultimately,' as the CBI's 1991 report on competitiveness (CBI 1991, p. 43) points out, 'it is the emphasis that UK manufacturers place on management training and development which will determine the extent of progress in this area.'

It is not obvious how traditional education and training can be changed to recognize the importance of communication: this Handbook may contribute to the debate.

A few programmes of management education have been modified to cover the topic of communication. Business schools in North America and Europe have been re-examining the content of management education, to look for ways in which some of the 'softer skills' such as communication and interpersonal skills can be incorporated into their programmes. For some years, Cranfield University's School of Management offered an elective covering public relations, public affairs and corporate communications to MBA students in the second half of their degree programme, and a similar change has been made more recently at City University Business School in London. But these courses are elective courses, taken by choice rather than as core courses. Although students taking the courses believe them to be highly relevant to management practice, covering core material, the subject of communication has yet to make a place for itself in the core management education programme.

Executive training and development activities tend to concentrate on group dynamics, on the ways in which top teams operate, rather than on skills such as communication which, again, are taken for granted or seen as too basic to merit detailed discussion at this level. Practical exercises that may form part of executive training require communication between participants, and the communication that takes place is discussed when experiences of the exercise are reconsidered.

There is strong demand for training that equips senior managers to communicate with and through the media, but this is concerned in the end with information transmission, with how to convey the organization's point of view or position without giving away information that might reflect adversely on the organization.

In the meantime, there is a role for consultants who specialize in work on *15* 'communication problems'. They are compelled to keep abreast of current practice and thinking regarding the uses of communication in organizations, and in many cases to carry out original research to take knowledge of the practice on. Smythe, Dorward, Lambert, The ITEM Group and Hedron, among other British communication management consultancies, and Towers Perrin, the international strategic human resources management consultancy with strong interests in internal communication, exemplify this approach. Smythe, Dorward, Lambert has set up a training activity as a result of its consultancy experience to transfer the knowledge it has acquired to others in the practice.

LOOKING AHEAD

The requirement to improve communication will move on to the management agenda, partly as a result of changes in the way businesses and other organizations are now having to structure themselves and operate. Appropriate education and training for communication will recognize that communication is a fundamental task in management, as well as in daily life and personal development.

Many organizations of the future will be more loosely-structured, with a changing membership bound together at a distance by electronic and intermittent communication. Emotion-based values, such as trust and commitment, will bind these organizations together, and these will be built through communication, reputation and behaviour.

For some managers, these suggestions will still seem too 'soft'. In the emphasis on results and precise business targets set in the face of increasing competition, how can time be taken to build trust and commitment?

Against this reservation, arguments produced in studies like the RSA's *Tomorrow's Company* (1995) suggest that success in future will in fact *depend* on taking the time to build relationships with all stakeholders. In this, communication has an obvious role to play, and there is a need to develop improved skills in communication now.

HOW TO FIND OUT MORE

Competing with the World's Best, CBI Manufacturing Advisory Group, CBI, London, 1991
'Communicating for change', *Internal Communication Focus* by C. Coulson-Thomas, Feb/March 1992
'Down the organisation', by D. Drennan, *Management Today*, June 1988
Employee Involvement – Shaping the Future for Business, CBI/KPMG, London, 1990
'Employee communications in the 90s: greater expectations', by J. Foehrenbach and S. Goldfarb (1990), *IABC Communications World*, May/June 1990
Enquiry into competitiveness of UK Manufacturing Industry, Department of Trade and Industry, London, January 1994
Getting the Message Across: improving communication between companies and

investors, Innovation Advisory Board, Department of Trade and Industry, London, 1993

Excellence in Public Relations and Communications Management, J. Grunig, L. Erlbaum and Associates (eds), Hillsdale, New Jersey, 1992

Economist Intelligence Unit Special Report by C. Hampden-Turner, Economist Intelligence Unit, 1990

Communication: why managers must do more, Hedron Consulting Limited, London, 1993

Culture and Organisations, by G. Hofstede, McGraw-Hill, Maidenhead, 1991

Culture's Consequences: international differences in work-related values, by G. Hofstede, Sage, Beverly Hills CA, 1980

Innovation in Manufacturing Industry, House of Lords Select Committee on Science and Technology, HMSO, 1991

Innovation – the Best Practice, Department of Trade and Industry, CBI, London, 1993

Institute of Directors, *Guide to Boardroom Practice on Employee Involvement*, London, 1983

Excellence in Public Relations and Communication Management International Association of Business Communicators, Data Report and Guide, 1991

The Benefits of Being an Investor in People, Employment Department, 1993.

New Developments in Employee Involvement by Mick Marchington, John Goodman, Adrian Wilkinson and P. Ackers, Manchester School of Management, UMIST and Department of Employment, 1992

New Priorities in Employee Communications, CBI, 1978

The UK Innovation Lecture, by Akio Morita, Department of Trade and Industry, London, 1992

'Listening – the most neglected of neglected management skills', by K. Murray, speech prepared for the Institute of Personnel and Development Conference, Harrogate 1995

British Social Attitudes, Social and Community Planning Research, London, 1991

Tomorrow's Company: the role of business in a changing world, Royal Society for the Encouragement of Arts, Manufactures and Commerce, London, 1995

How to Understand and Manage Public Relations, by J. White, Business Books, London, 1991

Strategic Communications Management: making public relations work, by Jon White and Laura Mazur, Addison-Wesley, Wokingham, 1995

United States Banker by F. Seitel, November, 1990

'Working in Britain: a survey of working people's attitudes', *Market and Opinion Research International*, London, 1985

World Competitiveness Reports 1993 and 1995, World Economic Forum and International Institute for Management Development (IMD), Lausanne

Price Waterhouse/Cranfield School of Management Project Report, Cranfield School of Management, 1991

Is Anyone Listening? The strategic management of internal communication in UK organizations, by Linda Gatley and David Clutterbuck, Business Intelligence, London, 1996

2 IC and the healthy organization

Susan Foreman, *lead tutor in Marketing with research and consulting interests in Internal Marketing, Henley Management College*

This chapter contends that the health of an organization at the turn of the millennium will depend on the vitality of its communication in the 1990s. It argues that everyone in the organization has a responsibility to manage different aspects of communication proactively; and that since organizations continually change, communication must also change and evolve to anticipate the needs of the new structures that will emerge.

The dynamic organizations of the future will be concerned less with transmitting messages down through the hierarchy than with creating relationships and developing collective communication based on conversations inside the organization. Their communication strategies will focus on producing an integrated package made up of three essential components:

- the *atmosphere* for communication
- the communication *process*
- the communication *methods*.

Effective communication combines these different elements. More often than not we stress the latter element, the specific methods, tools and techniques that can be employed to communicate internally. The different media, channels and the technology available to develop and implement the formal communications programme represent just one aspect of communicating inside organizations. In the challenging futures we face, this functional approach to communication will be inadequate unless it is conducted in an atmosphere that supports communication.

Communication cannot be reliant solely on tools and techniques but must emphasize the dialogue between people. The organizational context of the communication and the ambience of the business as a whole influences how we communicate and how the messages are received. 'Interpersonal communication is the essence of the organisation because it creates structures that then affect what else gets said and done by whom' (Weick 1987). Communication is therefore an ongoing process, in which the messages we all communicate continually influence our working practices and help to shape the nature of the workplace. Some consider we should be preparing for the next millennium by prioritizing organizational communication. 'Without communication there would be no organising or organisation' (Schall 1983).

THE CHALLENGES OF ORGANIZATIONAL CHANGE

The coming of more flexible organizations

One of the key challenges in the 1990s is the design and the development of flexible organizations in which communications are no longer structured on the basis of hierarchy and functions and where communication takes place horizontally across the organization. Indeed, organizations are more inclined to manage on a team basis where functional specialists are members of many different teams that meet for specified periods (Hirschhorn and Gilmore 1992).

Leaner and flatter organizational structures organized on an inter-functional basis diminish the traditional lines of authority and control in organizations and lead to the development of new forms of communication. Managers spend an increasing amount of time working across traditional boundaries with peers over whom they have no authority. Impersonal contacts, thus, give way to relationships based on trust and cooperation. The ability of employees to complete work is increasingly dependent on the quality of the communication shared in the new networks. 'Effective communication in cooperative effort rests on more than a simple exchange of information; people must be adept at anticipating the responses of other groups' (Rosabeth Moss Kanter 1989).

Uncertainty and new expectations

The word 'change' seems to have been ringing in our ears for at least a decade. Restructuring, delayering, downsizing, rightsizing and reengineering strategies have bombarded the workplace. These initiatives have a direct impact on people employed to manage and work in new structures. In many instances they are taken on board by our employees with some trepidation. There are uncertainties for different groups of employees. One group of survivors will remain to manage the 'new' organization. Some employees spend time in a vacuum wondering whether they are in danger of losing their jobs or whether the nature of the job will change. The remainder seek other forms of employment to reduce the feeling of uncertainty or because they are forced to do so. 'Effective managers strategically use communication to manage tough organisational changes' (Young and Post 1993).

Restructuring of organizations combined with the threat of recession and competition on an international scale is creating the need to change. Some organizations are turning themselves inside out, creating the need for collaboration and the need for them to play a strategic role in communication. A balanced approach is necessary internally to satisfy the employees' need for security. Communication with satisfied employees (who all have a responsibility to satisfy the needs of the external customer) is more likely to convert employees' concern into support for the organizational changes ahead. 'Good communication will make employees less resistant to change' (Young and Post 1993).

There are a number of reasons for communicating in the organization, the most important being to facilitate the free flowing exchange of information, ideas and views. Information may be conveyed but understanding is the required outcome. Accurate information communicated accurately in the organization helps to reduce misunderstandings and discrepancies and reduces the impact of information disseminated through informal channels.

The changing legal requirements for communication – those which underpin the employment contract with the organization – should not be overlooked. These include the general terms and conditions of employment, health and safety information, and material on work objectives and performance.

The need to communicate strategic views

Communication has developed since the days of conveying the coffee room chatter to more sophisticated systems that convey information about everything from the company performance, customer information, organizational change, environmental and social initiatives to employee information on training and development.

We operate in a fast-moving and turbulent environment where more and more employers use the internal communications systems to direct attention towards business objectives. This reinforces the formal messages on quality initiatives, business performance targets and the competition. However, do we understand what the employees want to know, and does it matter? In order to be effective, communications should be supported from the top and should be internally customer-focused, that is, with the emphasis on the employee.

The need for senior involvement

The strategic role of communications, with responsibility from the top of the organization, is becoming increasingly recognized. By the turn of the century top management will need to champion the cause of internal communication and will need to lead by example. Support from the highest level in the organization is necessary to show middle management that communicating effectively is not just another initiative to live through until the next management fad comes along, but something that is 'the most important managerial activity in this company' (Young and Post 1993). In many respects the contribution from the top is a fundamental and integral part of the success of the internal communications strategy. Specialists in communication should help management think about its relationships with employees and how the latter can help to contribute to the changing organization.

Shifting the emphasis of communication management

In addition to support from the senior management, the emphasis of communication should be on understanding the relationships inside the organization rather than managing the company newsletter. Given that 'Communication is the fundamental activity through which social interaction is accomplished' (Orlikowski and Yates 1994), the role of the communications specialist will place emphasis on employee relationships. The relationships that develop during internal communication contribute to shaping the working atmosphere. Through continuous communication both managers and employees not only learn about priorities and values, but also contribute to the atmosphere. This is less of a media role and more of a coordinating and facilitating role, one that emphasizes a communicative climate.

The need to develop competence

Typically, the insurance company Sun Life (featured in Pickard 1995) has recently targeted communications as part of a culture and change programme. Its success has been commented on widely in the media. Communications is now seen as part of everyone's role in the organization. A key aspect of the process was the development of competencies that were integrated into everyone's existing job specifications. Employees are not just encouraged to communicate but to communicate effectively and this is woven into the review and appraisal systems. The process is accompanied by unswerving support from top management to end one-way communication regardless of its source and to concentrate on the receipt of information, not just the dissemination of information.

Responsibility must be shared

'I think that everyone realises that communication is much too important to be left solely to the communications specialist. Everyone has a commitment and should play an equal part in making sure that the company communications are effective' (Pickard 1995).

Everyone in the organization is involved in communication. Rather than imposing a structure for managing internal communications in a flexible and a boundaryless organization, the responsibility for communications needs to be a shared one. If you communicate with others in the organization there is a responsibility to frame messages so that they are consistent and can be understood by the recipients, and to use timely, relevant channels of communication. As with any communications system there may be noise in the system, for example managers conveying messages may dilute the impact, impose their own interpretation or convey partial messages.

Internal communications responsibility at a functional level finds its home in many parts of the organization, marketing, human resources, public relations, corporate affairs, corporate communications to name a few. Its natural home seems to be difficult to find, however, in the team environment of the new flexible organizations: it may be acceptable to find a home across these boundaries.

COMMUNICATION METHODS ARE CHANGING

Traditional methods of communication give way to techniques that are compatible with flexible organizational structures. A multi-functional approach requires the matching of organizations' and employees' objectives. Employees differ between organizations and between one another. Just as we accept that customers in the external environment, beyond the boundaries of the organization, are heterogeneous and should be treated accordingly, we also need to acknowledge that employees have different needs, different behaviours and different relationships within and with the organization. Some employees have routine jobs where there is low performance ambiguity. Others have complex jobs: here ambiguity is high and it is difficult for the organization and the employee to evaluate their performance. At one end of another dimension, some employees may fully understand and support the goals of the organization, whilst at the other the goals of the employees and the organization may be incongruous. Other aspects of level, role, function or seniority in the organization show where the differences may exist in this diverse internal marketplace.

External signposts

Recent trends in communication in the external sphere give us signposts to the future in the corporate communications world. The trend is away from the broadcast media where the distribution coverage may be absolute but targeting of messages to specific groups is limited, making it difficult to shape a relationship with employees. A relational approach to communication would emphasize the need to:

- demonstrate commitment to employees
- develop continuous contacts with employees
- focus on the benefits of working together
- satisfy employees.

The benefits are numerous: organizations may see improvements in lower levels of absenteeism and lower turnover in staff. The retention of employees with whom they have developed a relationship is a more efficient way of managing people than the continuous recruitment of new employees.

More interactive cultures

In adopting a relational approach aimed at two-way communication, the Rover group has in recent years undergone a change in culture, which amongst other factors emphasizes the need to develop relationships with shopfloor work teams and the management. In the past communication had been unidirectional, from the top to the bottom, based on the dissemination of information and instructions. The 'new' way of working focused on listening to employees, understanding their needs and acknowledging their expertise, and using these exchanges to develop relationships (McCarthy 1994).

Two-way communication holds 'concerns' for both management and employees. Many organizations resort to employee surveys to provide evidence of two-way communication. Whilst this is a start, and can be used to understand the needs of employee groups, surveys often highlight grievances and can be difficult to interpret. The future lies in interactive mechanisms that facilitate upward communications, not in the traditional sense, but in terms of mutual or relational communication. That creates bonds through social interactions, meetings, question and answer sessions and so forth. The short-term view is that this type of activity is resource hungry; financially, in terms of the cost of the physical communications tools, and in human terms. Top management endorsement needs to be supported with the resources to make it happen.

The future is in personalization of communication. Communications should tie in with the issues important to different groups of employees. What matters to them in conjunction with what matters to you. Take a customer-focused approach to employees; identify the themes important to them and use words, analogies and metaphors that have meaning to the recipient of the communication.

EMPLOYEES ARE CHANGING

Everyone in the organization is the recipient of internal communications. In a sense all are customers. To meet the needs of customers in this internal market-place it is necessary to understand the organizational context, the employment conditions, requirements and nature of the job. If the communications programmes meet the needs of the internal customer then the propensity to achieve effective communications is enhanced and the successful management of change issues, mentioned earlier, is fulfilled.

To be effective, communications should be based on conversations employees share. Companies need to converse with employees at their level of understanding and interest. The more personal the message, targeted at the individual or the team or work group, the more likely it is to catch the attention of the workforce. Broadcasting impersonal messages to the whole organization tends to switch people off, leaving management with the impression that employees are not interested. Regular interaction with management will develop closer bonds and encourage the team approach to develop.

Relationships need clarifying

Just as organizations follow a system for managing change, so a comparable format is needed to share it with the different groups within the organization. Rolls (1993) suggests that in promoting 'dialogue and participation' and to 'make the connection' organizations should take the 'themes, issues, words, metaphors and relationships' used by people in all levels in the organization so that their contribution is explicit.

Beneficial Bank has reinforced the connection with different groups in the organization. In its annual report it describes how over 1500 employee suggestions (out of 3000) have been implemented. In the main body of the annual report it names each and every employee and outlines customer and employee case histories that emphasize the relationship within the organization and its impact on the external customer.

Active participation is the goal

Interaction with groups on many levels is required and here communication comes to the fore. The messages will be different to reflect the different needs of these employee groups. However, visible channels of communication will facilitate the management of change. The objectives of the communication will be to give information and develop awareness of the challenge ahead. The next stage will be to move beyond the cognitive to the conative level – in other words to create a sense of personal involvement, where commitment is gained (and given) on an altogether more emotional basis. Beyond that comes the affective level, where feelings and attitudes flow through into active participation.

The importance of informal methods

In addition to the formal communication issues we need to recognize that informal communications of all kinds prevail in our organizations. Regardless of the size of the business, the grapevine conveys information throughout the organization and is an important element of our socialization into an organization. Employee behaviour is influenced by the messages that are conveyed in this way and the source of the message. It influences how we respond to different people, the way we respond to the job and the role we have in the organization. It is a part of the organization that needs to be understood by people at all levels of the organization.

Those responsible for developing corporate communications strategies and plans should be aware of the power of the grapevine and other forms of informal communication. Some people suggest that they should not be overlooked in communicating with employees, especially when it is crucial to guard against inaccurate and damaging information spreading throughout the organization. My own view is that it is dangerous to regard them as 'tools' – at the very least, a wise person would treat them with respect and keep a safe distance.

The values communicated in the formal channels of communication should be matched by the values being demonstrated on an everyday basis, otherwise uncertainty will be created in the employee's mind. Messages lack credence when a formal announcement conceals a hidden agenda. The difficulty in interpretation caused by conflicting signals hinders effective employee communication. Avoid this simply by communicating honestly and consistently with the different constituencies in the organization.

PERCEPTIONS OF VALUE ARE CHANGING

Communication concerns more than the cash and cost. The scope of internal communications in an organization is vast and it pervades all activities. It is a misnomer to confine it to the realms of the corporate literature newsletters, employee surveys or videos. The process of internal communications is more a collection of attitudes and the prevailing culture in the organization than the amount of financial support.

Expenditure on communications is an investment; an investment of time and money that should, like any other investment activity, contribute to the performance of the business as a whole. However, budgets for internal communications rarely compare with their external counterparts. Financial support is necessary but it is a component of a communications package rather than a driver of the initiatives. The financial support enables those responsible for communications to produce videos and newsletters and use these methods, tools and techniques to differing levels of sophistication. However, they cannot reflect the costs and the value of top management support, the satisfaction gained from two-way communication and the worth of developing internal networks of relationships.

CONCLUSIONS

Communication is at the heart of the organization: it is the key to organizational success. It exists in everything we say and do, and also in things we don't say and don't do. It is the essence of the organization; it is all pervasive.

Communication needs to be more than one-way or two-way – it should be relational in nature. It is not sufficient merely to transmit messages, we should ensure that they are received and understood. While numerous methods of communication are available, they should be implemented in an atmosphere that supports mutual communication throughout the organization on a continuous basis.

Effective communication requires an understanding of employees' needs at all levels in the organization. To develop bonds between employees, there needs to be a firm foundation for interaction which can only be based on an appreciation of each other. Informal methods of communication are rarely acknowledged officially, but the messages that circulate both formally and informally should be compatible. It is often acknowledged that the more frequent the formal communications, the more informal sources abound

(Torrington and Hall 1991). The two sources are not mutually exclusive: rather they exist in tandem.

Finally, while the responsibility for communications may lie with a specialist group, support from senior management must be overt, and participation from all levels in the organization is essential. It is one of the key elements on which the success of an organization is dependent.

HOW TO FIND OUT MORE

Communication in Organisations, 2nd edition by D. Fisher, West Publishing Co. 1993.

'The new boundaries of the "boundaryless" company' by Larry Hirschhorn and Thomas Gilmore, *Harvard Business Review*, May–June 1992, pp. 104–14.

'Empowerment in action', by B. McCarthy, *Personnel Management*, **26**(10), pp. 60–1, 1994.

'The new managerial work' by Rosabeth Moss Kanter, *Harvard Business Review*, November/December 1989, pp. 85–92.

'Genre repertoire: the structuring of communicative practices in organizations' by Wanda J. Orlikowski, Joanne Yates, *Administrative Science Quarterly*, **39**, pp. 541–74, 1994.

'Harvesting the office grapevine' by J. Pickard, *People Management*, **7**(9), 1994.

'Employee communications has a change of heart' by J. Rolls, *HR Magazine*, **38**(10), pp. 132–3, 1993.

'A communication-rules approach to organisational culture' by Maryan S. Schall, *Administrative Science Quarterly*, **28**, pp. 557–81, 1983.

Personnel Management – A New Approach, by D. Torrington and L. Hall, Prentice Hall, Englewood Cliffs, NY, 1991.

'Theorizing about organizational communication' by Karl E. Weick, in F.M. Jablih, L.L. Putnam, K.H. Roberts and L.W. Porter, (eds), *Handbook of Organizational Communication*, Sage, Newbury Park, CA, pp. 97–122, 1987.

'Managing to communicate, communicating to manage: how leading companies communicate with employees' by Mary Young and James E. Post, *Organizational Dynamics*, Summer, pp. 31–43, 1993.

3 Understanding today's UK audiences

Susan Walker, *managing director, MORI Human Resource Research*

This chapter reviews the trends that have emerged from opinion research carried out over more than a quarter of a century among UK organizations' internal audiences. It questions, for example, whether the fact that employees' satisfaction with communication has not risen in 25 years means that increasing efforts to communicate have been a waste of time. Or is it rather that the effort needs to accelerate to outpace expectations?

We live in the age of the sound bite. Newspapers like the *Sun* make popular reading. The messages from research into literacy standards are mixed: some judge them to be falling while others indicate little substantive change. So the preference for 'easy' reading and listening may not be based on inability, but on choice. Time pressures too have their part to play – how many of us hear the comment 'But I haven't time to read that', especially in the context of work.

What does this mean for communication in the workplace? Organizations may still want to send their messages, but does the workforce want to hear them?

On the surface at least, the answer is affirmative. In a 1994 MORI Human Resource Research survey, a nationally representative sample of full/part-time employees was asked face to face about the importance of internal communication. Nine out of ten found it to be important. This view was consistent among both managerial and blue collar workers. Also in 1994, MORI Human Resource Research surveyed employees in nine leading UK organizations on changes in work environment and communications.

Group discussions in the workplace substantiated the value of internal communication, with people making comments like:

'Communication cuts down the barriers between management and the shopfloor.'

'Keeping you in touch gives you a sense of worth.'

'If you are well informed then you can do your job better and the company benefits.'

'Good communication kills rumours.'

'A well-informed employee feels more confident.'

'If you're not kept well informed then you're more likely to become a 9-to-5er.'

IS ENOUGH RESOURCE GOING IN?

With this kind of need, backed by good business and people management reasons, organizations might be assumed to put internal communication high on the agenda. Indeed they often do, but seemingly to little avail.

MORI normative data (from 300 employee surveys, 1969 to present, incorporating best and worst scores as well as average within sector) show that only just under half of Britain's workforce considers itself to be kept informed. This average figure, however, hides the bad news that some organizations are performing significantly worse (the lowest encountered by MORI being 17 per cent) while others achieve admirable scores, the best being 84 per cent (Figure 3.1).

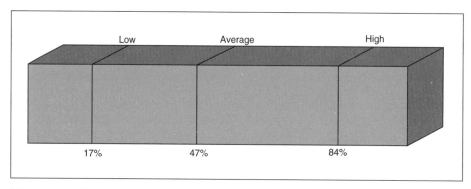

Figure 3.1 Internal communications: the best and the worst

Source: MORI normative database

Perhaps more disturbingly, that average has not moved significantly in 25 years (Figure 3.2). So what does this mean in the context of the additional communication people must be receiving – corporate videos, house journals, briefing meetings, e-mail, communication managers, communication consultancies?

It means that all this additional expenditure and all these additional resources are just keeping pace with people's expectations, which have been

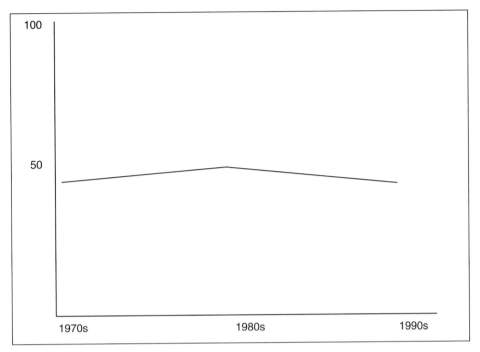

Figure 3.2   Level of communication over 25 years
Source: MORI normative database

and are rising as fast as the growth in the internal communication industry itself.

IMPROVING MEDIA

A contributory factor must be the growing efficiency of the media worldwide. At home people see news from round the world, sometimes within minutes of it happening, from an assassination in the Middle East to a hurricane in the Midwest. News is reported directly and succinctly.

Contrast this with internal communication within most organizations. A draft is prepared. It goes up to the directors' floor. Down again with amendments. Words are added, phrases become ever more tortuous to disguise the real (and often unpalatable) message. Time goes by. The grapevine carries the news, or some approximation of it. Eventually the definitive version appears: too late, too long and too complex. Credibility of the official communication sources falls even further.

THE IMPORTANCE OF CONTEXT

It is vital, therefore, when reviewing the area of internal communication, that you understand the wider context in which it operates. What are the   *29* developments in the social and working environment that can influence communication? This question needs to be considered in understanding the UK audience of today – and more importantly of tomorrow.

This chapter examines the social background, change in the working environment, its effect on communication and the differing audience needs within organizations. It is based both on observations during work with a wide range of organizations carrying out employee surveys, normative data built up from those studies and our own research both quantitative and qualitative among the UK workforce.

There is no need to go further than my local pub to be reminded of times past. On its wall is a series of photographs dating from the 1930s. These are portraits of staff members from one organization with their years of service printed with their names. Bill, the gatekeeper, 47 years; Muriel, accounts, 42 years; Betty, typist, 39 years. They look into the camera with quiet pride on their faces. But these are from a past time when loyalty, pride and dedication were prized by both employee and organization.

ALIENATION FROM THE WORKPLACE

These words are being replaced by employability, empowerment and personal development. What impact does this have on employees? A MORI survey within the working population asked about loyalty. Just over a third believed that their loyalty towards their organization had reduced while four in ten also considered that their organization's loyalty towards them had fallen.

Does this matter? In certain quarters the answer is a resounding 'No', with some organizations claiming that the concept of loyalty is outmoded and no longer part of their contract with employees. This may be the way of the future – and one that is accepted by the young people coming into the workplace – but for many this link of loyalty has been broken without any meaningful relationship to take its place.

This sense of alienation is reinforced by what we hear from employees through the research carried out in a wide range of organizations in both the public and private sectors. A frequent phrase is 'I don't enjoy coming to work any more'. Even taking the 'looking back with rose-tinted glasses' syndrome into account, there is a new outlook about working life. Will the workforce adapt to the 'new reality' or are we seeing a terminal disaffection?

FRAGMENTATION IN SOCIETY

Research by MORI Socioconsult shows an increasing fragmentation in British society that threatens to make life more complicated both inside and outside the workplace. The divide between young and old is growing in terms not only of behaviours but also of values. This shows itself, for example, in changes among the 18 to 34 year age group such as young women beginning to adopt more 'male' behaviours. (For more information see *Freedom's Children*, Demos, 1995.)

This work also reveals that people's strongest sense of identity is with their family, friends and neighbours. Where they do relate to the workplace, this is more with their colleagues than with the company itself. Their first instinct is to give priority to private life, finding more fulfilment from their personal lives than success at work.

But for many, mitigating these natural instincts is the basic need to work to make a living. Faced with the direct choice, more would put their personal life before their work but a significant proportion are not able to do so.

Today – and possibly tomorrow – this choice will face more people as working life becomes more demanding and stressful. What will their response be?

DEPRIORITIZATION OF WORK

We are finding a developing trend towards the deprioritization of work, illustrated by people foreseeing themselves spending more time on outside interests and 'a better way of life' (Figure 3.3). Over half the workforce would give up work if able to do so. This has significant implications for organizational communications, particularly its future direction.

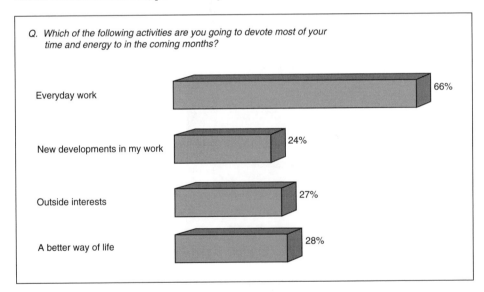

Figure 3.3 Priorities

Source: MORI Socioconsult

At present working life is overshadowed by the a high level of concern about job security and fear of redundancy, a situation that shows little sign of improvement. Indeed for many, their worst fears have been realized and downsizing and delayering have cost them their jobs.

British life has divided into the 'haves' with a job and the 'have-nots' without. So what of the fortunate people in work? Three-quarters of the workforce have   *31* been touched by reorganization and change, with its effect felt strongly by over half.

CONTROL THROUGH FLEXIBILITY

Especially in such times people look for more control over their lives, so it is not surprising that a preferred way of employment is flexibility in working time (although, as we shall see later, not the flexibility that most organizations have in mind).

In the main, people would like to stay in their present job, although some recognize the value of training and the ability to extend their skills base (Figure 3.4a). Most disliked are the very ways that organizations are pushing ahead: homeworking, job share, contract employment and the new concept of 'port-folio' work (Figure 3.4b).

The much-heralded concept of 'employability' is not welcomed. There are indications that this is certainly the case with older workers for whom

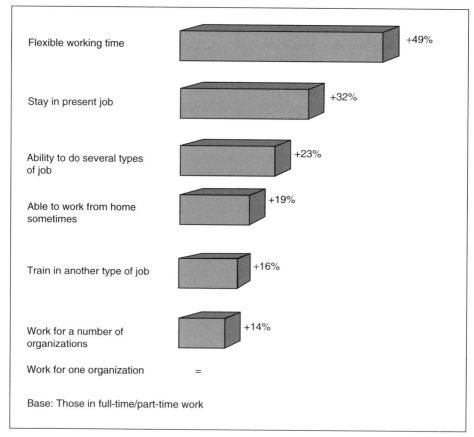

Figure 3.4a   Ways of working: preferred

Source: MORI general public research

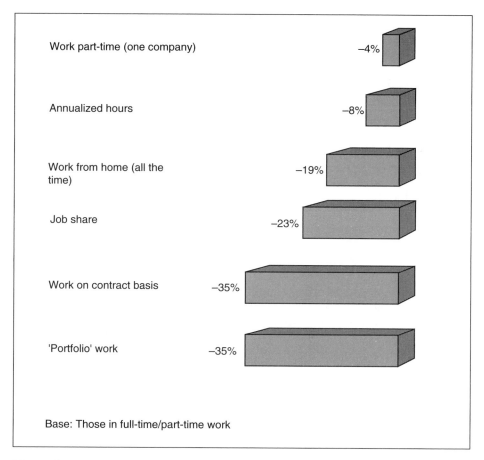

Base: Those in full-time/part-time work

Figure 3.4b   Ways of working: disliked

Source: MORI general public research

employability will never replace job security. Managers in one organization were surprised when the results of their survey showed that over half their workforce were looking for a job for life, revealing that their recent campaign about the necessity and benefits of 'employability' had fallen on deaf ears.

COMMUNICATING CHANGE

It would, however, be a mistake to assume that the British workers are Luddites. They recognize that change is inevitable and accept that for many this will bring new opportunities. The problems lie within the management and communication of those changes. People tell us that they could cope with the change if only they knew what was going on.

Looking at the correlation of the importance placed on internal communications with workplace change, we find it valued most in such times. But it is precisely in such times it is seen to work least effectively.

This was proved by a recent survey by MORI Human Resource Research within a successful, expanding company. The research was to be carried out over three days through group self-completion sessions. Before this happened we learned that an important announcement about possible redundancies would be made during the same period of time. The organization concerned decided not to change the survey dates although aware of the likely influence on the views expressed.

We were able, therefore, to analyse the results separately over the three days to judge the impact as staff heard the unexpected news. Not surprisingly, the scores for most of the questions worsened from day one to day three, especially for such aspects as job satisfaction and security. However, the largest reduction was for internal communications, although it could be argued that those people on day three were better informed than those on day one. The subtext in the message was clear: 'We don't like what we hear, so mark down communications'. The system gets the blame for the content.

This real life example is reinforced by findings from the MORI normative database. Communication is seen to suffer in times of change, particularly credibility. Another disturbing finding is that, on balance, marginally more employees disbelieve their senior management than believe them. Much of this relates to the atmosphere of distrust during change and the suspicion of a 'hidden agenda'.

People are becoming more cynical about their organizations generally. Although understanding of objectives is not high, it reduces further during periods of change as illustrated by comparisons with the MORI change norm; Figure 3.5 shows the average scores from organizations experiencing change.

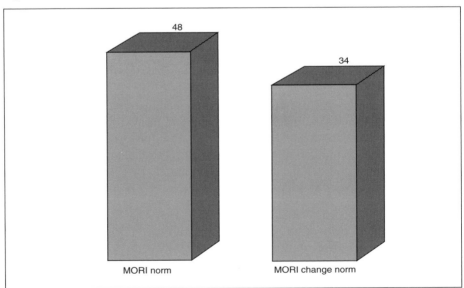

Figure 3.5   Understanding of company objectives

Source: MORI normative database

If change is now an integral part of working life – as most accept it is – what are the long-term implications for communication?

Another question: how will the trend towards part-time and contract work affect employees' perceptions of information related to objectives, strategy and mission statements? Will they really buy into two or three sets of values depending on where they are working? Our studies indicate the answer is likely to be negative, providing more challenges for the communications function.

Such evidence suggests that the creation and communication of a single corporate culture and values will become ever more difficult unless these are kept very direct and simple. If they do appeal to the 'hearts and minds', the expressed values or vision of an organization could be a significant factor in attracting potential employees. For this to be the case, however, organizations will have to overcome the barrier that no amount of communications can solve. Employees may know the values, and buy into them, but are usually disillusioned to see them totally absent in the behaviours around them.

THE NEED FOR SEGMENTATION AND TRAINING

All these findings make it clear that the developing social and working culture will call for different communication techniques. A more focused approach will also be needed to meet the divergent needs of the various audiences within organizations.

Go into any newsagents and look around. A wide variety of newspapers and magazines is on offer, appealing to young and old, special interests, ethnic groups, hobbies and so on, in a wide range of designs and approaches. Contrast this with the house journal or briefing system of most organizations. Just the single approach to appeal to the 16-year-old joiner and the 64-year-old long server, the sales director and the new clerk, the literate and the semi-literate, the *Sun* reader and the *Financial Times* reader.

As the internal audience becomes more disparate, there is a growing need to tailor communications to separate audiences. In the past this has sometimes found little favour as it appears to run counter to single status and equal opportunities. Now the talk is of 'diversity' with differences recognized and valued, providing the opportunity for the internal communicator to consider the needs of its internal publics.

It is already happening in the outside world. In areas with large ethnic communities, health advice and other public information is produced in a range of appropriate languages. When was the last time in the UK you saw a corporate mission statement in a language other than English, even in a factory where it is the second language? The fact that young people from different ethnic backgrounds are now being educated in the UK may mean that this issue lessens in the future, but at present it still needs to be considered.

In a wider context, as we think more European and more international, is it right that English often continues to be the prime language for communications? In other words, to translate or not? Much depends on the objectives of   *35* the enterprise. If it seeks to be a strongly central corporate entity, then it might be more appropriate to reinforce that message by using English as the main business language. If each of the separate organizations in its own country retains and projects its own image, then the relevant language may be more suitable. A flexible approach is called for: the needs of the audience and the various skill levels of audiences in different countries should be assessed before a decision is taken.

QUANTITY VS. QUALITY

New technology helps to make all these possibilities practicable. This, however, brings another potential danger: e-mail is one example. The ease of sending and receiving messages brings floods of missives – not all necessary reading for the recipient. The deluge of e-mail that greets many returning to their desk may be symptomatic of the 'watch your back' syndrome: make sure that *everybody* gets the message and then you can't be accused of missing anyone out. Better safe than sorry.

Indeed the plethora of communications in some organizations may also result from the safety-net school of communication that threatens its very effectiveness. During several communication surveys, internal audiences pleaded for better targeted, succinct information relevant to their needs. This very much ties in with the developing need to communicate with different audiences in an appropriate way, rather than adopt the scatter gun approach.

This also applies to differences by sector. We find, for example, that those people working in the service sector are much more likely to believe the information provided by their employer than those in the public sector. Another reason to understand your audience before formulating strategies and systems.

LATERAL AND UPWARD COMMUNICATION

So far we have mainly discussed communications as information passed downwards in the traditional way. However, equally important aspects of the communication process are lateral and upward communications. Even in organizations where communication is working relatively well, the most difficult challenge can be to create and maintain a process for listening.

Again this becomes more difficult in times of change. The perception that opportunities for employees to make their views known are poor ties up with the often strongly held belief that speaking up can damage prospects within the organization. This view is most prevalent where change and reorganization is happening. But is this just a perception? Senior management personnel often laugh at this, commenting that they 'did not get where they are today by holding back criticisms'. No organization likes to admit that 'Yes people' progress. It does not fit in with the empowerment movement. However, senior management personnel are also heard to describe some comments or actions as 'career limiting' while in a changing environment a critical comment is viewed as destructive rather than constructive. Witness the macho renaming of a 'problem' as an 'opportunity'.

The establishment of an effective two-way process cannot compensate for a reality where the outspoken are seen to be punished. The cult of *kaizen*, or continuous improvement, depends on ideas and suggestions at all levels and it is impossible to listen only to feedback that the organization wants to hear. There will also be more difficult messages to deal with from today's UK audience.

However problematic it may be to achieve, effective communication that works well both ways has tremendous power to contribute towards business goals. Our research shows links between those who rate communication highly with job satisfaction, motivation and loyalty. These are powerful reasons for organizations to prioritize communications.

IS 'CORPORATE PRIDE' STILL A FACTOR?

Today's audience, however, has become streetwise. It complains of PR style communications, wordy messages that camouflage the truth or do not align with what it hears and sees in the external media.

A sense of corporate pride is important to today's audience. This is clear from the way employees describe where they work to others. Some actually hide the truth, ashamed of being associated with their employer. Others actively want everybody to know – like the pictures on the pub wall described earlier. Communications can help them achieve this sense of pride, informing them of the victories but also explaining the failures so that they feel equipped to stand up for their organization externally.

We recently carried out two studies for different firms that had both experienced radical change. In one the 'pride' score was the lowest ever seen, in the other, the highest. The difference between the two? The management of the process, which included a high priority for internal communications.

THE INTERNAL AUDIENCE AS AMBASSADOR

There are bottom line benefits other than faith that an employee with a sense of pride is also a more effective worker. Our corporate image research shows that the best ambassador for an organization is the person who works for it. In a study of 30 leading companies and organizations measured on MORI's familiarity and favourability scales, favourability was analysed by the different sources of image. The results are shown in Figure 3.6. Awareness of advertising had little overall impact; media coverage and High Street visibility were influences, as was product experience. The most influential factor, however, is knowing a member of that organization's workforce.

Thus our internal audience is a powerful force. In the future, its needs will fragment and develop. Internal communication must adapt to play an effective role in tomorrow's organization. But the basic requirements people ask for time after time remain the same. And those requirements are very simple, *37*

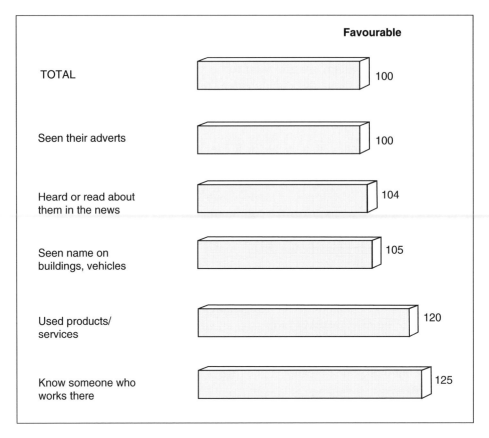

Figure 3.6   Effect of source of knowledge on favourability (average of 30 major companies)

Source: MORI corporate image study

although our research shows them difficult to achieve. They ask for communication which is timely, relevant, targeted, honest and direct.

4 Matching internal and external image

John Williams, *managing director, Fishburn Hedges*

This chapter argues that internal communication is a powerful force for shaping and sustaining corporate image. It explores two recent cases where high profile UK organizations – one a charity, the other in financial services – have been successful in shifting their market position, largely because they first succeeded in involving their internal audience.

Internal communication does not exist in a vacuum, and I believe, therefore, should not be conducted in a vacuum. Messages communicated internally will fail if they do not complement those communicated externally; internal attitudes and needs should be taken into account, and measured, alongside those of external audiences. While this may seem common sense, and would be accepted by communicators in many companies, it is at present far from standard practice.

THE OPPORTUNITY BEING MISSED

Employees make a crucial contribution to the external image of their organization, in two principal ways.

First, indirectly – because the image of any organization, in whatever field it operates, is founded in *what it does, how it does it*, and *how well it does it*. Clearly, what shapes those outputs is in part the quality of employees' work, the sum of their skills and efforts.

Second, more directly, in any service organization, employees *are* the product – they deliver the service directly, and interact with the customer. The customers' image of the organization – and their propensity to stay customers – will be shaped more by the people that deal with them (directly or indirectly) than any other single factor.

In fact, virtually all organizations today, including manufacturers, have come to think of themselves as service organizations – it is a long time since IBM, for example, has thought of itself simply as a maker of business machines. Certainly, the concept of internal supplier/customer relationships is now almost universally acknowledged. And in theory at least, it is generally accepted that all front-line employees, whatever their day-to-day role, are permanent ambassadors – and communicators – for their organization with external audiences.

For all these reasons, marketing, sales and general management divisions are increasingly taking an interest in the management of the morale, motivation and skills of employees. What was once seen largely as the domain of human resources is something that other departments want to monitor and manage.

This is particularly true in organizations where the company name – the corporate brand – is the same as the consumer brand, for example in banks and building societies, retailers, airlines and most public and voluntary organizations. And managing the reputation of a *company* is a much more complex issue.

Writing in *Admap* magazine in 1989 Stephen King, who was the founder of account planning at J. Walter Thompson, said: 'Unlike the classic brand, a company brand is not a standard article. It is a changing collection of people, values, styles and behaviour. What binds them together is very intangible – a complex set of norms, conventions, methods, examples, organisational patterns, rules and leaders'. Thus part of company brand management is managing and shaping the culture, which is why the contribution of internal communication is now inseparable from the interests of external image and identity.

Another reason that this is now an issue is that thinking about the management of corporate reputation has changed.

First, there has been a growth in the acceptance of stakeholder theory – that an organization is accountable to a wider range of interested parties than just customers and shareholders. Placed at the top of this extended list are employees, because there is a growing belief that they have a right to be better informed of what the organization is doing, and will be better motivated, more loyal and more productive if they are part of a more open and communicative culture.

Second, there is a belief that employees are behaving more like external audiences, and therefore should be managed as such. Their expectations of length of employment have changed: the lack of job security has made them more wary. There is greater recognition that they are not just employees but consumers and shareholders and citizens in their own right, and their desire to challenge and question companies, including the one that employs them, does not stop when they sit down at their desks.

Also, employees are exposed to more than their own companies' internal communications: they are as much, if not more, a consumer of their companies' external communications – as well as those of the competition – as any customer or prospective customer. When a privatized utility looks at its workforce, it sees not only employees, but also shareholders and local customers, and the management of internal communications must take account of that.

BARRIERS TO SUCCESS

It may be easy to accept these principles, but creating a process to act on them is not easy. There are three major barriers to achieving consistent, coherent and effective communications to internal and external audiences. These are to do with structure, attitude and the process of internal communications.

Structural barriers

The structures for managing internal and external communications are often quite different. Those involved have responsibility for different people and different departments. Historically, internal communications and image have been the responsibility of the personnel or human resources department, whereas the management of external image has been in the remit of marketing, sales or corporate communications. These departments have traditionally had very little to do with each other and are peopled by executives with different backgrounds, attitudes and priorities. Too often HR and communications/ marketing departments rarely talk to each other and hold different and some-times even conflicting agendas.

Attitudinal barriers

The old paternalistic view was that employees should be grateful for their jobs and had no right to be told more than they needed to know to do their work. There was no interest in what they thought. Pay and conditions were the necessary motivation. This attitude is being swept away, but led less by the case for managing image than by the need to improve productivity through total quality management.

But the real test of how far management practice has changed is in the use of employee surveys. In managing external image, research is considered vital. There is usually a substantial research budget for attitude tracking, qualitative research and new product development. Yet practice internally is patchy. Many organizations still very rarely research their employees. Many fail to use the research to set communications targets and then follow up. Worse, there are organizations that find the results of their employee surveys so bad that they feel unable to share the findings with senior management, let alone act on them. This can create a gulf in process between those managing external and internal communications.

Processes and tools

This ambivalence towards listening to the internal 'customer' is reflected in the process and tools of internal communication. They are often produced and   *41* distributed as a series of individual and uncoordinated communications ranging from the cascade briefing to the company magazine. Often, no one person or department is responsible for the coordination of all internal communications, let alone their integration with external communications. Often responsibility for published communications, such as the staff newspaper or video, lies with corporate communications, but not necessarily the *strategic* responsibility for the messages contained within. In many companies the editing of staff publications is seen as a chore and not as valuable an exercise as those devoted to external communications.

PRINCIPLES OF BEST PRACTICE

Managing image as a totality

The first principle of best practice is for organizations to accept that the corporate brand and image must be managed as a totality. This requires giving responsibility for it to one senior executive or department and for them to be empowered to coordinate all those responsible for shaping corporate communication, internal and external. In service companies this responsibility most logically lies with marketing.

Cross-functional input

Second, this strategy should be developed in conjunction with the human resources function, so that it has the opportunity to identify where and how it can contribute to the process.

Regular research

Third, organizations need to treat their employees as they would their consumers, as an audience to research, in order to identify and satisfy their needs. If you accept the principle of 'employee marketing', your first reaction is 'Well what do our staff think and feel? Does this support or hinder our corporate objectives?' As a result, research staff regularly, track their attitudes and set objectives; but note, as with external marketing, not all problems will be solved by communications. The challenge and frustration of internal research is that it often identifies more fundamental problems that only the senior management of the company as a whole can tackle. But that is no excuse to bury the results.

GOOD PRACTICE IN ACTION

Current examples of good practice tend to come from organizations that want to change their external image, and recognize that to do so successfully will depend on achieving a parallel change in their internal culture. Switches in corporate identity, in particular, provide an opportunity to conduct a thorough review of communication practice and to bring internal and external communications closer together.

More than just a name change

A good illustration of this process in action is provided by Scope, one of Britain's biggest charities, with a total annual income of over £70 million. It was founded as The Spastics Society by parents of children with cerebral palsy in 1952. Scope's operations now embrace over 200 local groups, schools, residential and therapy centres, lobbying, and a full marketing and fund-raising operation.

For many years, The Spastics Society had been concerned about its name. 'Spastic' had become a term of abuse. Earlier studies, both external and internal, had recommended a new name, but the momentum for change could not be created. Resistance reflected the high risk to income of a new identity, and a lack of a robustly-researched case for change.

In 1990, an external consultancy was commissioned to conduct a comprehensive review of the options, through an audit of all principal stakeholders. These included representatives of every significant external audience, including trustees, people with cerebral palsy, disability activists, parents and carers, GPs, medical specialists, local authorities, MPs, corporate donors and journalists. This review was supplemented by quantified research among the general public. In parallel, staff at all levels were interviewed and a quantitative survey of staff attitudes conducted.

The report's main recommendation was that the name was increasingly unacceptable and a primary barrier to growth. The response from outside audiences was 'This is an organization that is *not for me*'. Internally, staff responses confirmed they were aware of the tensions in the continuing use of the name. They also endorsed some of the criticisms of external audiences that the organization needed to undergo more in-depth change (for example in having a more effective equal opportunities policy that brought in more disabled people).

At that point, the charity could simply have made some executive decisions, but it recognized the need and the opportunity to go further with its internal audiences. It looked to build a detailed consensus among staff and members, primarily the local groups of the Society, constitutionally the decision-makers in the organization, about what needed to change, and on the process of change. This was achieved through a series of roadshows up and down the country where the survey findings were presented and workshops held to explore the issues raised.

Staff were not only encouraged to challenge and debate the findings, but asked to address some of the strategic decisions that arose from them, for example what should the organization's priorities be and what image should it have? Staff were also encouraged to brainstorm possible alternative names.

The result was a high level of staff acceptance of the need for change, which   *43* helped underpin the decision in principle by the local group membership in November 1992 at its AGM to work towards a change of name.

From that point on, staff were briefed regularly on progress as names were short-listed through research among key external audiences. The final decision on the name Scope was taken by an EGM in March 1994. While preparations for the launch – set for 3 November 1994 – would focus on how best to project a new and unknown name on to external audiences, it was seen as essential that staff became comfortable first. So there was no attempt to keep the new name under wraps. The organization immediately began referring to itself as 'soon to be Scope' and distributed regular briefing literature on the countdown to the launch.

Moreover, the Society adopted a deliberate policy of maximizing the number of people in the organization actively involved in planning for the launch. Cross-departmental working teams worked on different aspects of implementation and promotion. As a result, people were familiar, comfortable and positive about the name before the public launch, which ensured optimum enthusiasm and support when it was finally introduced.

Rebranding from the inside out

Another example of the importance of internal audience in corporate rebranding – this time without a change of name – is United Friendly, the life and general insurer.

Founded in 1908, United Friendly is a publicly-quoted company, though still family-owned in that the majority of voting shares lie with descendants of the founder, whose grandson is chief executive. Until 1993 it was focused almost exclusively on policyholders in lower income households, paying small regular premiums for a range of motor, household, life insurance and pensions products.

Accordingly, United Friendly's business has been built on 'home service' insurance – direct cash collection of premiums from people's homes. Today, however, the company offers a broad range of products where premiums are increasingly paid by direct debit, but it remains true to the principles of highly personalized customer service. Marketing had been concentrated on its 2500 strong salesforce, serving over 1.5 million clients through a traditional branch network structure and a head office in central London. As a brand, therefore, United Friendly had advertised very little and achieved limited awareness outside its customer base.

In 1993, however, the company saw an opportunity to widen its franchise by acquiring a life company that was a specialist distributor with a totally different profile – the emphasis of its salesforce was financial planning, served by a wider range of products, and aimed at a more sophisticated and affluent audience.

It was decided to market the combined and newly-expanded range of products under a single unified brand identity. The name United Friendly would be strengthened in the market and a new brand strategy developed around it. In doing so, the company recognized the need to take its internal audiences along with it. Extensive research among both head office and field sales staff was therefore carried out alongside external research.

The results were significant in that they revealed not only the expected uncertainties that follow any large acquisition, but also poor communications between the head office and sales staff of the original United Friendly operation. It emerged that there was a sense of two quite separate cultures. On the positive side, however, the expanded group was seen to offer new opportunities and a feeling that the company was 'going places'.

Thus the external marketing brief, aimed at 'relaunching' the organization to a wider audience, was complemented by a brief to unite the organization into a single, more service-oriented and mutually supportive culture. Hence while the relaunch was led by the director of marketing, he worked closely with the director of human resources, and when the launch strategy was presented to the board they made a joint presentation, which included proposals for tightening cascade and feedback procedures, and for greater training at all levels.

And it was the internal dimension – as much as any external pressures – that led directly to the decision to incorporate within the marketing communications programme a change of corporate identity. The rationale was that there should be a vision of a new 'United Friendly' – crystallized in a physical identity – shared equally by staff and customers, old and new.

Among steps taken to help bring staff on board with the changes was a television advertising campaign, included for the first time within a significantly increased marketing budget. The campaign strategy offered an unusually integrated solution that put staff at the very heart of the communication, based on the premise that they were, and should be recognized as, a significant part of the brand. Under the idea of 'Person to Person', the campaign's purpose was to demonstrate that all United Friendly's products are sold through personal contact and personal knowledge. The treatment featured staff talking about the company and conveyed a picture of a very real and personable, yet professional organization.

It was an approach that opened the door to maximum staff involvement. Casting the commercials involved many volunteers and the whole process was videoed over a six-month period so that at the launch presentation to staff, when the advertising and new identity were unveiled, the film of the making of the 'new' United Friendly could be shown and the rationale could be explained clearly and simply. In the meantime, monthly updates on the progress of the campaign and corporate identity change were sent out in two series of special briefing papers.

The outcome? A highly charged and motivated workforce, utterly in touch with and committed to the strategic changes being made – indeed, altogether more united and friendly. This was confirmed in formal postlaunch staff research.

If there is one lesson to be learned from both these examples, it is that a properly integrated communications campaign, one that reaches out to and *45* engages equally internal and external audiences, is a most powerful way to manage and promote an organization's image and reputation.

HOW TO FIND OUT MORE

The New Guide to Identity by Wolff Olins, The Design Council/Gower, 1996

The Corporate Image: strategies for effective identity programmes by Nicholas Ind, Kogan Page, 1990

Corporate Reputation: managing the new strategic asset by John Smythe, Colette Dorward and Jerome Reback, Century Business, 1992

The Virtual Corporation by William H. Davidow and Michael F. Malone, Harper Business Press, 1993

How to Understand and Manage Public Relations by D. White, Century Business, 1991

'Whose hand on the heartbeat?' by Jon White, *Human Resources*, Winter 1991/2

Advertising Excellence by C.L. Bovee, McGraw-Hill, 1995

Freedom's Children by Helen Wilkinson and Geoff Mulgan, Demos, 1995

Institute of Practitioners in Advertising (IPA), 44 Belgrave Square, London SW1X 8QS 0171 235 7020

Institute of Public Relations, The Old Trading House, 15 Northburgh Street, London EC1V OPR 0171 253 5151

Chartered Institute of Marketing, Moor Hall, Cookham, Maidenhead, Berks SL6 9QH 01628 524922

5 The impact of computer-based communications networks

Paul Samuels, *formerly head of IC, Digital UK*

Thanks to the convergence of technologies in three industries – telecommunications, computing and electronics – the desktop computer is now as useful for communication as it has been for applications like data analysis and word-processing. This chapter analyses the impact that this is having on organizations, strategically and structurally.

Soon, most people at work and many at home will have access to some form of desktop device, and via that to information carried by other computers linked together in a network. Such a development heralds big changes for organizations and individuals alike. It opens up a wealth of new opportunities for communication, which in turn will usher in a range of new working practices and radically change many people's lives.

The key lies in the setting up of computer networks both inside and outside organizations. One of the largest in the public sector is the Internet. Many organizations are now establishing their own networks, offering a range of on-line services. These external networks will eventually become a primary source of organizational and industry information.

Once people, wherever they are in the world, can exchange information instantaneously – using not only text or speech, but also video, graphics and other kinds of sounds – profound changes are needed in the shape and style of organizations with which they interact.

Properly managed, access to such computer networks can be the means for creating organizations that are not only more participative but vastly more efficient and effective. Poorly managed, it is just as likely to lead to worse communication, not better.

That is why the development and implementation of internal networks, as well as judgements about their synergy with external networks, cannot be left to the IT department – nor even to internal communication specialists. To gain the full benefits of this revolution in communication, the involvement of the whole senior management team is essential.

WHAT IS AVAILABLE

The range of communication services that can be offered on computerized networks is unlimited and can be adapted to meet an organization's particular needs. The services currently available and their basic capabilities are listed below. Part III of this Handbook looks in more detail at the strengths and weaknesses of some of these new media as methods of communicating and of managing communication.

Electronic mail

Instant transfer of messages and documents worldwide between people on the same private network, or with access to the same public network.

Facsimile

Transmission of documents to addresses not yet capable of accessing or receiving information using electronic mail but which do use traditional fac-simile machines.

Video conferencing

Meetings conducted via computer terminal screens using multimedia facilities – as opposed to using special equipment and dedicated rooms.

Business television

Live or pre-recorded business television programmes that are broadcast across the network.

Electronic libraries

News and information, often edited and updated centrally, that can be used in much the same way as televised teletext, except it is more flexible and faster. A front page screen lists the information available by subject headings. Predominantly it is a text service although some networks provide multimedia electronic libraries.

Computer conferencing

Any user on a network can open a 'conference' on any topic and other users can contribute. Particularly useful for organizations that want to invite feed-back on topical issues.

Electronic daily news service

A daily summary of any media news that features the organization, its industry and competitors. This is then provided on the network for access by all users. It can also include highlights of worldwide news, stock prices and the latest organizational press releases.

Electronic newsletters and journals

Initiated internally or externally by any individual or group wishing to provide news, information and features on their particular specialist area. They can then be distributed on-line to predetermined distribution lists.

Reader's Choice

One area of concern for current users of computer networks is the plethora of information and news they receive on a daily basis, much of which is not relevant to their work. This can be alleviated by setting up some form of Reader's Choice. Each user on the network completes an electronic proforma that details their specialist areas of interest. This is held centrally. Any specialist newsletters and journals are also sent on-line to a central electronic distribution point which creates distribution lists based on users' proforma information.

THE IMPACT ON ORGANIZATIONAL STRUCTURES

In traditional organizations, all the key information is pulled to the top of the organization and senior management make decisions that drive resources, responsibilities and control down to the front-line units.

By contrast, computer networks allow communication to flow freely through-out an organization cutting through hierarchial and bureaucratic obstacles. Consequently, the organizations that have benefited most from the introduc-tion of these new networks have also changed their fundamental structure.

The successful modern organization has been compared to a biological organism rather than a centrally controlled machine. Computer networks act as veins ensuring a steady flow of information and communication to every point of the organism.

Organizations using the new networks successfully share several character-istics.

Flatter structures

More organizations are breeding knowledge workers – people who have become almost independent specialists within their own area. These people *49* expect to receive information speedily and directly from source in order to do their jobs effectively. As a result, organizations have found that they no longer need a large number of middle managers controlling and often censoring information, and have created fewer tiers of management. The new networks ensure information can reach anyone who needs it.

Individuals want to network

With flatter structures, the walls are also coming down between the various specialized departments and functions. The popularity of total quality management (TQM) and re-engineering has seen organizations placing emphasis more on horizontal processes than vertical relationships. This has encouraged employees to network throughout the company, irrespective of the traditional boundaries. The computer network allows employees to contact any individual they feel has the specialized knowledge that will help them in handling their job.

Global standards

Large numbers of companies and organizations, regardless of size, now operate in an international framework. Manufacturing plant, sales and distribution outlets may be on opposite sides of the globe. Colleagues or parallel organizations around the world may have the vital piece of information necessary to move a project forward. The new computer networks allow employees to communicate and share information around the world, at any time of the day, 365 days a year.

Project teams

An increasing amount of the work carried out by organizations is done on a project basis. A team with the appropriate resources and skills is put together to complete a particular enterprise and disbanded when it has done so. In this respect the new organization is often compared to a symphony orchestra or hospital where large groups of specialists, who direct and discipline their own performance, come together as required to work towards a common goal. As computer networks develop a growing number of so-called virtual teams are also being set up. These may be composed of specialists from around the world. However, they are virtual in that they never physically meet. All their communication is conducted across computer networks.

Openness

Where greater participation and involvement is desired, it is necessary to build an environment of trust. That means making information more widely available. The computer network gives people much greater access to an organization's information database.

SEGMENTING INTERNAL AUDIENCES

Organizations that want to go down the networking route need to begin by considering the relative importance of the audiences with whom they need to communicate.

Employees

The employee audience is likely to be segmented into smaller groups depending on whether individuals are working for the organization full-time, part-time, as contractors and so on. Certain groups may need to be excluded from accessing information regarded as highly sensitive.

Organizational partners

To help improve their effectiveness, organizations are forming an increasing number of alliances and strategic partnerships. Many organizations also operate through dealers and other third parties to market their products and services. An on-line connection to these partners helps to facilitate sharing of information and faster decision making. The network allows the employees of an organization and its partners to communicate directly with each other.

Financial institutions

Most sectors of the financial industry, including banks, insurance companies and investment houses, have had sophisticated computer networks installed for many years. However these have almost all been data and graphics-driven and have not offered the sophisticated video and audio interactive facilities that are currently coming on-line. It will become invaluable for organizations to have on-line connections with their various financial institutions, although access is likely to be restricted to specific groups.

Suppliers

Many organizations already have on-line network connections with their principal suppliers, although again these are mostly data and graphics-driven. Various groups and individuals within an organization will have their own portfolio of suppliers. Facilitating a network connection can ensure a faster and more efficient service between both parties.

Media

Organizations often have to respond so rapidly to changes in the market-place and external events that information may reach the external media before it has been fully communicated internally. An effective computer network helps

51

to alleviate this situation as media releases can be communicated over the internal network prior to their being sent externally. It is still uncertain how conventional media channels will operate in the emerging digital environment although it is probable that interactive computer networks will eventually become the predominant communication medium.

Government and other influential groups

Most organizations create relationships with a broad range of groups with whom it would be invaluable to share not only a networked communications link but also specific information. This link could include groups such as a university or government department, a local chamber of commerce or consumer organization.

Customers

Organizations can communicate directly with the ever-increasing number of customers who own their own PC and modem. They will be able to provide sales and marketing information, take orders, respond to enquiries and organize on-line research.

General public

Organizations can increasingly communicate with the general public across the computer networks already established in the public arena. Using this new channel gives organizations more control over their external communication than is offered currently by working through traditional media outlets.

THE IMPACT ON WORKING PRACTICES

The computer is the essential work tool of the late twentieth century and an important aspect of the computer is that it is not location specific. Since the nineteenth century, newly-invented forms of transport such as the train, the car and the aeroplane have introduced more and more mobility into people's working lives. But the economic and social effects of commuting are becoming untenable. Air pollution, traffic congestion and environmental degradation are becoming too high a cost to pay for the daily migration of employee productivity. By contrast, computer networks provide the ability to move work to people by moving ideas and information.

It is now possible to send and retrieve work from anywhere in the world, and just as efficiently at home as from an office. And when these computers are linked to multimedia capability – including videoconferencing for example – not only do opportunities open up for highly effective communication vehicles, but the value of commuting into a centralized workplace decreases.

Flexible workers (not to be confused with flexi-time workers) are on the increase. They are full-time employees who simply do not require a permanent workplace. The introduction of such working patterns leads to significant cultural changes that present communication professionals with specific challenges.

Bringing employees together

Flexible workers are just that, flexible, so they could be working in many different ways:

- *office based* – spending most time at their organization's main office
- *location based* – having a home office as well as spending time in the office
- *home worker* – spending most of their time working from home
- *mobile worker* – based at home but travelling to work at different locations
- *site worker* – based at home but travelling to work at customer sites.

Bringing such employees together, say for a social occasion, presents its own problems.

Cascading messages

Most communication research concludes that the manager is employees' preferred source of organizational information. However, in organizations that have enterprise-wide computer networks, it is found that electronic mail, and other on-line information services become the preferred source of information. Indeed, some organizations have found that introducing computer networks can disenfranchise the manager altogether as the main source of communication.

Ensuring good decisions

Greater responsibility is being given to employees, particularly those in customer-facing roles. Many are expected to use their initiative in situations that previously would have been prescribed in organizational procedures manuals, held by managers and supervisors. Today, rather than being bombarded with corporate-wide generic messages, employees need be given only a broad decision-making framework plus whatever flow of information is needed to do their job.

MAKING IT HAPPEN

The strategic impact on organizations of the new computer networks can be summarized as:

53

- a more democratic and participative work culture
- convergence of external and internal communication
- a more flexible and self-reliant workforce.

Making communication work within this new organizational paradigm takes careful planning. Two committees need to be established: a steering committee and an action committee. The *steering committee* is concerned with the goals and strategy while the *action committee* is responsible for the implementation. To ensure that the two work in harmony, a member of the steering committee should also be the chairperson of the action committee. Both the steering committee and action committee should have direct lines into the senior management board (Figure 5.1).

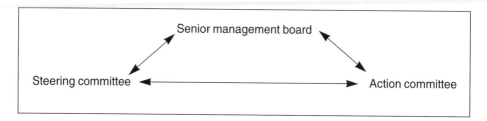

Figure 5.1   Board and IT implementation

THE STEERING COMMITTEE: WHO'S ON IT AND WHAT IT HAS TO DO

Given that the success of the organization will be strongly linked to the success of the new computer network, it is essential that the chief executive or managing director chairs the steering committee.

And as computer networks begin to play an increasingly important role in communication with a number of audiences, integration between the human resources, marketing and corporate communications functions will grow. The directors representing these functions should be involved.

The steering committee will need to consider certain core issues.

Business objectives

The purpose of providing access to computer networks is to support the goals of the organization. The steering committee's task is therefore to explore opportunities for achieving business goals more effectively using the computer network. That will involve developing an understanding of the networks' capabilities and their potential impact.

Existing technologies

54   The steering committee will need to evaluate the current technology used by

the organization for communication. Often, the full capabilities of existing technology are not being used because users lack knowledge or have insufficient technical support. Current technologies need to be considered in the light of the objectives for the computer network and technical compatibility.

Audiences

The needs of the various audiences who will use the network must be evaluated. Decisions will have to be taken on the level of service each will be offered and the degree of openness to be allowed.

On-line services management

Some of the services made available on the network need to be managed centrally. The steering committee will determine the make-up of this group and the scope of their work. The key personnel within the group will be communication professionals with experience of on-line services.

Timescales

A timescale needs to be agreed and an implementation plan produced.

Budget

The real cost of computer networks is not the initial expenditure on hardware and software but the ongoing systems costs. Many of the leading computer manufacturers have built features into their systems that have been designed to cut maintenance costs. Many organizations have also contracted-out the management of particular applications, the help-desk function, or the whole network, in an effort to control costs.

Use IT suppliers to help produce a budget for the network. Get their help in going beyond initial capital costs to take into account the full costs of the network over its expected lifetime, particularly labour costs.

THE ACTION COMMITTEE: WHO'S ON IT AND WHAT IT HAS TO DO

The implementation, or even a major upgrade, of a new computer network will have a substantial impact on an organization. It is therefore essential that the implementation is handled in stages.

Preparation

The preparation stage should focus on communicating the reasons for introducing the network, the individual and organizational benefits and an outline of the timescale. This stage should not be rushed – many such initiatives have failed because insufficient consideration was given to preparing people to accept or indeed welcome them.

Revelation

This stage should reveal the details of the network, including its capability to change people's patterns of work and communication. Its emphasis should be on training.

Communications technology is becoming increasingly simple to use and in time the communications facilities on a network will be as easy to use as a telephone. However, apart from learning how to use the network from a technical standpoint, people will also need to be trained in the new network guidelines and standards that will have to be established. It will also be essential to set up separate training programmes for special groups such as flexible workers.

Transmission

The final stage is the installation of the network, including the hardware and software. If the preparation and revelation stages have been implemented successfully then the transmission stage should allow the organization to benefit immediately from its new computer network.

HOW TO FIND OUT MORE

In the Age of the Smart Machine: the future of work and power by Shoshana Zuboff, New York, Basic Books, 1988
The New Realities by Peter Drucker, Heinemann, 1989
The New Organisation by Colin Hastings, IBM McGraw-Hill Series, 1993
The Empty Raincoat by Charles Handy, Hutchinson, 1994
The Virtual Community by Howard Rheingold, Secker & Warburg, 1994
Communication Futures Technology: the impact of technology on internal communication by Anthony Goodman, Kate Lye and Kevin Gavaghan, Smythe Dorward Lambert, 1994
Cyber Business by Christopher Barnatt, John Wiley & Sons, 1995
Being Digital by Nicholas Negroponte, Hodder & Stoughton, 1995
Creating Tomorrow's Organisation by David Birchell and Laurence Lyons, Pitman Publishing, 1995

Part II

EFFECTIVE COMMUNICATION STRATEGIES

6 Setting objectives

David Clutterbuck, *chairman, The ITEM Group*

It is no longer enough to demonstrate professionalism in the delivery of communications. The ability to put together a clear, credible communication strategy, one that demonstrably adds value and links closely to corporate goals, is more and more a necessity for any IC professional who wants respect from top management. This chapter takes you through the strategy setting process, from appreciating political realities and styles, to its critical conclusion – a successful presentation to the board.

Like any other strategy, a communication strategy cannot exist – and therefore should not be conceived – in isolation. It should be (and be seen as) an integral part of the mechanics of ensuring that the strategy of the organization succeeds. (If no one in the senior management structure takes responsibility for developing a communication strategy, that is in itself a strategic decision – to manage without the integrative power of planned communication.)

The communication professional should therefore be able to sit down and create a communication strategy as an immediate outcome of the organization strategy. In practice, it's rarely that simple, for a number of reasons.

Many organization strategies are themselves inadequate for the purpose

They may be too vague, insufficiently related to what is really going on inside and outside the organization, or, in some cases, virtually non-existent. Especially (but not only) in small and medium-sized enterprises, top management may have a fairly clear idea of the general direction it wishes to take the company, but nothing that clearly expresses the strategy and its implications for the component parts of the organization.

In such circumstances, objectives tend to be relatively arbitrary, based heavily on past performance rather than on potential, and fairly easily distorted either by the whim of the chief executive or by functions and departments for their own ends.

The IC function may find that its priority task is to help the board or the executive team articulate the organization strategy in a form that *all* functions in the business can understand, relate to and use in developing their own strategies and objectives.

Even where there is a clear business strategy, this is only the top layer

Beneath it the IC function must build a strategy that supports needs from around the business. There will be specific demands for support from line managers and other functions, for example, who need communication help to deliver their strategies, and from cross-functional project teams, set up to deliver specific changes, which will also have special communication needs.

The role of the IC function is to juggle these needs, agreeing with its internal customers strategic objectives that are both achievable and closely in line with the business direction. Given that key figures in the company may have very different views of relative priorities, this can be a delicate set of negotiations. Without a senior manager who has strong personal influence, it may be impossible to arrive at a consensus.

The strategic process is rarely as well-developed in companies as the board would have outsiders believe

Still relatively little use is made of techniques such as scenario planning to identify and plan for alternative futures – most serious problems still tend to come as surprises.

In developing their business strategies, the majority of companies operate at one or other of the operational extremes illustrated in Figure 6.1.

For the IC manager, the absence of a single right approach to strategy creation has a number of implications.

- Where strategic styles do not encourage active participation by staff functions, initiatives only appear on the IC agenda once they have already been decided. IC's role then becomes one of implementing around goals and priorities already cast in concrete.
- Where wider involvement is the norm, the challenge becomes one of harnessing rampant creativity around shared priorities. IC can have a significant role to play in making the process of consultation structured and meaningful, time-effective and cost-effective. In particular, it can help to define the framework and facilitate the processes for gathering and analysing input from numerous sources.
- Where there is no visible strategic statement, the priority for the IC function is to get close enough to senior management thinking to model

Top down Top management creates the broad strategic objectives and asks managers below to expand it – but not to challenge the general direction or targets.	**Bottom down** Top management invites unit and function managers to develop strategic plans and then looks for the common-alities. There is usually a very broad framework or vision to work within.
Caucus Strategy is the job of a chosen few at the centre.	**Broad church** Lots of people have a contribution to make towards strategic thinking.
Ends directed Emphasizes the *what* – provides strong picture of what success would look like. Places great value on vision. Sales and marketing have the main influence.	**Means directed** Emphasizes the *how* – the mechanics of achieving the dream. Staff functions such as HR, IT and Internal Communication may be involved as drivers rather than advisers or deliverers.
Unified Top management feels it is important that everyone understands and commits to the big picture.	**Fractured** Top management only expects people to understand and commit to their particular part of the strategy.

Figure 6.1   Operational extremes

an approach on it. Recent management initiatives, culture change pro-grammes and so on all hold important clues. Using one or two influential and communication-conscious senior managers as sounding boards is a practical move.

Whatever the predominant strategic planning style of an organization, if the contribution of IC is to be valued, it is important to recognize and work it. In due course, it may be possible to promote change in the process, but that can only be accomplished from within.

Within the IC function itself, however, there is no need to follow the pre-dominant strategic planning style. The manager will be more effective in developing strategic objectives if he or she makes some clear decisions about, for example, whether to spend time gathering the views of a wide range of internal customers or simply to discuss priorities with the top team.

CREATING LINKS WITH ORGANIZATION STRATEGY

An effective IC strategy will link with the organizational and other departments' strategies at four levels.

- *Mission* The mission, along with the vision and values, that provides the rationale and fundamental purpose for the organization.

61

- *Objectives* The pragmatic medium- and long-term goals that stem from the mission.
- *Strategy* The broad processes by which those objectives can be achieved. Strategy provides the focus for investment of the key resources of finance and people. It also assigns priorities within the organization's stakeholder groups.
- *Tactics* Campaigns, budgets and plans, usually within the short-to-medium term.

The primary aim of the communication strategy must be to add value at each of these points. This can be achieved by a number of means:

- capturing the concepts in a manner that makes them readily communicable (i.e. understandable, deliverable and able to influence) to the various stakeholder audiences
- establishing the mechanisms for feedback to senior management and ensuring that they are efficient and effective
- developing and implementing IC plans that reflect the organization's strategic priorities.

CRAFTING STRATEGY TO FORM A SOLID BASIS FOR PLANNING

Turning these broad aims into genuine value added is primarily a matter of prioritizing and integrating using a strategic activity grid as illustrated in Figure 6.2.

Along one axis of the grid lie the strategic objectives. Along the other are the communication objectives. Both will vary from organization to organization, but the latter might typically include:

- gaining commitment to the organization's direction
- increasing and maintaining motivation
- giving people the right information to do the job
- ensuring people have the right skills to do the job
- supporting the desired corporate culture
- maintaining and increasing top team credibility
- encouraging teamwork
- supporting functional/business unit campaigns
- advising on communication technologies
- ensuring effective systems of feedback.

With this 'wish-list' matrix, the IC manager can now consult a senior manager to check on priorities and budgets, which will allow the generation of a communication plan (see Chapter 7). Given that budgets are never infinite, judgements will need to be made on a number of criteria, including absolute and unit cost, the number of strategic objectives and purposes supported and

Business objectives / Communication objectives	Quality improvement (achieve EQA)	Investment in people	Effective change management	etc.
Stimulate upward feedback	Make the suggestion scheme work	Encourage people to identify development opportunities for themselves	Identify which and where resistance to change is occurring	etc.
Gain commitment to business vision and goals	Educate people in quality concepts. Recognize quality achievements	etc.	Help people understand how changes fit with the business vision	etc.
Improve communication and teamwork between functions	etc.	etc.	etc.	etc.
etc.	etc.	etc.	etc.	etc.

Figure 6.2 Strategic activity grid

The boxes of the grid will be used to select the relevant tools for each job. These can be media (e.g. magazines, conferences) or activities (e.g. internal consultancy, training, research). Any current activity that doesn't find a place in the grid (i.e. that doesn't fulfil both a communication purpose and a strategic objective) is probably not worth doing.

The next stage is to add (usually in a different colour) any tools that *could* usefully be added to the grid. Both existing and new tools can then be costed, and graded accordingly.

the people resources available. The question 'How will this add value to the organization?' underlies all these discussions.

A decision will also have to be made on where the emphasis should lie between the strategic and tactical, administration and delivery (Figure 6.3).

	Administration	Delivery
Strategy	Policy	Consultancy
Tactics	Administration	Communication training Media production

Figure 6.3 Deciding on emphasis

Practical experience in other staff functions shows that it is difficult to gain credibility by trying to give equal priority to all four areas of activity. In general, the more willing top management is to cast the IC in the policy/consultancy roles, the more sense it makes to contract out admininstration and delivery functions either to the line (i.e. away from the corporate centre) or to an external contractor.

UNDERSTANDING THE DRIVERS AND BARRIERS

The strategic activity grid provides a solid basis for constructing a detailed plan of action, with budgets and schedules. Before doing so, however, there are still a few additional pieces of the jigsaw to gather together.

The first is to identify what will boost and what may hinder effective communication within the organization. These 'drivers and barriers' can take many forms, but will normally include the culture, the people, the procedures and systems, and the resources available. A SWOT analysis (looking at strengths, weaknesses, opportunities and threats) is a useful means of identifying this data.

Understanding the drivers and barriers enables you to assess how different types of messages and different circumstances will affect the quality and quantity of communication. This in turn helps decide how much resource needs to be invested to achieve communication objectives, for example how many times a message needs to be repeated through different media.

The SWOT analysis

To carry out a SWOT analysis you will need to develop a realistic picture of the environment in which the IC function operates. By realistic, we mean:

- based on valid research or other credible data
- objective – experiments show that most managers tend to accentuate the positive and underemphasize the negative, for obvious reasons (this can be particularly true of 'promotional' departments, such as IC, public affairs and marketing)
- at the right level of detail (this is a matter of judgement and most people get it right after a few attempts).

Your picture of the environment might typically include the following.

An analysis of the organization's attitude towards IC

Is it hostile, positive or neutral? Neutral may be the worst position of all, because it implies people do not think IC matters. At least if they are hostile, it shows they care and provides an impetus for meeting their concerns.

One-on-one interviews, questionnaires and focus groups are all useful techniques for gathering this data. Typically, you will find substantial variations in attitude across the organization. These can usually be aggregated into segments of the internal audience, giving you the opportunity to revisit each segment to find out *why* they are positive, negative or neutral.

An assessment of the IC brand

Closely linked to general attitude, the brand is a summation of people's perception both of the 'proper' role of IC and of the quality of its performance. Given that IC is increasingly being requested to help other functions improve their own branding, it behoves IC to at least try to set an example.

Establishing an internal brand takes time, but is almost always worth the effort. Get IC staff and the internal customers to answer some of the following questions.

- What do internal customers think of our:
  - competence/professionalism?
  - ability to motivate?
  - relevance to their most pressing problems?
  - interest in those problems?
  - integrity?
  - responsiveness? (e.g. whose timeframe do we operate in – ours or theirs?)
- What factors affect the way internal customers think of us?

To support this broad data, it often helps to gather anecdotal evidence illustrating perceptions. The questions 'Why do you feel that way?' and 'Can you give me an example?' may open up the floodgates of frustration, providing valuable insights.

An evaluation of top management's understanding of communication and its role in making it happen

To what extent does the top management team need to be educated in this regard?

Just because there are one or two champions of IC, it does not mean that the top team as a whole is on board. And senior managers tend to have a far lesser understanding of the dynamics of communication than they think. This is true even when the chief executive and chairman appear and think themselves to be highly supportive. Not only may they not be aware of where else IC can contribute, but the broad requirement for consensus at the top may result in the blocking of valuable IC initiatives, simply because the CEO needs time to sell them to colleagues.

An evaluation of communications competency generally in the organization

From top management down to the shopfloor or front office, communication skills are essential, if only in getting the job done. Yet most organizations have no objective measures of how competent people are at communicating, nor of how well communications occurs. This information is vital both in making the case for IC expenditure and directing where it should be spent. The barrier until recently has been the lack of effective methods of assessing communica- *65* tion competence at an organizational, team and individual level. This lack is rapidly being overcome – not least by pioneering work by ITEM and some of its leading edge customers.

An evaluation of the primary communication vehicles

In a number of studies of media in leading UK and European companies, we have identified a common pattern, which we call *objective decay*. Key media, such as team briefings or employee periodicals, are set up with a small number of core goals in mind. In the best-managed IC functions, these objectives are clearly stated and communicated both within management and to the intended audience.

Over time, however, senior management changes, the organization's structure and priorities evolve. New tasks are assigned to the medium; tasks for which it may not have been designed, but convenience is a compulsive argument. Before long, the original objectives have been diluted or forgotten, but their influence remains.

Reviewing media against their objectives on a regular basis should be a standard requirement of the IC function. In practice, it happens far too infrequently. The increasing demand by top management for measurement data is bringing about change here, but there is much to be gained from ensuring that the initiative for measurement and review comes from the IC function itself.

Equally important at this point is to question both whether the objectives set now match the organization's priorities and whether the media used are the most suitable for communicating those objectives. Close consultation with top management is essential here.

An evaluation of organizational receptivity

This piece of jargon simply means how receptive different internal audiences are to different types of messages. Receptivity may be affected by local culture, educational level, previous experience (e.g. having trusted a company promise before and been severely disappointed), the nature of the work discipline (people in IT and in the legal section may interpret an apparently straight-forward message in very different ways) and so on.

Of course, you cannot map an audience's receptivity to all messages, but you can begin to identify how it is likely to react to some of the core messages to be broadcast over the next year or so.

For example, if a group of employees has been through a period of intense and painful change, are they likely to want to listen to news of yet more radical change on the way? And if they listen to it, are they likely to be accepting, welcoming, neutral or resistant?

An evaluation of the link between internal and external communications

Are the same messages being broadcast by IC and Public Affairs/Marketing?

Are the mechanisms to ensure a seamless communication adequate and effective? Have they been put to the test?

An evaluation of the link between IC and other, internal-facing functions

ITEM's experience with staff functions of all kinds suggests that IC rarely puts much effort into educating other functions in how to use centrally-controlled communication media to best effect. Is there a forum for examining such issues? Does IC have a clear understanding of the communication priorities of each of the other functions it supports?

An assessment of 'make or buy' opportunities

Unless the organization has a blanket embargo on the use of third-party suppliers, it is useful to examine the pros and cons of resourcing externally. Critical questions in this evaluation include:

- what are our priorities?
- can we deliver these from our own people resources and still have capacity to handle other, perhaps more essential activities?
- what is the cost comparison, with and without overheads and other hidden costs?
- can an outside provider bring objectivity or expertise not easily generated from within?
- what are the politics of this decision?

Gathering all this data for a comprehensive SWOT analysis may take weeks or even months the first time around. So the SWOT analysis needs to begin at least six months ahead of the target date for producing the communication strategy. Ideally, you should involve as many as possible of the IC staff (to gain their ownership of and commitment to the results). You may also wish to involve a cadre of selected internal customers. You will certainly need to keep the chief executive informed.

AT LAST, THE STRATEGY

The strategy should be an automatic outcome of all these deliberations. It will typically be put together over a series of iterations, with multiple short discussions and a small number of intensive retreats (perhaps just one) to tie the ends down and ensure agreement among the key IC staff.

The strategy can take a variety of forms, but one of the most common and easily adaptable is as follows.

1. *Executive summary*
   What needs to be done, why, and at what cost? What choices have to be made by the top team in allocation of resources?

2. *Where are we now?*
   Using measurement wherever practical, identify the strengths, weaknesses, opportunities and threats for the organization in communication terms.
3. *What can IC do to help build on the strengths, overcome the weaknesses and threats, and seize the opportunities?*
   This section should be highly results-oriented. The key criterion is will this investment of time and resources support the business objectives?
4. *Who do we need to communicate to, to achieve these objectives?*
   This involves sensitive audience segmentation.
5. *What media should we use?*
   Look at new media and review existing media.
6. *How will we measure the effectiveness of our efforts?*
   Consider both quantitative and qualitative measures.

SELLING THE COMMUNICATION STRATEGY INTO THE ORGANIZATION

If you have gone through the strategy creation process conscientiously, you will already have involved many key people. None the less, the finished strategy must itself be sold, as an entity, into the internal market.

Of course, the strategy document itself must exemplify best practice communication: it should be clear, precise and well supported with accurate, credible data; it should show strong understanding of strategic, financial and operational issues as well as an easy familiarity with the language and concepts of strategy.

But as in any form of selling (or indeed any form of communication), documents are only one tool. Your next step must be to put together a communication plan for the strategy itself – part of which will be to secure senior management champions who will in turn help promote the strategy on your behalf.

7 Developing a plan: the basics

Mike Long, *managing director, The ITEM Group* and
Tony Newbold, *specialist business writer*

*Taken together, the next two chapters provide a complete and compre-
hensive approach to developing a communication plan, which you can
easily modify to suit your own needs. Before looking at each of the common
planning steps in detail, this chapter helps you consider some questions that
will be fundamental to the success of your efforts.*

WHY HAVE A PLAN?

One of the most common reasons for the failure of change initiatives within
organizations is inadequate communication. There are many reasons for this –
unwillingness to cooperate; political machinations; lack of vision and direction
at the top; but above all, the lack of a plan for communicating the key messages
and feeding back reactions.

The communication plan answers these challenges by providing clear direction and coordination. Without it, there is a strong likelihood that all activity
will tend to randomness – reacting to day-to-day events. A plan provides a
structure to work to, makes it clear who is responsible, with defined budgets
and schedules, and gives a benchmark for performance measurement. It helps
you ensure that you are getting the maximum impact for your budget by
orchestrating different media and messages to reinforce each other.

It also shows that you are in control of your job, makes establishing your
case for a budget much simpler and helps build credibility with key decision
makers within your organization.

And when the inevitable happens, and radical change does occur in your
organization, you will have a rigorous process in place for communicating it in
a way that suits your culture.

WHAT DOES A COMMUNICATION PLAN LOOK LIKE?

The plan will normally outline:

- the main messages to be communicated
- what you intend to do
- the methods to be used
- resources needed
- measures of success.

The exact content and appearance of the plan will depend on the nature of your audiences and the culture of your organization. Generally it will be a formal document, well presented (since you need to practise what you preach) and in sufficient detail to be useful to its readers. It can also begin to establish an identity for internal communication within your organization.

WHO IS THE PLAN DESIGNED FOR?

1. *Yourself* You use it as a working tool. It sets out your personal and public agendas, and provides an opportunity for you to clarify your thinking by following its discipline, and to schedule your communication activities to best effect.
2. *Your team* Involve your team in developing the plan, as their ideas, support and commitment will be vital.
3. *The person you report to* You will need their buy-in and sign-off, both in terms of the messages and the media used.
4. *The top team* Their support is essential since effective internal communication is likely to be one of the keys to their success.
5. *Key players in the organization* These are people who have an interest in communication activities, and are not always the same as the top team. For example human resources may be closely involved through the communication of personnel issues; sales and marketing may have a strong interest in gaining support for new initiatives or feeding back performance results; customer services may be concerned about messages coming from the organization via employees.
6. *Everyone in the organization* People will relate better to communication activities if they can see the reason for them. By being involved in the communication plans that affect them, people will be more likely to buy in to both the process and the messages, and see that the organization is committed to communication.

Not everyone wants, or needs, to see the whole plan. But you may choose, for example, to highlight parts of it via existing internal media, and this can have as much to do with marketing the activities of internal communication as with informing people.

The decision about which of these audiences sees which part of the plan rests mainly on the politics of your organization and your own strategic imperatives.

WHAT DOES THE PLAN DO?

The plan spells out:

- objectives
- priorities and strategy
- audiences
- targets
- key messages
- tactics
- media
- feedback systems
- responsibilities
- resourcing
- timings
- measurements.

This list may look daunting, but many of these sections can be quite brief, and you may find that in practice several topics can be grouped into one section.

WHEN DO YOU NEED A PLAN?

Most communication plans run for a year, to reflect the organization's own business year and planning process. Ideally, the plan should be used throughout the year to measure achievement against objectives, and can be updated as appropriate. It is important that the plan is flexible enough to keep up with changing strategic priorities. As the person running internal communication, you need to be on the 'inside track' of strategic changes, otherwise you will not be in a position to support these.

SHOULD YOU GET EXTERNAL HELP WITH THE PLAN?

External consultants can help you to develop new thinking and produce maximum impact. Choose someone you feel comfortable with, who has a proven track record in communication and in dealing with organizational politics, but remember that no one knows the organization better than you. Consider benchmarking your communication process against someone you consider a leader in the field.

Once you have considered these questions, you can start developing your plan.

8 Developing a plan: a step-by-step approach

Mike Long, *managing director, The ITEM Group* and Tony Newbold, *specialist business writer*

This chapter outlines a typical communication plan. It suggests how to develop or find the information to complete each step, and discusses the issues that are likely to arise. You will find cross-references to subjects covered in more detail elsewhere in this Handbook.

This chapter describes a thorough and comprehensive approach to communication planning. A 20-step process for developing a plan is set out in Figure 8.1 (see pages 74–75). Depending on your own needs, you may want to vary the order of the steps, and your own timescales may dictate that you carry out some of the steps in parallel.

STEP 1   RESEARCH

In the early stages, you need to set yourself a clear vision for your communication plan. Ideally, this should be rooted in research (see Chapter 6 and Part V: Measuring success).

STEP 2   SET COMMUNICATION OBJECTIVES

The starting point for these objectives could be the priorities set out in your organization's business plan, if you have one. In any event, you can develop a clear set of objectives fairly easily, based on the strategic needs of your organization.

The most straightforward approach is to write down all the things you *need* to do, *ought* to do, or *would like* to do.

Need to do

This list should reflect the way the organization works; legal responsibilities; commitments made in the company mission and values; and actions tied in to your own performance objectives. In some organizations there is a formal charter that spells out the organization's commitment to communication.

Typical actions would include:

- communicate the half-yearly/annual results to everyone in the organization within 48 hours of their announcement
- provide regular updates on share schemes, pension schemes
- provide information on organization restructuring to everyone within 48 hours of the first announcement.

Ought to do

Actions that reflect best practice or would present you in a good light.

Typical actions would include:

- ensure over a three-month period that your target audience knows and understands the organization's vision and values
- communicate the essentials of the business plan to all employees within one month of its board approval
- publish monthly sales league tables.

Would like to do

The things you would like to do if budget and time allowed.

Typical actions would include:

- deliver all urgent corporate messages to all sites within 30 minutes
- link remote sites through three good human interest stories each month
- recognize monthly achievements relevant to your target audience.

Each objective starts with an action ('do this'), and defines what will be done, the audience and the timescale involved.

STEP 3   SET PRIORITIES AND STRATEGY

From your list of objectives, select the priority areas that will be the drivers behind your communication activities for the year. Choose those that are likely to have the greatest impact on your organization's performance. There is no point in ending up with a long list. You will be unlikely to deliver effectively on more than six major objectives. Some of the others will probably fall out as subsets of the main ones.

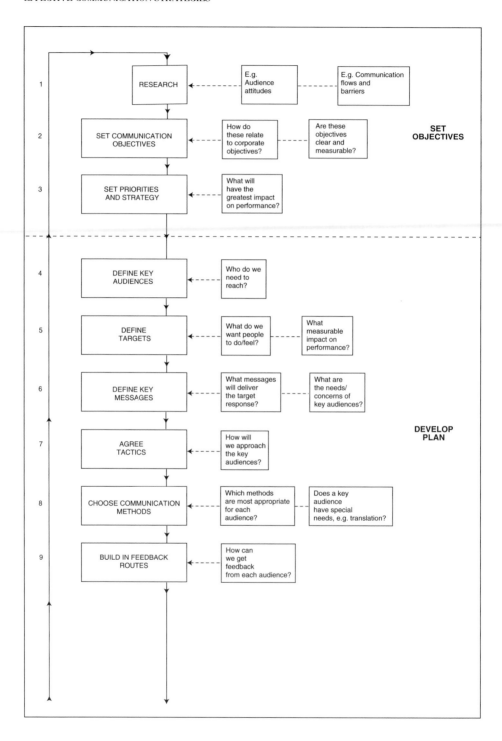

Figure 8.1   Developing a communication plan

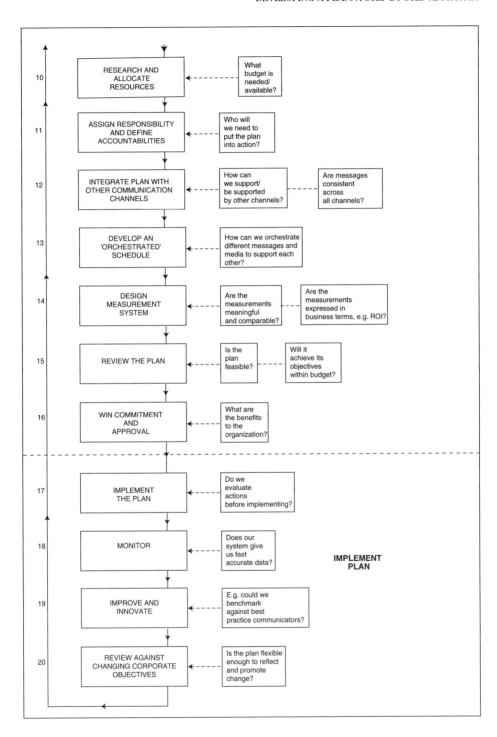

Figure 8.1   concluded

Once you have your priorities mapped out, it may be sensible to restate your communication strategy before you start getting distracted by detail. The strategy explains in outline *what* you are doing and *why*, whereas the plan explains in detail *how* and *when*.

The strategy may be something as straightforward and timeless as the following:

- establish key messages and audiences
- plan and implement clear and cost effective methods of delivering those messages
- create the infrastructure for continued efficient delivery
- ensure that all responses are fed back
- measure the effectiveness of all messages.

Alternatively it could be simply: 'to continue as in previous years, but this year working more closely with line management to focus on the following objectives'.

Or the strategy could be more detailed, for example outlining your approach to:

- regular communication
- campaigns on specific issues
- marketing the internal communication function
- who gets told what
- how rapidly messages need to be received

and so on, but without straying off into the detail of the plan.

See Chapter 6 for more detail on strategy.

STEP 4   DEFINE KEY AUDIENCES

Now that you have decided what your priorities are, and have set your general approach, it is time to consider your audiences. Who are you trying to communicate with? Who do you need to reach to achieve your objectives?

Likely audiences include:

- all employees
- senior management
- groups of employees by function for particular purposes – for example sales people, IT people
- groups of employees by project – for example everyone working on a particular model of car, albeit on different sites
- groups of employees by geographical area – for example everyone in the US subsidiary
- groups of employees by financial interest – for example employee shareholders, pension holders, bonus scheme members

- other stakeholders
  - general shareholders (usually non-institutional)
  - suppliers
  - collaborative partners
  - agents/brokers/third-party users
  - large/long-standing customers
  - retired employees
  - families of employees
  - the local community.

It may be impractical to communicate from the centre to so many different groups. Sometimes it will be done locally or functionally, with your support, in which case this needs to be taken into account in the plan.

STEP 5   DEFINE TARGETS

Now that you have defined the audiences you want to influence, you need to consider what you want them to do as a result of the communication:

- what attitudes are you seeking to create?
- what sort of behaviours do you want to promote?
- what perceptions do you want to change or challenge?
- what information do you want to convey to improve understanding?

Any communication is likely to fulfil one of three objectives: educate, motivate or inform. Whatever the objective, it is vital to have provable and quantifiable outcomes, so that you can demonstrate success.

For each of your communication objectives, create a measurable target. Often the simplest way to do this is to picture what success would look like in any particular area, and then describe the elements that would make it up. The relationship between the objectives and outcomes could be as follows.

Objective
- communicate the half-yearly/annual results to everyone in the organization within 48 hours of their announcement

Outcomes to check
- messages delivered on time
- received by the target audiences
- understood by them
- target attitudes adopted
- target behaviours observed
- target actions defined and checked
- feedback channels established
- feedback received and acted on.

You can now start generating the chart that will act as the heart of your action plan for communication (Figure 8.2). Where appropriate, each step will add another category to the chart. Filling this in helps you ensure you have thought through all issues in detail.

Audiences	Targets

Audiences: who you want to reach.
Targets: what you want the audience to achieve or feel as a result of the communication.

Figure 8.2   Planning chart

STEP 6   DEFINE KEY MESSAGES

Now that targets are set for communication activities, you need to consider the messages that will trigger the right response from your audiences to make them achieve the organization's objectives.

For example if your organization is seeking improved quality and customer service and reduced costs, you need to develop a campaign of messages that will raise awareness of these issues and help people to meet challenging targets.

These targets must be expressed in clear, measurable terms. One of the real dangers lies in creating impressive communication vehicles, and then discovering that senior management will not allow you to say anything meaningful or give you access to targets or figures. The vehicles become devalued as the messages vital to the organization's success are replaced with bland success stories. Far too many organizations plump for the softer, palatable 'nice to' communicate messages at the expense of what they really 'need to' communicate.

Usually you would expect key messages to relate to each part of the organization. For credibility from all audiences, there needs to be a clear link between your messages and corporate strategy – after all, if the message is not important to the organization, why are you pushing it?

Messages that would normally be considered as priority could include:

● the mission or vision of the organization
● any factors which are critical to the achievement of the vision – including regular progress reports and areas for improvement

- people issues – including audience feedback, and training and development
- community involvement.

Communication works when you are meeting the needs of your audience. To some extent, it is *their* needs and concerns that should drive the agenda for communication. There may be many issues that concern the people you are addressing that the organization in the past has ignored, or swept under the carpet. These issues may be affecting morale, motivation and performance, and your plan needs to address sensitive issues, because if they matter to people, everyone will be talking about them.

Once again, it may help to condense your original list of messages into six or seven themes, to generate a coherent plan that anyone can grasp.

Now that you have a list of key messages, you can add these to your planning chart, where appropriate, highlighting different priorities for each specific audience (Figure 8.3).

	Audiences	Targets
Key message 1		
Key message 2		
Key message 3		
Key message 4		
Key message 5		
Key message 6		

Figure 8.3 Planning chart: key messages

STEP 7   AGREE TACTICS

Tactics are simply short cuts to a more successful implementation of your strategy.

Umbrellas

The communication plan should provide a universal logic that consolidates messages across the organization so as to avoid confusion, cynicism and initiative overload. An 'umbrella logic' or campaign will give coherence and should also help to present a unified image.

Theming

Choosing valid and attractive themes gives your communication campaign real focus. For example, you may know that an organizational drive for empowerment or customer care is likely to happen in month five, and plan accordingly. Or you may prepare or force the issue by providing an outline series of themes for the year up front. This is simple to do and the list can be easily varied as required through the year to meet emerging needs.

For example, the following are all likely core topics for any organization:

- customer focus
- growing the business
- growing our people
- systems or processes to improve effectiveness
- teamwork
- innovation
- quality
- winning in our markets.

Clustering

Clustering is a variation on theming, and allows you to subgroup mini-campaigns so that they still fit the general picture.

These are the kinds of issues that need to be considered:

- frequency
  – how often do the various kinds of messages need to be carried?
- over what period?
- to which audiences?

Whichever tactics you choose to use, it is important to make it clear to people why you are communicating, what's in it for them, and how the message affects them.

STEP 8   CHOOSE COMMUNICATION METHODS

Once you've grouped your key messages into coherent themes, you can start planning *how* you will communicate them, for example choosing which communication methods and media will work best with which audience.

For each audience and message consider:

- what would be the best way of conveying each of the key messages?
- what methods do we currently use and how cost-effective are they?
- what is the 'shelf-life' of the campaign?
  – a one-off event like the announcement of the annual results would be delivered in a short burst across a variety of media
  – messages on a continuing subject, such as customer care, need a regular drip feed over an extended period.
- how many different methods would be appropriate?

- different media can reinforce each other and also 'refresh' messages over time
- individuals react differently to specific media, for example while some people may prefer the visual impact of video, others may react better to a detailed written document that they can read at their own pace.

Most surveys show that the majority of people prefer face-to-face communication, in the case of employees, ideally from their immediate boss. Clearly this is time-consuming, but it should be the preferred starting point because it gives an ideal opportunity for two-way communication and checking understanding.

Cascade briefings or briefing groups, with all their imperfections, can still create a strong base for any communication strategy. Around them you can build the infrastructure of other (less regular) opportunities for direct dialogue, and indirect message carriers – the core brief itself, handouts, magazines, videos, audiotapes and so on.

The wide range of options available for direct and indirect methods of communication are discussed in detail in Part III of this Handbook. Ideally, you want to be in a position to choose the methods most likely to suit:

- your objectives
- the nature of the messages
- the needs and attitudes of your key audiences
- feasibility within your budget and schedule.

One key audience need may be for translation. This is increasingly important, both because of transnational workforces, and because of different language groups within the same country or workplace. There are some basic questions to be answered:

- what size are the different language groups?
- what proportion of your target audience do they represent?
- how well do they understand English?
  - you may need to carry out a language audit to find out
- what proportion of the material will you translate?
  - for example, some multilingual magazines carry short translated summaries alongside the full original text
- which languages will the material originate in?
- how will it be translated?
- how will you check the translated text for cultural fit?
- do you need to have the translated copy available at the same time as the original?
- who will pay?

If you are working within a large organization with operations in a number of different countries and different languages, and you choose only to translate where the largest headcounts lie, you are sending out strong, indirect *81* messages to the others, with the risk of alienating them.

Add the media you intend to use as a column in your planning chart, thinking about their suitability for different audiences and messages (Figure 8.4).

	Audiences	Targets	Media
Key message 1			
Key message 2			
Key message 3			
Key message 4			
Key message 5			
Key message 6			

Media: best medium to convey this message to the audience.

Figure 8.4   Planning chart: media

STEP 9   BUILD IN FEEDBACK ROUTES

Feedback systems are essential to ensure that communication is not just one-way. They also allow you to make continuous adjustments to your communication media to meet changing needs and perceptions. And they provide useful information about the performance of internal communication, which may help your cause.

Feedback systems might include:

- focus groups
- analysis sheets (feedback forms)
- telephone hot lines
- reply coupons or letters pages in publications
- listening groups
- letters
- suggestion schemes.

Part III of this Handbook shows how you can create opportunities for feedback even with traditional one-way media.

Add a column for feedback mechanisms to your planning chart to ensure that you have a way of gathering reactions to each key message and from each target audience (Figure 8.5).

STEP 10   RESEARCH AND ALLOCATE RESOURCES

Most communication activities are time-intensive and resource-hungry.

	Audiences	Targets	Media	Feedback
Key message 1				
Key message 2				
Key message 3				
Key message 4				
Key message 5				
Key message 6				

Feedback: how response will be encouraged/received.

Figure 8.5   Planning chart: feedback

Organizations that fail to plan their communication adequately will pour away their budget through fire-fighting or use a large proportion of it on a high-profile flagship vehicle such as a corporate video or a large event, and have little left to sustain ongoing communication activities. Therefore, now that you've identified the media you want to use, you need to cost in detail how you would resource these.

Effectively, you are making the business case for each communication activity. You need to challenge each option, making sure it is the best way to invest your budget and that it really will deliver the maximum desired impact for your money. Going through this thought process will help you prepare your argument when justifying your budget.

Consider what resources your plan needs in terms of:

● people
● skills
● money
● equipment
● space.

To help define your role in internal communication, consider these questions:

● is your role hands-on, or do you provide support for other functions within the organization?
● what can most effectively be subcontracted?
● which areas, if any, would benefit from specialist external advice/ involvement?
● what can best be done in-house?
  – by your team
  – by others within the organization.

For example across the organization you may have existing resources you can call on to stretch your budget:

- an internal design function which will produce magazine pages/artwork
- copywriters
- distribution facilities on which to piggy-back – for example internal mail
- internal printing facilities.

The additional advantage of involving as many people internally as possible is getting their buy-in and support. For example involving employees on the editorial boards of newspapers and magazines will help you increase your credibility, especially if the employees are seen to be setting the news agenda.

When making your decision about whether to buy in skills and services consider the following:

- will internal resources be available when we need them?
- are internal resources costed on the basis of how much they actually cost the organization, or are certain factors left out?
- are there sensitivities that rule out bringing in outsiders, or are there political reasons that make it desirable to bring outsiders in?
- will outside experts be the *value* choice once quality, creativity and flexibility are taken into account?

When considering the budget, you also need to take into account any related training needs and how these would be met. For example, leaders of briefing groups may ideally need some training to ensure maximum effectiveness.

Budgets tend to work in one of two possible ways:

- 'what we spent last year', then add some
- zero basing, where everything is re-calculated from nil each year.

Either way, you still need to make a strong business case to justify the budget you are proposing. A well-thought out and fully-costed budget strengthens your argument, especially where backed up by cost-benefit analysis, citing consequences of poor communication.

A well-presented budget will also help you to resist (or win extra funding for) unexpected demands from colleagues for extra campaigns during the course of the year.

Ideally you should cost out each item against the schedule. Costs are likely to fall into the following categories:

- bought in goods
- bought in services
- overheads
    - salaries
    - occupancy costs: rent, rates, phone etc
- expenses

- internal costs from other divisions
  - for example, training, print or graphic support.

Sometimes part of the costs can be offset by:

- external advertisements in a magazine or audiotape
- recharging costs to subsidiaries or functions, for example, some organizations make operating units pay for their share of internal magazines on a per capita basis: it makes no difference to the organization, but it may help your budget.

Because communication is at the heart of any activity to change the way the organization works, you need to budget for the unexpected. Set aside a contingency fund to finance activities to cope with 'unexpected' events such as corporate acquisitions, takeover bids, redundancies, last-minute sales drives and changes of corporate direction.

Remember your plan is only a detailed route map. The day-to-day demands of business dictate that there should be enough flexibility in the plan to cope with the unexpected.

It is still hard to demonstrate a bottom-line benefit from internal communication activities. Attempts have been made to do this, with varying degrees of ingenuity and sophistication. Showing that you are willing to be measured on this basis sends the right message to your backers, and tying communication objectives tightly to those of the organization as a whole makes your case more secure. You still may not be able to *prove* your impact on the bottom line, but your research can show improvements in attitudes and behaviours, which can only act towards improved efficiency and corporate objectives.

Above all, budgets need to be transparent. It can be all too easy to lose track of costs in time-intensive communication activities, especially if you have only part-time access to in-house staff. For example if a manager repeatedly changes an article in an internal magazine, it is helpful to be able to tell him or her how much money that indecision is costing the organization.

Add a column for resources to your planning chart to ensure that you have a complete overview of the resources you will need to communicate each key message (Figure 8.6).

STEP 11   ASSIGN RESPONSIBILITY AND DEFINE ACCOUNTABILITIES

Where communication activities are competing for an executive's time, they can often be pushed on to the back burner. It is very important to set out clearly who is responsible and accountable for delivering key aspects of your communication plan.

Where organizations have introduced key competencies for individuals, communication usually features as a primary area. As part of the organiza-   *85*

	Audiences	Targets	Media	Feedback	Resources
Key message 1					
Key message 2					
Key message 3					
Key message 4					
Key message 5					
Key message 6					

Resources: people and budget needed to produce media selected for each message.

Figure 8.6　Planning chart: resources

tion's commitment to communication, you could consider having a named member of the top management team to champion a particular theme, for example one manager being the public face accountable for ensuring that messages about quality are communicated.

As with any action plan, the person responsible needs to know:

- what they have to do
- when they have to do it by
- how success will be measured.

Add a column for accountabilities to your planning chart to ensure that you have a named individual in charge of every core action, and that nothing can 'fall between the cracks' (Figure 8.7).

	Audiences	Targets	Media	Feedback	Resources	Accountabilities
Key message 1						
Key message 2						
Key message 3						
Key message 4						
Key message 5						
Key message 6						

Accountabilities: named individuals responsible for ensuring messages are communicated.

Figure 8.7　Planning chart: accountabilities

STEP 12   INTEGRATE PLAN WITH OTHER COMMUNICATION CHANNELS

By this point you have the skeleton of your plan in place, but before you start setting deadlines in your schedule, you need to think about the impact of other communication media on your target audiences.

Communication does not operate in a vacuum. Although you run internal communication you do not control every memo, every press release, every brochure, every advertisement, or any other means by which people form an impression about your organization.

You need to ensure that your plans support, reflect and react to what people receive through other communication vehicles and be aware of opportunities or issues coming up, for example:

- if a TV crew has been in-house filming a documentary, celebrate the coverage and encourage people to watch the film
- if you know there is going to be negative press coverage, act to circumvent this by giving people the organization's viewpoint before they read about it in their newspapers.

Some organizations fully integrate their internal and external communication, ensuring consistency and coordination of messages. In others, the two functions are completely divorced. Even where this is the case, the teams involved in internal and external communication need to work closely together, especially in areas of sensitivity such as redundancy announcements.

Whatever the case, there are always grey areas surrounding who takes responsibility for communicating specific messages. For example, who deals with employees' families and the local community?

If your organization is large, it may be that other functions (IT, distribution, sales, marketing, human resources and so on) already have well-established communication vehicles of their own. They may guard their interest in these jealously, or they may be only too willing for you to work with them. Either way, you need to take account of their needs and potential support in the plan.

There may also be the question of trade union activities. You may find yourself competing with them in terms of speed of messages delivered and of who gets in first with the information.

The important point is to see everything from the viewpoint of your target audience. It is constantly receiving information from different parts of the organization and outside. The organization's credibility is undermined if messages are inaccurate or inconsistent. You need to coordinate carefully to make sure your schedule includes key events. For example, you can support the messages of a new advertising campaign by running 'teaser' articles before the launch and in-depth coverage once it is under way.

STEP 13 DEVELOP AN 'ORCHESTRATED' SCHEDULE

You can now develop your plan into a schedule, setting out the proposed actions for each month. This approach will quickly expose any gaps or patchy coverage. Since the main complaint within most organizations is not about lack of communication, but poorly focused communication, the objective of scheduling is to produce a planned, even spread, with the appropriate messages delivered at the right time. Are there points where there is information overload, and other parts of the year where not much is happening? Also consider the logistics of managing the peaks and troughs of your communication plan – are you making best use of your resources?

Just as you can work with colleagues in different functions to coordinate and support messages through their media, so you can work with the media under your own control.

'Orchestrate' your campaign carefully, phasing in messages and different media for best effect, as illustrated in Figure 8.8. For example, a customer-service campaign could follow this route:

- short 'teaser' articles in the organization's magazines to raise awareness
- dedicated video and team briefing to give a high impact launch
- in-depth supplements in the magazines to explain the concept in detail
- regular progress reports towards the set targets, communicated across all media with target graphs marked up on posters and notice-boards
- travelling roadshow to reinforce the messages of the campaign, and offering advice to prevent enthusiasm tailing off.

Using different media, and repackaging messages in new and innovative ways will help keep your campaign alive. Also, the weaknesses of some media can easily be compensated for by supporting them with other devices. For example little detail can be conveyed in active sessions like team briefings and presentations, but details can be passed on in attractive documents, which the audience can refer to at their own pace.

STEP 14 DESIGN MEASUREMENT SYSTEM

Effective measurement requires valid pictures of 'before' and 'after'. At its most basic this might mean a survey of key audience opinion every two years. Within that, a series of milestones is needed to measure progress on a more frequent and regular basis.

Typical formal assessment systems are:

- audits of communication effectiveness
- opinion surveys
- mini-audits on particular issues, for example a forthcoming reorganization
- readership surveys.

TIME

	1	2	3	4	5	6	7	8	9	10	11	12
Key message 1	Mag. ►	TB	R: PLYMOUTH	PB	R: LONDON		PB	R: YORK		PB	R: GLASGOW	
Key message 2	C ►		TB ▼ Mag.	TB	PB	TB	PB	PB		PB	PB	CD ►
Key message 3	CD ►		▼ Mag.		Mag.►	TB	V ►	N ►	N ►	N ► C ►	C ►	CD ►
Key message 4						Mag.►	TB	TB N ►		Mag.► N ►		
Key message 5						Mag.►	TB	N ►		N ►		
Key message 6								Mag.► V ►	PB	TB	PB	PB

Key: Mag. = Magazine TB = Team briefing PB = Progress briefing R = Roadshow N = Newsletter C = Conference
CD = Conference document V = Video and document.

Figure 8.8 Timing chart

Performance must be measured against the key objectives you have set. Before you can measure performance you must know the following.

For the communication team
- who is responsible
- what standards are appropriate
- how performance can be measured against those standards.

For those receiving the messages
- did the messages get through?
- did they have the intended impact?
- were they understood?
- are these the preferred ways of receiving information?

Measurements can be made on at least two levels: corporate and local. There are also measurements for the messages themselves. For example:

- *relevance* – appropriateness, clarity of purpose
- *clarity* – coherence, understandability
- *credibility* – believability, trustworthiness
- *response* – registered impact.

Having researched the opinions of your key audiences you need to demonstrate a commitment to acting on the findings, and quickly feed the details of your research to your audiences.

There are also more general measurement issues:

- are there systems to check whether broader objectives, for example change of behaviour and attitude, have been met?
- do you measure internal customers' perceptions of your service?
- which award schemes can you enter as a measure of peer group value? For example, the Institute of Public Relations *Sword of Excellence Awards*; the International Association of Business Communicators *Gold Quill Awards*; the British Association of Communicators in Business *Communicators in Business Awards*. (See appendix to Chapter 16 for addresses)

The more data you can cite to prove the impact of your communication activity, the more likely you are to have the facts and figures you need to justify your next budget.

For detail on measurement systems and techniques see Part V of this Handbook.

Add a column for measurement systems to your planning chart to ensure that you have a way of evaluating how successfully key messages have impacted on each target audience (Figure 8.9).

	Audiences	Targets	Media	Feedback	Resources	Accountabilities	Measurements
Key message 1							
Key message 2							
Key message 3							
Key message 4							
Key message 5							
Key message 6							

Measurements: system for judging success of each activity.

Figure 8.9   Planning chart: measurements

STEP 15   REVIEW THE PLAN

At this point you have a draft plan and draft figures. Before you present it to senior management, test it out on colleagues who will be involved in its delivery. Challenge every assumption, make sure that objectives and measurements are clear and in place. Make any further revisions you feel are necessary.

Does it feel right?

Check your plan against these questions:

- does your draft plan feel workable?
- is it something you feel happy to commit to?
- will it satisfy the top team?
- does it look like the kind of document they can relate to?
- will it help deliver the organization's business objectives?
- will it support your own personal and career development?

If not, this is the time to sit down and pick it apart:

- why is not delivering what you need?
- what feels wrong about it?
- what should it do that it doesn't?
- is it too ambitious?
- is it too vague, with unquantifiable targets and generalized statements in place of key messages?
- is the mix right of educate, motivate, inform?
- does it contain a viable mix of new and innovative approaches?

Does it look right?

Once you are happy with the detail of the plan, you need to give some thought to its presentation. Is the plan a good advertisement for your communication capability? It should begin to develop the image that you want internal communication to reflect.

Most organizations have some form of desktop publishing or word-processing software that will allow you to present an attractive layout, cost-effectively.

The minimum standards should be:

- readable typesize (11 or 12 point) and attractive typeface
- wide margins
- possibly 1.5 or double line spacing
- strong use of graphics where appropriate
    - for example colour Gantt charts for schedules

- card covers and wire-o or comb binding
  - this looks professional and is easy to read and work from.

As a final check, try your document out on someone who has not been involved in developing it. You and your team are now so familiar with your plan that you need someone with a completely fresh pair of eyes to make sure that it makes sense when read 'cold', and to spot any last-minute errors.

STEP 16   WIN COMMITMENT AND APPROVAL

Head up your plan with an executive summary, simply one page highlighting six or seven key bullet points. As context, it may make political sense to remind people about your achievements over the past year, awards won and so on, boosting the credibility of your plan.

Getting the plan approved

At some stage you will have to present the plan to one or more of the senior team. Ideally you should have 'pre-sold' it by discussing tactics on relevant areas with key influencers in advance. This can also involve sorting out any financial contribution their function may make to campaigns.

Any kind of formal or semi-formal presentation should be backed up by visuals and examples – either in the form of OHTs or visuals and graphics. Any formal presentation would also involve handing out copies of the plan (at the end of the presentation to prevent your audience reading ahead).

STEP 17   IMPLEMENT THE PLAN

Once the plan is approved, you are ready to implement it. In reality there will usually be a seamless transition from last year's communication activities, unless for some reason you want to send a clear signal of radical change. Because you are budgeting for the whole year, communication activity should not level out towards the year end as the budget runs out.

The measure of your planning is how well it works in action:

- were key players adequately brought in to the plan and did they feel involved?
- were all the activities feasible in the budget and timescale?

STEP 18   MONITOR

You need to keep track of how successful each activity is throughout the year. Gather feedback from the audience and research their reactions and attitudes.

The ultimate test for your plan is a review at the end of the year. Many details will have changed as events unfolded. This is inevitable. But how well did you deliver against the objectives? How closely did you meet budgets and   93 schedules? Most important of all, how well did you meet the needs of your customers?

STEP 19 IMPROVE AND INNOVATE

On the basis of your monitoring activities, look for areas to improve, and take instant action. Look for new ways to present and package messages. Benchmark your activities against what you see as best communication practice, whether it is a competitor, someone in an unrelated industry or even an advertiser talking to customers. Are there lessons you can learn from how they communicate?

STEP 20 REVIEW AGAINST CHANGING CORPORATE OBJECTIVES

In today's fast-changing corporate environment, planning even a year ahead can be difficult. Your plan needs to be flexible enough to keep pace with the changing strategic priorities of the organization.

Ideally, internal communication managers should be in a position where they can demonstrate their strategic understanding of the organization, being brought in on decisions early enough to be able to advise senior managers on the most effective way to present the message. The more professional your approach to communication planning, and project management in general, the more likely it will be that you will be let in on decisions early enough to communicate them with the best impact.

So, even during the course of the year the plan is open to change, and can be radically revised. But the start of each corporate year is the time to step back and work through the process again, re-evaluating the organization's objectives.

Part III

TURNING STRATEGY INTO ACTION

Introduction to Part III

Tony Newbold, *specialist business writer* and
Eileen Scholes, *director, The ITEM Group*

This part of the Handbook is designed as a reference section, giving a brief introduction to the key methods of communicating – including face-to-face communication. It should help you think through how best to apply different media and wherever possible how to make internal communication interactive. As well as outlining the potential offered by new technologies, we look at traditional media in a new light.

To help you reach your decisions, and compare across media, each medium is broken down into the following format:

- *Strengths*
  the medium's inherent advantages
- *Opportunities*
  innovative uses
  how it can be made more involving and interactive
- *Weaknesses*
  the medium's inherent disadvantages
- *Pitfalls*
  common mistakes when misusing this medium
- *Budget issues*
  some of the cost factors you will need to consider
- *Timescales*
  some of the time factors you will need to consider
- *Activities*
  step-by-step checklist of tasks you will need to undertake
- *Feedback*
  how you can build feedback routes into the medium

- *Measurement*
  how you can measure the effectiveness of your communication
- *How to find out more*
  guidance on books, resources and associations you can use for further
  research into this medium

The following list shows how the different media have been classified. (See
Contents for relevant page numbers.)

Face-to-face communication
Formal meetings
One-to-one meetings
Team briefings
Mentoring, shadowing, secondment and visits
Walking the talk
Managed meals

Events
Conferences
Presentations and speeches
Roadshows, themed events and business simulations
Workshops and seminars

Print communication
Magazines and newspapers
Newsletters
Manuals, guides and handbooks
Brochures and reports
Briefing packs

Electronic communication
Telephone and voice mail
Fax
Audiotape
Audioconferencing
Moving light screens
Video
Videoconferencing
Videotext
Internal television systems
Direct Broadcast by Satellite (DBS)
Time-shift broadcast

Computer-based communication
Letters and memos
E-mail, bulletin boards and on-line conferences

Multimedia
Video with interaction
Documents on disk or via modem/network
The Internet

Organizational communication

Corporate identity
Symbolic communication
Participative structures
Working environment
Public display
Award schemes
Focus groups, surveys and research
Grapevine
Networking
Public relations, news management and marketing
Advertising

9 Face-to-face communication

Tony Newbold, *specialist business writer* and
Eileen Scholes, *director, The ITEM Group*

FORMAL MEETINGS

Despite the innovations of new technologies, the personal interaction that takes place in face-to-face meetings remains an essential part of all human activity. Yet meetings are also classic time-wasters, with people leaving them feeling that nothing has been achieved.

This is often because not enough preparation has gone into the event, for example agreeing the aims, and circulating the agenda and any written materials in advance. Meetings can and should result in clear actions, responsibilities and deadlines, so that not only can the project move on, but people can feel motivated to play their part.

Strengths

- rapidly developing a shared vision
- gauging progress towards a vision
- gathering and exchanging information
- practical demonstrations or exercises are possible
- receiving immediate feedback
- clarifying accountabilities and agreeing actions
- fast problem-solving, for example at project team meetings
- strengthening relationships

Opportunities

- set agendas
  - give all participants a chance to influence the objectives of the meeting

- manage participation
  - an effective chairperson will draw out all participants by inviting them to contribute, or by asking questions
- share presentation
  - divide the burden of presenting information and produce documentation to help add variety and involve more of the participants
- circulate reading materials in advance
  - everyone needs notice so that they can read, digest and assess relevant materials to be able to make a full contribution to the meeting
- use techniques such as brainstorming to tap creativity and involve everyone
- involve customers or people outside the team, for example from different functions or departments, to bring a fresh perspective
- break the meeting into subgroups to tackle particular issues and reconvene
- messages from the meeting can be angled and communicated on to target audiences, making them feel involved

Weaknesses

- can be time-consuming
- difficult to coordinate diaries – may result in delay
- traditionally poorly handled, resulting in low expectations from participants

Pitfalls

- late starts
  - typical of internal meetings, this adds greatly to the real cost
  - time discipline is vital, so do not be tempted to be too generous when waiting for latecomers
- poor location
  - for example poor lighting, noise, inadequate seating
- unclear aim
  - objective not agreed/agenda not circulated in advance
- irrelevant topics
  - have you invited the right people for this subject area?
- overloaded agenda
  - better to have shorter meetings more often, than infrequent long meetings
- the meeting dives into detail
  - detail is better handled through written communication, circulated before or after the meeting
- wrong time balance
  - for example too much time is devoted to a low-priority issue
  - individual items may be too long, resulting in fatigue and boredom,   *101*

     you may be able to break them down into smaller, better-defined subjects
- schedule in natural mind-breaks, even at short meetings, giving people a chance to recharge before the next topic
- think carefully about allocating time in the agenda, you can be flexible on the day, but you can postpone a tricky item rather than sacrifice the rest of the business of the meeting
- poor chairing, carrying the risk of
  - overrunning, or some items being rushed through
  - sidetracking
  - conflict
  - poor participation with a few people dominant
  - no agreed outcomes or actions

Budget issues

- time spent on meeting preparation, and producing and circulating documents
- participants' time at the meeting
  - are all these people needed?
  - would a smaller group achieve more, faster?
- any travel cost and time
  - could the meeting be handled by an e-mail conference, a round-robin memo, or phone and fax?
- opportunity cost incurred while participants are at the meeting
  - for example lost production or sales
- meeting room overheads, refreshments, materials
- time spent on minuting the meeting and producing summary documents

Timescales

- formal meetings need at least two weeks to set up to allow people to organize diaries, consider the agenda and read any preparatory material
- for regular meetings plan two or three weeks ahead
- you can arrange urgent on-site meetings almost immediately

Activities

- define the meeting's objective
- determine if this objective can be better achieved in any other way
- propose meeting date and venue
- agree meeting date and venue
- circulate agenda, any documentation to read and any actions to be carried out before the meeting
- run the meeting, making sure that everybody is fully involved
- manage the time carefully, summarizing conclusions and agreeing action points before moving on to the next item

- summarize and close the meeting, highlighting any action points, deadlines and accountabilities
- circulate minutes of the meeting, including any actions to be taken as a result

Feedback

- immediate feedback at meeting
- include a questionnaire when circulating the meeting's minutes

Measurement

- compare the meeting's outcome to its stated objectives
- research to identify best practice meetings and key benchmarks
  - share this information around the organization, and if appropriate use 'star players' as coaches
- conduct regular cost-benefit analysis to judge effectiveness
  - so many of the real costs of a meeting are hidden that this is a useful discipline

How to find out more

How to Win Meetings by Greville Janner, Gower, 1990
Positive Management: assertiveness for managers, by Paddy O'Brien, Nicholas Brealey Publishing/The Industrial Society, 1992
'Effective communication' by Paul Sandwith, *Training and Development* (USA), January 1992
Effective Meetings by P. Hodgson, Century, 1993
'Don't communicate – involve!' by Anne Evison, *Training and Development* (UK), June 1994

ONE-TO-ONE MEETINGS

As with all forms of face-to-face communication, one-to-one meetings involve maximum exposure for both participants, but also the highest potential for communicating and checking understanding.

In a management context they represent a significant investment of management time, and as such tend to be used for specific purposes such as recruitment and appraisal interviews, coaching, counselling and mentoring. The success of the meeting hinges chiefly on the ability, experience and training of the manager running the meeting, and the thought he or she has put into planning it.

Strengths

- personal and direct
- can deal with sensitive or 'off-the-record' subjects

- closely targeted on the needs and interests of both people
- should be highly interactive
  - questions, answers and feedback on both sides
- instant feedback and reaction
- you can check understanding and agreement on the spot, without interruption
- can be informal and relaxed to build relationships and motivation
- practical demonstrations or exercises possible

Opportunities

- be aware of how your body language can reinforce what you are saying
- talk through visuals or documents together
- be flexible enough to tailor the meeting more closely to the emerging needs of your partner
- listen actively and ask open questions
- summarize regularly to check understanding and agreement
- one-to-one meetings can be very frank and revealing
  - for example with careful planning exit interviews can give very valuable 'from the horse's mouth' information about how the organization is working

Weaknesses

- time-consuming
- can be threatening for both parties
  - their skills and personalities are on the line
- relies on ability and credibility of the manager/leader
- sometimes old hostilities and personality clashes can arise, which would be tempered by the presence of a neutral mediator or diplomat

Pitfalls

- assuming that because the other party is not saying much, they are in agreement
- not recording the meeting
  - both parties leave with an entirely different view of what had been agreed
- paying so much attention to running the meeting that you are not listening to what the other person is saying

Budget issues

- time spent on meeting preparation and circulating documents
- participants' time at the meeting

- travel cost and time
- opportunity cost incurred while participants are at the meeting
  - for example lost production or sales
- meeting room overheads, refreshments, materials

Timescales

- can be instant, sitting by someone's workstation
- formal one-to-one meetings, like appraisal interviews, require weeks of notice, so that both parties can prepare

Activities

- set objectives
- for formal one-to-one meetings agree a time, and a quiet venue
- ensure that you will not be interrupted
- allocate time for different subjects
- if there is anything relevant for the other person to prepare or read, ask them to do this before they come
- run the meeting, making it as participative as possible, checking agreement and understanding as you go
- summarize the outcome of the meeting, agreements reached, and actions to be taken
- where appropriate, follow up with a written summary of what was agreed

Feedback

- immediate feedback at the meeting
- follow-up questionnaire
  - giving anything but positive feedback at a one-to-one meeting itself could be interpreted as a challenge or personal criticism of the manager
  - it may be safer to direct honest and open feedback into a formatted questionnaire with a rating system, giving *both* sides an opportunity to 'mark' the meeting

Measurement

- compare the meeting's outcome to its stated objective

How to find out more

Effective Meetings by P. Hodgson, Century, 1993
How to Win Meetings by Greville Janner, Gower, 1990
Talking from 9 to 5: How women's and men's conversational styles affect who gets   105

heard, who gets credit, and what gets done at work by Deborah Tannen, Virago, 1995

Tough Talking: how to handle awkward situations by David Martin, Pitman Publishing, 1993

TEAM BRIEFING

Team briefing has had its critics. However, it is a consistently popular way for organizations to cascade information out from the centre, through a network of managers, supervisors and team leaders, to reach all employees.

Used effectively it can offer the best of all worlds, being an ideal way to promote employees' understanding of key issues, and providing a platform to feed back information and views to the centre.

While many organizations use regular team briefing, the same principles can be applied to special one-off briefs, for example to address issues concerning a product launch, reorganization or relocation.

Strengths

- core business and organizational issues presented within a consistent framework but in a local context by a local leader
- face to face, employees' usual preferred method of communication
- small, familiar group environment
- reinforces and builds on the natural work group structure
- can be highly interactive, with questions asked, ideas prompted or challenged, and consensus arrived at on the spot
- understanding can be checked immediately
- corporate messages can be interpreted in ways that make them directly relevant to the needs of the local audience
- team-specific issues can be raised and discussed
- enables teams to set goals and agree how to organize their work
- provides a forum for employees to raise concerns, ask questions, and feed back their opinions and ideas

Opportunities

- has the potential to become the 'hub' of the organization's communication structure
- carefully formatted, can initiate new cultural styles and initiatives, e.g. greater interactivity, involvement
- properly adapted and personalized to the needs and interests of the workforce, can help to align personal and business goals, inspire new commitment, energy and enthusiasm
- where appropriate, individuals can brief the others on their area of expertise

- carefully-constructed briefing materials (see briefing packs, p. 140) support busy managers, enabling them to take ownership of messages
- provide photocopyable briefing sheets for passing out to employees as reinforcement or to provide detailed information
- involve the team in recording and minuting their own briefing
- build in a question and answer session
  - briefing packs should include answers to likely questions
  - encourage managers to be honest if they do not know the answer, and provide a rapid support service so that they can promise to find out
- consider circulating briefing packs simultaneously at different levels, minimizing the inevitable delay with many-layered cascades
- chance for IC to get early access to senior management thinking on core issues

Weaknesses

- success is largely dependent on a complex range of wider organizational and cultural issues, like management structure, communication structure and equipment, relationships between the centre and operations, and whether interpersonal skills and 'bottom up' contributions are valued and rewarded
- time-consuming and therefore costly
- relies on being able to pull a team together in the same place at the same time
- not suitable for conveying complex data
- relies on individual managers and leaders to be motivated and have the presentation and leadership skills to brief effectively in a 'formal' setting
- managers may distance themselves from unpleasant or difficult news, even to the extent of attacking and undermining senior management decisions

Pitfalls

- inconsistent messages given out (misdirects energy, loses credibility)
  - poor access to/support for senior management
  - low calibre/inexperienced creator of core brief
  - managers do not know how to use the core briefing pack materials correctly
  - lack of access to training
- can expose shortcomings of inexperienced or weak leaders or managers, or those used to simply giving intructions, affecting their credibility in other contexts
- opting for 'professional' or more senior level delivery loses the 'local' feel
- slow cascades

- even with today's flatter hierarchies, it can still take a long time for the brief to trickle down from top management to line employee
- if there is not as short a time as possible between the first and last person to be briefed, the grapevine will take over
- information dams
  - the cascade effectively breaks down if managers unilaterally decide to withhold information
  - careful monitoring is needed to identify and improve the information flow
- irregular briefing
  - the briefings must be regular and deadlines kept to or the system will suffer and credibility will be lost
- boring delivery and irrelevant detail
  - poorly designed core brief
  - caused by managers not preparing adequately, not personalizing the briefing pack material for their own team, or even reading it aloud verbatim
  - monitor and measure to ensure all managers are performing to a consistently high standard, consider training for those who are not
- large groups
  - if the team is larger than a dozen, break it down into subgroups
  - ideal group size for participation is six

Budget issues

- calibre of core briefing creator
- time spent preparing and circulating core brief
- time spent on meeting preparation and circulating documents
- participants' time at the meeting
- travel cost and time
- opportunity cost incurred while participants are at the meeting
  - for example lost production or sales
- meeting room overheads, refreshments, materials

Timescales

- team briefing can be very flexible depending on the needs of your organization
- regularity helps establish it as a valued communication method, for example on a rolling weekly, fortnightly or monthly programme
- some organizations may find it difficult to brief in less than two weeks because of the time needed to generate and approve briefing packs
- urgent briefs can be prepared, distributed and delivered almost immediately, if the system is prepared for this.

Activities

- define objectives and outline content
- create core briefing pack (see briefing packs, p. 140), and submit for approval
- revise core briefing pack
- distribute core briefing pack
- local manager/leader combines core brief with local information and issues
- local manager personalizes core messages, making them more relevant to the local team
- manager hands out briefing pack summary for team
- manager conducts briefing, including question and answer and feedback sessions
- team minutes the briefing and any action points
- manager checks up on any unanswered questions and feeds back
- link into HR systems – induction, recruitment and promotion criteria, training, provision/appraisals/training needs analysis – to promote improved capability
- encourage senior managers to promote and validate the system whenever possible

Feedback

- immediate feedback at the briefing
- team leaders should also feed back their own opinions and pass back any relevant feedback from the team to the source of the brief

Measurement

- survey to measure retention of key messages
- employees rate team leader on his or her communication skill
- use focus groups to discuss attitudes to the briefing process and its effectiveness
- study under regular communication audit
- vital to measure and compare performance of different managers, and establish best practice managers as role models

How to find out more

The Industrial Society, Robert Hyde House, 48 Bryanston Square, London W1H 7LN 0171 262 2401
Team Briefing, The Industrial Society
A Briefer's Guide to Team Briefing, The Industrial Society
Video: *Talking to the team*, The Industrial Society/Video Arts
The Effective Communicator by John Adair, The Industrial Society, 1988

'The benefits of talking shop' by Lucie Carrington, *Personnel Today*, 17–30 May 1994

Employee Communications by Patrick Burns, The Industrial Society, 1994

MENTORING, SHADOWING, SECONDMENT AND VISITS

The key to communication is understanding another's needs, and putting yourself in their shoes, so that sender and receiver are literally 'on the same wavelength'. Mentoring, shadowing, secondment and visits all give a closer insight into each other's expectations, and help build and strengthen relationships.

Enabling greater personal contact between people of different grades and functions helps to enhance communication skills as well as promote communication across, up and down the organization. This helps to challenge preconceptions, and give a real picture of the work of different functions.

Strengths

- personal and direct
- gives people a 'hands-on' feel, a direct sharing of experiences
- fully interactive

Opportunities

- visits from customers to meet employees, give talks, work in project teams and give their feedback on performance
- customer placements
  - representative employees visit customers to gain insight into their operational needs
- mentoring provides an opportunity for direct two-way communication between protégé and coach
- shadowing
  - key employees shadow or swap with managers in different jobs, or different operations
  - this experience should be followed by written or face-to-face reports, including to the employee's own team
- site and function swaps
  - key staff swap between operations for short periods to give an insight into how other areas work
  - promotes understanding of other functions and departments
- local visits from senior management, ideally getting a sense of life in the field, watching and talking to employees about their views and concerns (see walking the talk, p. 112)
  - while it is important to take a fairly structured approach, the schedule needs to be flexible enough to allow informal contact with employees
- work placement

- for example senior directors from companies like McDonalds and DHL are seconded for a day a year to work in the field – it gives them real insight into the issues faced in the front line, and sends a strong team message to employees

Weaknesses

- time-consuming
- disrupts the host's normal schedule

Pitfalls

- no automatic follow-up
  - it is important for people to feel that their views have been listened to, and taken into account
- 'what on earth are *you* doing here?'
  - if the objectives of the contact are unclear from all sides, it reduces the task to a 'social' visit

Budget issues

- time spent on preparation and contact
- lost working time

Timescales

- simple, short-term projects like in-house work placements can be set up within a week
- in general, time is needed to ensure that everyone is prepared, the objectives thought through, and where appropriate, the event is fully planned

Activities

- clarify objectives
- negotiate with target host or coach
- agree procedures and deadlines
- initiate the project and monitor
- plan and initiate any follow-up actions

Feedback

- direct feedback through personal contact

Measurement

- regular evaluation of the exercise by all participants
  - for example by questionnaires or surveys

How to find out more

The European Mentoring Centre, Burnham House, High St, Burnham, Bucks
  SL1 7JZ 01628 662517
Everyone Needs a Mentor by David Clutterbuck, IPD, 1985
Mentoring in Action by David Clutterbuck and David Megginson, Kogan Page,
  1995
Mentoring by Reg Hamilton, Industrial Society, 1993
Mentoring: A guide to the basics by G. Shea, Kogan Page, 1992

WALKING THE TALK

'Walking the talk' is a popular and vital part of people management. Typically,
it involves managers scheduling time to walk around the workplace, talking to
their team members, coaching and checking performance, motivating and
listening to concerns, and gauging opinions.

Done well, it should help build an atmosphere of trust and strengthen
relationships, giving the impression of a manager who is both on the ball and
on the team.

Strengths

- enables immediate upwards feedback
- handled well, it is a good opportunity to boost credibility
- acts as a safety valve, enabling people to let off steam
- demonstrates concern for others' views
- provides high visibility through direct and personal contact
- shows that you are in touch with the workplace

Opportunities

- apply the principle in reverse by keeping an open door policy
- prepare a clear agenda for the conversation, but give people room to
  raise issues of their own
- extend the idea up and down the chain, visiting chief suppliers and
  customers

Weaknesses

- relies heavily on the interpersonal skills of the manager
- assumes manager has easy access to the people on the team
- usually treated as a fairly unstructured exercise, hard to measure, with
  anecdotal benefits
- employees may feel rejected if not talked to
- some people may feel intimidated
- exposes managers with poor attitudes or weak interpersonal skills

Pitfalls

- *'Of course I know my team are happy: they'd tell me otherwise'*
  - leaders sometimes assume their team members can be completely open with them, and not intimidated by their status
- *'I just go in there and press the flesh'*
  - walking the talk depends upon having a clear objective for talking with people, taking note of their views and feeding those views upwards
- *'Oh no, what have I done wrong now?'*
  - people need positive reinforcement
  - if the main reason you talk in depth to an employee is to correct them, you need not be surprised if they are guarded or defensive when talking to you
- *'We're expecting royalty'*
  - local leaders sometimes brief their teams to be on best behaviour and tell them what subjects to avoid, ensuring the visitor an upbeat but unrealistic experience
- *'Time to get out the dirty washing'*
  - cynical employees may take the opportunity to stir trouble, or undermine the visit
- *'Going through the motions ...'*
  - managers pay lip-service to the process, demotivating people by not really listening to them

Budget issues

- management and employee time

Timescales

- immediate, though a complete sweep of employees will need to take place on a rolling schedule

Activities

- set objectives
- careful preparation to think through the approach you need to take to get the results you want from individual team members
- watching, talking and listening to selected employees on a regular basis
- rehearsing to peers, or by yourself with a tape-recorder to see how you sound

Feedback

- immediate, in conversation with the team member
- keeping employees informed of any actions resulting from the conversation

113

Measurement

- attitude or opinion survey before and after the walkabouts
- some managers use a log to assess how useful any data gathered is, and its impact on the organization's performance

How to find out more

The One Minute Manager by Ken Blanchard and S. Johnson, Fontana, 1983
Interpersonal Skills by Astrid French, Industrial Society, 1993
The Industrial Society, Robert Hyde House, 48 Bryanston Square London W1H 7LN 0171 262 2401

MANAGED MEALS

Managed meals make use of people's 'dead time' by talking to managers over a meal. Small groups discuss strategic issues with senior managers over special 'meals' on a rotating basis, demonstrating management commitment to face-to-face communication.

Ideally they set people in the right frame of mind for creative, unhindered discussion, and provide a relaxed atmosphere and environment. Like all social occasions there is a real opportunity for bridge-building, and getting to the heart of the matter, though if badly handled it can seem rather ritualistic, formal and unnatural.

Strengths

- high perceived value
- opportunity for frank upward communication
- demonstrates concern to hear views
- opportunity for relaxed, open and honest direct feedback
- opportunity for all members of a team or organization to catch up with news, share experiences
- can be used to reward and recognize people's performance

Opportunities

- off-site venues
  - for example at a hotel, or at a customer or supplier's premises, or even combined with a day-trip or picnic
- special events held during meal breaks
  - can be used for series of sessions, for example using outside speakers or a 'surgery' on benefits topics, making use of people's 'dead' time

Weaknesses

- the logistics can be complicated
  - the right mix of people, in the right place, at the right time, with the right menu
- people may feel pressured into attending, but forcing them would be counterproductive
- likely that because of the timing it will take place partly in someone's own time
- danger that poor food may undermine the exercise
- danger that free food may be the main motivator for their attending
- can have an unnatural 'captain's table' feel to it
- some people may find the idea offensive – 'I choose who I eat with'

Pitfalls

- *'Why wasn't I invited?'*
  - if the events are being run on a sub-section of the internal audience you want to reach, you need to make it clear that it is a *representative* sample, and not being chosen has no reflection on your status, contribution or potential

Budget issues

- people's time
  - for example breakfast or evening events could be scheduled partly in working time, partly in people's own time
- cost of venue, food, service

Timescales

- ad hoc lunches can be arranged almost instantly, but more organized team lunches may take at least a month to set up

Activities

- set the objective for the meal
- explore the logistics
  - time, place, number of people, length of meal, catering arrangements
- determine who should be invited, and how

Feedback

- direct feedback during the meal
- keep the attendees informed of any action resulting from their feedback

Measurement

● measure change in attitudes

HOW TO FIND OUT MORE

The Industrial Society, Robert Hyde House, 48 Bryanston Square, London W1H
    7LN 0171 262 2401

10 Events

Tony Newbold, *specialist business writer* and
Eileen Scholes, *director, The ITEM Group*

CONFERENCES

Much of the real 'business' of conferences tends to happen in the bars, restaurants and hotel lobbies. These are the places where relationships between colleagues are forged, renewed and strengthened. But a good conference can achieve more than teambuilding. With thorough planning and clear objectives, it can be a powerful force for motivating and channelling the talent of the entire organization.

Strengths

- builds group identity
- promotes a shared organizational vision
- wins commitment to change, or the launch of new products, because everyone feels part of the process
- opportunity for peers from different areas or departments to come together
- promotes social and professional networking
- chance to reward, recognize and motivate people

Opportunities

- pre-conference preparation
  - conduct research to identify what target audiences want or need to know
  - ask delegates to read relevant documentation and choose which

optional seminars and syndicates they want to attend
- set them practical tasks in preparation for workshops or seminars they are going to attend
- syndicates and workshops
  - breaking out into smaller groups to give more scope for participation
- games and simulations will add variety and deal with management issues in more creative and interesting ways
- outside speakers
  - lend credibility or boost motivation by bringing in a 'best practice' expert or a high-powered speaker from outside
- open fora
  - senior managers circulate between small syndicate groups, giving people a chance to ask questions about all aspects of the organization
  - ideally fora should address a combination of pre-conference suggestions and questions arising from the conference itself
- post-conference action plans
  - delegates sign up to action plans, demonstrating their commitment to what was agreed at the conference, and transferring any learning back to the workplace
- social functions
  - ultimately these can make or break the atmosphere at a conference, and for many delegates are often the highlight
  - the social binding, grazing and teambuilding at parties has a positive impact, but ideally should be the final event of the conference, as the 'morning after' needs to be fairly undemanding
- conference voting systems
  - electronic voting systems are becoming more common, enabling 'straw polls' and votes on issues from the audience, giving instant feedback
- post-conference cascade
  - promoting the vision and learning of the conference to the wider organization
  (see audiotape, p. 151, video, p. 157, multimedia, p. 176, briefing packs, p. 140)

Weaknesses

- requires a great deal of preparation
- relatively high cost, especially if lost work and opportunities are taken into account
- one of the most demanding and politically-exposed project management tasks
- reveals weak speakers
- gaffes are very public
- external venues too public or insecure for sensitive subjects

Pitfalls

- disappointing expectations
  - the very public loss of face in 'cancelling' or 'shrinking' a conference either in length, or numbers of delegates
- deciding the logistics before the objectives and content
  - you may be scraping the barrel to fill a two-day programme, when one day would do
- poor venue choice
  - service is as important as facilities; even today Basil Fawltys seem to be everywhere
  - after drawing up a short list, visit the venues (including unannounced visits to see how they *really* operate); meet the staff who will be looking after your delegates
  - put yourself in the delegates' shoes
  - imagine the logistics of the venue when dealing with your number of delegates (noise level, movement between rooms, telephone availability, serving times in the restaurant, and so on)
- poor financial management
  - agree venue costs in *fine* detail
  - watch out for 'hidden extras' or variable costs at the venue like on-site photocopy charges, equipment hire
- *'but I thought you were talking on'*...
  - presenters often automatically agree to speak to the brief given them, and then on the day talk about something entirely different, because they don't attend to the task until the last minute
- poor attendance
  - all conferences have 'graveyard' slots, notably early morning, post-lunch and in the final sessions
  - the problem is exacerbated by the fact that poorer speakers tend to be given the poorly-attended slots
  - it's possible to buck the trend by closing the conference with a keynote speech
- information overload
  - many presenters are tempted to shoehorn as much information as possible into their presentations, overloading the audience
  - persuade them to move the detail into supporting documents (see presentations and speeches, p. 122)
- poor pacing
  - an ideal conference includes a mix of subjects and presentation styles
    - this is a strength that should be built upon
  - aim to mix contrasting views, stimulating debate
  - place strategic breaks where the programme needs them, not when the venue 'deigns' to grant them
- lack of logic
  - where possible group presentations into themed sessions

119

- dire presentations
  - while presentation training can help, some people simply cannot present, and undermine their own credibility and embarrass themselves, the audience and the organization as a whole
  - different presentation styles may help weaker presenters, for example by having them interviewed on video or working in partnership with a stronger co-presenter
  - a senior manager needs to take ownership of the programme, weeding out, vetting and project managing the presentations to ensure that standards are consistently high
- poor involvement
  - many conferences fail because instead of *conferring*, people use them as an opportunity to talk *at* their colleagues
  - although most programmes rely heavily on speeches, good speakers involve the audience as they talk, asking for examples, reactions and questions
  - programmes need an element of choice; aim to expose delegates to situations where they must take active part, such as workshops, seminars and syndicate groups

Budget issues

- deciding who *really* needs to attend
  - can information be conveyed more effectively to non-attendees by video or briefing documents?
- anticipate *all* venue charges
- determine the balance of internal and external resourcing
- choosing the right conference production company
- equipment hire
- travel and accommodation
- project management and administration time
- delegates' attendance time, travel time and any opportunity cost
- producing branded notepads, programmes, promotional material
- technical facilities
- set design and construction
- time and materials on speeches, presentations, videos, workshops and syndicates
- contingency budget
  - because you are dealing with a fixed deadline, you need to budget for last minute emergencies, such as 'rush fees' for slide production, or hiring a special piece of equipment
- cost of external speakers, presenters and facilitators
- time and materials on supporting documentation
- time and materials on follow-up, feedback, measurement and analysis

Timescales

- a practical minimum of at least two months, but large conferences should be planned at least a year in advance
- better venues are booked well in advance

Activities

- set and agree objectives of conference
- decide who needs to attend
- plan proposed conference content, length and logistics
- win agreement for budget
- choose a venue big enough for the audience
- approach potential speakers and agree speech outlines with them
- distribute and manage invitations
- organize any accommodation and supplementary activities
- organize any support materials needed
- set up at venue
- if possible, run through and time presentations
- organize set and speakers

Feedback

- questionnaires after individual sessions
- full questionnaire at end of conference
- follow-up questionnaire back at the workplace, away from the 'high' of the conference

Measurement

- track the speed and quality of information passed out to non-attendees, if appropriate
- measure attitude change before and after conference

How to find out more

How to Organize a Conference, by Iain Maitland, Gower, 1996
How to Organise Effective Conferences and Meetings by David Seekings, Kogan Page, 1992
The Complete Conference Organiser's Handbook by Robin O'Connor, Piatkus, 1994
'Positive interaction' by Bridget Kelly, *Managing Service Quality*, November 1992

Association of British Professional Conference Organisers, 100 Park Road, London NW1 4RN 0171 723 6722
Association of Conference Executives, Riverside House, 160 High St, Huntingdon, Cambs PE18 6SG 01480 57595

PRESENTATIONS AND SPEECHES

Presentations and speeches are the principal media at most events. While the information content they can carry is fairly limited, they can have a powerful impact on an emotional level, especially when supported by striking graphics, lighting, sound, choreographed events and stagecraft.

Strengths

- personal and direct
- good for creating an emotional commitment, motivating audiences

Opportunities

- autocue, with speech text projected onto a screen or lectern
  - enables the speaker to make regular eye contact with the audience, making them feel more involved
- use a link-person to be the audience's representative on stage, summarizing key points and asking for clarification when needed
- roving mike
  - allows experienced presenters to circulate the audience, asking for questions, comments or examples
  - imposes a useful discipline, because giving someone a microphone indicates that only that person is supposed to be speaking
  - gives audience members a feeling of equal status with the speaker
  - etiquette is important; organizers should try to ensure that no one 'hogs' the microphone and that a variety of people manage to talk
- written documents
  - these will be the lasting memory of the presentation
  - use these to carry any facts and figures you want to convey but were too complex for your speech, and include paper copies of your overheads or slides
- video and audiotape
  - these can capture the flavour and style of the presentation, recording them for a wider audience

Weaknesses

- poor at conveying complex ideas, facts and figures
  - use written documentation to support the key messages of the presentation
- high risk, high exposure
  - a poor performance will embarrass the speaker, the organization and the audience
- limited to conveying only a few key messages

- in most cases, limited scope for widespread participation, although taking every opportunity for interaction will help, for example asking questions

Pitfalls

- *'what I want to talk to you about today is…'*
  - many speakers fail to put themselves in the audience's shoes
  - they don't even ask who the audience is
  - they don't research to find out what they want to hear
  - if they've been given a brief they may well ignore it
- lack of a clear brief from the organizer, including the audience's profile, and any information about their needs
- eleventh hour presentation style
  - many presenters underestimate how long it will take them to produce their presentations, and can result in extra costs for 'rush' fees for overheads
  - organizers need to check regularly on progress, for example asking to see a synopsis at an early stage to ensure that it matches the brief
- mix and match
  - presenters try to recycle a mix of old presentations, and cannibalize any material they can find
  - this runs the risk of not meeting the audience's needs, and it becomes obvious when there are sudden changes in style, tone and subject matter
- overrunning
  - a common problem, resulting from lack of preparation and focus
  - it looks unprofessional, inconveniences the audience and any co-presenters and carries the risk of skipping over key messages
- diving into detail
  - experts disappear down detailed sidetracks that the audience may not be able to follow
  - the problem can usually be tracked back to the synopsis, which attempts to cover too many points in too much detail
- prose
  - although most professional speakers will use a script or notes, the aim is for spoken English
  - many speeches sound like turgid academic or business reports, with very little active language, great formality and endless subclauses that make the spoken sentence almost impossible to follow
- style over substance
  - presenters fall in love with a glitzy theme, and bend their messages to fit
  - too much glitz can get in the way of clarity
- stage fright
  - this is surprisingly common, especially among managers

- nervous presentation style and body language transmits to the audience, making them nervous too
- avoid alcohol or tranquilizers
- there is no 'cure' as such, other than a combination of painful experience, rehearsal and specialized presenter training courses
● runaway train
- nerves and lack of preparation can cause presenters to deliver their material at a relentless pace, incomprehensible to the audience
- timing is vital, and the only accurate way to time a presentation is to rehearse thoroughly

Budget issues

● time and materials on producing the speech, and supporting documents and visuals
● venue costs
● time spent at the venue
● travel time and cost
● time spent on follow-up, for example sending further information on request to delegates

Timescales

● many presenters do produce speeches literally the night before, which is precisely why the general standard is so low
● to stand out from the crowd, you need to start compiling a presentation at least a month in advance
- the more time you have, the more opportunity you have to put the script down and come at it afresh, improving the quality of your revisions

Activities

● set objectives
● confirm time and venue for your presentation
● write any written support you may want to give your audience – leave-behinds and handouts
● outline the content of your presentation
● revise outline
● draft presentation
● revise draft
- read draft aloud for timing and to reveal areas where it does not flow
● draft out visual support
● produce visual support, for example overheads, slides or any props you can use
- depending on how you are producing your visuals, you need to finalize

their content fairly early in the process as they can take one or two weeks to produce
- revise draft and if necessary reduce to bullet points or write speaker's notes on cards
- rehearse and revise
  - keep doing this until you are satisfied that the speech has impact and that it's at the target length

Feedback

- tape record or video-record a rehearsal
  - *you* will be your own most powerful critic
- test your presentation on colleagues or family
- gauge immediate audience reaction on the day
- if appropriate, give the audience sheets to fill in on your performance

Measurement

- retention of key messages
- speaker performance by questionnaire

How to find out more

Effective Presentation by Antony Jay, Pitman, 1993
Janner's Complete Speechmaker by Greville Janner, Century, 1991

ROADSHOWS, THEMED EVENTS AND BUSINESS SIMULATIONS

Roadshows, themed events and business simulations are increasingly popular ways of reaching internal audiences with high profile materials and imaginative practical sessions.

Strengths

- themed events can 'spice up' ordinary messages
- a roadshow delivers consistent messages, touring to reach people at different sites with the same materials
- business simulations give people a chance to 'discover' messages for themselves as the simulation unravels

Opportunities

- annual event
  - opportunity for senior management to meet people, rather like an AGM for shareholders, concentrating on the organization's performance

- question and answer fora
  - opportunity to raise issues and concerns with the 'people who know'
  - frequently-asked questions can be summarized and used as the basis for further research, or the answers established
- roadshow presentations
  - for example senior managers out on the road to different locations
  - especially important in organizations where senior management is centralized, far from many employees/suppliers/franchisees etc

Weaknesses

- relatively high cost
- a roadshow can take a long time to reach a number of sites
- different themes tend to appeal to different people
- managers are taken away from their jobs for long periods

Pitfalls

- simulations too generic or too specific
  - business simulations work best when they relate directly to the needs and experience of the audience
  - opting for a generic exercise carries the danger that the simulation won't *directly* relate to any one audience, but it should at least be recognizable to all
  - opting for a specific exercise carries the danger that the simulation may relate well to one group, but not another
  - where possible, simulations should be a mix of generic skills and issues, customized for specific audiences

Budget issues

- roadshow
  - designing and producing the roadshow and exhibition
  - organizing, producing and presenting roadshow events
  - travel costs, time and accommodation
  - creating any support materials, for example brochures
- themed events
  - creating and testing the theme
  - project managing and producing the event
  - creating any support materials
- business simulations
  - creating, testing, revising and using the simulation
  - producing any support materials, for example handouts and workbooks

Timescales

- allow at least three months to plan roadshows, themed events and business simulations, depending on the scale of the project

Activities

- set objectives
- design event, roadshow materials or simulation
- implement and assess

Feedback

- feedback gathered through discussion at roadshows, and participation through themed events and simulations

Measurement

- retention of key messages
- profile of audience reached by roadshow

How to find out more

How to Organise Effective Conferences and Meetings by David Seekings, Kogan Page, 1992

Association of British Professional Conference Organisers, 100, Park Road, London NW1 4RN 0171 723 6722
Association of Conference Executives, Riverside House, 160, High Street, Huntingdon, Cambs PE18 6SG 01480 57595

WORKSHOPS AND SEMINARS

Workshops and seminars are used as a semi-formal way to involve people more actively at events. The two terms are moving closer together, as seminars become more participative and less academic.

Strengths

- small groups
- personal contact
- highly interactive
- practical and focused
- flexible
  - you can use workshops to concentrate on specific, local team issues, or to give local people perspective on the wider organization

Opportunities

- involving the wider team
  - if appropriate to the objective, invite customers or suppliers to give their input too
- customizing the workshop
  - ask people to prepare before the workshop, bringing along a project or task of their own that reflects their individual needs
- sharing the seminar workload
  - moving away from the academic image of a seminar, as effectively speech-giving to a small group, to a full participation event, with tasks allocated between all participants
- winning levels of buy-in from broad agreement through to acceptance of proposed solutions and actions

Weaknesses

- time-consuming
- likely inconsistency between events as the outcomes and success depends on the work and attitudes of the individual groups

Pitfalls

- the wrong people
  - workshops and seminars need to attract the people who will be able to make a difference, and motivate them to do so, otherwise you risk 'preaching' to the 'converted' or the 'disenfranchised'
  - an inappropriate topic would alienate the audience

Budget issues

- opportunity cost of people's time
- time and materials in preparing, designing and running
  - many materials will be generated by the teams at the workshop, and these will need to be edited after the event
- time of all participants
- cost of venue and refreshments

Timescales

- allow at least a few days to book time in people's diaries, and to design and set up a workshop
- allow one month for a seminar

Activities

Workshop

- set objectives
- produce and distribute the agenda or outline
- select participants
- select and organize venue
- identify exercises and demonstrations
- design workshop and schedule
- produce any supporting materials
- run the workshop
- record actions and issues arising
- edit and circulate materials produced by the teams
- follow up any agreed actions

Seminar

- set objective
- produce and distribute the agenda or outline
- select participants
- ideally, all participants should have a clear role, for example a presentation to make
- chair to ensure full participation
- produce any supporting documents or visuals

Feedback

- immediate feedback at the event
- questionnaire when back in the workplace to gauge the application of key messages in daily work
- distribution of agreed actions, and follow-up meetings to see how they were carried out

Measurement

- retention of key messages
- performance improvements in target areas

How to find out more

How to Run Seminars and Workshops by R. L. Jolles, John Wiley & Sons, 1994
Workshops that Work by Bourner, McGraw-Hill, 1993

11 Print communication

Tony Newbold, *specialist business writer* and
Eileen Scholes, *director, The ITEM Group*

MAGAZINES AND NEWSPAPERS

With IC's range widening to include more face-to-face communication, regular publications (periodicals) generally have taken something of a back seat.

For most organizations, however, their regular newspaper or magazine still acts as the symbol of their existence as a community. It is one of the few forums where everyone – managers as well as others – comes together on a virtually equal footing as members of 'a club'. As such, it can become a clear 'voice' for the organization, embodying its values and beliefs.

Thanks to the flexibility of publications, content can be funny, sad and serious all at the same time. It can cover a range of subject matter, from important management statements to pictures of a social event.

Modern-style publications place emphasis on the exchange of best practice and a greater element of interaction all round. And, though the vast majority are print-based, many are adding video, or multimedia or Intranet formats.

Format distinctions between newspapers and magazines have become blurred in recent years. In the past, the choice between a newspaper/magazine format for employees was simply based on 'what we assume our people read outside'. For manufacturing and retail staff, for example, managers' knee-jerk assumption was (and to an extent still is) 'tabloid'.

Several developments have opened up opportunities to approach this issue in more sophisticated ways, starting from what the business wants to achieve. One big factor behind the new flexibility is that changes have been occurring on the news-stands.

Despite the tabloids' self-created high profile, publishers know that the real growth in the British reading market over the past 10 years, across all social groupings, has been in magazines. The women's magazine sector has grown – while also becoming more fragmented – but the most startling growth has been in men's and special interest magazines. Evidence of this increasing interest is that most newspapers themselves, including many tabloids, now include magazines as part of their offer.

The conclusion has to be that most people (men and women) who regularly buy and read publications, regularly access both newspapers and magazines with equal ease and familiarity.

So – when to use which?

If you want to maintain interest, manage expectations and maintain credibility with a particular audience, the important decision is *why* and *in what circumstances* people would choose to read the publication – and therefore in which format.

Consider some of the principal differences in expectation inherent in the two formats.

Newspapers

- rely on high-impact material (headlines and photography)
- style, language and assumed education level is closely targeted to particular socio-economic groups
- high frequency (low frequency of internal newspapers often seen as a joke by employees)
- here today gone tomorrow treatment of subjects
- don't bother to keep or take home
- tend to 'come down on one side' on issues
- must have lots of small snippets (requires large contact networks; heavy on time/cost to collect)
- 'behind the news' treatments less about 'understanding' than adding narrative detail and extra human interest
- real newspapers are printed on cheap, relatively flimsy paper stock – newsprint: organizations tend to confuse readers' expectations by upgrading the paper quality

Magazines

- less concerned with 'new' information, more concerned with people and issues 'in the news'
- readers share an interest but can come from all education levels, backgrounds, e.g. *Motorcycle News*
- seen as a mix of seeking increased understanding, 'behind the scenes' information/education, entertainment
- 'keep it and read again' feel

- more flexibility – more scope for feature treatments as well as shorter items
- less 'news' expectation, only topicality
- bi-monthly frequency seen as 'normal' on a magazine
- easier to go up or down in size – works equally well at either 12 or 16 pages
- colour taken as standard
- usually higher quality print stock than newsprint

Strengths

- familiar format and style
- can be read anywhere at any time
- reaches all audiences
- easy to distribute personal copies
- flexible in terms of content and style

Opportunities

- letters pages, anonymous, if appropriate
- questions and answers with senior managers, revealing areas of complaint
- clear, regular format – people can find the information they need quickly
- targeted publications
  - 'opt-out' pages enabling customized content, for example special pages for individual sites
  - entire publications aimed at a particular group of employees, customers or suppliers
- reader services
  - discounts, for example trips, products and services, small ads, free samples
- special issues and inserts
  - newspaper and magazines become special 'brands' which recipients recognize instantly
  - their strength can be built upon by issuing supporting documents under the same brand, or special 'stop press' newsletters to address urgent issues
- print on demand
  - improvements in print technology, and its flexibility mean that it is becoming increasingly feasible to create printed media with shorter print runs, aimed at the needs of niche groups
  - a master copy of the magazine or newspaper is stored on disk or digitally scanned at a centre and transmitted to sites across the world, the sites then print it – this cuts out any distribution delay, meaning that everyone gets the news fast, and at the same time.

Weaknesses

- relatively slow
- although they may mimic the format of news-stand newspapers and magazines, the content is almost bound to be of less general interest, and the design and journalistic standards can be inferior

Pitfalls

- newspapers can give a 'downmarket' impression, and use 'downmarket' content
- they can be perceived as propaganda, even when not
- legal, honest, decent and true?
  - management can indeed fall into the trap of behaving like media barons, spreading their own propaganda
- traditional newspapers/magazines actually have very little direct reader involvement; classically-trained journalist/editors may find it hard to change their approach

Budget issues

- for large organizations it may be possible to subsidize the magazine or newspaper with advertisements
- project-managing an internal newspaper or magazine is complex and time-consuming
  - it may be more cost-effective to put the day-to-day work out of house, while retaining strategic editorial control
- print costs can vary greatly depending on the format, paper size, type and weight, and the number of colours used
- paper costs are subject to substantial fluctuations

Timescales

- first issues usually take between one and two months to establish the format, design and content, as well as contact networks; thereafter frequencies can vary from weekly to quarterly

Activities

- research needs
- set objectives and editorial policy
- appoint editorial team, or select supplier if appropriate
- establish and test design and format
- outline content
- ideally, plan features and articles well in advance
  - keep flexibility to incorporate topical issues

- commission articles, photography and illustrations
- approve raw text
- lay out text, illustrations and photographs in a proof
- circulate proof copies for minor corrections and proof-reading
- circulate colour proof for final checking
- print and distribute

Feedback

- immediate feedback on the latest issue from people on the editorial teams or a sample group of readers
- readership surveys
- opinion surveys
- communication audit

Measurement

- effectiveness in achieving communication objectives
- reader appreciation
- retention of key messages

How to find out more

Editor's Handbook, British Association of Communicators in Business Ltd, 2nd Floor, Bolsover House, 5/6 Clipstone Street, London W1P 7EB 0171 436 2545
Creative Newspaper Design, by Vic Giles and F. W. Hodgson, Heinemann, 1990
'Are house journals just hot air?' by Ian Spurr, *Involvement and Participation*, Autumn 1990

NEWSLETTERS

In contrast to newspapers and magazines, newsletters tend to be concerned with the exchange of more directly useful, factual information, like a portable bulletin board. They are an ideal medium for reaching small target groups, including site-specific audiences. They can provide support for internal newspapers, magazines or other media by enabling rapid updates under the same brand.

Strengths

- fast and immediate
- relatively cheap
- conveying short, focused bulletin-like material
- targeting specific audiences
- helping to reinforce the identity of the target group
  - for example service staff, team leaders or computer specialists

- strong on regular factual information
  - for example competitor analysis, new business won and so on

Opportunities

- give access and time to desktop publishing equipment, enabling groups to create their own newsletters, for example quality teams
- build in standard involvement mechanisms such as letters pages

Weaknesses

- budgets tend to rule out an 'editor' so it becomes a 'chore' for a volunteer or admin. support
- can look amateurish or cheap, especially if poorly laid out
- difficult to carry advanced graphical or photographic material without access to specialized equipment
- little opportunity to feature any subject in depth

Pitfalls

- deadlines can be missed and the newsletter can appear infrequently if no one has clear responsibility for it
  - damages credibility and loses readers
- messages undermined by poor editorial style or layout
  - this can be overcome by training in layout and editing

Budget issues

- can use existing word-processing equipment
- printing letterhead in advance to photocopy or laser-print on to
- if printing, producing camera-ready artwork, cost of litho-printing
- time spent in word-processing or desktop publishing material
- time spent on distribution

Timescales

- a basic newsletter can be created and photocopied onto branded paper almost immediately

Activities

- set objectives
- commissioning/writing material
- commissioning illustrations
- editing and sub-editing
- laying out pages

- finalizing approval
- proof-reading
- printing master copy
- photocopying
- distributing

Feedback

- return slips
  - comments box
- letters
- questionnaires/research
- correspondents' awaydays

Measurement

- measuring distribution of the newsletters
- retention of key messages
- level of participation

How to find out more

How to Publish a Newsletter, by Graham Jones, How To Books, 1994

British Association of Communicators in Business Ltd, 2nd Floor, Bolsover House, 5/6 Clipstone Street, London W1P 7EB 0171 436 2545

MANUALS, GUIDES AND HANDBOOKS

Manuals, guides and handbooks are often thought of as being very much the dusty, neglected corner of internal communication. But whose fault is that? Far too many are dull, incomprehensible and badly produced, and hardly ever 'sell' the actions people are supposed to take. If the 'leave the brains at the gate' culture still exists, it's in the world of the stuffy old manual.

There is a sense of false economy in that organizations will invest massively in a new process or a machine, but rush the job when it comes to producing the accompanying manuals, guides and handbooks that will put it all into action.

An attractive, well-written guide should pay for itself, as more people understand and feel committed to the actions they are expected to take, avoiding costly mistakes or inefficiency.

Strengths

- clear purpose
- familiar style and format

- informative and instructional

- provides a permanent record and reference
- forms the basis for training and quality procedures
- acts as arbiter in difficult situations
- screen versions are easily updated and accessible

Opportunities

- integrate messages into other media
  - for example put the messages of a manual in your organization's diary
  - run regular guides through newspapers and magazines
- link to an over-arching communication campaign
  - for example an awareness campaign to climax with the launch of the document
- use alongside multimedia
  - for example when training in a practical discipline, like correct lifting techniques, a multimedia programme could run a demonstration of how to do it, while the employees keep a handbook as their permanent record
  - multimedia is becoming a strong format for on-line and disk-based guides (see multimedia, p. 176)
- revamp 'standard' media
  - the employee handbook, for example, can be more than just a dull collection of statutory information relating to contracts of employment; it can be a motivational, involving tool in its own right

Weaknesses

- perceived as dull and old-fashioned
- hard to mix motivational messages with the instructional

Pitfalls

- written by experts ...
  - many guides are put together by the people directly involved in the process they describe – too close to the process and the accompanying jargon
  - calling in someone from outside the project team to document the process can give valuable improvement lessons for the project itself, as a fresh mind may throw up new issues
  - in any event, drafts of the manuals need to be tested on the target audience for clarity and understanding
- over-documenting
  - many manuals and guides mushroom into huge indigestible tomes, thoroughly documenting the process, but completely intimidating the target audience

Budget issues

- scale of production, for example paper stock, binding and so on
- scale of research
  - to some extent driven by the needs of the target audience and the size of their document

Timescales

- three months from initial research through to produced documentation

Activities

- set objectives
- research the process
- produce and test outline against the document
- produce first draft, test against process and test with target audiences
- revise draft and test
- produce manual
- support with awareness-raising campaign if appropriate

Feedback

- have clear contact points printed in the documentation

Measurement

- effective implementation of the process
- survey users before and after implementation

How to find out more

How to Write a Staff Manual by S. L. Brock and S. R. Cabbell, Kogan Page, 1990

BROCHURES AND REPORTS

Brochures and reports are among the most highly finished of internal media, ranging from information about particular sites, to employee versions of annual reports.

They can increase the credibility of the organization, and convey its values and key messages – even fairly complex ones like financial performance targets – through powerful combinations of text and graphics.

Strengths

- high quality

- high impact
- motivational
- opportunity for fine detail illustrations, design and photography
- gives the reader a personal copy, to take home, keep for reference or show to others
- readers can go at their own pace, re-reading to check understanding

Opportunities

- employee annual reports or business plans
  - adapted from the annual report, highlighting progress against performance targets
- useful for 'orientation' of potential, new or existing employees/suppliers etc

Weaknesses

- relatively high cost
- may date quickly

Pitfalls

- *'they spent how much on this?'*
  - a glossy report may seem to some an expensive solution
- overdesigning
  - there can be a temptation to experiment with ever-more adventurous design in order to make the report stand out
  - the danger is that the visual effects will act against, rather than for, readability

Budget issues

- quality of production, for example paper stock, binding, number of colours and so on
- quantities produced, and likely 'shelf life', i.e. how many copies will you need to print over the predicted lifetime of the brochure or report?

Timescales

- a basic brochure could be generated in a month, but allow three months for a more sophisticated version

Activities

- set objectives
- research the content

- produce first draft
- source illustrations, photographs and design
- revise draft
- lay approved text out in design
- approve final proofs
- print and distribute

Feedback

- contact points throughout brochures and reports
- tear-off slips for replies or requests for information

Measurement

- retention of key messages
- survey to gauge audience reaction

How to find out more

How to Communicate Your Message: the PICKUP guide to promotion by David Carter and Paul Stirner, HMSO, 1993

BRIEFING PACKS

Briefing packs are the foundation of successful team briefings (see Team briefing, p. 106). A core brief sent out from the centre can help ensure that key messages are delivered in a consistent and timely (even simultaneous) way, right across the organization.

Strengths

- makes life easier for the briefer by providing the core information and giving guidance on running the briefing
- makes delivery of information consistent
- gives the centre greater control over what information is shared, and how
- providing the briefing system is settled, packs can be created and distributed to briefers in a matter of minutes via fax or e-mail.
- allows use of the full range of media, depending on resource and need, in conjunction with face-to face-techniques
- relatively simple to measure effectiveness and spot gaps

Opportunities

- different levels of pack can be created depending on need: e.g. for communication of major restructuring, regional managers may pass on

detailed lists, first line managers may use video or a desktop presenter, individuals may receive their own pack
- dedicated packs can be created for briefings that need to be repeated for different groups over time, introducing a particular process or product: these can become quite sophisticated, using audio-visual materials, booklets and so on
- local input into a centralized brief
  - ideally only part of the brief should include mandatory messages from the centre that must be covered: the rest of the agenda can therefore be driven by local needs in selecting optional messages or covering topics of local interest
- customization of messages
  - the system can be flexible enough for briefers to interpret and package messages in a way right and relevant for their audience
- agenda setting by teams
  - teams across the organization can be encouraged to put forward their ideas for subjects to be covered in the team briefing
- prepared answers to likely questions
  - briefers can use guidelines on how to answer questions likely to arise from particular topics

Weaknesses

- relies on the skill – and goodwill – of briefers to use the pack effectively
- producing a full set of documentation can be slow and time consuming
- briefers can rely too closely on the core briefing packs, failing to customize the briefing for their own team

Pitfalls

- information overload or underload
  - hitting the right degree of emphasis on specific topics requires careful thought and consultation, for example by setting up a sample group of briefers to help identify which topics need to be covered, and in what detail
- no news
  - because of cycles in the organization's work, it may be that briefings may be overloaded with information in some periods, quiet at others: keeping to a regular format, for example including regular progress reports, will help ensure that there is always something tangible to report on, and planning ahead will help to minimize any imbalances in the amount of material available
- misunderstanding
  - briefers may be using the packs with little preparation, and need to be able to grasp the key messages as quickly as possible, without the danger of ambiguity or misunderstanding

- patronizing instructions
  - the centre may be so keen on consistency that instead of guidelines, the briefing pack gives over-detailed and restrictive instructions on how to run the briefing
- domination by the centre
  - because the centre produces the packs there may be a danger of the agenda being skewed towards Head Office life, and not adequately reflecting the needs and interest of employees as a whole
  - the briefings need to be flexible enough to incorporate a large proportion of material of purely local interest
- prioritizing the pack over the process
  - producing well-presented briefing packs will have little impact if the cascade process itself is flawed, or if briefers lack the skill and the confidence to run a briefing

Budget issues

- time of briefer, team and people monitoring the success of the briefing
- pack production and distribution costs

Timescales

- virtually immediate for urgent briefing packs
- plan main topics up to three months in advance for monthly briefs, include subsidiary topics up to a week in advance and keep a 'stop press' sheet to be inserted for any last minute additions

Activities

- determine key messages
- research local environment
- identify best format for the briefing pack
- prioritize the messages, allocating time for them at the briefing
- structure the briefing, aiming to give interest and variety, while covering the key messages in appropriate depth
- draft the briefing pack, creating any supporting visuals or documents
- edit the packs and win approval
- circulate the packs
- monitor performance

Feedback

- build feedback route into the briefing itself
- include specific questions where the briefer needs to report back on the team's views

- include space in the pack to record comments, ideas and actions arising from each point of the briefing, and include a summary action plan format to capture actions and responsibilities arising from the meeting

Measurement

- gather briefer's reactions to the pack and their ideas for improvement
- measure the success of the briefings themselves
  - for example, did the briefing take place by the deadline?
  - for example, how well were key messages understood by the target audience?

How to find out more

- Most materials on team briefing will contain guidance on pack preparation

12 Electronic communication

Tony Newbold, *specialist business writer* and
Eileen Scholes, *director, The ITEM Group*

TELEPHONE AND VOICE MAIL

The increase in the number of direct telephone lines has led to most of us becoming more and more accessible to phone calls, as people bypass switchboards and secretaries. Organizations have taken longer to adapt to the resulting changes, for example in failing positively to encourage colleagues to answer each other's phones. In some cases, the answer can be more technical – diverting calls to the department's answerphone, or using a more sophisticated voice mail system.

The communication professional has to bring together the right mix of hardware, software and telephone skills training to make sure the organization is communicating effectively, internally and externally.

With the continued advance in telecommunications, the choice of options can be bewildering. Well aware of the problem, the industry is more than willing to talk through how its technological solutions can meet your needs.

As with all media, the best defence against such confusion is to have your objectives clearly set out before talking to the 'experts'.

The industry is working towards number portability. The day will shortly come when one telephone number will cover all your telecommunication devices, whether it's your mobile phone, your pager, your fixed phone, your mobile laptop or fax. Even now, using the call diversion technologies available on digital networks, you can divert your calls to another number, with no inconvenience to your callers.

New applications are constantly being found for techniques like audiotex, originally designed to present a menu of short recorded messages to callers, allowing them to select the option they want using a tone phone.

Strengths

- telephone is personal, immediate and interactive, with the ability on both sides to ask questions and check understanding
- now increasingly mobile, phones make use of dead time, such as when travelling
- allows shorter, more informal messages, simpler requests
- confirming arrangements, reaching agreement
- telephone useful for 'off the record' or casual conversations
- big advantage of voice mail is that you can 'broadcast' the messages to a number of people
  - for example making sure that a management team handles a crisis in a consistent way
  - this is especially useful for urgent communication when dealing across time zones
- audiotex is a cost-effective way of giving callers a range of possible information options from one telephone number
- audiotex, answerphones and voice mail offer callers an instant response when no one is available to take calls

Opportunities

- set and monitor standards for all telephone behaviour including answering, message-taking and message leaving to ensure consistency of quality
- offer opportunities to develop telephone skills, for example learning how to summarize to edge conversations gently to a close
- tailor different combinations of services to different audiences
- targeted messages via audiotex
  - keep recorded messages short, a maximum of two minutes, and where possible break into short segments
  - update the messages frequently, so there's an urge to 'keep up with the news'
  - tone phones mean that you can select certain options offered you, tapping into different information
  - you can program some systems to generate call data, judging the relative demand, and profiling people who call for particular services
- vote lines
  - telephone logging numbers to record how many people favour a particular course of action
  - for example choosing which charity should benefit from next year's social responsibility fund

Weaknesses

- a lack of control, with the possibility of time-wasting and distractions at either end

- relies on notemaking for a record
- messages can become vague without visual stimulation
- with ordinary telephone calling you choose a good time for *you* to make the call, but it may not be the right time for the receiver
- despite familiarity with answerphones, many people still have great difficulty leaving a coherent message on one, largely because callers are prepared for interaction
- audiotex and helplines rely on the motivation of people to call them
- audiotex options rely on the wide availability of tone phones

Pitfalls

- creating opportunities to indulge in small talk and 'social grazing' by phone
- one side forgetting that they may have more information in front of them than the other
  - check the other understands
- believing that the phone is quicker than writing, when for complex tasks the fax or e-mail may be more time-effective
  - for example talking through corrections to a long report, when it would be far easier and clearer to mark the changes to the report itself
- feeding information through in a disorganized way
  - telephone conversations can be unstructured with distracting ideas popping out at random
- people may fail to see the need to prepare for a conversation, in the way that they would with written communication
- compelling receiver to make notes
  - even shorthand experts have a hard time keeping up with phone conversations, because natural speech contains blind allies and confusions
- 'mechanical' answerphone and audiotex messages
  - people are less likely to use these services if the message greeting them sounds like an officious android
- endless audiotex options
  - while the virtue of a flexible audiotex system is that you can offer many options to callers, the more you list the more confused callers will be as they wait for the option closest to their need

Budget issues

- telephone usage is becoming easier to monitor through improved management information systems which means choosing the best telephone option is becoming an increasingly complex decision
  - draw up a short list of your top three suppliers and set your selection criteria
- for voice mail, you may need to do a cost-benefit analysis on the basis of

equipment hire or purchase, versus time-savings and boosted efficiency

Timescales

- for substantial telecommunication changes, spend at least a month researching the field
- demand fast delivery and installation from the time you place your order
- once established, all these media can be used immediately and are easy to update

Activities

- research needs and set objectives
- research solutions
  - hardware, software and training
- install communication systems
- monitor use
- look for training gaps and target training on improving performance
- monitor telecommunication press for details on new products and services

Feedback

- where recording systems are available, invite callers to leave their comments
- offer helplines, access lines and list telephone numbers in all relevant documentation, improving accessibility

Measurement

- number of times audiotex, voice mail and answerphones are used

How to find out more

- Talk to telephone companies

Telephone Skills by Maria Pemberton, Industrial Society Press, 1988

Quality Calls: making the most of the phone (video-based open learning), Industrial Society, 1995

FAX

Fax machines are an indispensable item for organizations of all sizes. Newer models may be integrated with phones, answerphones or personal computers, and use standard paper.

Strengths

- direct, clear and immediate
- now that plain paper faxes and faxes linked to laser printers are becoming more widespread, there is little difference in look and feel from a letter
  - short faxes may be cheaper than post
- leaves sender and receiver a written record
- a multi-fax system can send one fax to a range of destinations virtually simultaneously
- international communication
  - a cost-effective way of communicating across time zones
- faxes can be sent and received by computers and mobile laptops
- 'brands' each fax page with your identity across the top
- some laser printers can now serve computing and fax needs
- more home use means that flexible working becomes increasingly possible, including to overcome short-time crises like rail strikes

Opportunities

- grade your faxes
  - introduce an 'urgency' grading system
- the fax ident is an opportunity to brand your communication
  - if your fax automatically codes the time sent, ensure that you update the clock in line with time changes
- introduce dedicated fax lines
  - maximize access and interactivity, and speed up receipt and attention
- cover during down time
  - to ensure constant access, consider diverting your fax automatically, when it is engaged or being maintained
- fax newsletters
  - immediate updates to keep in touch with satellite offices, or people who work from home
- fax information services
  - faxing out information on request
  - some organizations link this to a system that recognizes tone phones and computer services; the callers press for the relevant option from a menu and the specific information sheet is faxed to them
  - you can use this discretely to 'market' your own services
- fax briefings
  - support team briefing by using fax to distribute the core briefs, enabling last minute 'stop press' items

Weaknesses

- having a fax exposes you to junk-faxes
  - you pay in wasted fax paper for other people's marketing, so avoid

having your number published in a fax directory, unless you have an overriding reason for doing so; consider a faxbarring system that will accept faxes only from recognized numbers
- black and white only
- poor, slow and costly photo reproduction
  - newer machines are better at handling photographs and fine illustrations, but older machines are not good at handling faxes with large shaded areas, for example text and photographs on dark coloured papers
- time wasted in recalling, checking arrival, resending

Pitfalls

- speed scrawl
  - people tend to handwrite them at speed
- permanently engaged
  - because large organizations do not adequately invest in fax machines, many fax lines are jammed, wasting time as senders pile their documents in queues waiting for the line to be freed
  - some phone systems enable an automatic divert to another machine if the line is engaged
- losing fax
  - relying on the internal post to circulate faxes can be a little risky
  - the curly fax paper has an alarming habit of creeping down the back of the fax machine, out of sight – a fax 'catcher' should minimize this problem
- out of sight, out of mind
  - given the logistical problems and opportunities for error with faxes, surprisingly few people take the service-minded step of ringing to check that their fax has arrived – if nothing else this step will draw attention to your fax
  - because 'faxing' is the 'easy' last stage of producing a document, and relies only on a number, people can quite happily send faxes to the wrong destination, wasting time and causing embarrassment
- jam today, jam tomorrow
  - fax jams are still common and particularly frustrating in the case of long documents
  - consider faxing in segments – it may cost more in fax header sheets, but it makes the document more digestible all round
- the ident 'giveaway'
  - people sometimes forget how much is revealed by the fax ident
  - fudging a missed deadline? – your ident may carry the correct time (unless of course you reset the clock in your favour)
  - seamless subcontracting? – if your internal or external customer is unaware that you've subcontracted the work, they will soon realize it when they see someone else's fax ident

149

- the 'idiot'-proof fax
  - deciding which machines to buy or hire rests on the balance of functionality vs usability – some fax machines offer barely-used features that simply confuse users
  - few organizations bother to train employees how to use features on fax machines, for example clocking up wasted hours as people laboriously tap in the last number, when they could use the redial button
  - common sense is not that common, as you realize when you receive a blank fax because the person at the other end has put their work wrong-side down on their fax machine
- 'more than my job's worth to touch that machine'
  - most fax machines suffer much abuse, and even the most basic maintenance is rarely carried out; the result is that organizations habitually send out dirty faxes, without knowing it, until a horrified executive finally sees the illegible mess that the client received
  - keeping the fax clean also helps to prevent jams and breakdowns, but most of all gives a clearer copy to the receiver
  - some faxes react badly to the common practice of pencilling the fax number to call on the back of the first page – it can rub off as the paper passes through the roller, sprinkling graphite around the machine

Budget issues

- assess the hire vs. buy decision
- consider upgrading to paper-based fax by comparing the real cost of photocopying floppy, fading documents
- rather like the movement from mainframes to personal computers, it could make sense for many organizations to move from high capacity centralized faxes to decentralized simpler faxes, spread across the organization, saving people's time

Timescales

- in theory, faxing direct from your computer screen to another computer screen is almost immediate
- at the other end of the timescale, writing, printing and sending a fax to many areas of Eastern Europe, for example, will give you much time for reflection and practice with the redial button – the only saving grace being that the postal service there is equally unreliable

Activities

- set objectives and plan
- research needs, volumes and types of faxes sent
- research fax solutions
- site fax machines and monitor usage and quality of faxes sent

Feedback

- build in a reply section to any communication sent

Measurement

- check fax quality by testing both with customers and with internal fax machines
- usage from fax/telephone bills
- examine *how* people are writing faxes
  - time taken to generate and send vs. alternative methods such as phone

How to find out more

Talk to telecommunication/equipment suppliers

AUDIOTAPE

An almost universal medium, audiotape is well established in internal communication fields such as magazine programmes and open learning. It's familiar, relatively cheap and, if carefully produced, can personalize and bring issues alive that would die on the printed page.

Strengths

- intimate, direct and personal
- personalizes and dramatizes issues, which makes it ideal for motivational speeches, debate and demonstrating personal commitment
- people listen in their own 'dead' time, at their own pace, for example when commuting to work
- high perceived value; people are less likely to throw cassettes away than paper communication
- almost as flexible as print, and more personalized
- cost-effective for reaching large numbers of dispersed audiences
  - for example sales forces
- one-off events
  - for example distributing a short motivational, personal speech from top management in times of crisis
- small and convenient for portability
- can reach anyone worldwide with access to a cassette-recorder
  - audio-cassette mailing fast and cheap

Opportunities

- invite listener comment and let them set the agenda
- feature listeners heavily in the recorded features

151

- take comments from a dedicated answerphone or phone line
- support or follow up with documentation to carry any detailed information
    - for example the tape could carry the motivational 'end of year' message from the management team, while the accompanying document lays out the facts and figures
    - alternatively, interweave the structure of the tape and the document, cross-referencing between the two, as in traditional open-learning packages
- in line with equal opportunities it's also a cost-effective way of recruiting and informing visually handicapped people.

Weaknesses

- poor at conveying complex information, because listeners cannot take it in without visual stimuli, and cannot 'read' at their own pace
- difficult to 'browse' through
- unit cost typically higher than parallel print documents
- could be seen as poor relation to video

Pitfalls

- danger of producing tape programmes that:
    - sound as if they use 'written' rather than spoken English
    - have an unclear structure
    - comprise long, unbroken items
    - are longer than the audience's average commuting distance
- can damage management credibility if their performance is poor or overtly propagandist

Budget issues

- low-budget programmes can be turned round rapidly in-house by using a high-speed copier (only practical for audiences smaller than 20)
- if you are aiming for a professional-sounding result, in most cases it will make sense to get tenders and creative proposals from audio producers, removing the need for you to budget for initial equipment such as recorder, microphone, headphones (plus mixer and editing deck if not editing in a studio)
- in any event, producing audiotapes takes a great deal of project management time
- other likely costs include:
    - studio hire including engineer/editor
    - bulk copying
    - printing on to the cassettes (on-body printing)
    - printing an inlay card to go in the cassette box
    - distribution costs

Timescales

- almost immediate for a simple programme, recorded, edited and bulk duplicated on your own equipment, for example recording a chairman's address for circulation
- at least six weeks for planning, producing and circulating a basic 20-minute magazine programme

Activities

- set objectives
- set and agree content
- set up and record interviews/reports/footage
- arrange for scripts and inlay card to be written
- arrange for inlay card to be designed
- win approval of scripts and footage
  - circulate transcripts of the quotes to be used if necessary
- produce any supporting documentation or inlay card
- record presenter's script
- edit master tape
  - cut the recorded footage together with any scripted recording, musical stings, etc
  - cut the final tape to target length
  - win approval for edit if necessary
- bulk copy cassettes
- distribute cassettes

Feedback

- listeners can record messages/comments on tape and return

Measurement

- survey to measure retention of key messages, understanding of issues

How to find out more

Contact internal communication agencies for production consultancy.

AUDIOCONFERENCING

Anyone with a telephone can set up an audioconference from their desk. Most modern telephone exchanges and telephone companies offer conferencing facilities.

There are also specialist devices and companies available to help you link together groups of people sitting at tables around special audioconferencing microphones. Like a real conference, groups can be split into seminars, reconvened, split into other groups – regardless of where they are in the world.

Strengths

- cost-effective way of linking groups of people across the world
- brings together any group of people you need to have a meeting with where time or travel costs may be an issue
- relatively quick and easy to set up, depending on the number of participants and the technology used

Opportunities

- record the conference, circulating it to absentees
- digital switching means that the equipment can switch faster from speaker to speaker, improving interactivity
- circulate the agenda and any other vital reference documents in advance to help structure the conversation

Weaknesses

- needs careful management to ensure one party or group is not dominating the meeting
- takes time to get used to audioconferencing etiquette
  – for example identifying yourself before you speak
- impossible to monitor participants' activity
- requires visual support for interest and to convey detailed information
- seen as a poor relation to videoconferencing
- relies on variable line quality worldwide

Pitfalls

- temptation to patch in too many lines, reducing participation

Budget issues

- most modern business telephone systems allow you to combine two or more internal lines with an external call
- 3-way calling is available on modern digital telephone exchanges, enabling you to combine 2 external lines with your own, if you have the symbols # and * on your telephone
- hiring specialists to manage the conference for you
- investing in audioconferencing equipment

Timescales

- almost immediate if arranging a small conference call from your own phone

Activities

- set objectives
- agree meeting time and circulate agenda
- explain the ground rules of audioconferencing to anyone new to the technique
- distribute any visuals or documents that will be needed
- organize any additional equipment, for example whiteboards that can 'fax' their images
- call participants and welcome them individually to the conference
- manage the audioconference, cuing in participants and ensuring that no one is dominating the event

Feedback

- gather feedback as people 'leave' the conference
- fax 'happy sheets' to survey immediate reactions

Measurement

- cost-benefit analysis vs travel time

How to find out more

- Check instructions on your phone system for the ability to conference call
- Talk to your telephone company
- Talk to specialist audioconferencing companies

MOVING LIGHT SCREENS

Moving light screens vary in size from the vast screens used at football events and pop concerts to the 'running strips' used in shops, stations and reception areas. An echo of Times Square, they still have enough novelty value to conjure up the image of romance and urgency, of dealing rooms and journalistic scoops.

In reality, the 'news' carried on moving light screens is much more mundane, but organizations are beginning to find that this is a powerful way to convey short messages, from the organization's latest share price to the number of calls handled by a department, from sales to date to performance against target.

Strengths

- immediacy, acting as a constant 'bush telegraph'
- regular update on a standard range of information
  - for example key performance indicators, cost savings made
  - for example the winners of regular competitions
- silent medium
- clear, updatable public display
- simultaneous 'broadcast' to multiple sites
- no distraction
  - people glance at it in their own time

Opportunities

- the modern equivalent of welcome boards – being able to customize messages in reception, for example people's names
- listing the events happening across the organization today
- tie in with external databases
  - use the system to display key information
  - for example stock market news on related organizations
- competition news
  - news headlines about related or competing organizations
- reinforcing culture
  - for example running the mission statement on a rolling basis, to remind the audience

Weaknesses

- can carry only brief, simple messages
- only referred to for short periods
- a fairly passive medium, relying on 'casual' interest in dead time
- will become moving wallpaper, ignored by the audience if the information is not kept fresh and interesting
- it is difficult to distinguish urgent messages from the routine
- even with modern technology, not very readable
- needs a fairly large display area, and careful consideration needs to be given to sightlines and the surrounding interior design
- the movement can be irritating, if viewed all day from a peripheral position

Pitfalls

- yesterday's news
  - often the information is not updated, because it is considered a low priority task
  - the whole point of the system is that it is *immediate*, there are more effective ways of conveying routine information

- long sentences
  - consider the speed of character movement for readability and under-standing
- font mania
  - making the text less readable by pushing the font functions to the limit

Budget issues

- hire vs buy decision on equipment
- installation and maintenance
- licensing of any external data used
- time spent producing and updating text

Timescales

- once established, updating messages should be almost immediate

Activities

- set objectives
- draft text
- edit text to readable length
- where possible and appropriate, adjust speed and pause times
- test text – checking that it is readable by the target audience
- approve text
- put text on-screen

Feedback

- response to on-screen requests, for example publicizing a telephone number to call with feedback

Measurement

- survey to measure retention of messages
- study to identify how quickly and widely the messages spread, and the routes they follow

How to find out more

- Research moving light screen suppliers and compare products.

VIDEO

The increased reliability and availability of video has made it an essential medium, supplanting temperamental and fiddly media like film, film strips and   *157* slide-tape packages. Ranging from low cost training videos to broadcast-standard production, video is a flexible medium. The spread of camcorders is now making in-house video filming possible, though watchable video-editing is still relatively expensive.

For most organizations, producing a corporate video is a rite of passage that brings credibility and status. Consequently, many organizations produce corporate videos with vague objectives, in the belief that they *ought* to have one. Many corporate videos are expensive, glossy and call on the latest video graphics and presentation techniques, others are more limited. The beauty is that the style chosen reflects the culture, and more than with most media, you can show rather than say.

Strengths

- high impact, good at conveying emotion
- immediate and direct
- gives a holistic view of the organization; locations, people, products, services, processes, actions
- excellent for training demonstrations
- can reach anyone with access to a video-recorder

Opportunities

- regular video magazine programmes
- support with documents to carry complicated detail
- build in comment slots to magazine programmes
  - people film reports/pieces to camera on their own camcorder, or one loaned by the organization
- 'owned by employees'
  - employees may buy in to a video if the concept, ideas and presentation involve them
  - this also legitimizes looking a little low-budget – if Carol of finance is doing the presenting, the expectation is that this is not going to be of broadcast standard

Weaknesses

- poor at conveying complex information
- easy to look amateurish
- people tend to expect broadcast quality
- relatively high cost
- difficulty in scheduling 'viewing' periods
- short shelf life
- a linear medium, making it difficult to find specific material (contrast with the video content of multimedia)

Pitfalls

- using too many video gimmicks which can get in the way of the message
- all things to all people
  - corporate videos tend to be used for a variety of purposes, from sales to education links, from lobbying to induction, which means that they can end up rather bland
  - there is also the danger that one key audience will be put off, for example using a 'salesy' corporate video for graduate recruitment
  - consider edited options for different purposes

Budget issues

- project management time
- equipment purchase/hire
- fees of scriptwriter director and camera crew if appropriate
- editing fees
- video stock
- duplication, packaging and distribution

Timescales

- allow at least two months for basic video production

Activities

- set objectives
- plan
- produce a script outline
- approve outline
  - take into account logistics, for example there is no point suggesting multiple locations if the budget will only run to filming at one site
- produce full script
- approve script
- produce any supporting documentation
- hire director and camera crew and explain what you are trying to achieve
- organize filming, minimizing disruption
- off-line editing
  - create a rough version of the programme to make sure that the proposed edits work and send the right message
- on-line editing
  - extremely expensive, building up a master tape by laying down material in sequence
  - extensive editing can add greatly to the budget
- duplicating master

Feedback

- print contact name/number on the video package
- survey for target audience's reactions

Measurement

- retention of key messages and understanding of key issues
- audience appreciation

How to find out more

Using Television and Video in Business by Andrew Crofts, Mercury, 1991
Interactivity: designing and using interactive video, by M. Picciotto, I. Robertson and R. Colley, Kogan Page, 1989

International Visual Communications Association (IVCA), 3rd Floor, Bolsover House, 5/6 Clipstone St, London W1P 7EB 0171 580 0962

VIDEOCONFERENCING

Advances in telecommunication technologies, and the spread of fibre optic networks and digital exchanges across the UK make videotelephony more of an affordable reality. Dedicated videoconferencing units are being used by more organizations as reliability improves and costs fall.

Videophones are already on the market, but not yet in widespread use.

The obvious trend is towards integrating all telecommunications into desk-top computers, with the video signal just another window on your screen. The freedom of holding a videoconference by instant dial-up access will make approving a pack design as easy as holding a telephone conversation.

Strengths

- meetings between small groups worldwide without incurring travel costs
- minimal travel time
- bridge-building across geographical and language barriers
- enables speedier decision-making

Opportunities

- video-record conference for reference, or to circulate to non-participants
- carefully 'chair' conference to ensure full participation
- involve and unite different sites or cultures, for example two companies preparing for a merger or two research departments collaborating on a task
- circulate documents and samples in advance, to save over-reliance on viewing via the camera

- use extra cameras to transmit illustrations, for example a camera dedicated to slides

Weaknesses

- still relatively costly
- not quite as good as face-to-face contact
- poor understanding of teleconferencing 'etiquette' can create a chaotic atmosphere
- need to wait for a critical mass of compatible videoconferencing units or high-quality videophones, enabling wider use and greater familiarity
- video quality on videophones currently fairly poor
- timeslots are expensive
    - promptness is sometimes a problem

Pitfalls

- can be seen as 'gimmicky'
- over-reliance, or inappropriate use
    - there is no substitute for face-to-face meetings in terms of building and maintaining relationships
    - just as you would probably not feel comfortable employing or buying from someone you had only 'interviewed' by videoconference, they would not feel that they had met you properly either
- out of sight, out of mind
    - some people take the need to be at a meeting less seriously because it's local
- time zone insomnia
    - the fact that members of distant videoconferences save travel time and money is significant, but it still may leave one group working in the middle of the night

Budget issues

- videoconferencing suites available for hire in many large towns
- videoconferencing hardware dropping in price
- low cost one-to-one videoconferencing increasing through use of video-phones
- ISDN/phone link costs

Timescales

- the only limitations are the availability of videosuites and of the people involved in the meeting

Activities

- set objectives
- research potential suppliers
- hire vs buy decision about whether to install suites or hire facilities
- raise awareness of videoconferencing and offer training

Feedback

- instant feedback at meeting

Measurement

- cost-benefit analysis vs travel time

How to find out more

Using Television and Video in Business, by Andrew Crofts, Mercury, 1991

International Visual Communications Association (IVCA), 3rd Floor, Bolsover House, 5/6 Clipstone St, London W1P 7EB 0171-580 0962

VIDEOTEXT

Many organizations are considering running in-house videotext services, rather like the screen-based services offered by television broadcasters such as CEEFAX, ORACLE and 4-TEL.

With screens scattered throughout the organization, text can be updated almost instantaneously. Using a rolling format, one page moves automatically to the next after a set time. The sequence of pages repeats until updates are made.

Strengths

- 'high tech' appearance
- can be updated immediately
  - for example to make an 'announcement' to employees
- particulary useful in organizations with a high public profile where there is a need to convey news to an internal audience before the media does
- provides clear text summaries, reaching everyone in public areas
- can reach scattered sites in continental Europe and worldwide
- uses TV sets which may also be used for other purposes

Opportunities

- reaches all parts of the organization simultaneously

- 'free screen'
  - boosts involvement in the medium by throwing over some of the pages to employees
- makes use of the grapevine – the 'did you see?' syndrome

Weaknesses

- relies on the target audience to have the time and feel motivated to read the pages
- not everyone may have equal access to the text screens
- low resolution screens seen as poor quality

Pitfalls

- *plus ça change...*
  - there may be little to fill the text pages, resulting in the same pages appearing with monotonous frequency, or the same page staying on screen *ad infinitum*
- yesterday's news
  - often the information is not updated, because it is considered a low priority task, while the whole point of the system is that it is urgent
- danger, artist at work
  - there may be a temptation to create a graphic impact with what is essentially a text-based system – very hard to pull off successfully
  - the graphic support, rather like crude typewriter pictures, added to which you have a limited range of colours and the results can be crude and garish
  - worst of all, selecting background colours that make the text hard to read
- *'got a screen to fill'*
  - overloading the screen with too much text or too many graphics, making it unreadable
- *'any idiot can write on a screen'*
  - as a public medium, with few of the audience doing more than glance at the screen, the text needs to grab the reader and convey its message instantly
  - professional writing skills will enhance the retention of key messages, producing shorter, 'snappier' text

Budget issues

- after initial start up, relatively easy to maintain, with comparatively low running costs

Timescales

- 'pages' can be updated almost instantly from a computer keyboard

Activities

- set objectives
- design the general 'rolling format' of pages
- decide who will draft text for the pages
- create a system for approving text

Feedback

- invite feedback over the screen
- review content and reactions with a sample group taken from the target audience

Measurement

- awareness and use of the medium
  - for example how often a day someone reads the screen
- retention of key messages

How to find out more

- research sites, existing or potential
- research human resources, for example existing editors
- research information needed
- for an explanation of potential, look at HyperCAST web site http://www.hypercast.co.uk

INTERNAL TELEVISION SYSTEMS

Internal TV systems can be used to run a schedule of internal programmes throughout the day, or at specified viewing hours. Overplayed, this can have something of a 'big brother' feel, with all the TV monitors on-site showing pictures of happy workers, or handing down corporate messages.

However, it is particularly useful for multi-site and multinational organizations, which need to reach everyone at once with consistent messages, and to break down barriers between people at different locations (see the following section on Direct Broadcast by Satellite). It can also be used in foyers for visitors and for live broadcasts of annual general meetings to remote shareholder groups.

Strengths

- familiar, popular medium
- high impact
- programmes easy and quick to digest
- immediacy
- showing locations, actions, processes

Opportunities

- possibility of live two-way television
- video or telephone links to bring in questions or input from other sites
- training, product demonstrations
- branch networks

Weaknesses

- as with any other TV station, the broadcast hours are expensive to fill
- could be perceived as a luxury at times of cost-cutting
- can have a 'big brother' feel
  - in some systems even the volume is fixed so that the TV cannot be turned down
- can distract people when they should be doing other things
- 'watch with mother' – the only way you can be sure people are watching is to sit down with them and watch the programme
- it's hard to match broadcast quality, so your version can appear rather amateurish to the audience in terms of picture quality, production values and presenter style

Pitfalls

- 'voice of god' propaganda
  - internal TV should not be an ego-trip for senior managers, neither should it be too overtly biased to management messages
  - the TV audience is sophisticated and can spot items that look unbalanced
  - if you've chosen to take a fairly independent stance in your programming, you stand the risk of losing management support
- talking heads
  - because of logistics and costs, internal TV programmes often rely on long, staged interviews with senior managers which can become sterile
  - worse, some dispense with the interview and have the manager talking direct to camera, difficult to do unless they are well trained
  - many interviews are poorly-edited, but the edit points in an interview are actually a good opportunity to 'cut away' to footage or stills of real things to liven the programme up
  - even abstract concepts like quality have a physical or human dimension to illustrate them, for example performance measures or simply shots of people working

Budget issues

- large initial investment in equipment

- large production budget needed to feed the system with regular programming

Timescales

- most programmes will take three months to produce
- when programmes are off-air, the screens can be used to carry text (see videotext, p. 162)

Activities

- set objectives
- commission and plan programmes (see video, p. 157)

Feedback

- feedback at live events
- audience surveys

Measurement

- retention of key messages

How to find out more

Using Television and Video in Business by Andrew Crofts, Mercury, 1991

International Visual Communications Association (IVCA), 3rd Floor, Bolsover House, 5/6 Clipstone St, London W1P 7EB 0171 580 0962

DIRECT BROADCAST BY SATELLITE (DBS)

Satellite technology can encode and broadcast live or recorded programmes, direct to an organization. You can use this as a fast way of distributing video magazine programmes around multiple sites, with each site recording the signal on a video-recorder at a pre-arranged time.

You can also link live events happening across different locations, for example drawing together a network of stores for a sales launch, or enabling your chief executive to talk simultaneously to everyone at all sites.

Strengths

- high impact
- high potential for interactivity
- carries the kudos of live TV
  - it is still unusual, and impresses audiences

- emotional and motivational
- reaches an entire audience at one go
  - has the unifying effect of a nationwide event
  - circumvents the grapevine because everyone experiences the same material simultaneously
- instant distribution
  - no delay or uncertainty waiting for tapes to arrive
- reaches audiences at geographically diverse sites within the satellite's footprint
- encryption helps to prevent security breaches

Opportunities

- schedule in input from remote locations
- 'low cost' live input by viewers telephoning in questions to the presenter
- use for one-off events such as merger announcements, product launches
- interactive training
  - questions relayed live by telephone to a central trainer

Weaknesses

- high cost
- poor on complicated, factual messages
- technologically complex, especially linking live sites together
- requires basic equipment at all sites (dish, decoder, video-recorder)

Pitfalls

- cost may outweigh benefit of immediacy
- more cost-effective broadcast mechanisms may be available (see the following section on time-shift broadcast)
- 'we borrowed Eurovision's satellite'
  - live video and audio feeds from remote locations are technically difficult to pull off, and rather like the Eurovision song contest, may leave your presenter beached with no one to talk to

Budget issues

- may be cost-effective if it replaces cost of regional conferences and road-shows
- filming video material including number of locations
- renting or buying equipment, for example receiving (downlink) dishes
- live or recorded
- number of locations to link 'live'
- equipment and transmission costs

- outside expertise and production
- down time as staff watch the programmes

Timescales

- most events and programmes need at least three months' planning
- emergency live broadcasts can be arranged quickly

Activities

- set objectives, outline plan and target timescale
- invite proposals from DBS specialists
- select proposal and review
- script and plan event in detail
- book satellite time
- organize equipment, film crews, presenters
- organize satellite uplink from any sites sending equipment for broadcast
- rehearse event, especially any input from remote locations
- run the event

Feedback

- instant feedback on day
- ongoing audience reaction survey

Measurement

- survey to measure retention of key messages

How to find out more

Using Television and Video in Business by Andrew Crofts, Mercury, 1991

International Visual Communications Association (IVCA), 3rd Floor, Bolsover House, 5/6 Clipstone St, London W1P 7EB 0171-580 0962

TIME-SHIFT BROADCAST

Because most people now have video recorders, there is an opportunity for organizations to transmit programmes for their target audiences to record off-air. For example the BBC can transmit programmes in the early hours of the morning, using the frequencies used by BBC1 and BBC2. The target audience simply set their video-recorders, and watch the material when *they* want.

Strengths

- kudos and near-immediacy of broadcast TV
- reaches home-based audiences over a familiar and trusted medium
- can be a low cost method of distributing video material
- audience views at its own pace and convenience
- audience does not need to set a new channel on its video-recorders

Opportunities

- showcasing major events, such as organizational changes, annual general meetings
- updating skills
  - for example standardizing training for a dispersed profession such as nursing
- back up with documentation, for example workbooks for open learning

Weaknesses

- relatively high cost
- programmes must meet broadcast technical standards
- relies on target audience's motivation/ability to record programme
- an insecure medium, as it is broadcast to everyone with a television

Pitfalls

- could be seen as 'downmarket' television

Budget issues

- for non-urgent situations, more straightforward to send video-cassettes
- the savings made by not having to duplicate and distribute videos may not outweigh the costs of hiring transmitters

Timescales

- production issues as with video (see video, p. 157)
- requires advance booking

Activities

- set objectives
- negotiate and book slot on transmitters
- programme production process as for video (see video, p. 157), but to broadcast technical standards
- notify and motivate target audience

Feedback

- reply-paid cards

Measurement

- survey target audience to establish profile of those who recorded it, and those who ultimately watched the recording
- survey to measure retention of key messages

How to find out more

Using Television and Video in Business by Andrew Crofts, Mercury, 1991

International Visual Communications Association (IVCA), 3rd Floor, Bolsover House, 5/6 Clipstone St, London W1P 7EB 0171-580 0962

13 Computer-based communication

Tony Newbold, *specialist business writer* and
Eileen Scholes, *director, The ITEM Group*

LETTERS AND MEMOS

We are assuming that most business-related letters these days are typed into a computer. Whatever the medium, e.g. paper or screen, the letter format remains an effective way of conveying information concisely. Although a traditional and formal way to communicate, the language used is more frequently 'plain English' and colloquial.

At its worst, the memo is the last preserve of the 'Sir Humphreys' of this world, using a strange language known as memo-ese. By contrast, today, the Post-it note is undoubtedly one of the greatest communication tools. Stick it on, scribble a message, and there's an instant memo.

Strengths

- letters are generally more private than many other methods
- can carry complex information
- gives you and the receiver a permanent record
- helps people focus on the action you want them to take
- allows you to think through and revise what you want to say, putting emphasis on the right points
- can be very persuasive
- word-processed letters can be customized quickly for specific people

Opportunities

- direct mail to people's homes

- 'open-mail' systems, which enable people to send letters and memos through a central clearing house, direct to senior managers; replies pass through the clearing house, which directs them to anyone who may have their identity protected by a code system

Weaknesses

- takes time to plan and write
- depending on people's personalities and educational backgrounds, written messages can be over-formal and bureaucratic, taking too long to write and too long to read; others can be too abrupt or poorly expressed, leading to misunderstanding
- passes the action over to the receiver who may take a long time to reply
- one-way communication
- relies on efficient postal services; no record of sending or receipt on standard letters
- insecure

Pitfalls

- tendency to become over-formal
- mistakes undermine your credibility; proof-read your letter carefully
- word-processing has introduced its own brand of errors; check carefully for nonsense which can pass through a spellcheck; check set letters that you 'cut and paste' together, you'll be so familiar with the content that you may miss pasting errors

Budget issues

- cost of generating, printing and sending letters and memos
- cost of time taken to send by different methods

Timescales

- internal memos depend on the efficiency of the internal post
- next day delivery

Activities

- set objectives
- review the standard of letter writing in your organization
- consider establishing a house style, and creating model letters for common situations
- consider offering training

Feedback

- survey people's preferred means of sending and receiving messages
- survey people's views on the standard of written communication in the organization

Measurement

- compare the feedback responses over time

How to find out more

Letters at Work by A. Barker, Industrial Society Press, 1993
The Only 250 Letters and Memos Managers will ever need by R. Tepper, John Wiley & Sons, 1994

E-MAIL, BULLETIN BOARDS AND ON-LINE CONFERENCES

The fact that average computers are becoming more powerful, and able to communicate with each other, has meant that many of the traditional communication media are simply transferring to computer. For example, the humble memo or letter has achieved a new lease of life as electronic mail (e-mail). From your desk, you can send letters, complete with whole file attachments, almost instantly to computers across the building, or across the world, with equal ease. Similarly, the notice-board now has an on-line equivalent, with the content being updated by the users, and people can 'interact' at on-line conferences, as opposed to propping up the bar at conference venues.

As information technology penetrates further into organizations, more and more people will acquire access to these services, marginalizing still further those denied computers.

Strengths

- immediate, with a record of when created, when put on-line, and when accessed by the receiver
- can give people direct access to anyone, including senior management
- the ability to personalize general or routine messages
- once the facility is established, a cost-effective way of linking people worldwide
- avoids additional paper circulating the organization
- on-line conferences provide an opportunity for many people to give instant feedback, brainstorm and problem-solve
- bulletin boards and special interest fora provide a defined area for fast information-giving and problem-solving
- fast way of distributing text documents, such as newsletters, as well as pictures, logos and powerpoint shows, which can be printed locally or when needed

173

- attractive, particularly for younger groups
- a thriving subculture, with a relatively informal 'netiquette', with its own somewhat 'Americanized' style and shorthand
  - for example IMO ('In My Opinion'), BTW ('By The Way'), WRT ('With Regard To'), FWIW (For What It's Worth), ROFL (Rolling on The Floor Laughing), BCNU (Be Seeing You), :)   :(

Opportunities

- use computer 'kiosks' in public areas like the staff restaurant to give access to people without their own computer
- extend parts of the e-mail system to customers and suppliers, speeding all-round communication
- back up key communication with written support, such as a directory of all bulletin boards or fora
- support by archiving and indexing useful data

Weaknesses

- only reaches people with *informed* access to a computer, although others can rely on hard copy printed out nearby
- there is a temptation for users to send far too much, irrelevant, un-targeted and unsolicited mail
  - training and awareness campaigns can help ensure that people target their mail
  - bulletin boards and fora can grow so fast that nobody has a clear idea what they contain
  - ideally someone needs to police and audit the system, identifying the material that should be archived from the dross that must be deleted
- no physical presence means that people may neglect to check their e-mail; software can provide automatic prompts, so that users see when their mail comes in
- it is so fast that it can become a main route for the grapevine (see grapevine, p. 207)
- needs to be downloaded to disk or laptop to be read at home or when travelling
- discipline needed to ensure that people do not waste time 'surfing' the company's bulletin boards, fora and conferences

Pitfalls

- *'well, it's free, isn't it?'*
  - people see e-mail as 'free' communication, creating an undisciplined approach
- *'why do I need to talk to you?'*

- its speed and ease can make people feel that they don't need to make face-to-face contact
- *'just dashed off an e-mail'*
  - e-mail is about as close as written contact gets to the speed of speech, and there is a tendency not to edit, revise or even read e-mail memos before they are sent

Budget issues

- many organizations will already use a Local Area Network (LAN) to link local communication or a Wide Area Network (WAN) to link all sites, if not investment may be necessary for full networking
- alternatively, remote users, such as home workers, could log in via modem and phone line to 'pick up' their e-mail
- time spent using and administering the system
- off-line e-mail reader/writers will save phone time on external e-mail

Timescales

- e-mail communication is virtually instant, but there is no guarantee when – or indeed *if* – the receiver will read it
- on-line conferencing ideally works in real time, ideas building on each other, or strands can be picked up later, perhaps by people working on the other side of the world

Activities

- set objectives
- raise awareness and offer training in e-mail etiquette
- regulate the growth of e-mail
- oversee the running of conferences and bulletin boards

Feedback

- build feedback sessions into conferences
- within each forum or bulletin board, have a help section devoted to training and supporting users

Measurement

- it is vital to survey people to ensure that they are getting the information they want
- people accessing e-mail documents can be measured automatically
- compare effectiveness with other media
- measure how long it takes for readers to access their mail from the time it is created

175

How to find out more

The Virtual Corporation by William H. Davidow and Michael F. Malone, Harper
Business Press, 1993

MULTIMEDIA

Multimedia is a sweeping, all-encompassing term, and as such looks likely to
survive the rapid technology shifts already affecting the equipment involved in
producing it. At the moment it refers to computers combining text, video,
sound, animated computer graphics, telecommunications, usually using a CD-
ROM drive (compact disk – read only memory). There's yet to be a breakthrough application to make multimedia machines 'must haves' for everyone,
and early users ran into numerous technical problems.

However, the hardware and software are settling down and the integration of
all media into one is releasing tremendous synergy. For example it is revolu-
tionizing computer-based training, by offering users very realistic simulations
to participate in. We're all used to the help systems lying behind our software,
but it is very reassuring to have a human face on screen calmly explaining what
you have to do – the latest packages can feel like dealing with the Hal computer
from *2001*.

If, as psychologists say, we retain about 20 per cent of what we hear, 30 per
cent of what we see, *50 per cent of what we hear and see*, the potential is there to
create 'documents' with real impact.

For example a multimedia presentation on the organization, circulated on
CD-ROM or available on a network, could be used as the 'bible' on how the
organization works, with different levels of information for different purposes.
The advantage is that it is not linear – users determine what they see and in
which order. It could be used, for example, as a general overview at induction,
or explain in detail the working of a particular process to an experienced project team. The networked version could be progressively updated, replacing
old modules with new ones – minor changes would not mean discarding the
entire programme, as it would with a corporate video.

Strengths

- combines strength of all media
  – print, video, CD-ROM, software
- totally flexible from users' point of view; they can choose which options
  they want to see, and in what detail
- none of the users' time is wasted handling any material they do not need;
  they gain instant access to what they want
- high impact presentations, using more of the audience's senses, aid
  retention of messages

Opportunities

- post conference support
  - see the speech being given, read it in synopsis or in full on screen, or print it out, view the slides, or any combination of these
- simulations for on-the-job training and education
  - for example using a sound card and a microphone to record a sequence into a dramatized situation, such as recording a response to an angry bank customer
  - lets the trainee practise interactions without the need for time-consuming 'real-time' role-plays
  - possible to keep a record of a person's progress through a module
- use multimedia 'kiosks' in public areas like the staff restaurant to give access to people without their own multimedia computer
- use for interactive marketing
  - for example displays in foyers, exhibitions, hands-on museum exhibits
  - person using it becomes fully involved with your 'advert'
- back up multimedia with written support, preferably giving the audience a route map showing how to find your way around a multimedia package

Weaknesses

- multimedia software is not very user friendly, and not always compatible with specific hardware
- multimedia authoring is something of a new skill, and many people are learning 'on the job'
- multimedia can put a great demand on the memory of machines; even when the memory is boosted to compensate, power-hungry material like video sequences can slow down performance
- a multimedia project represents a huge investment of time and specialist skill
- we know how to produce the individual media within multimedia, but we're still learning how to put all those parts together to best effect
  - it's rather like knowing the words of a language without knowing the grammar
  - there are few successful models to guide people on how to structure multimedia 'documents'
  - thinking in a non-linear way is demanding; you no longer have the security of a 'beginning', 'middle' and 'end', because to a large degree the 'structure' is defined by the audience

Pitfalls

- blue sky technology
  - designers enjoy the challenge of using the latest multimedia software and will push it to the limit, with the danger that the objectives of the

    programme, and its budget and schedule, will be lost in the name of 'art'

- burying options
  - some 'documents' lose flexibility by building in long, linear sequences, effectively hiding the material from the users, or forcing them down a particular path to reach the information they want
- upgrade-mania
  - multimedia authoring software is ever-improving, but it is not always easy to upgrade existing presentations into the new software, which shortens its effective shelf life
- 'whose profession is this anyway?'
  - by definition, multimedia works across all disciplines
  - ideally you need a project team strong in all the media represented, run by someone with a clear unifying vision
  - without a strong, shared vision, multimedia teams can pull in opposite directions, or worse, omit one of the disciplines, for example software experts writing text or directing videos, or writers believing they can create graphics
- quite a high level of computer needed to run it

Budget issues

- supplementing existing hardware
  - upgrading current hardware vs buying new multimedia hardware packages
- authoring software
- buying in or subcontracting the main project skill areas involved in multimedia authoring

Timescales

- equipment and off-the-shelf software can be bought and running almost immediately
- at least three months' intensive effort from a multidisciplined project team to create a professional-looking multimedia program

Activities

- set objective
- write plan and approve
- storyboard
- test the storyboard on a target sample audience
- 'build' a crude prototype
- test the prototype on a target sample
- source and create material
  - video, audio, computer animation, graphics and text

- build a prototype combining all elements

- test the new prototype on a target sample
- revise and de-bug
- when approved, press on to CD-ROM and distribute, or place on a network

Feedback

- invite feedback on screen via e-mail, print and fax/mail, for example as a prompt when the user exits a multimedia program

Measurement

- retention of key messages
- study to check usability and to see which options are most popular

How to find out more

Association for Educational and Training Technology, Centre for Continuing Education, City University, Northampton Square, London EC1V 0HB 0171-253 4399

International Visual Communications Association (IVCA), 3rd Floor, Bolsover House, 5/6 Clipstone St, London W1P 7EB 0171-580 0962

VIDEO WITH INTERACTION

The danger with standard video is that it is becoming so familiar and seductive that it can leave the audience unchallenged, just passively absorbed in letting the material wash over them with the same degree of attention they pay a TV soap (or indeed, not even that much).

The philosophy of interactive video is to challenge the viewers, asking them to make certain choices or posing questions before they proceed. This has entered a new era through computer-based multimedia (see multimedia, p. 176) but there is still a role for using ordinary video-recorders, structured for interaction.

Strengths

- relatively low-tech, accessible to anyone with a video-recorder
- helps to illustrate, structure and punctuate events
- good for conveying target behaviours, improving performance
  - can show the outcomes of different courses of action
  - makes abstract choices concrete by showing the consequences – demonstrating 'what-if' scenarios

Opportunities

- boost involvement through questions, choices and exercises
- use interactive video for specific purposes
  - for example recruitment, induction, training
- by using two or more videos you can simulate the effect of choosing different routes, as with computer-based interactive video
- for full interaction treat it like an open learning package with worksheets and follow-up exercises

Weaknesses

- because video is a linear medium, it cannot match the level of inter-activity available via multimedia (see multimedia, p. 176)
- the structure is fairly rigid; it assumes you want to go through all the exercises and questions with each audience
- difficult to access specific parts of the tape

Pitfalls

- 'the blindingly obvious choice'
  - some interactive videos can be rather patronizing, with very obvious choices, resembling old-style government public information films
- 'Hobson's choice'
  - because the element of choice offered is frequently very limited, the user's true course of action may not be represented

Budget issues

- cost of designing and producing interactive video programme, and its supporting documentation
- cost of viewing facilities

Timescales

- minimum of three months for a good quality product, tailored to need

Activities

- set objectives
- pull together team to design, test and produce programme
- duplicate, use and monitor
- arrange viewing facilities

Feedback

- questionnaires after use

Measurement

- compare with objectives
  - for example improvement in target behaviours by comparing with measurements taken before the programme is used

How to find out more

International Visual Communications Association (IVCA), 3rd Floor, Bolsover House, 5/6 Clipstone St, London W1P 7EB 0171-580 0962

DOCUMENTS ON DISK OR VIA MODEM/NETWORK

The amount of time and effort wasted by people re-inputting text, or even recreating content from scratch, is truly alarming. Through a simple operation, that text can now be shared on disk, or sent via modem or over a network, anywhere in the world.

We are yet to see a quantum leap in sharing data in this way, despite the increased compatibility of systems. To some extent the problem is attitudinal rather than technological. People are reluctant to share information that they've worked hard to get, or which gives them some power, or takes effort – even the smallest – to share.

But sharing data for the good of the organization *will* be for the good of the organization, and in theory for the individual involved, as they'll benefit in turn from the work of others.

Unfortunately, most information sits in eccentrically-named files, buried seemingly at random in an individual's subdirectories, doing the electronic equivalent of gathering dust. How many of us can say that if we disappeared under that proverbial bus, anyone else in our organization could find their way around our filing systems?

This communication blockage will be removed only if business as a whole can sort out the ethical and intellectual property issues – in short who has *practical* ownership of a document.

If someone generates a document in the organization's time and using its resources, then surely that organization has a right to expect that person to store that document in a way that the whole organization can benefit from it? The technology exists: the potential benefits are great, but the intellectual and psychological challenge is enormous.

Strengths

- high portability of information

- instant delivery via network or modem
- high capacity on disk, easily posted across the world
- rapid sharing of knowledge, spreading of best practice
- documents can be customized, and used for different purposes by different receivers

Opportunities

- introduce document control systems
  - for example showing who created a document, when and where it was generated, the draft number, the software it was written in
  - it is hard enough to keep track of different drafts of the same document, but even harder with multiple sites producing their own version of documents
- create a file index
  - to prevent organizations constantly reinventing the wheel a central index describing key files on the network would provide the best starting point for any project
- standardize file naming and file describing protocols
  - people could search the organization's database for self-explanatory filenames, or by keywords
- introduce a 'clippings' service
  - use software to enable people to set their systems to 'browse' the organization's databases on a regular basis, identifying all documents containing keywords of their choice
  - useful for skills updating or for monitoring developments in a particular field
- how fast you can retrieve and manage key information is a vital source of competitive advantage, and if you are doing this right, it makes sense to push this message to your outside customers through marketing or PR

Weaknesses

- lack of central control
  - individuals edit and rewrite documents as they want
- lack of control over own files
  - it may be hard to convince people that anyone else should have access to their work
  - they may overcompensate by password-protecting too many of their files
- not much good for technophobes
  - it could marginalize anyone lacking the necessary computer or research skills
- distributing electronically relies on the receiver to take action to access and use the file
  - as opposed to passively receiving a physical document

- people like paper – it's familiar, physical, they can write on it, and it's easy to file
  - in most cases there will be a hard copy duplicate of documents
- exposure to the Data Protection Act
  - in theory, certain sensitive data should not be computerized in any way
- increased risk of virus damage
  - computer security protocols are becoming increasingly important as information is shared from system to system, over disk or networks

Pitfalls

- not the paperless office
  - systems still crash and disks corrupt from time to time
- untrained people
  - outside the computer industry, the standard of computer training tends to be low, with many users just expected to learn as they go
- overloaded networks
  - organizations often push overloaded networked systems past their limits, with too many users making demands at peak times, slowing tasks down

Budget issues

- cost-benefit analysis of local vs central document production
- investment in dedicated communication lines (Local Area Networks or Wide Area Networks)
- alternatively, investment in software to link PCs on-line via modem when needed
- training and resource

Timescales

- most organizations can now transfer files on disk between systems
- to transfer data on-line from one system to another means the time taken to buy, fit and learn to use a modem

Activities

- research and setting up of appropriate etiquette and work systems
- set objectives
- awareness campaign to highlight the cost of re-inputting text and citing cases of unnecessary re-work
- training campaign, if needed
- setting up a central information resource
- networking systems if appropriate

183

Feedback

- most software will verify and confirm that a file has been successfully transferred – posting a disk relies on a call to check that it has arrived and works
- if you are using someone else's files, it is usually courtesy and good practice to let them know what you're doing – they may also be able to offer further help

Measurement

- cost-benefit analysis for different methods of transferring data
  - for example rather than printing and sending a paper document around the world, you could simply send the text electronically, and print out locally
- record of files being used and transferred

How to find out more

- identify bulk senders and receivers of text within and outside the organization, talk through their needs with them
- invite suppliers in (competition is tough so they'll happily do it for free) for advice and awareness sessions
- identify parallel organizations that are sharing data effectively and visit them to see how they do it

The Virtual Corporation by William H. Davidow and Michael F. Malone, Harper Business Press, 1993

THE INTERNET

The Internet is a global network of over 20 million users, ranging from government offices to corporations, from individuals and universities to businesses of all kinds.

At the time of writing, it has yet to prove its practical worth as a business tool, but the potential is too exciting to ignore. Even now, the network is so huge, that finding your way around it can seem impossible, rather like seeing the big toe of an elephant, and trying to imagine the whole beast from it.

To make it more of a challenge the Internet thrives like a grapevine, and has an organic, totally flexible 'structure'. It makes mapping it out difficult, and means that most of the literature in the field dates very quickly.

What it does do is bring the world to your desk over a local gateway. That is, for the cost of a local call, you can use the modem on your computer to tap into a node on the global network through a service provider. It will handle the connection, and give guidance on where to find particular information.

Alternatively, with the right hardware and software, you can access the

Internet directly yourself by making an agreement with a site you are interested in, and dialling their number.

In a business context, once connected to the network, you can use it to search newspaper or magazine databases for all the articles written on a particular subject, scan business reports, check the financial health of a company, keep up to date with share options, and in the same way find the best rail route from Dresden to Darlington.

The Internet unites people of like interests and expertise, pooling the world's information resources. Increasingly intelligent and sophisticated search programs are helping to manage the information, making the systems capable of filtering out just the data you are looking for.

At the moment, rather like real surfing, surfing the Internet is a highly skilled process – sometimes you hit the crest of a wave and find the very information you're looking for, but at other times you may be paddling through more than a little software 'sewage'.

Strengths

- ever-growing
- appeals to the computer-literate within your internal audience
- access to outside databases/contributors worldwide
- e-mail gateway for customers and suppliers

Opportunities

- closer contact with customers, suppliers and peers
  - for example on-line conferences, bulletin boards, help fora (see e-mail, bulletin boards, etc., p. 173)
- can provide an instant on-line research resource

Weaknesses

- software to access it is still rather unfriendly
- requires fairly high skill levels
- needs software protection protocols to be strictly followed
- security issues
  - danger of sensitive files being accessed from the network
  - danger of virus being introduced into the organization
- real cost ignored
  - people tend to think of the cost of a local call, but pricing structures can be more complicated
  - expect high charges for access to premium databases

Pitfalls

- finding yourself chasing novelty value

- to some extent the Internet is still an incredible solution looking for an application
- opening up a browser's paradise
  - part of the Internet's emotional attraction is the fact that so little of it has been explored
  - browsing and exploring is somewhat addictive, and can be expensive in both time and extra usage charges
- sex, lies and videogames
  - unlike service providers such as CompuServe, an on-line information service that helps structure access to the Internet, the Internet itself is not under anyone's specific control; organizations are running into the problem of people accessing very dubious or sensitive material, spreading commercial rumours and, most commonly, simply downloading and playing the latest computer games
  - any organization with a computer needs a clearly defined computer security policy, and this needs to be strengthened and enforced when you are able to access outside networks
  - put disciplinary guidelines in place to discourage people from abusing the system – it may not prevent them from inadvertently downloading a virus, but it will at least stop them from using 'pin up' windows, and playing games in work time

Budget issues

- most organizations will already have the necessary and simple hardware – a modem and computer
- investment in software to improve access to the Internet, and ability to search for data
- subscription to a gateway service
  - for example membership of an ISP (Internet Service Provider) such as CompuServe or UKONLINE to give you local access to the network
- time spent in learning how to use the software, and identifying useful contacts and databases around the Internet
- faster modems (at least V34, 28,800 bps) save time

Timescales

- given that you can access it with fairly basic hardware, most organizations already have potential access to the Internet
- signing up with a gateway service provider will take around two weeks

Activities

- set objectives
- research hardware and software requirements
  - talk to your IT department
  - read computer magazines for contact addresses

- take out a subscription to a gateway provider if appropriate
- go on-line to carry out tasks, for example global on-line research or e-mailing outside your own organization

Feedback

- instant feedback on-line or via e-mail

Measurement

- measure usage and popular destinations
- cost-benefit analysis of different research methods, for example in-house vs out-of-house, library vs on-line services

How to find out more

The Internet Guide for New Users by Daniel P. Dern, McGraw-Hill, 1994
The Virtual Corporation by William H. Davidow and Michael F. Malone, Harper Business Press, 1993

CompuServe, 1 Redcliff St, PO Box 676, Bristol BS99 1YN 0800 289378
UKONLINE, The Maltings, Charlton Road, Shepton Mallet, Somerset, BA4 5QE 0645 000011
HyperCAST Services UK, 30–31 Newman Street, London W1P 3PE 0171 580 3739

14 Organizational communication

Tony Newbold, *specialist business writer* and
Eileen Scholes, *director, The ITEM Group*

CORPORATE IDENTITY

Everything an organization does says something about its values and personality (see the sections on symbolic communication and working environment, pp. 192 and 198). This is nowhere more apparent than in the visible components of an organization's corporate identity – in its crudest form its corporate colours, logo, headed notepaper, lorries, uniforms and so on.

Consciously revising your organization's corporate identity is often a classic, if extremely valuable case of 'the tail wagging the dog'.

It's only when we sit down to decide what we want to 'say' about ourselves that we start examining the fundamental and painful questions about our organization:

- *who* are we?
- *why* are we here?
- *what* are we trying to do?
- *how* do we do what we do?

According to the corporate identity industry's godfather, Wally Olins, it is the 'yardstick' against which an organization's products, behaviours and actions are measured.

Typically, people think about corporate identity as the *physical* things that can be updated, the signs, uniforms and so on, but its advocates believe it does much more. It can provide a clear symbol that things have changed. It can also redirect and re-energize employees and reinforce the commitment of other stakeholder audiences.

Corporate identity is now a booming field, with the public sector heavily involved, from healthcare trusts to individual schools, from the 'new' universities to government agencies. The successful players are highly specialized. Developing corporate identity is a combination of management consultancy and design expertise. To the extent that it's usually not wise to cut your own hair, it may be a mistake to handle a corporate identity revamp in-house – you're just too close to the problem.

Strengths

- re-energizing
- communicating change
- motivating
- restating the organization's values

Opportunities

- involve internal audiences in research and testing
- involve them in the communication campaign
  - for example a party on the day of the launch
- as a public relations exercise, donate obsolete stationery to charities of employees' choice
- involve employees in auditing everything that needs to be updated
  - the list may be daunting, and this will be an opportunity to decide if all the variations of memos, forms, letterheads, compliments slips and so on are *really* needed, thus avoiding criticisms that too much is being spent on the change

Weaknesses

- the cost, with leading players charging at least a million for a corporate identity programme
- the change will be cosmetic if it is not a true reflection of the organization and its values
- this may mean it has to follow or be accompanied by a programme to change attitudes and behaviours
- can be seen as a waste of money or a luxury option in times of cost control
- a soft target for people to attack, very hard to quantify in terms of benefits
- requires superb project management and logistics skill
- you can't please all the people all the time
  - if you were successful with your last corporate ID, people will take time to be persuaded to your new one

Pitfalls

- inadequate research
  - in hurrying the research phase, you miss the important opportunity for involvement and testing designs, resorting instead to arbitrarily imposing a solution
- patchy update
  - inevitably, corporate identity has to be phased in over a period, but nothing looks more unprofessional than a mix of identities; wherever possible, make sure no one can use an old identity by mistake
- using a cheap supplier
  - a second-class identity represents a second-class organization
- local empires
  - departments and sites may try to make unauthorized adaptations of the corporate standards
  - diluting the 'brand' by introducing too many variants
- unclear or hidden corporate standards
  - in many cases, internal audiences are ignorant of the fact that there *are* standards controlling how logos are used, documents laid out, and so on; put a clearly written corporate standards file in every department, explaining in plain English how the identity should appear, and include a contact number for colour copies of logos, bromides, etc.; for immediacy, circulate the standards on disk or network them
- too often
  - 'fiddling' with the identity, or relaunching the whole identity too often, literally does create 'identity crises', moving the cultural goal posts and leaving internal and external audiences confused about what the organization actually stands for
- lack of vision
  - there is a danger of conservatism, merely 'tweaking' the existing identity because of organizational inertia
  - the objectives may be too vague or abstract, for example, 'we want to be a "world class" organization'
  - blandness – 'me too' identities based on other design models rather than organizational values
- fashion
  - some corporate identities become classics, others date because they are too closely tied to what is in vogue in graphic design at the time
- short shelf life
  - it's easy to forget to plan ahead for contingencies, for example how many companies wasted paper on 'phone day', by not predicting stationery usage?
- ugly, uncomfortable uniforms
  - walk down any high street, and even today you will find some spectacularly demeaning uniforms, some even designed to match the carpets
  - question the need for uniforms in the first place

- people are only going to feel confident and motivated if they've been involved in choosing the design of the uniform, and it's very clearly been tested

Budget issues

- time spent defining objectives, working up proposed identities and testing them
- time spent in planning and implementing the identity
- materials bill including new signage, livery, packaging, products, publications, vehicles, advertising/marketing materials
- cost of awareness campaign
- if you have in-house capability, it's a question of how far you involve outside consultants
  - for example they may help with the initial design concepts and research and you handle the practical implementation

Timescales

- for large organizations, introducing a new corporate identity will take a minimum of six months

Activities

- set objectives for the new identity
- define, commission and test designs by seeing how they are perceived by target groups
- run an awareness campaign as a 'teaser' for the new launch
- draw up an implementation plan
- put the plan into action
  - explain to people what the identity means for them
  - update the physical materials – logos, livery, uniform, stationery, T-shirts and so on
- audit the identity
  - ensure that all evidence of previous identities has been removed, including 'personal' stocks of old letterhead, forms, etc. which may creep back into the system
- research periodically to make sure identity has not dated

Feedback

- invite employees, customers, suppliers, shareholders for their input into the design
- survey all target groups as you develop the identity

Measurement

● comparing reaction of target groups against identity

How to find out more

The Corporate Image: strategies for effective identity programmes by Nicholas Ind, Kogan Page, 1990

Corporate Reputation: managing the new strategic asset by John Smythe, Colette Dorward and Jerome Reback, Century Business, 1992

The New Guide to Identity, by Wolff Olins, Gower/The Design Council, 1996

SYMBOLIC COMMUNICATION

Consistent messages are vital in communication. The challenge in internal communication is that what we say is often not what we do. Action speaks louder than words, especially in the context of employee communication, where the audience can be suspicious of organizational propaganda. Bold promises, cynically made, are received on the ground even more cynically.

Symbolic communication is not so much a medium to control, more as they say, 'a way of life'. It covers everything from the organization's values, the management style, the way employees are treated through to the corporate body's social responsibilities. As such it's the territory of everyone from general management consultants to organizational psychologists, from ergonomists, even to anthropologists.

Employees (and suppliers) are whole people, so if they're demotivated and not performing, the diagnosis has to be a holistic one. There will be a wide range of reasons why people are unhappy, and why the star performers you are after wouldn't touch your organization with a bargepole. Regular and detailed attitude surveys will start to give you clues why (see p. 283).

This section will look in more detail at some factors lying behind the organizational façade and give examples of some of the practical steps you can take. Actions do speak loudest of all, but they are also the hardest medium to control.

Organization values

What messages do you send people about the values of your organization? For example via:

● job titles
● visible status symbols
  – for example type of office, thickness of carpet, size of window
● how redundancy is handled
  – coldly handed a bin bag and escorted from the premises

- with sensitivity, investing in outplacement
- uniforms
  - the style denotes the public image the company has of itself (which may not match the audience's notion)

Management style

What messages do you send to people through the way managers are allowed or encouraged to behave? For example:

- commanding or empowering
- means of address
  - for example on first name terms with all
- tacit acceptance of aggression, bullying and victimization
- socializing with the team, or keeping their distance
- tolerating humour or welcoming it
- leading by example
  - a leading Japanese businessman recently said, 'I would be ashamed to take a pay rise higher than my team'
  - 'mucking in when crisis hits'

Buildings and facilities

What message do people pick up from your buildings? For example:

- choice of office
  - a high-tech unit on a business park
  - an imposing tower block
  - a friendly Georgian house
- the state of the building
  - how secure can people feel if the organization appears not to invest in maintaining the building?
- number of people per square foot
- overloaded infrastructure
  - poor ventilation, inadequate heating, little natural daylight, lack of meeting places, poor telecommunication, computing, toilet and kitchen facilities
- can employees be *effective* within it?
  - if you're not 'empowered' even to open a window, you hardly feel valued in your job
- catering facilities
  - the acid test of single status restaurants is not the layout, nor the principle that management and workers can eat together, but whether they actually *do*
- extra facilities like open learning centres, workplace nurseries and access to sports facilities

Employee respect

How do employees (and suppliers) feel they are treated? For example:

- balancing needs
  - are they respected as whole people who need to look after family as well as work interests?
- personal and career development
  - does the organization play an active role in supporting it?
- decision-making
  - are your people involved, especially in decisions directly affecting them?
- listening
  - do people feel that they can really make a difference?
- dress code
  - is it demeaning, or can it be deliberately subverted, for example 'dress down' days when employees can dress casually?

Social responsibility

Where does the organization stand in terms of business ethics, supporting charities, and working with the local community? For example:

- supporting the local community
- running office/works tours
- family days
- encouraging voluntary work, secondments to local charities
- building links with schools and colleges
- producing educational packs

Strengths

- symbolic communication is at the heart of the organization
  - positive impact here will communicate to employees and beyond
- symbolic communication is active – the organization is 'putting its money where its mouth is'

Opportunities

- any new management style has to be demonstrated from the top by senior management
  - reinforce this with an awareness campaign
  - introduce upward appraisal
- if you have a depressing, inefficient building, consider handing the problem over to the people who work in it – they know best what they need to perform effectively

- take every opportunity to consult people on issues that affect them
  - people will only buy in to decisions if they have been explained to them
  - imposing decisions is counterproductive in the long run because people can find a million ways to undermine situations that they do not agree with

Weaknesses

- symbolic communication is essentially a symptom rather than a cause – you can be aware of it, but ultimately you need to tackle the fundamental problems that are holding back your people
- it can take a massive investment in a communication and change programme to have a big impact on how an organization behaves

Pitfalls

Alienation

- by challenging the status quo, you may unsettle those who are comfortable with it
  - for example introducing empowerment to a culture where managers traditionally have control will make managers feel insecure

Human engineering

- organizations are like delicate ecosystems – changing any element in the environment, whether it's the way employees are treated, the building, the management style or its social responsibility policies, can have an unpredictable effect
  - some people may like the change, others will not

Budget issues

- funding attitude research

Timescales

- the quest to manage attitudes with greater awareness through symbolic communication is ongoing

Activities

- set objectives
- attitude change campaigns and training workshops

Feedback

- use all media to gather feedback

Measurement

- it is difficult to define the items that make up symbolic communication but it is easy to measure the impact it has through attitude and opinion surveys (see focus groups, surveys and research, p. 205 and Chapter 20, p. 283)
- you can also measure changing factors in the organization through regular exit interviews

How to find out more

The Power of Empowerment by David Clutterbuck and Sue Kernaghan, Kogan Page, 1994

The New Guide to Identity, by Wolff Olins, Gower/The Design Council, 1996

PARTICIPATIVE STRUCTURES

Whatever your political stance on unions, they were a direct channel of communication to employees and an identified structure for employee representation.

Apart from within multinationals, the notion of works councils being imposed from Europe may now have somewhat receded, but best practice suggests that employees *do* need a way to be more involved in the running of organizations. How far can empowerment go, if employees' scope for decision-making is so limited?

Rather than being feared, face-to-face communication between management and some sort of employee representative group can help explain the background to difficult decisions, even if organizations are not going to go beyond such legal obligations as exist to consult employees on certain issues.

Some companies favour shared ownership as a means of stimulating participation, sometimes offering employees shares at a discount rate, but while this is financial participation, there's not much opportunity to have a say in the business outside the AGM.

Other organizations favour joint consultative committees, working in partnership together to tackle business issues. Then there is the plethora of ad hoc teams, such as service or quality improvement teams, concerned with particular tasks.

Strengths

- creates a climate where ideas and commitment are valued
- route for upward feedback from target audiences

- channel for management to deal directly with the people concerned
- demonstrates a clear commitment to consultation

Opportunities

- jointly produced documents or jointly run projects that are in the mutual interest of the organization and the target group
  - for example producing guides on personal safety
- involving group representatives in aspects of the communication process
  - they may be more trusted
  - they can help keep internal media on track with the issues employees care about
  - for example employees could be members of editorial committees

Weaknesses

- management fear lack of control and misinterpretation of messages
- time-consuming
- everything relies on the assumption that the people on the committees are truly representative of employees
- can create expectations of involvement in decision-making which managers are not prepared to cede

Pitfalls

- once a consultation process is established, it may be perceived as a right and be very hard to take away or ignore
- the process needs to be managed carefully to avoid creating a bodged, compromised outcome, all too obviously the product of a committee of diverse views
- singing one's own praises on consultation, either within or outside the organization, before you're sure the target group would agree with you

Budget issues

- time spent preparing and meeting

Timescales

- if consultation is not in place it may take many months to set up a successful process

Activities

- set objectives
- research best practice in employee consultation to choose a model appropriate for the culture
  or
- run meetings within existing infrastructure

Feedback

- regular meetings act as a forum for feedback
- employee attitudes surveys

Measurement

- impact of employee consultation on the organization

How to find out more

Employee Communications and Consultation, ACAS Publications, 1994, 01455 852225
Your Employees – Your Edge in the 1990s, Smythe, Dorward, Lambert, 1990
New Developments in Employee Involvement by Mick Marchington, John Goodman and Adrian Wilkinson, Employment Department, 1992
'Employee communication and participation' by Chris Brewster and Ariane Hegewisch, *P+European Participation Monitor*, Number 7, 1993
'Writing wrongs with democracy' by Anat Arkin, *Personnel Management Plus*, April 1994 (study of John Lewis' consultative and communication mechanisms)
'Employee involvement: employees' views' by Christine Tillsley, *Employment Gazette*, June 1994
Empowering People at Work by Nancy Foy, Gower, 1994

Involvement and Participation Association, 42 Colebrooke Row, London N1 8AF 0171-354 8040
ACAS, Head Office, 27 Wilton St, London SW1X 7AZ 0171-210 3000

WORKING ENVIRONMENT

Most organizations want their employees to contribute more ideas and be more creative. For example they go to great lengths to run award schemes which reward ideas and innovation (see award schemes, p. 203) and service improvement teams, yet it may be the organization itself that is stifling creativity.

From outside, many organizations look like they were deliberately designed to stamp out any creative thought, from rigid rulebooks to dingy conditions, from the soulless office to performance management systems that put the emphasis on *management* rather than *performance* (see symbolic communication, p. 192).

It's no surprise that some of the best breakthroughs happen through conversations. One thought will spark off another. The art is somehow to capture the benefits of the sort of creative interplay that goes on around coffee machines across the world, as well as what emerges in more formal meetings.

Strongly creative people by definition find a way around the rigidities of the bureaucratic organization. They break all the rules, rub the boss up the wrong way, and make themselves generally hell to manage.

But what about most employees? What can be done to release their creativity?

Strengths

Workplace

- immediately visible as a sign of commitment to the well-being and productivity of individuals
- affects *everyone*, not just those who typically read or listen
- no special expenditure needed – just thought
- stimulates appropriate behaviours unconsciously

Working methods

- improvements in working methods reflect and support other positive activities like quality and customer care

Opportunities

- involve individuals in improving their work area
  - ideally ask them to plan what they would do within a set budget
  - each area or team will establish its own identity and set up creative corners

Weaknesses

- it's hard to define creative behaviours
  - by definition creativity does not lend itself to reductive competency statements
- creative tensions are a necessary part of any creative process, but can be counterproductive if managers are unskilled

Pitfalls

Workplace layouts

- replacing one rigid structure with another
  - organizational needs and teams change constantly, so any new layout needs to be just as adaptable
- *'but this is what you asked for'*
  - as with any consultation exercise, make sure that you've consulted everyone who will be affected, not just those who shout loudest

Working systems

- *'what's really valued here?'*
  - competency statements are notorious for being vague and unclear
  - define clear performance standards
  - be wary of off-the-peg competency statements, test them first on your employees
- *'if I'm not paid extra for it, why do it?'*
  - you can't itemize every behaviour
- *'my boss'll never give me credit'*
  - if the performance standards are clear, there should be less variation in how managers rate employees
  - build in an arbitration process, and make the performance management system more objective by 'cross-marking'
- *'my boss only listens to them'*
  - be wary of favouring employees perceived as 'creative'; you may be setting up élitism, and holding back other employees

Budget issues

- cost of creating new, flexible layouts; in fact, hot-desking and utilizing restaurants as meeting areas are cost-saving exercises

Timescales

- ties in with existing initiatives

Activities

- set objectives
- research to identify what employees feel would help them be more creative and make more of a contribution to the organization
- look for a more flexible approach to office design, mixing employees, breaking down 'little empires'

- for example organizations are introducing central areas where employees can 'hot-desk', simply dropping in to use a workstation or meet with colleagues
  - one of the benefits of hot-desking is that people from different functions automatically network with each other because there are no fixed territories
- set up working areas in the restaurant or 'public' areas like an atrium, utilizing space that is not fully utilized through most of the day; this can be a pleasant, informal working or meeting place
- clarify objectives, goals and standards and then empower employees to meet them however they want to
- if people feel they can add value, and have more scope to operate, they are more likely to take risks
- pool talents, for example cross-functionally, as new perspectives 'bouncing off each other' may create fresh ideas
- where appropriate, encourage employees to work from customers' sites, improving their understanding of customers' needs, which they can communicate back to the organization

Feedback

- employee involvement in designing a more creative environment

Measurement

- productivity measurements
- analysis of successful creative ideas
- monitor use of communal areas

How to find out more

The New Guide to Identity, by Wolff Olins, Gower/The Design Council, 1996
The Virtual Corporation by William H. Davidow and Michael F. Malone, Harper Business Press, 1993

PUBLIC DISPLAY

Notice-boards carry everything from the menu in the staff restaurant, to flat shares, car sales and quality submissions. A quirky hybrid of bureaucratese and street talk, part of their charm is that they are 'public', open to everyone.

Posters are a clear way of conveying a simple message, especially in industrial environments.

Strengths

- notice-boards give sense of community, familiarity and joint ownership   *201*

- posters leave a constant reminder
- equal access to everyone

Opportunities

- involve employees in taking ownership of the notice-boards, clearing off old messages when they become dated
- dedicate part of a board to anonymous feedback on specific issues, letting off steam
- posters can be made interactive, for example requiring people to fill in key organizational measurements in terms of sales, clients served and so on

Weaknesses

- notice-boards and posters are a fairly passive medium, relying on people to read them as they pass by
- remember notice-boards are a public medium, so all visitors will see them

Pitfalls

Notice-boards

- not updated or managed
  - become messy and chaotic, carrying curling sheets
- not formatted
  - just an information dump
- inconsistent design
  - difficult to find the information you need
- not read at a glance
  - need to be visually striking and easily read

Posters

- posters can seem a little too propagandist or patronizing, 'now wash your hands'
- siting is vital – you may want to choose restaurant and coffee areas as key sites, where people are more relaxed, or test out the sight-lines of people at various locations
- watch out for off-the-shelf posters: question if they talk the same language as your people
- posters can be quite a crude form of communication, able to handle only simple messages
  - they can be the internal communication equivalent of 'shouting', or there is a temptation to crowd them with far too much detail

- update all public display material regularly, otherwise it literally becomes wallpaper

Budget issues

- time spent updating notice-boards
- poster production

Timescales

- notice-boards can be updated almost immediately
- posters can be designed and printed in a few weeks

Activities

- set objectives
- updating notice-boards
- designing, printing and siting posters

Feedback

- 'open up' areas of notice-boards for free communication between people

Measurement

- awareness survey to see if key information has been spotted on posters and notice-boards
- monitor usage of notice-boards

How to find out more

- take note of other people's notice-boards when you visit – develop a feeling for what makes a good or poor notice-board display

AWARD SCHEMES

Award schemes are long-standing ways of recognizing and rewarding people for appropriate behaviours and peak performance. They require intensive communication campaigns to support them, but the benefits are high in terms of both practical results and general motivation.

Strengths

- promoting involvement
- creating role models
- acting as a fast channel for good ideas

Opportunities

- combine with e-mail or multimedia to create on-line guidance for participants: for people who do not have access to a computer, create interactive kiosks in public areas
- involve potential entrants themselves in setting the standards and criteria for awards

Weaknesses

- can be demotivating for frequent, unrecognized submitters
- benefits hard to analyse

Pitfalls

- people feel their ideas have disappeared, or feel unrewarded for their effort
  - reply to all suggestions
  - send a holding letter if there is any delay in assessment
  - if an idea is not adopted, or a reward not given, write explaining why
- inconsistent reward
  - clear criteria and guidelines, or a central overseeing committee are needed to ensure that standard judgements are made and standardized rewards given
- *'whose idea was it anyway?'*
  - different people may come up with similar ideas, resulting in dispute
  - individuals might put forward ideas generated by their team
- *'surely it's just your job to do that?'*
  - it is difficult to set guidelines on where an award submission is merely someone doing their normal job, and where it is beyond the 'call of duty' and should be recognized

Budget issues

- setting up the scheme and administering it
- communication campaign support

Timescales

- ongoing support for the system

Activities

- set objectives
- research how best to run the scheme
  - for example benchmark against leaders in the field
  - for example find out what reward employees would value

Feedback

- survey employees to establish awareness of the scheme, reasons for participating or not participating, and the target behaviours and attitudes that are looked for

Measurement

- number of ideas generated
- number of ideas implemented
- cost savings or improvements made
- proportion of target employees involved

How to find out more

The Industrial Society, Robert Hyde House, 48 Bryanston Square, London W1H 7LN 0171-262 2401

FOCUS GROUPS, SURVEYS AND RESEARCH

Successful internal communication rests on having a clear understanding of an audience and its needs. In the past, many organizations would have been content to rely on 'instinct'. Today, our more information-based society calls for conclusions based on research, including full communication audits, regular attitude and opinions surveys, and focus groups to give a face-to-face dimension to research on specific issues.

Much depends on the statistical validity of the numbers and groups you sample, and ideally you need to cross-check different sources of data for validation. A mix of quantitative and qualitative research will give you 'meat on the bones' as you try to turn the findings of your research into practical communication. You should also take into account the need to compare data, either historically or with other organizations.

See Part IV of this Handbook for further details on research methods.

The important point to realize in this context is that doing research in itself communicates to your audience.

Strengths

- thorough and independent research will give credibility to your communication plan
- data can help convince management that the internal communication function is providing the strategic information it needs when determining change programmes
- research can generate attitude benchmarks against which future successes can be measured

- creates a forum for people to express opinion and suggestions
- makes people feel they have been consulted

Opportunities

- focus groups, as opposed to print surveys, bring people together, create links and enable people to swap ideas
- spot surveys give you an instant picture of how people are reacting to a particular issue
- surveys via e-mail give instant responses, and save having to input the data
- consider giving small incentives for people to do the research
  - for example stickers, pens and so on
- turn conclusions into a board presentation, gaining more visibility for yourself and demonstrating the strategic potential of communication activities

Weaknesses

- a thorough research project can be expensive and slow
- small sample sizes may be unrepresentative

Pitfalls

- not acting on issues raised
  - if the organization refuses to respond to concerns, it should at least explain why
- not feeding back the results
  - the natural assumption will be that the results were so bad you couldn't release them
  - ideally the full report on the results should be available on request
- unclear or ambiguous survey design
  - surveys always need to be tested on the target audience to make sure they generate the sort of output you need
- incomparable data
  - poor planning in determining what to measure limits the use of data, making it hard to compare with other data sources, or identify trends over time

Budget issues

- costs of research and feedback
- costs of communicating the results

Timescales

- a thorough opinion survey will take anything from two months and more to implement

Activities

- determine research objectives
- select research groups
- design research method
- carry out research
- analyse results
- feed back results to employees
- report results to senior managers
- take action on priority areas highlighted by research
- monitor improvement made in priority areas

Feedback

- keep an open door policy on research, with a clear contact point for unsolicited opinion and views on both content and method

Measurement

- historical data, for example changes in key attitudes
- benchmark against other organizations using similar research methodology

How to find out more

- contact organizations such as The Industrial Society for examples of research carried out by other companies
- check whether any research has already been done within your organization

GRAPEVINE

Organizations tend to have a healthy respect for the grapevine. They recognize that they can't destroy it, but they also fear that it will undermine the credibility of their own communication efforts – by painting a picture that internal audiences perceive as being the 'real' story.

In an ideal world, if as an organization you're being open and honest with people, the grapevine acts positively by *reinforcing* your messages, giving them added credibility in the language people use to talk.

Grapevines thrive where there's a communication vacuum – the perfect climate for sensational speculation, organizational paranoia, gossip, rumour-mongering and conspiracy theories.

The grapevine is there for social bonding and psychological needs as much as for an actual, deliberate need to share information. In fact, most organizations have multiple networks of grapevines, some of which will be entirely separate, restricted to specific social groups, professions or locations.

The grapevine needs to be included in any communication strategy as part of the media mix. You won't be able to control it, but you may be able to *influence* it, or at least predict and prepare for its impact. You can also act to circumvent it by creating even faster communication flows. In any event, you can't afford to ignore it.

Strengths

- highest credibility of any information source
- fast
- reaches everyone and in their day-to-day language
- acts as a 'safety valve'
- people select the information relevant to them
- personalizes messages, making them relevant to the listener
- highly reactive and interactive, a social medium
- can be used to give credibility to messages conveyed by formal communication methods

Opportunities

- open-door policy
  - you can work to become a focal point on the network
- establishing and demonstrating trust
  - building yourself into the network to monitor it
- encouraging formal grapevines
  - for example unedited free-form bulletin boards on the e-mail system, anonymous helplines, space on notice-boards
- providing fora for people to 'let off steam'
  - face-to-face meetings, making sure all media have places for anonymous feedback
- gauging opinion
  - attitude surveys (see focus groups, surveys and research, p. 205 and Chapter 20, p. 283)
- internal recruitment
  - 'planting' forthcoming vacancies on the grapevine
- promoting informal behaviour change
  - dropping disciplinary hints, circumventing the need for more public and official disciplining

Weaknesses

- its weakness (or virtue, depending how you look at it) is simply that it *is* beyond management's control

- it is totally organic, and evolving continuously – by the time you've identified one grapevine route, another will have sprung up
- you have no control over who it reaches or when
- the grapevine may be stronger in particular parts of the organization, or have a differing bias
- there is a real danger of sensitive information leaking outside the organization

Pitfalls

- if you make the grapevine propagandist, you will look Machiavellian and untrustworthy
  - a new grapevine will simply bypass your own 'unreliable' one
- even if you do plant messages, there's no control over how they will be interpreted
  - there's a natural tendency to sensationalize and dramatize messages
- it can undermine the organization's formal structure and hierarchy and be used to destroy individuals

Budget issues

- time spent reviewing and feeding into grapevine

Timescales

- almost immediate

Activities

- set objectives
- sketching out informal communication flows
  - which routes do messages take?
  - are there people who are evidently key transmitters?
- testing timescales
  - how long does it take for messages to reach different parts of the grapevine?
- promoting an open style of management
  - management by walking around etc. (see walking the talk, p. 112)
  - creating feedback mechanisms
- circumventing the grapevine
  - developing ever-faster methods of communication (see e-mail, p. 173, letters, p. 171, telephone and voice mail, p. 144, walking the talk, p. 112, moving light screens, p. 155)
- setting up crisis hotlines
  - special dedicated telephone lines with recorded messages or staffed to reassure callers

Feedback

- instant feedback via grapevine

Measurement

- how quickly messages are conveyed
- how effectively messages reach all target audiences
- how accurately messages are conveyed

How to find out more

Employee Communications and Consultation ACAS Publications, 1994, 011455 852225

Effective Employee Communications, by Michael Bland and Peter Jackson, Kogan Page, 1992

'Acknowledge and use your grapevine', by David Nicoll, *Management Decision*, **32**, (6), 25–30, 1994

IPD LIS Services, 35 Camp Road, Wimbledon, London SW19 4UX 0181-263 3355

Advisory Conciliation and Arbitration Service (ACAS), 27 Wilton St, London SW1X 7AZ 0171-210 3000

NETWORKING

Like the grapevine, networking is a valuable communication route, running up, down and across the organization, across sites and across functions. In contrast to the grapevine, however, networking is not primarily about passing on gossip or 'news', but about people seeking out individuals who have the skills, experience or information to help them.

Ideally, both partners will have something to gain from the relationship, looking for advice from each other, support and coaching, or simply someone to bounce ideas off.

The organization can encourage networking as a valuable development tool, an outlet for peers to consult each other, and an opportunity to share best practice across the organization.

Strengths

- people benefit from the skills and experience of others, regardless of their position in the hierarchy
  - meritocracy vs bureaucracy
- breaks down all barriers
  - functional, departmental, geographical, hierarchical, social
- marries well with the 'flattening' process most organizations are going through and with the increased use of e-mail and other forms of computer networking

Opportunities

- promote networking in specific forms
  - for example mentoring
- encourage networking through training courses
- stress publicly that it is a valued skill
- extend networks to customers and suppliers
- more active steps can be taken to facilitate networking where co-location of key people is impossible, for example providing dedicated teleconferencing or modem facilities

Weaknesses

- researching and building a reliable network takes a long time
- maintaining and using the network is time-consuming
- the network constantly changes shape and structure
- if you are bouncing ideas off someone lower than you in the hierarchy, it may be seen as a sign of weakness
- once someone on the network gives you advice, they may be surprised or offended if you don't take it
- the risk of ideas being stolen/opposed
- both parties have to see a clear gain in prospect
  - relies on 'enlightened self-interest', what's in it for me?

Pitfalls

- conflict can arise where someone powerful in the hierarchy is undermined by someone more skilled in the informal network

Budget issues

- networking tends to develop informally but you can invest in training and support to facilitate it

Timescales

- a full-scale network will take some time to develop, but relationships can start almost immediately

Activities

- set objectives, research and plan
- individuals build their own networks
- do what you can to ensure contact details are generally available

Feedback

- direct and immediate feedback between people on the network

Measurement

- no formal measurement but can be included as a general question in a survey of communication sources or looked at within an audit process

How to find out more

- set up informal conversations with line managers about the extent to which multidirectional contact does or does not take place
- explore whether such contact would add value, in their opinion
- look at existing communication and reference materials to assess its potential for facilitating networks

PUBLIC RELATIONS, NEWS MANAGEMENT AND MARKETING

Public relations, news management and marketing campaigns are key factors in the success of organizations in the public and private sector. It is essential that internal and external communication sends consistent and coordinated messages. Just as internal audiences are exposed to the organization's external communication, so the public may also gain access to internal communication.

In an ideal situation internal and external communication strategies are woven together, and there is close cooperation between the two areas of responsibility.

Organizations tend not to be proactive in news management and consequently the coverage tends to be a firefighting reaction to bad news. Attempts to get press coverage are still largely limited to press releases on new products or performance achievements. But *people* make a good story too, and in theory internal communication people are in the right position to identify them. News management also means that internal audiences should hear any news ahead of the media. All too often, the first internal audiences hear about job losses and site closures is on the news.

Strengths

- subliminal and cumulative effect of marketing messages
- external news is probably the most credible source of information
- reaches people through the media sources they choose

Opportunities

● set objectives

- involve everyone in public relations activities and stories, giving them credit for their work, for example invite them to suggest public relations ideas
- newsgatherers may want to put a human interest factor into stories, that is employees
- employees themselves do newsworthy things
  - expand personnel database to include likely candidates and their newsworthy activities
- give internal audiences on-line access to a database outlining the organization's position on key issues, and facts and figures about the organization's values, aims and performance
  - a cut down version could be used for induction purposes

Weaknesses

- public relations and marketing may be treated with some scepticism by some internal audiences
- the organization can trigger an initial interest from the news media but thereafter it's out of its control

Pitfalls

- *'do they mean us?'*
  - the image given by the news coverage may seem biased to an internal audience, creating resentment or cynicism
- *'they want to hear the real story'*
  - there may be unwelcome follow-up to any story which ignores the 'inside' view
  - the media is only too happy for whistleblowers to report the misdemeanours of their organizations

Budget issues

- time spent planning and coordinating internal and external communication

Timescales

- the demand for topicality determines a fast turnround
  - the PR department may need access to 'newsworthy' employees very quickly to meet the needs of the media

Activities

- set objectives

- coordinating with, and supporting the PR department or suppliers to offer newsworthy material
- making sure that internal and external messages are consistent
- coordinating with marketing department to spread awareness of forth-coming marketing campaigns

Feedback

- evaluate as advertising

Measurement

- coverage of key messages in external media
- success of marketing campaign
- extent and quality of news coverage

How to find out more

Manage the Message: how to write communications that get the results you want by Bryan Thresher and Jim Biggin, Century Business, 1993
How to Understand and Manage Public Relations by D. White, Century Business, 1991
'Whose hand on the heartbeat?' by Jon White, *Human Resources*, Winter 1991/2

Chartered Institute of Marketing, Moor Hall, Cookham, Maidenhead, Berks SL6 9QH 01628 524922
Institute of Public Relations, The Old Trading House, 15 Northburgh Street, London EC1V 0PR 0171-253 5151

ADVERTISING

Advertising – corporate, product and recruitment – strengthens the image internal audiences have of the organization. But this works both ways. Employees are ambassadors for their organizations – their behaviours have the potential to give the advertising credibility.

Strengths

- aligns external and internal views of organization
- high external profile/visibility
  - can add credibility and build pride
  - if positioned correctly, it is good news for employees, as it shows confidence and commitment on the part of the organization
- reaching internal audiences via the external media, usually when not at work
- reinforces internal messages

- helps to dramatize, personalize and demonstrate the organization's values

Opportunities

- involving employees in the advert's production
  - for example real employees on screen or working to define the original concept
- employees and other relevant internal audiences should know in advance about advertising
  - this gives an additional feeling of being 'in' on something
  - prepares them to receive comments and questions from others

Weaknesses

- the advertising content may be treated with some scepticism
- it should not be used as a substitute for communicating direct

Pitfalls

- the reality gulf
  - internal audiences will become cynical if the picture painted in adverts is too idealized
- 'glitz'
  - there may be resentment at an obviously high advertising spend, especially at times of cost-cutting
- *'that's news to me'*
  - people feel resentful and out of touch when the first they know about a new product, service or claim is when they're told about it in an advert
- *'what are we promising now?'*
  - very real worry that customers' expectations are being raised to un-realistic levels

Budget issues

- advertising is effectively free for internal communication purposes, though making people aware of forthcoming campaigns is an essential task

Timescales

- short timescales to coordinate advertising and internal communication campaigns

Activities

- set objectives
- making sure that internal and external messages are consistent

Feedback

- encourage internal audiences to comment on advertising

Measurement

- perception of company, organization, product or service by internal audiences before and after campaign

How to find out more

Advertising Excellence by C. Bovee, McGraw-Hill, 1994

Association of Graduate Recruiters, Sheraton House, Castle Park, Cambridge CB3 0AX 01223 356720
Institute of Practitioners in Advertising (IPA), 44 Belgrave Square, London SWX 8QS 0171-235 7020

Part IV

DEVELOPING GOOD COMMUNICATORS

15 Understanding how communication works

Richard Varey, *director of the BNFL Corporate Communications Unit at the University of Salford*

This chapter is intended to give IC managers a better understanding of what happens when people attempt to communicate with each other, which in turn should help them support organizations and people in trying to improve communication competency. It discusses aspects of communication between people at a subconscious level as well as at the level of conscious attitude and behaviour.

Few organizations would claim they have 'the communication problem' beaten. We tell ourselves that 'better communication' and 'more communication' would solve many of our organizational problems and improve our business results considerably. Yet we can't do it!

Our best efforts to deal with the 'simple' problem of communication often leave us frustrated and confused. Our goodwill somehow just isn't enough to ensure mutual understanding and agreement or to achieve the results we expect and desire.

Much of the difficulty stems from our tendency to take communication for granted. After all, communication is such a basic human activity, why should it require any more attention in our busy lives than, say, breathing or sleeping? We just do it, automatically.

The reality is that very many attempts to communicate – particularly in a work context – go badly awry. They confuse where they are intended to make clear; they turn people off rather than motivate; or they may miss their mark entirely.

In fact, to be effective communicators we need to be fully aware and mindful of what is involved so that we take up an appropriate communication attitude. We need to develop certain skills – we even need to become amateur social psychologists. And if we want in any way to 'manage' communication in work relationships, we need to pay more attention to the nature of communication itself.

COMMUNICATION AND INFORMATION

Understanding the difference between *communication* and *information* is the central factor.

Communication encompasses all the processes by which information – facts, intentions, feelings, attitudes, and ideas – is transmitted and received between people. Good communication involves a learning process since a change in behaviour results. This suggests that true communication can take place only if there is an exchange of information with feedback through interaction, i.e. a dialogue. Therefore, it is both interactional and transactional.

The most widely accepted model of communication shows a message transmitted from a source and received at a destination. At any point between the source and the destination the signal can be lost, distorted or interfered with, just as with a radio or TV signal.

One definition of communication is 'the capacity of an individual (or group) to pass on feelings and ideas to another individual (or group)'. This is in keeping with the original meaning of the term 'communicate' which comes from the Latin *communicare* which literally means 'to share'. Thus communication is the sharing of meaning. We implicitly recognize this when we speak of giving information *to*, while communicating *with*, others. Yet we often don't behave this way by taking account of others in our communication attempts.

> We are keenly aware that we said what we did because of what she said. But it may not occur to us that she said what she did because of what we said – just before, yesterday, or last year.
>
> (Tannen)

The point is, rather than the *message sender* transferring some fixed meaning of their message to a receiver, the meaning is ascribed by the *receiver*.

Communication, then, is not simply a tool; all relationships require communication and all communication requires the existence of a relationship. It is a two-way process in that the receiver acts on information, attitudes, and ideas by contributing his or her own, and by changing or rejecting what they receive. Ideas are shared, not moved. In contrast, the use of one-way 'communication' assumes passivity and reactivity on the part of the receiver.

RELATING INFORMATION TO ACTION

It is also essential to distinguish between *knowledge* and *information*. Communication does not simply concern the dissemination of information as hard 'facts'; it is fundamentally a process of gathering information about our social world to enhance knowledge and understanding and to aid thinking and decision-making.

Traditionally, the emphasis has been on the creation and transmission of effective messages, that is on communication content. More recent thinking has turned the spotlight on behaviour as part of the communication process. Communication includes the total behaviour of the two or more people engaged in the process of interaction.

The meaning of a communication is the response you get.

(Anon.)

The meaning of any message is determined by who is interpreting the message at the time. The meaning is not contained in the message but exists only as an interpretation in the mind of the person who is decoding the message, that is in the response to the message. Furthermore, communication is not simply a process of information transmission but also one of selection of content. Both sender and recipient make choices. The intended meaning put into a message by the sender, and that taken out by the recipient, are both 'correct'.

If communication is to take place between people there must be enough similarities in their interpretations for them to share a common meaning. (Reporters in war-torn former Yugoslavia are well informed, but how many of us share their experience and are therefore capable of wholly understanding their messages?)

Simplistic models of communication may include *feedback* in recognition of the interplay between communicators. This fails to deal with the complexity of social interaction and the essential nature of communication as a goal-centred activity.

Just as important is *feedforward* which is also present in real communication as we attempt to assess a situation and predict the other person's behaviour at some future time, for example 'What's the best way to tell the boss I'm not going to make target this month?'

Feedforward is both proactive and continuous, since it takes place during the interaction. We call it 'thinking on our feet'.

COMMUNICATION AND ROLE-PLAYING

Our *communication style* is strongly influenced by the *roles* we assume or are assigned by others, particularly family and occupational roles.

A role is a repertoire of behaviour patterns that are used in a specific con-text, while all other irrelevant behaviour is deliberately suppressed. For instance when asked 'who are you?' or 'what are you?' we often give the name of our role as we see it, for example 'daughter' or 'manager'.

Let's take the manager's role.

We all have a mental model of what being a manager entails. The traditional picture is of someone forecasting, planning, organizing, commanding, staffing, directing, coordinating, reporting, budgeting and controlling. It has also been widely associated with someone who appears tough, objective, striving, achieving, unsentimental and emotionally inexpressive.

This picture is in line with the traditional male role, which does not readily acknowledge or disclose the real self, to himself or to others. It echoes the fact that in the past, men have generally been trained to assume an *instrumental role*, to relate more on an I–It basis (rather than an I–You basis) than do women, and to believe that they can and should ignore their own feelings and avoid the 'distraction' of overly intimate personal knowledge of the others' feelings and needs.

Such impersonal, role-to-role relationships concentrate on content rather than relational detail, and so emphasize objectives, outcomes and performance measures. Social aspects of the relationship are seen as irrelevant and unproductive, and are down-played. Hence the concentration on effective message delivery rather than personal interaction and building relationships.

The management theorist Douglas McGregor described these authoritarian characteristics as 'Theory X'. Subscribers to Theory X believe that workers have to be told what to do and how to do it. The alternative approach is represented by 'Theory Y' in which the manager shares problems and their solution through delegation.

In Theory Y, managers are associated with:

- dependency on the activities of others
- managing people – a social role
- motivating people to identify the right things to do
- gaining their cooperation to do them well and then better
- learning to do new things, with and through other people
- taking responsibility for the quality of others' work.

So, at one extreme – Theory X – the manager decides and tells, while at the other, the manager delegates decisions to subordinates, within limits he or she defines.

There are any number of other roles that we may adopt, and they explain why it is so difficult to communicate.

According to Eric Berne, when a person takes up the **adult** role, reasoned discussion, logical argument, and fact-finding are employed before coming to a decision. Feelings are a response to the present moment, rather than allowing past experiences to determine present behaviour.

The **parent** role may be supportive and nurturing or it may be critical, disapproving, teaching or preaching. Managers who treat their staff as if they are naughty children shouldn't be surprised if they adopt a **child** role and behave in a childish manner.

Of the two broad approaches referred to, the task-oriented command and control style of management is becoming increasingly unacceptable (Figure 15.1). People's expectations about their social and work world are changing.

A growing portion of the available workforce is reconsidering its expectations of work and the appropriateness of supervision as a function of

People-oriented	Task-oriented
Employee-centred	Production-centred
Democratic, autonomous	Autocratic, authoritarian
Concern for people	Concern for production
Initiating	Laissez-faire
Supportive, protective	Belittling, exposing
Consults, joins	Tells, sells

Figure 15.1   People and task orientation

management. Quality of work life is becoming more important than career progression or remuneration. Managers are required to provide a work environment and conditions that enable subordinates to use as much of their relevant knowledge as possible and to do better tomorrow (Figure 15.2).

From	To
Producer	Server
Cost-watcher	Measurer of performance
Profit hound	Outcome securer
Strategy-taker	Strategy-maker
Legislator	Value-adder
Administrator	Leader
Intervenor	Role model
Expert	Learner
Instructor	Informer
Controller	Coach of better performance
Forcer	Empowerer: provider of authority and accountability
Inspector	Enabler: provider of information and training
The boss	Team player
Reactor	Originator
Policer	Coach
Middle-man	Service leader
Problem-finder	Opportunist

Figure 15.2   The new manager role

Even the notion of a distinction between manager and managed may disappear. A recent prediction by a prominent UK policy analysis unit suggests that by the year 2000, around one in five workers will be 'a manager', working in self-managed teams in which people come together on the basis of their expertise to complete a project, and then move on to another. In such a scenario it is clear that the manager's role must shift fundamentally, particularly in relation to how information is received and worked on by individuals in the team (Figure 15.3).

The Japanese would claim they have for some time had a head start on western cultures in this respect.

223

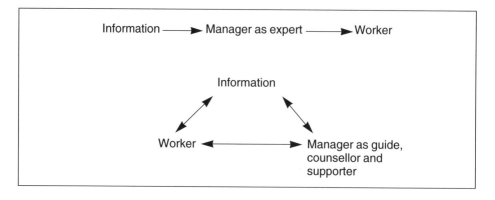

Figure 15.3   Contrast between the manager as 'expert' and 'guide'

For you the essence of management is getting the ideas out of the heads of bosses and into the heads of labour.... For us, the core of management is the art of mobilising and putting together the intellectual resources of all employees in the service of the firm.

(Konosuke Matsushita 1979)

Increasingly managers are having to change their role, or have it changed for them by social and competitive forces.

Push and pull

Two forms of language are used by managers. Managers use 'push' language to tell people (what is, what is not, what to do). Managers do this because they believe that their competence as a manager is about knowing all the answers. They see their 'communication' problem as that of getting the 'answers' out of their own head and into those of their subordinates. 'Pull' language, on the other hand, is used by leaders to question, and to learn. Many managers believe, however, that this reveals a weakness since curiosity is equated with ignorance.

Consider the contrast between *telling* and *participating*, as illustrated in Figure 15.4. Try listening for the language used by your colleagues as a means of identifying their assumed communication role: do they initiate, elicit, check or direct?

COMMUNICATION AND PERCEPTION

Take any group of people and you will find differences in attitudes, perceptions, experiences, morality, philosophical orientations, emotions and general psychological dispositions or personality. We also attach different, very personal, feelings and expectations to words when we use language to communicate.

'Push' language	**'Pull' language**
Propose	Seek information
Give information	Test/check
Shut out	Build
Inform/instruct	Elicit ideas
Criticize	Suggest
Assess	Reaction
Suggest	Feelings
Evaluate	Innovating
Disagree	Support/direct
Defend/attack	Bring in
Persuade	Encourage
Manipulate	Influence
Win/lose	Win/win
Order	Interest
Penalize	Reward
Tell	Share

Figure 15.4   Contrast between 'push' and 'pull' language

Communication, at the very best, involves a compromise of meaning between individuals.

(Burgoon et al., 1994)

Our attitudes can and do change as we encounter new people, new ideas and new experiences, but we may not even be aware of them much of the time. They are formed by a whole range of factors: gender, race, age, education, social and economic status, interests, experience, social relationships, beliefs, values, personality and intelligence. Each is capable of having a profound impact on how people see themselves and each other, on how they interpret information and how they see their role as a communicator in different situations.

Each is therefore also a potential source of similarity and difference between people who set out to communicate with each other.

In general, the degree of similarity people perceive between themselves and others tends to determine who will communicate with whom and the likelihood of successful communication. Complete similarity might suggest there would be little to talk about, but people who are similar do tend to share common interests that provide topics for communication, whereas those who are extremely dissimilar may lack the common experiences or vocabulary necessary for effective communication.

People often make the wrong assumption to start with. The evidence suggests that most of us *assume* similarity until evidence shows us otherwise – and sometimes not even then. But when it comes to people we like, we often overestimate the degree of similarity between us and them, and believe that others we perceive as being similar to ourselves are attracted to us. Conversely, when in conflict, we may overestimate the differences between us and others.

225

Such misperceptions provide fertile ground for miscommunication. Effective communication is possible only when there is enough common ground for understanding, balanced by enough difference to produce dynamic interaction. Even then of course, what is relevant to one person may be irrelevant to another!

COMMUNICATION, PERCEPTION AND THINKING

The process of communication involves both *perception* and *thinking*. Perception is the collection of information from the outside world by our senses (sight, hearing, touch, smell, taste). Thinking is what we do to convert information into action: it is the processing of that information by the brain, storage of the information in memory and the production of some form of physical or mental response. Seeing this as a process, with any number of influences bearing down on it, should help you to appreciate that the way in which you perceive and think may be different from that of others and will influence your ability to communicate with them (Figure 15.5).

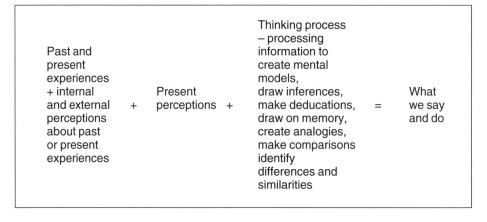

Figure 15.5   Perception, thinking and behaviour as a process

The role of perception

What we perceive as 'reality' may not be reality for others. We cannot safely assume that we are all alike in what we 'see'.

Perceptions differ because:

- our senses have a limited capacity for receiving information
- this capacity differs between people
- we select or filter information
- we organize and interpret information according to our own past experiences or 'frame of reference' and the situation or environment in which they occur

- we tend to generalize from our past experiences
- we see patterns in information
- our perceptions are affected by our emotions, attitudes, feelings and aspirations.

We feel insecure and are prone to become defensive when other people seem unable to acknowledge our point of view or interpretation of a situation. An empathetic relationship is required if we are to fully understand the other person's point of view.

The role of memory

Research has shown that our information retention capacity is very limited. Most of us will forget 40–50 per cent of new information within 24 hours, and up to 80 per cent after seven days, unless we take steps to shift it from short-term memory to long-term memory.

The general view is that we can sustain retention of seven items in short-term memory, to allow thinking, but this is limited to three if the information is presented visually or if meaning is sought. Rest periods after about 20 minutes have been shown to have a significant effect in improving concentration. This is the so-called attention span.

The role of listening

Research suggests that we typically spend about 40 per cent of our waking hours in listening; 35 per cent talking; 16 per cent reading and 9 per cent writing.

In practice, however, most of us are poor listeners and this reduces our effectiveness as communicators, since listening is a primary requirement of communication.

Communication is a two-way process; it requires at least one talker and at least one listener. There is a need to listen to understand the other's views, and a need to talk effectively so that others will listen. There is, therefore, an equal responsibility for ensuring effective communication.

Listening is difficult and takes training. Managers need to make a conscious effort to improve their listening ability by training themselves – and those for and to whom they are responsible for communication – in specific listening skills such as anticipation and recognition of barriers.

The role of 'selection'

It is often surprising to hear a colleague describing the meeting you have both just attended. Two individuals witnessing the same event may give widely different accounts of it. This may be partly because they paid attention to different parts of the event, or partly because there was some *subliminal*   227 *perception*. Another explanation may be that we pay attention to some things and not to others.

Many people are unaware that communication is a highly selective process and that selectivity greatly affects their communication.

Clearly, we cannot:

- attend to a message to which we are not exposed
- perceive and interpret a message to which we have not attended
- retain a message that we have not perceived.

Yet, we tend selectively to expose ourselves to messages that reinforce our existing attitudes. Ideas and information that reaffirm our pre-existing ideas and attitudes bolster our image of ourselves and what we 'know'. Moreover, we remember more accurately messages that are favourable to our self-image than messages that are unfavourable.

Our expectations of information affect how we perceive it – praise from a friend is always better received than from someone we think dislikes us. What we have been told about others also affects our perceptions.

The role of thinking

If we don't all perceive the world in the same way, neither do we all have the same capacity for or style of processing information.

Thinking is crucial to converting information into action, but thinking in a logical and analytical way, which most of us aspire to be able to do, is not the only or indeed the predominant mode of human response: some people may be inventive thinkers, involved thinkers, intellectual thinkers and so on.

And because we all have different ways of thinking, our communication efforts are often misrepresented, adding to situations where other people sometimes seem not to be on our wavelength.

Whatever our preferred mode of thinking, we all share some potential barriers to clear thinking. Figure 15.6 lists some common examples.

UNDERSTANDING AND ALIGNING

People need to know and want to know different things. In a work context, information is often broken down into three categories:

- *need to know* – information needed to do work properly
- *should know* – information that is desirable but not essential
- *could know* – everything else.

This model emphasizes information rather than interaction. But even in the apparently simple act of passing over information, we encounter a number of barriers.

General tendency	Explanation
Generalization	Trying to reach a globally-applicable conclusion based on one or two experiences. This distorts our mental maps and prevents us from making distinctions.
Deletion	Overlooking, tuning out, or omitting information in arriving at a decision or opinion.
Stereotyping	Treating others as though they were a single group sharing identical characteristics.
Projection	Assuming that someone shares the same characteristics as ourselves.
Prejudice	Predicting attitudes and behaviour.
Distortion	Allowing prejudice to twist our perceptions.
Discounting	Evaluating new information as irrelevant, especially when it is contrary to our prevailing view.
Conformity	Allowing group customs or standards to dictate our behaviour.
Compliance	Going along with a view we don't subscribe to in order to win a reward or avoid punishment.
Autistic hostility	Becoming hostile when we do not understand the other person's reasoning, and making no attempt to do so.
Mirror-image	Seeing ourselves as well-intentioned and right thinking, and our 'enemies' as mistaken and malicious.
Halo effect	Extending someone's credibility beyond the original subject or situation in which their credibility was earned.

Figure 15.6   Barriers to clear thinking

Language based on words – both spoken and written – is a limited device for producing mutual understanding. Managers in particular need to develop the skill of getting underneath the skin of the people they work with.

First, they need to know how they themselves perceive information most easily, and how they prefer to organize and process the information (how they think). They should then take steps to determine the way other people do this.

This also has significant implications for educators and trainers, since information and delivery systems must be designed to meet the needs of the individuals and groups who need and want to know.

Words mean different things to different people in different contexts. It is vital to avoid jargon if you want to communicate outside a given circle.

We also differ in the way we talk to each other. Our personal *conversational style* has a strong influence on our communication effectiveness. The individual way in which we pace and phrase our conversation leads people to draw conclusions about our personality, abilities, intentions and motivations (e.g. 'he sounded a bit dodgy').

We create communication problems for ourselves and others by taking our own conversational style as the norm. To be good communicators managers need to change or drop those conversational devices that may be inappropriate to some people – rather than drawing negative conclusions about people from the way in which they respond to what has been said. For example being blunt may win respect in a macho culture but may offend in other cultures, and may result in a negative response, even though no offence was ever intended.

Another example of the dangers of placing emphasis on information to the detriment of interaction is the careful use of 'please' and 'thank you' in Britain, and its much less frequent use in countries like America or Spain. This is sometimes thought rude where no rudeness was intended, only directness.

As social communicators, managers need to understand, to be understood and to know whether they have been understood. We often assume that people do not understand us, when, in fact, they disagree with us. Equally, we sometimes too readily accept assurances that people are in agreement with us, when a lack of understanding remains the problem.

Our behaviour is often a reaction to the apparent motives we attribute to others. Sometimes we may be right in those assumptions, but we could be wrong. We can also be mistaken in expecting other people to be cooperative, for example, simply because we ourselves are cooperative by nature.

One final point on behaviour: *our communication behaviour is often influenced strongly by our need to justify our actions.*

OVERCOMING COMMUNICATION PROBLEMS

How can anyone deal with the complexities of all the situations just described? Calls for 'more communication' and 'better communication' or repairs to 'communication breakdown' do not tell us much about what to do to improve our communication competence and effectiveness.

Communication competence requires:

- the motivation to communicate and to engage in appropriate communication behaviour
- emphasis on achieving outcomes
- sensitivity to the expectation of the context
- flexibility to adapt to the environment
- skills in using communication methods and techniques
- knowledge of communication and how to communicate.

Anyone can start to acquire such competence by thinking of communication as a cooperative learning process.

Discussion is clearly important. Facts are rarely able to tell their own story without comments to bring out the meaning. Discussion builds understanding, by supplementing each participant's information with the information possessed by other group members. It stimulates different perspectives, allows conjectures and provides opportunities for criticism and refutation. This speaks in favour of team briefings, for example, and cautions on the sole use of e-mail as a means of communicating.

When BP employees were asked what makes a good communicator, two-thirds said the person communicating *must want to do it*. In other words, that person must have a positive attitude to open interaction and the motivation to behave this way. Learned skills and inherited ability were seen as much less able to explain good communication behaviour.

A cooperative climate makes for good communication. In a competitive climate each person strives for his or her own outcomes, often at the expense of others. When more people seek goals than can achieve them, competition is a very common behaviour pattern. Is your organization a place of scarcity of resources or a feast of plenty?

Mirroring is helpful. This is where we match certain behaviours of the other person, such as voice tone and tempo, breathing, movements and body postures. Some of us do this naturally (strike up a rapport), but it can also be practised.

Our beliefs about another person are usually based on insufficient evidence, therefore they are often false. We are poor at predicting and understanding why he or she does what he or she does. Unfortunately, the way we present ourselves is often based on erroneous notions of the other's abilities, interests and knowledge, and that means we are unlikely to communicate.

Psychometric testing can help. Such tests are now being used to identify individual differences in thinking, learning and interpersonal styles, including management styles, so that communication can be enhanced through tailoring and segmentation to meet varying needs and expectations. The Myers-Briggs Type Indicator is one of the better known tests.

Self-disclosure also helps. It alters perceptions, reveals similarities and differences in our thoughts, feelings and hopes, and reveals the needs of others.

Managers should make themselves known to other people – show something of the personal or human side to their nature so that people can see where they are coming from. Research has shown that those of us who disclose the most are much better at establishing close communicative relationships with other people. Women seem to disclose more personal data than do men.

Such open communication is admittedly risky, and dreaded by some, since it lets others know how the speaker has experienced life. Yet communication, when authentic, can enrich each other's experience, permitting agreement, disagreement, comparison and contrast. The disclosed experience of another person lets us see, feel, imagine and hope for things we could never even have imagined before exposure to the discloser's revelations.

Keeping an **open mind** is also good advice if we are to free ourselves from outdated and inappropriate ideas that can hamper communication effectiveness. It helps to be context-sensitive, aware of ourselves and always receptive to new information.

The sign of good communication can be found in our ability to answer the *231* question: 'Does my encounter with another person enlarge me, diminish me, or does it not affect me?'

Communication tends to be a satisfying and effective process when we:

- know what we want to achieve through communicating
- have developed our ability to capture as much information as we can so that we can respond flexibly, matching our behaviour to the response we want
- emphasize the process, not simply the content or vehicle
- dovetail what we want with what the other person(s) want(s)
- understand the way in which others might think, and shape our messages appropriately, taking care to check that real understanding has been reached
- take account of the fact that educational levels differ greatly and affect what people are able to comprehend
- establish a rapport based on mutual trust in our competence and in our recognition of the needs of the people with whom we wish to communicate.

Of course, credibility as a communicator can be conferred only by the other party, and two or more people may respond quite differently to the same communicator.

People are likely to form a judgement of a communicator based on their apparent knowledge of the subject under discussion. But credibility is also influenced by perceptions of character, composure, sociability and extroversion.

Open communication can also make for better communication since it provides greater scope for people to become involved in the process. Open communication requires that all stakeholders to a choice between alternative courses of action are encouraged to state their needs and wants before authority to decide is exercised. Subjective opinion and disagreement are allowed as part of the learning and decision-making process.

Often, however, misunderstanding does not arise through 'poor communication'. The real experience of working in any organization is that it comprises a variety of interest groups who wish to pursue their own objectives. Good communication then is not about reconciling interest, but rather about exposing divergent interest and conflict in an open forum. This should help improve understanding and provide agreement on some issues.

Communication can also be improved if we remain aware that it is more than the efficient and effective transmission of information: it is also a 'social' activity, and this social role is equally important at work.

Some time ago I developed the acronym ACUMEN to describe how managers could improve working relationships with their work groups.

ACUMEN = Appreciation + Communication + Understanding + Motivation + Encouragement + Negotiation

These are all aspects of communication and it seems to me now that we need to shift our thinking on communication. It is not simply a facilitating mechanism for managers: in so many ways, it is what management is.

EXPLODING SOME COMMUNICATION MYTHS

- *Problems are all due to 'communication breakdown'.*
  Not true. People are different and this often causes problems in relationships, but this is not necessarily a communication problem. The failure to influence someone certainly need not always be a communication problem .
- *More communication will always solve problems.*
  Not true. People who dislike each other may move further apart by continuing to communicate.
- *Communication is free.*
  Not true. Communication is not without its costs, and in some situations may not be worth the effort.
- *No communication effort is no communication.*
  Not true. There is always communication, intended or otherwise.
- *Communication is 'good' or 'bad' in itself.*
  Not true. It is the way we attempt it and our intentions that matter.
- *Communication is simply about producing more effective messages.*
  Not true. Competent communicators must listen, understand and only then, deliver.

HOW TO FIND OUT MORE

Games People Play: the psychology of human relationships by Eric Berne, Penguin Books, 1964

Human Communication, 3rd edition, by M. Burgoon, F.G. Hunsaker and E.J. Dawson, Sage Publications, 1994

The Mind Map Book by T. Buzan with B. Buzan, BBC Books, 1993

Communicating for Managerial Effectiveness by P.G. Clampitt, Sage Publications, 1991

Quantum Learning: unleash the genius within you by B. DePorte and M. Hernacki, Piatkus Publishers, 1992

If You Take My Meaning: theory into practice in human communications, 2nd edition, by R. Ellis and A. McClintock, Edward Arnold, 1994

Communication in Organizations, 2nd edition, by E.R. Emmet, West Publishing Co, 1993

Corporate Communications Management: the renaissance communicator in information-age organisations by D. Gayeski, Focal Press, 1993

How to Talk So People Listen by S. Hamlin, Harper & Row, 1988

I'm OK – You're OK by T.A. Harris, Pan Books, 1973

The Transparent Self by S. Jourard, Van Nonstrand Reinhold, 1971

Experimental Learning: experience as the source of learning and development by D.A. Kolb, Prentice-Hall, 1984

Influencing with Integrity: management skills for communication & negotiation by G.Z. Laborde, Syntony Publishing, Palo Alto, 1987

Mindfulness: choice and control in everyday life by E.J. Langer, HarperCollins, 1989

The Personality Test by P. Lauster, Pan Books, 1976

Mind Skills: giving your child a brighter future by D. Lewis, Souvenir Press, 1987

Communication Models: for the study of mass communication, 2nd edition, by D. McQuail and S. Windahl, Longman, 1993

Common Ground: a course in communication by R.K. Sadler and K. Tucker, Macmillan Company of Australia, 1981

Understanding Misunderstandings: exploring interpersonal communication by R. Shuter, Harper & Row, 1979

Interpersonal Communication Competence by B.H. Spitzberg and W.R. Cupach, Sage Publications, 1984

That's Not What I Meant!: how conversational style makes or breaks your relations with others by D. Tannen, Virago Press, 1986

'Managing personal qualities: a service quality management and social imperative' by Richard J. Varey, unpublished working paper, 1993

Corporate Communication and Business Performance by Richard J. Varey, Stanley Thornes, 1995

Managing for Peak Performance: a guide to the power (and pitfalls) of personal style by A. Weiss, Ballinger Publishing Co., 1989

16 What are communication skills?

Tony Newbold, *specialist business writer,* and
Eileen Scholes, *director, The ITEM Group*

This chapter begins with a quick look at why it's worthwhile trying to develop communication skills and whether it's possible to put them in neatly-defined categories. The bulk of the chapter, however, gives you the 'basics' on more than 30 commonly talked-about skill areas related to communication at work. For rapid reference, it lists skills in alphabetical order.

According to CBI director-general Adair Turner, 'the skills of a country's people are the only long-term foundation for economic success'. Organizations whose employees become aware of the power of good communication and learn to communicate well can expect to profit substantially by improved efficiencies, effectiveness and innovation, and through raised morale and commitment.

The benefits to individuals are also clear. Of all the skills learned at work, those connected with communication are among the most transferable to home and private lives.

Aren't most people as good as they're going to get?

Most of us can run. But anyone who has to run as part of their job – say a professional footballer – soon finds themselves in the hands of a coach, learning to run all over again, acquiring and honing new techniques, maybe even dismantling 'naturally-learned' habits and style. In today's sophisticated work environments, people are having to take a similarly professional approach to improving their communication skills, which look certain to be in greater and greater demand.

What exactly are we talking about?

People throw around the term 'communication skills' as if we are all sure what it means. Can anybody put together a definitive list?

The answer, at the present time, would seem to be no.

It is plainly not useful to restrict the definition to something as basic as *using language*, for example, whether writing, reading or speaking. Already, the switch from information paucity to overload means learning new ways of 'reading', more akin perhaps to sifting (surfing, even) and editing. What is acceptable or effective in written communication is also changing: putting one's point across successfully on e-mail is a far cry from composing letters or reports, or even old-style memos. And teleconferencing, while becoming ever more akin to real meetings as technology improves, may well always call for different sets of body language or interjection skills, for example.

Surely the list of communication skills should not stop either at what trainers call 'interpersonal skills', starting with something like active listening, for example, checking understanding or summarizing, and going all the way up to assertiveness. It makes sense to recognize newer composites of communication skills – those required, for example, in modern work situations like appraisals, presentations, seminars, brainstorming sessions and focus groups.

You can easily go still further. Thanks to the development of the personal computer, keyboarding – once a skill only secretaries and journalists learned – has become more universal. A case could similarly be made for organizations soon needing to spread capability in formerly 'specialist' communication skills, for example in generating slides or newsletters, even Internet home pages.

Can you classify them?

With such a plethora of options, it is natural to attempt some form of classification or at least to identify priorities. Not surprisingly, there appears to be no genuine consensus about how to do this either, at least for the moment. (Indeed, who is to say, as styles and media develop, there ever will be?)

Dr Jon White, for example, in Chapter 1 of this Handbook, divides communication skills into sense-making, listening, presentation, media handling, self-awareness and empathy. At a more fundamental level, Richard Varey in Chapter 15, though he offers no actual breakdown, clearly sees developing awareness of one's own prejudices, for example, as well as openness, alignment, and role-playing as key skill areas.

A more literal classification than either might be:

- generic, applied in all aspects of life and across all media, e.g. asking questions
- allied to particular media, e.g. scriptwriting
- driven by a particular purpose, e.g. taking part in appraisals
- behaviourial, e.g. using body language.

Then there is 'communication style'. Changes in motivational patterns at work are said to be calling for new communication styles from managers and managed alike – out with 'top down' and 'command', for example, in with 'upward', 'teamworking' and 'consultative'. Organizational psychologists, in particular, are constantly finding new ways to analyse and describe people's behaviour by 'communication style' – leaving the way open for assessment and training to strengthen 'weaker' areas. The ITEM Group has itself recently commissioned research aimed at defining the all-round communication competence needed by the '360° communicating manager'.

So what did we decide?

We opted out and chose the easy way – alphabetical. If you attempt to read through from A–Z, you are likely to find yourself confused. Conversely, it should be easy to access the information as occasion demands, which is more the scenario we have envisaged.

We have also included a mixture of all kinds of skills, at a variety of levels, that seem to be important right now.

Clearly, both the order and the selection of skills could be determined differently, and probably will be in any future edition of the Handbook. Constructive suggestions from any quarter are welcome.

However, we have at least tried to develop a useful consistency of approach to content. Looking at each skill area, we asked:

- what is its nature and significance?
- how might you know if it is not being practised effectively?
- briefly what form might development take?
- where can you go next for information?

For more detail on developing communication strategies and plans involving skill training, see Part II of this Handbook. For more about specific media and how to manage them, see Part III. For consultancies and training relating to the subjects discussed, consult the *Human Resource Management Yearbook*. This is published by AP Information Services, 33 Ashbourne Avenue, London NW11 0DU 0181 458 1607.

The communication skills discussed are listed below.

Answering questions
Appearance
Appraisal
Asking questions
Assertiveness
Body language
Brainstorming
Briefing
Communicating through manuals and guides

Counselling
Delegating
Editing
Facilitating
Getting feedback
Giving feedback
Keeping it simple
Leading discussions
Letter, fax, memo and e-mail writing
Listening
Media management
Meetings
Negotiating
Networking
Neuro Linguistic Programming (NLP)
Presentation
Reading
Report writing
Speaking
Speech and scriptwriting
Summarizing
Telephoning
Transactional analysis

Answering questions

Skill training is plentiful and readily available in this area: the challenge is to expand its use from the application for which it has mostly been developed – helping those who handle external audiences, for example the media.

The point about questions is that, whatever the context, they always provide a powerful platform for influencing people – as long as they are competently handled. For a start, the person (whether 'for' or 'against' you) has opened up the opportunity for a reply. Moreover, when people ask questions, they reveal their areas of concern, and their attitudes.

On the down side, just as happens in external media handling, an obviously inadequate or evasive response produces damaging effects – like undermining credibility and boosting cynicism. TV journalist Jeremy Paxman says that what drives him when he is interviewing a politician is the thought: 'Why is this lying bastard lying to me?' Many internal audiences are no less aggressive in their thoughts – if not necessarily in open forum.

To make the case for better training, focus minds by citing past 'gaffes' in internal communication and their expensive consequences. Promote the view that answering questions is a highly productive skill, but one that takes knowledge and practice to acquire.

Training helps people learn how to avoid:

- giving 'off the cuff' answers
- bluffing 'rather than lose face'
- jargonized 'management speak' (something to hide?)...

... and instead how to:

- anticipate which issues are important enough to drive someone to ask a question
- prepare an informed and consistent line of answer
- explore any certain ground, and then promise to find out any further information needed.

How to Get Your Point Across in 30 Seconds or Less, by M. O'Frank, Transworld, 1993
How to Take on the Media by D. Wragg, Kogan Page, 1993
Face the Press: managing the media interview by John Lidstone, Industrial Society Press, 1995
What's the answer? (video) Fenman Training 01353 665533

Appearance

Impressions made in the first few minutes are known to 'stick'. All kinds of assumptions are made about status, professionalism, state of mind – and from this, the credibility of individuals and the organizations they represent – all based on no more than an individual's clothing and accoutrements, combined with their hair and physical demeanour, possibly also their eating habits and personal hygiene.

Added to this, much stereotypical British 'class grading' of people by appearance continues today in work situations – despite widespread tendencies to equalization in UK society at large – and popular satire ridiculing it – particularly in the division between manager and worker. The UK scene is thrown into relief by the Japanese philosophy of uniforms for all, now being imported into many of their UK operations.

Most organizations have appearance 'norms', especially where customer-facing staff are concerned. In reality, all business relationships are affected by appearance and would be susceptible to improvement via specific training – yes, all the way to colour consultants who help people make the right sort of impact, through the blend of shades they wear.

Presenting Yourself – Men by M. Spillane, Piatkus, 1994
Presenting Yourself – Women by M. Spillane, Piatkus, 1994

Appraisal

Appraisals should be a useful tool in performance management: most organizations now do them and they represent a massive investment of time. But, far from being the opportunity for open and honest communication about performance everyone wants, appraisals (up, down, peer and 360-degree) are often dreaded by both 'sides' and end up a missed opportunity.

Getting the best out of appraisals calls for specialist communication skills – at present, only a few people win support in developing. Managers, for example, can learn how to give specific feedback on performance, how to concentrate on priority areas and on factors that appraisees can actually control, and how to agree specific planning objectives, resulting in a joint action plan.

As for the appraisal subject, it may be the only opportunity they have in the course of a year for an in-depth, private, one-to-one discussion with their manager/internal customer about areas of mutual concern. Few organizations have yet to think of giving them preparatory training, for example, in receiving criticism or assertiveness.

The empowering appraisal (video-based open learning), The Industrial Society, 1995

Appraisal and Appraisal Interviewing by Ian Lawson, The Industrial Society Press, 1989

The appraisal interview (video and CDI) Melrose Training Resources 0171 627 8404

Straight talking (video) Video Arts 0171 637 7288

The dreaded appraisal (video) Video Arts 0171 637 7288

How am I doing? (video) BBC Training, 1989, 01462 895544

Asking questions

At work in particular, few people know how to get the answers they need, as distinct from the answers they want. On a much bigger scale, how many forms, internal surveys and focus groups fail to generate the baseline quality of response that would be required in academic or external market research circles?

Effective questioning techniques exist and can be learned – open questions for broad responses, closed questions for specific or yes/no answers, reflective questions for checking and clarification, and so on. So can the arts of silence, of facilitation, of building trust so people open up, of steering communication – opening up a conversation at one moment, closing it down the next – of summarizing, and moving on to the next topic.

Effective Interviewing by John Fletcher, Kogan Page, 1992

Professional interviewing by Rob Millar, Valerie Crute and Owen Hargie, Routledge, 1992

Good question! (video) Fenman Training 01353 665533

More than a gut feeling (video) Melrose Training Resources 0171 627 8404

The Panel Interview (video) Melrose Training Resources 0171 627 8404

Interviewing skills (looseleaf training activity) Fenman Training 01353 665533

Assertiveness

Assertiveness is at the heart of successful communication, because it hinges on achieving mutual understanding and satisfaction with outcomes.

Passive and aggressive communicators waste time in an organization. The former rarely convey the full thrust of their message, causing delays, irritation and reworking. The latter tend to be less concerned with moving things along than with preserving their own status and power over others. Little is achieved apart from an ego trip on one side, and damage on the other, in the form of lost contribution at the time and hereafter from the 'victim(s)'.

By contrast, the assertive 'sender' respects the needs of the intended audience, goes through the mental process of assessing what they need to know, and how. The assertive 'receiver' has the skill and the confidence to challenge ambiguity or misunderstanding.

Assertiveness at work by Ken and Kate Back, McGraw-Hill, 1982
Assertiveness: a working guide by Paddy O'Brien, Nicholas Brealey Publishing/ Industrial Society, 1992
Positive management: assertiveness for managers by Paddy O'Brien, Nicholas Brealey Publishing/Industrial Society, 1992
Straight talking (video) Video Arts 0171 637 7288
Assertiveness skills (looseleaf activity pack) Fenman Training 01353 665533
Say what you want (video) Melrose Training Resources 0171 627 8404
Working with assertiveness (video) BBC Training, 1990, 01462 895544

Body language

Most people interviewed say they prefer face-to-face communication, and the existence of body language is one of the biggest reasons why. Scientists claim that up to 92 per cent of communication is non-verbal; the clues people pick up from the way we move our faces and bodies, as well as our physical appearance and so on. In particular, body language plays an important role in conversations, encouraging talkers by nodding, making regular eye contact, smiling, using 'phatic' communication like 'hmmm' and 'I see'.

People are often unconscious of the messages they are able to send or receive in these ways. Training in body language therefore covers subjects like eye contact, voice control, facial expression, awareness of personal space, posture and touch. It typically uses video to show people themselves in action.

Body Language: read the hidden codes and maximise your potential by Jane Lyle, Reed International, 1990
Body Language by A. Pease, Sheldon, 1992
Body talk (video) Fenman Training 01353 665533
Body language at work (video) Melrose Training Resources 0171 627 8404
What the window cleaner saw (video) Melrose Training Resources 0171 627 8404
The interview game – body language (video) BBC training, 1985, 01462 895544   *241*

Brainstorming

People with the skills to facilitate and to contribute readily to brainstorming sessions can contribute enormously to the process of achieving genuine innovation and continuous improvement. In effect, they 'release' the potential of ideas and knowledge that already exist in an organization. Brainstorm sessions using on-line conferencing allow colleagues anywhere in the world to build on the power of their ideas and imaginations in this way.

Such skills can be used extensively in team meetings and in personal and systems development activities to generate fresh approaches to a given topic. Ideas are generated as quickly as possible – usually shouted out and written on a flipchart – without any discussion. Only when all the ideas have been 'stormed' does the group start to evaluate them.

Training would look at how to define a topic: too narrow and the group may struggle for ideas; too wide and everyone may interpret the subject in different ways. It could also look at variations like 'brainwriting' where members write and display their own thoughts.

Brainstorming techniques are covered in most basic training and meeting skills texts. They are usually considered a vital ingredient in quality working and are likely to be accessible from quality associations or your own quality department.

Creative problem solving (looseleaf activity pack) Fenman Training 01353 665533

Briefing

Effective briefing techniques are crucial to the successful outcome of many transactions at work, the most obvious being delegation. Often either the content of a brief – 'garbage in, garbage out' – or the way it was expressed gets in the way of successful communication. Situations that get out of control in this way often become complex, building layer upon layer of misunderstanding, and are difficult or impossible to disentangle until the damage has been done.

Training covers being clear about objectives, planning how to pass on instructions, specifications and background in a structured way, anticipating difficulties of understanding. The persons being briefed can also be shown how to play their full role in looking ahead and asking critical questions.

- For more information on team briefing, see Chapter 9 of this Handbook. For more about describing tasks to someone else, see Delegating later in this chapter.

Brief encounters (video) Melrose Training Resources 0171 627 8404
Talking to the team (video) Video Arts 0171 637 7288

Communicating through manuals and guides

Organizations are frequently disappointed at the attitudes and awareness of their people when they install an expensive new system or equipment or launch a new initiative.

Frequently the problem lies not in the device or idea itself but in poor communication – either ignoring the fact that there is such a dimension to such occasions or giving the task to people with inappropriate skills. Sometimes, it is the lack of good internal marketing that is to blame. More often than not, the problem lies in the manuals and guides supposed to make installation and usage easier. Many are incomprehensible because they have been regarded as a last-minute task and produced by the team closest to the project.

The skills involved in perfecting such communications are really about communication management and begin with initial testing on a sample audience. This is to establish context for usage, current understanding, language levels and so on. 'Writing' is usually critical in some form and for preference should be done by a professional, but much useful information may be better conveyed through diagrams or pictures or sound or video. It may even be necessary to run initial familiarization courses.

Manuals that work: a guide for writers by M. Davis, G. M. Gray, and H. Hallez, Kogan Page, 1990
Producing employee handbooks by Barbara Dyer, Industrial Society Press, 1995

Counselling

In a work context, counselling techniques can be used to cross emotional barriers underlying performance problems. Such techniques are being seen as more and more important as the incidence of change increases within organizational structures.

Counselling is not about giving advice – quite the opposite in fact: the aim is to help people find out for themselves what's going wrong and identify a strategy for putting it right.

Nor is counselling a specialist skill. Managers can learn to counsel, for example, as they become more directly involved in leading and coaching their teams. As in any psychological area, however, a little knowledge can be a dangerous thing. The potential for negative impact, even damaging people, is high – if for example the manager crosses the boundary between what is legitimately a work performance issue and what is prying.

Training in this field remains fragmented, but the national body, the British Association of Counselling, can advise on accredited courses. It centres on learning how to explore the feelings of the employee by building rapport, listening carefully, empathizing and not passing judgement. It raises awareness of the commitment and care required.

Counselling your staff by W. Redman, Kogan Page, 1995

Counselling: a practical guide for employers by Michael Megranahan, IPD publications, 1989

British Association of Counselling, 1 Regent Place, Rugby, Warwickshire CV21 2PJ 01788 550899

The counselling interview (video) Melrose Training Resources 0171 627 8404

Can you spare a moment? (video) Video Arts 0171 637 7288

Successful interviewing (Vol. 3: counselling, confrontational and dismissal interviews) (video) BBC Training, 1989, 01462 895544

Delegating

Effective delegation, widely recognized as a key component of successful management and leadership, rests largely on communication skills. In contrast with the all-encompassing nature of empowerment, delegation is usually concerned with specific, one-off tasks with clear boundaries.

We tend to think of delegation working hierarchically, 'the crumbs of interesting tasks handed down to subordinates', but with flatter structures and the growth of teamwork, more delegation is peer to peer.

Good delegators know how to convey information, and to check that it has been understood and committed to. People often shy away from delegation, saying by the time they had briefed, they may as well have done it, or that no one can do the job like they can. Sometimes they may be right, but often this is a cover for insecurity.

Moreover, people who are not delegating because of a lack of confidence in their communication skills, may well be holding on to a range of information that would be better passed on, and so may be causing other, unseen communication problems.

Delegation features in much management training and examines how to 'sell' an action to someone else so that they buy into its successful outcome; how to explain the task, making sure they understand; how to monitor and evaluate their performance, and how to communicate with them effectively about progress.

- See also Briefing in this chapter.

Delegation by Andrew Forest, The Industrial Society, 1995

Delegating for results by Robert B. Maddux, Kogan Page, 1993

Assertiveness at work by Ken and Kate Back, McGraw-Hill, 1982

Effective delegation (video) Melrose Training Resources 0171 627 8404

Editing

Think how much your organization could save if people routinely determined which communication is *really* necessary. Imagine if meetings that weren't needed didn't happen, if reports that were destined never to be read weren't written; indeed that all manner of unnecessary or unsuitable activities and initiatives were aborted.

Editing is the skill of deciding the best way to communicate on a given subject. It looks at what to leave out as well as how to structure and express what goes in. Editing decisions are driven by the needs of the audience. What do they want or need to know? What's in it for them? *Are* we saying this? What is the best way of saying it? Is the structure aiding communication or hindering it? How much detail?

We are not just talking here about the physical act of editing a report, house journal or video, but rather the *way of thinking* behind editing. Anyone who wants to prepare successful communication to others in a formal work setting needs to develop the editing mindset – particularly as the more the culture of our organizations changes to become participative, the more people on the receiving end of communication will question and analyse it.

Communication audits provide the best evidence of where the organization would benefit from people knowing how to adopt a more disciplined approach to communication. Established processes can be looked at via brainstorming, or by bringing two sides of a regular communication face to face to explore each others' needs on timing, length, frequency and so on. The absence of specific communication skills (e.g. clear writing or speaking) at significant points in the process should surface at the same time.

Facilitating

The skills used in facilitation can be used to run participative training courses, focus groups, brainstorming sessions, creative meetings and 'break-out' groups from plenary sessions.

Facilitators can help groups generate ideas, articulate needs, derive and test solutions, set standards, resolve differences, reach consensus and declare commitment publically, or re-energize stalled communication processes. It is a very demanding role, calling for a range of communication techniques, especially in the face-to-face area.

The facilitator's unique virtue (as opposed to managers or leaders) is that they usually don't have a vested interest in the subject: their focus is on supporting the communication activity in a way that successfully involves and draws from everyone present. With this 'independence' constraint, anyone in an organization can act as a facilitator. It is an obvious area for managers to develop, as well as HR and communication specialists.

Training concentrates, for example, on diagnosing communication problems quickly and techniques for overcoming them – such as planning ahead of an important meeting by searching for areas of agreement between opposing areas of interest.

Faultless Facilitation by Lois Hart, Kogan Page, 1992
Facilitator's Handbook by John Heron, Kogan Page, 1992
Facilitating by Mike Robson with Ciarán Beary, Gower, 1995

Getting feedback

Anyone directly involved in doing a task has a unique insight into it and therefore has the potential to help improve the organization's performance. A capability to draw out open, honest comments from people in a work situation, as well as listen effectively, appreciate the implications of what is being said, and communicate it onwards, adds immense value to any organization.

Effective feedback depends on a combination of communication skills. It begins with establishing respect and trust, allied to accurate observation (remembering that not all communication is verbal) and asking questions. In some cases, it may involve leading effective discussions with groups or setting up ongoing systems. If the feedback needs to be passed on within the organization, it also requires recording and editing skills, as well as the ability to access and if necessary manage the chosen medium.

Effective feedback can be achieved through the efforts of a single person, depending on the circumstances, or require the combined skills of a team.

Effective Feedback Skills by T. Russell, Kogan Page, 1994
Marking the managers: a guide to upward feedback (video-based open learning), The Industrial Society, 1995
Feedback solutions (video) Melrose Training Resources 0171 627 8404

Giving feedback

Giving feedback, especially when it is negative, calls for yet another range of communication skills. The main principle is that the communication must be clear, specific and unambiguous.

In addition, the person giving feedback must take responsibility for thinking through in advance what they want the person on the receiving end to do or feel as a result, and question whether their approach will achieve it. For example, it would be counterproductive to criticize someone about something that they have no power to change. Similarly, if they are to be convinced of the need to change, people need specific examples to show the basis on which criticisms are being made. Too general comments like 'You're a bit abrupt with people, aren't you?' are most likely to lead to denial and defensiveness.

Nobody likes receiving criticism, so to communicate it effectively means making sure it is set in a properly balanced context, alongside appropriate positive comment. For example, 'I'm very pleased with the quality of your input overall. Sometimes you have been a bit too detailed, for example...'. On the other hand, given the opportunity to evaluate themselves, the person on the receiving end will often be more self-critical than the manager feels able to be.

Once criticism has been accepted or volunteered, the skill then becomes one of listening and of counselling, helping the person to imagine a more positive outcome and discuss possible changes to achieve it.

Marking the managers: a guide to upward feedback (video-based open learning), The Industrial Society, 1995.

Assertiveness at Work by Ken and Kate Back, McGraw-Hill, 1982

Feedback solutions (video) Melrose Training Resources 0171 627 8404

Feedback techniques (video) Fenman Training 01353 665533

Keeping it simple

Any organization will run more effectively and efficiently if it values communication that is direct, clear and unambiguous.

People often use long words or complex diagrams and images in the belief that simpler representations cannot adequately express the sophisticated thoughts they want to communicate. In fact, the opposite is often true: the simpler the language or the image, the more chance they stand of conveying their thoughts in the first place. By contrast too, people who use over-complex language or imagery are often derided, or thought of as pompous and untrustworthy.

Little training is available in this area, but the IC function has a key role to perform in setting standards – in 'defogging' the language and look of organizational literature, for example, and in using more active and less passive expression.

The Plain English Campaign sets a useful benchmark, the Crystal Mark, which it awards to documents that have passed through its filters for plain English. To improve the standard of communication, organizations can run their own campaigns, raising awareness of the issue and offering training.

Financial Times Style Guide edited by Colin Inman, Pitman, 1993

Plain English Campaign, PO Box 3, New Mills, Stockport SK12 4QP 01663 744409

Leading discussions

This particular set of skills has become increasingly important as more emphasis is put on fully-participative meetings, training sessions and break-out groups. Rather than being 'told', people are now 'discovering' answers and coming to their own decisions through discussion.

Typical training in this area involves preparing questions to prompt discussion on key points, keeping discussions on track, keeping the momentum going and managing time, and finally to reach agreement and record what has been decided. It is also important to manage the group, drawing out the quiet, and closing down the dominant, and manage conflict and emotions.

How to lead discussions is covered in most introductory texts on meeting skills and training.

Letter, fax, memo and e-mail writing

Written communication offers both sender and receiver the advantages of a thought-out and well-crafted exchange, as well as providing an item of record. Thanks to the new computer networks, written messages can now also be transferred between people with little or no waiting time.

The problem is that writing is supposed to be a 'basic' skill – so routine that most organizations put very little effort into evaluating or improving it. As a result, every year, many thousands if not millions of pounds are lost through time wasted, wrong actions being carried out, relationships upset, re-work and frustration all round.

Common problems include using inappropriate language and being unclear in content or purpose, but also using inappropriate media – writing a full letter when a memo would have been more effective (and vice versa), or a combination of e-mail and telephone, for example.

Tackling the problems may involve instituting regular checks, gathering a 'black museum' of where written communication went wrong, articulating and raising awareness of the standards expected, and recommending improvements. You may also offer in-house training or recommend external courses, which are plentiful. Model routine letters circulated on disk may help, especially if they are 'sold' to people on the basis that these should make life easier, as they will only need to adapt the model to their own use, rather than writing from scratch.

In addition, computer-based text editing programmes now exist, which make it relatively easy to carry out sampling or for individuals to identify the degree of jargon used in a piece of text or a speech, or to assess how complex is the correspondence being sent out to shareholders or suppliers or customers, for example. There is relatively little use of such devices at present, but we can expect to see it grow.

Manage the Message: how to write communications that get you the result you want by Bryan Thresher and Jim Biggin, Century Business, 1993
Writing Letters by Wendy Moss, NEC, 1995
The business letter business (video) Video Arts 0171 637 7288

Listening

Listening is often reckoned to be the most neglected communication skill. It should take all our attention because we're hearing, comprehending, analysing and storing information simultaneously.

Instead, anyone who has transcribed a taped interview they have been involved in will have come face to face with their own listening (in)abilities. Typical symptoms include interrupting, steering the conversation through your own agenda regardless of what the other person says, thinking of your next question while the other person talks, making assumptions and finishing their sentences.

Training includes understanding how to use and interpret body language such as eye contact, nodding and head tilting to show attentiveness, picking up clues from the speaker's body language, encouraging the speaker, being comfortable with silence, and understanding the barriers to listening and how to overcome them.

The listening manager, by Tony Lake (open learning pack) NEC/The Industrial Society, 1995
Effective listening skills (video) Fenman Training 01353 665533
Listen! (video) Melrose Training Resources 0171 627 8404
Listening skills (video) Video Arts 0171 637 7288

Media management

Media management covers areas like promoting good news and handling bad news, dealing with journalists (working for internal and external media), putting key messages across in interviews and creating systems for crisis management. In its widest sense it also takes in orchestration of available media to produce a properly reinforced campaign.

'Media training' is widely available, but is typically confined to practice in dealing with journalists or TV presenters through a series of demanding role-plays. At present, the remaining skills are largely available only in vocational training, for example PR and journalism, but some companies have developed in-house courses for managers.

How to Take on the Media by D. Wragg, Kogan Page, 1993
How to Get Your Point Across in 30 Seconds or Less by M. O'Frank, Transworld, 1993
Face the Press: managing the media interview by John Lidstone, Industrial Society Press, 1995

Meetings

Meetings represent a huge investment of time, effort and money, yet few organizations have come to grips with how to make them effective. Taking part in meetings is another communication skill that people are simply assumed to have.

Common problems include holding meetings as a knee-jerk reaction to handling a task when another medium might be more effective, poor preparation, lack of clear purpose, no target end time and imbalanced participation.

Training will typically cover:

- agreeing and clarifying the meeting's objective
- setting and circulating agendas and any preparatory work
- balancing the contribution of all individuals present
- asking questions and leading discussion

249

- being aware of personal and hidden agendas
- clarifying and summarizing viewpoints and opinions.

How to win meetings by Greville Janner, Gower, 1990
Impact at meetings (video) Melrose Training Resources 0171 627 8404
Meetings, bloody meetings (video) Video Arts 0171 637 7288
More bloody meetings (video) Video Arts 0171 637 7288
Effective meetings (looseleaf activity pack) Fenman Training 01353 665533

Negotiating

Negotiation is an increasingly valued and sought-after communication skill, for a number of reasons. Take, for example, the sweep of competitive tendering through the public sector, or the growth of cross-charging between departments and outsourcing or, more generally, the intensification of competition in most markets.

Negotiation is not about 'putting one over' on someone else: it is about achieving 'win-win' situations, where both sides gain something out of a transaction and neither loses face.

Typically training covers planning ahead, anticipating how the other party will respond, and knowing when and where to compromise. Negotiators need to think through the issue from the perspective of both sides, in short, understand what they and their opposite number really want. They need to know when to withhold and when to reveal key information and to develop strategies for countering likely moves.

Successful negotiation between colleagues, or with suppliers, is particularly important because of its ongoing repercussions – people bearing grudges are unlikely to promote successful team efforts.

Effective Negotiation by Colin Robinson, Kogan Page, 1995
Pocket negotiator, The Economist, 1993
Negotiate, the Art of Winning, by H. Mills, Gower, 1993
Tough Talking: how to handle awkward situations by David M. Martin, Pitman, 1994
It's a deal: negotiating skills (video-based open learning), Industrial Society, 1995
Negotiation skills (looseleaf activity pack) Fenman Training 01353 665533
Negotiating: tying the knot (video) Video Arts 0171 637 7288

Networking

Organizations are forever reinventing the wheel as best practice slips down the cracks between cliques and departments. Moreover, older, more formal hierarchical structures have rarely ever reflected the real power-base and usefulness of individuals.

As organizational structures have begun to flatten out, more opportunities are opening up for individuals at all levels to learn new skills related to building their own set of contacts – people who can give them access to additional information and support beyond what they gain through formal sources within the hierarchy.

People in general can be made aware of the benefits of networking and be encouraged to identify who would be useful to contact on what subject. But networking can also take place at a more formal level – say, between regional champions for customer service or quality. Similarly on cross-functional project teams, members can be encouraged to talk to key individuals in the different departments, reflecting the need to break down the barriers between the functions.

Other networks may be bound by different needs – women managers may come together for mutual support, in much the same way as the 'old boys' network' functions. Networks also extend outside the organization, such as through the membership of professional bodies or through benchmarking best practice with a partner organization.

Perhaps the most powerful encouragement of all to networking comes from technology, as more and more desktop computers become linked to each other, either within organizations or through publically accessible networks like the Internet. (See Chapters 5 and 14 of this Handbook for more on this.)

Power: Creating it, using it by Helga Drummond, Kogan Page, 1992

Neuro Linguistic Programming (NLP)

NLP embraces many communication techniques. A simple description would talk about the concept of mirroring, recognizing and reflecting the verbal and body language of your audience.

This draws on the observation of psychologists that when we are comfortable with someone, our body language and the terms we use begin to reflect theirs. For example, we may change the way we sit to be more like them, or if we notice they use aural imagery like 'I hear you went...' 'that sounds...' the theory goes that the hearing is their preferred sense and the best way to communicate with them.

Training typically encourages people to be more observant of this sort of clue, and gives practice in responding. Other common areas include analysing behaviour to make sure what is being said matches the clues given by the body, and evaluating eye movements to determine whether the speaker is talking about a real memory, or something they are creating.

NLP: the new art and science of getting what you want by H. Alder, Piatkus, 1995
Body talk (video) Fenman Training 01353 665533
NLP at Work by Sue Knight, Nicholas Brealey Publishing, 1995
Introducing NLP by Joseph O'Connor and John Seymour, Aquarian Press, 1993
Frogs into Princes by Richard Bandler and John Grinder, Real People Press, 1979
Practical NLP for Managers by Ian McDermott and Joseph O'Connor, Gower, 1996

Presentation

Presentation skills have become more important as organizational cultures move from a position where orders are 'obeyed or else' to one where agreement and commitment must be won.

Acquiring these skills takes knowledge and considerable practice, yet too many organizations still assume that any manager should be capable of presenting, on virtually any topic, to any audience, from more junior colleagues to the board.

The challenge is considerably increased by growing pressure for two-way communication at presentations, where the audience is involved as much as possible.

Most training courses will examine issues like audience analysis, content preparation, working with equipment and controlling the environment. They will also look at personal appearance, the use of posture and body language such as keeping regular eye contact with the audience, and breathing and voice control techniques.

Learning to prepare and use visual material is particularly important, especially now that audiences are becoming used to multimedia and video content. Sometimes the 'tricks' of the trade can be more low-tech, such as using relevant props to make the abstract concrete.

Presenting to camera for videos and internal television systems is also becoming more important, for employees as well as managers.

These media are growing in popularity, and internal audiences seem to like the implied ownership of the messages presented by 'one of us'. At the same time, today's sophisticated viewers are intolerant and critical of 'amateur' presenters – such a performance can easily distract from the message. A good video director will always 'nurse' a novice through a piece to camera, but for anyone who is going to present on a regular basis or play a prominent part in a 'flagship' video, it's worth considering sending them on a presenter training course.

- For more information on presentations, see Speech and scriptwriting later in this chapter.

Effective Presentation by Antony Jay, Pitman, 1993
Perfect Presentation by Andrew Leigh, Century Business Books, 1993
Loud and clear: speaking to groups (video-based open learning), Industrial Society, 1995

Most of the leading video producers have a range of videos on this topic.

Reading

Most people at work have very limited time to read the documents they receive, whether in print or on screen. If this becomes a problem, it makes sense for the organization to examine the root cause and determine if all these documents are really necessary.

But there are also skills that will help the individual cope with information overload. Learning how to prioritize, for example, deciding what should be read now, if not when, and in what detail, and what should go straight in the 'bin'. Skimming and speed-reading techniques will also help.

The big breakthroughs come when people in an organization learn to stop regarding reading as a passive 'receiving' task: if a document is incomprehensible, they challenge it. For example organizations often have documents in use for years with sections that no-one understands, even the department that created them. Encouraging widespread use of contact names and numbers on all documents is one way to improve the quality of language, by providing a fast route for queries and complaints.

Having said all that, it is too easy to assume that everyone in the organization can read and that all read equally well. In some organizations, literacy levels may be poor, especially where there is an additional challenge of English as a second language. One in six people in England and Wales lack basic skills such as literacy and numeracy – 6.5 million potential employees. The task here may be less finding access to training than persuading the organization to recognize the extent to which such factors are holding it back.

Multinationals also face problems in attempting to make transnational communication work. Again, the task is rarely as simple as finding the right 'course' and may require more innovative and tailored approaches.

Speed Reading in Business by Joyce Turley, Kogan Page, 1990
Rapid Reading by Janis Grummit, Industrial Society Press, 1995

Basic Skills Unit for advice 0171 405 4017

Report writing

Reports are often seen as the natural and automatic accompaniment to a project. Each year, organizations throw millions of person-hours into writing them. Leaving aside the question of whether or not they are needed, few of us receive formal training on how to do it, or receive any useful feedback from the readers.

The structure of reports tends to be fairly good, thanks to the tried and tested formats that have evolved – the executive summary saves readers having to read endless padding. Content, however, is often dull, poorly presented and sketchily edited, if at all. Reports produced by working parties or committees are often the worst: unless there is a strong editorial voice, they can degenerate into a mishmash of inconsistencies and writing styles.

There are many books and training packages on report writing. It may at least help if you were to set standards and a house style for reports in your organization.

How to Write Reports by John Inglis and Roger Lewis, Industrial Society Press, 1982

Report Writing by Judith Vidal-Hall, Industrial Society Press, 1995

Report writing (video or CDI) Video Arts 0171 637 7288

Report writing made easy (open learning activity) Fenman Training 01353 665533

The writing programme (video) Melrose Training Resources 0171 627 8404

Speaking

Speaking is a skill that can be improved like any other. Speed – too fast or too slow – is a common fault. Like high-pitched speech it is usually a product of nerves or stress.

Any sort of speaking – public, face to face or over the telephone – depends on good breath control. Training and relaxation techniques can help people speak in a steady, measured way, without the need for hurried breaths, and to achieve better voice projection. Training can also tackle issues like volume, pitch, diction and intonation.

People who use the telephone extensively are especially exposed as the telephone diminishes the quality of the voice still further.

As with body language, the perception of voices in part depends on cultural norms. If your organization works with many different nationalities, cross-cultural training can also help examine assumptions made about a person's attitude or mood on the basis of their speech patterns.

Speech and scriptwriting

Speech and scriptwriting are specialist skills. However, many people treat them just like any other form of writing, resulting in a dry, barely compre-hensible delivery.

A speech or script needs to be written for the 'ear'. It should sound natural, as close to spoken language as possible. Various techniques are available, for example recording a conversation with a friend about what the speech is to address. By reviewing the tape it's possible to capture the naturalness of speech, and convert this into notes or a full script.

Timing is usually very important in this form of writing: speaking from notes or cards can make it hard to predict how long the speech will be. A full script gives the speaker a chance to mark points of emphasis, and gives you the security of complete control.

Complete Speechmaker, by Greville Janner, Century Business, 1994

Executive Speeches by B. Filson, John Wiley & Sons, 1994

Summarizing

Summarizing is an important communication skill because it helps people make sure that they are on the same wavelength. It's an opportunity for listeners to demonstrate that they have been listening, and gives the speaker an opportunity to challenge any assumptions made. It's also a way of reinforcing messages and it can act as a punctuation point, signalling the move from one subject to another.

Sometimes summarizing is built into a question to establish mutual understanding of someone's position, for example 'So you're worried that it if we run the journal quarterly we won't be able to attract the advertising?'

Tips for summarizing are included in most training courses and books that offer meeting skills.

Telephoning

Telephoning has been part of daily life in western countries for decades, but organizations can still do much to improve the telephone skills of their people.

Telephone discipline is very important as the phone is often the main route of contact for customers or clients; it is an important part of the corporate image and a consistent approach is needed. A vague greeting, followed by a poor transfer will do little for your organization's credibility. Callers want to know who they're talking to, what's happening at every stage, and someone to take responsibility for handling their call.

One way of testing this is by 'mystery shopping' your company's phone etiquette. Look out for common problems like long delays in answering, getting 'lost' in the system when transferring, people sounding distracted, failing to identify themselves and failing to pass on details when transferring, so that the caller has to explain themselves over and over again.

Telephone systems are becoming more complex to use, but may offer potentially useful features like conference calling, if people know how to use them.

All the relevant skills are covered in the many courses, open learning packages and books on the subject.

Telephone Skills by Maria Pemberton, Industrial Society Press
Quality calls: making the most of the phone (video-based open learning), Industrial Society
Telephone perfection (video open learning) Melrose Training Resources 0171 627 8404
Positive telephone skills (video open learning) Fenman Training 01353 665533
Quality calls (video) BBC Training, 1991, 01462 895544

Transactional analysis

Like other behavioural theories, transactional analysis (TA) provides a useful model for communication. It describes human interactions from three basic perspectives: adult, parent and child.

On the face of it, all interactions at work should be 'adult' talking to 'adult'. *255*

Both parties should be treating each other with respect and communicating assertively, openly and honestly. Between bosses and subordinates, however, there is often a powerful 'parent/child' relationship in play. For example 'How many times do I have to tell you, you must do your time sheets!' will more than likely bring forth the reply 'How can I do my job when you're always hassling me about time-sheets?'

TA helps people question the nature of their relationships at work. Sometimes people get 'stuck' in particular roles that block communication and hamper their effectiveness. Once they are aware of the model, they may be able to 'step back' and consider how 'adult' their actions really are, and identify any signs of parent or child behaviour.

Introductory training should give opportunities to experience the difference between various approaches, and to analyse typical behaviours and situations on this basis.

I'm OK – You're OK by Thomas A. Harris, Pan, 1973
Staying OK by Amy and Thomas Harris, Pan, 1985

APPENDIX: PROFESSIONAL DEVELOPMENT

Where in the UK today is the skills need for IC professionals being met? In general, the answer appears to be that neither academia nor business has yet addressed the challenge fully.

The higher education picture, despite increasing numbers of related degree courses – media studies, marketing communication and organizational development, for example – remains patchy. At undergraduate level in particular, it looks likely to remain so until more progress is made in achieving a clearly defined role for the IC function, one that provides a distinct career path or a validatable component in any management career.

Until that happens, both specialist and generalist managers in the field will find that one of the most effective ways of developing themselves is to network with other internal communication professionals.

Where's best to start?

Over the past decade, the number of seminars and professional association meetings on IC has risen steeply.

Some of these events are staged by professional associations as a development service to members and as a recruitment vehicle. The Industrial Society, one the earliest organizations to acknowledge internal communication as a management function in its own right, sponsors the Employee Communications Association, based at its Bryanston Square address. The Institute of Public Relations has formed an Internal Communications Group which offers a specialized seminar programme and promotes IC's positioning within the public relations mix.

Seminar programmes are also run by the London-based chapter of the

International Association of Business Communicators (IABC), a worldwide organization with members in 40 countries.

In addition, several of the leading consultancies in the field now run courses and seminar programmes: many have formed active networking associations – such as ASPIC (Association for Strategic Planning in Internal Communication) – as a means of raising standards generally as well as awareness of their practices.

All these groups bring together in-house and consultancy practitioners operating in the private and public sectors. They provide topical focus and infinite networking opportunities for exchanging experiences and developing ideas on strategies. Events usually take place in London, some using guest speakers, some based on interactive working groups.

Two associations – the IABC and the UK-based British Association of Communicators in Business (BACB, formerly the BAIE) – run annual study conferences.

IABC's annual international conference typically has a US venue. It provides the opportunity for upwards of 1000 professional communicators to keep up to date with best practice at international level through keynote presentations and smaller syndicates. For the first time, in 1996, IABC UK also held a one-day conference in London, leading up to its annual awards dinner.

The BACB's conference is held at a different UK venue each year and is made up of sessions headed by leading practitioners and workshops covering many aspects of communicators' day-to-day work.

Opportunities for qualifications

Both the IABC and the BACB offer qualification programmes.

IABC Accreditation is designed to allow candidates to demonstrate their expertise across the range of business communications practice covering all constituencies: media, customers, investors, governments and employees. Candidates are required to possess a bachelor's degree and five years' continuous experience, or a combination of nine years' post-secondary education and experience before being considered.

Applications must be accompanied by a portfolio showing the range of candidates' strategic planning and programme execution ability with heavy emphasis on results achieved. This is followed by a written and oral examination requiring a minimum 70 per cent pass mark.

The BACB runs a series of one-day courses in the spring and autumn, mostly covering the more technical aspects of editing, but beginning to broaden into more management. Members are able to take advantage of certificate and diploma courses. The certificate is open to associates who can then progress to the diploma and full membership of the association. The diploma may also be taken by candidates who have attained a communications degree, the National Council for the Training of Journalists certificate or relevant NVQ certificates.

The Industrial Society also offers a course twice a year for internal communication managers based on a curriculum developed, piloted and run by British

Telecom. This is designed to ensure that internal communication is appreciated as a vital part of the communications mix and to increase its value and worth throughout organizations. Over three days, the course looks at all aspects of internal communication including the tools such as print and visual media, influencing skills, upward feedback and lateral communications.

One of the brightest hopes for the future comes from efforts by members of the Employee Communications Association to set up National Vocational Qualification units. Volunteers have analysed the jobs of people working within IC in 50 different organizations to compile a list of competencies, and researched existing NVQs in related fields such as public relations, customer service and marketing. A small number of people were due to take part in a pilot exercise at the end of 1996.

In addition to the work of these organizations there are conferences dedicated to internal communication topics offered by both professional training organizations and promoted by business magazines.

Reading the journals of the professional organizations mentioned above will contribute to your ongoing learning.

Contact addresses

Professional associations

British Association of Communicators in Business Ltd, 2nd Floor, Bolsover House, 5/6 Clipstone Street, London W1P 7EB 0171 436 2545

Institute of Public Relations, The Old Trading House, 15 Northburgh Street, London EC1V 0PR 0171-253 5151

International Association of Business Communicators UK c/o Watson Wyatt International, Watson House, London Road, Reigate, Surrey RH2 9PQ 01737 241144

The Conference Board, 845 Third Avenue, New York, NY 10022-6679, USA 001 212 759 0900

The Industrial Society, Peter Runge House, 3 Carlton House Terrace, London SW1Y 5DG 0171-839 4300

Publications

Briefing Plus, The Industrial Society, 48 Bryanston Square, London W1H 7LN 0171-262 2401

Communication World, International Association of Business Communicators, One Hallidie Plaza Suite 600, San Francisco CA 94102, USA 001 415 433 3400. An electronic version of *Communication World* is available on the Internet through an IABC World Wide Web page. The IABC has an active international forum on CompuServe under the Media page.

Communicators in Business, British Association of Communicators in Business Ltd, 2nd Floor, Bolsover House, 5/6 Clipstone Street, London W1P 7EB 0171 436 2545

Intercom, Employee Communications Association at The Industrial Society, 48 Bryanston Square, London W1H 7LN 0171 262 2401

Internal Communications Focus, Third Floor, Brigade House, Parsons Green, London SW6 4TH 0171 736 7111

IPR Journal, Institute of Public Relations, The Old Trading House, 15 Northburgh Street, London EC1V 0PR 0171 253 5151

17 Managing communication through supervisors

David James, *communication consultant, The ITEM Group*

Delayering – taking out tiers of middle management – has turned the organizational spotlight full on front-line managers, supervisors and team leaders. Most organizations are only just beginning to come to grips with the consequences. Few (there are some noble exceptions) have yet to review the style or structuring of their communications to suit the new circumstances; fewer still have addressed the subject of training, including communication training, for such managers. This chapter examines how we reached the current position and some of the principal contributions to thinking about it.

Remember *I'm All Right Jack*, the Boulting brothers' 1959 film satire on post-war industrial relations? The power of the shop steward; the manipulative behaviour of the directors; the personnel manager terrified of both. Although it has long since disappeared, the very awfulness of that culture and those conditions still bring a wry smile.

Instructive to communicators was a scene in which the company chairman exhorts a mass meeting of workers to 'export or die'. 'Wot's he on about?' asks one of the lads. Never have so many blank faces been caught on camera.

At the time, the failure to communicate at work was a common theme. Harvard Business School professor F. J. Roethlisberger, for example, observed that it was 'extraordinary' that any two people could communicate within an organization, given their likely differences in background, experience and motivation.

Perhaps managers and workforce are not 'divided by a common language' as they once were, but we continue to talk about the need for relevance and the alignment of values in industrial communication, and often have yet to achieve it.

SHOP STEWARD AS THE 'REAL' LEADER

Another memorable image from the film was that of the total trust the workers had in their shop steward (Peter Sellers), drawn to him like sheep as he marched through the works, calling them out on strike.

Shop stewards, a product of the First World War, represented the interests of union members in the workplace, listened to their grievances and even took them up with management, if necessary, if it was felt that the more senior trade union leaders had failed in this regard. Certainly, representing the feelings of workers did not come within the remit of Personnel. Personnel meant the engagement and dismissal of labour, pay negotiation, and little else. Even as late as the 1970s, most Personnel departments had few staff management appraisal and development responsibilities, and no hand in communication.

SO WHO DO PEOPLE TRUST NOW?

The interesting question, then, is to whom has the trust of employees been transferred in the interval, as the power of the shop steward has waned?

Only in small part was it transferred to the foreman, a role which industry encouraged for a time, not least because managers could shift to them part of their responsibility for communication. If messages were not received and acted on, it was the foreman's fault, notwithstanding the fact that he or she was a technical or process specialist, not a communicator.

No, trust has ultimately surfaced with the supervisor, front-line manager, or team leader. (For the purposes of this chapter, I will use the terms interchangeably.)

Surveys all over the world bear the same message: people trust their front-line managers and believe what they tell them, in preference to any other source – and by a very big margin.

The significance of this finding is profound. Organizations wishing to influence their people – in whatever way – are more likely to succeed if they accept that communication does not happen uniformly across the organization: that it is most likely to occur where trust exists – which in turn is most likely between supervisors and their teams.

The book, *Communicating Change* (1994), is emphatic on this point.

> Communication has the best chance of changing front line behaviour if it comes from the most desired and credible source, and that's not from the CEO – it's the immediate supervisor.

The authors, US communication consultants T. J. Larkin and Sandar Larkin, are not the first to say so. Others have expressed much the same sentiment, including a number of British management commentators, such as Eric Caines, writing in *Work 2000* (Stanworth and Stanworth, 1991).

> People in organizations promote the view that some high level of thought exists in the higher echelons of organizations, but that is not so – only people who can actually do jobs can talk sensibly about those jobs.

However, genuinely informed discussion in this field is in a sense only just beginning, as organizations are only now experimenting with the new task of communicating in channels left empty by the withdrawal of many middle management layers.

The particular authority of the Larkins' book stems from the depth of their empirical research. One thing is very clear: the fact that management needs to re-engineer its communication mindset comes 'screaming' from the page.

And with good reason. For despite all the evidence, UK organizations persist in *telling* or *presenting at* their people from the top, rather than using the rapport their front-line managers have with their teams to create a climate in which people voluntarily involve themselves to a greater degree in the organizations' aims.

The *1994 Industrial Society Survey of Employee Communication* reflected an over-reliance in the UK on the vehicles that were least effective at communicating with most people.

- *Notice-boards* – 97 per cent of companies put their communication faith in notice-boards, when only 6 per cent of their people considered them effective.
- *Traditional newsletters and house journals* – another favourite with management, these fared poorly, just 6 per cent of people considering them effective. Such vehicles – whether in print or using other media formats – obviously have a role, but it is much more likely these days to be to facilitate the communication of messages, top down and bottom up. Their future looks likely to be as a vehicle for generating and recording feedback and responses, and for playing a big part in identifying and transferring best practice.
- *Video* – few people considered video effective, and *e-mail*, although popular, has, as yet, questionable communication value in the full sense of the word.
- *Team briefing* – commonly used, but, again, only half the people interviewed thought the process effective. And this would appear to be the general experience of managers too.

WHO 'OWNS' THE MESSAGE?

This last fact might be thought to invalidate the Larkins' argument, because here, I suppose, the involvement of supervisors is most manifest. But there are also considerations of content and ownership. Is head office necessarily the most desired and credible information source in employees' eyes? Has it ever been so? Financial updates and organizational changes initiated by the chief executive and senior management, even when presented by a local manager, usually offer little of interest to people who really want to discuss themselves, their own contribution and the local picture.

There is absolutely no evidence, say the Larkins, that communication from CEOs in large organizations significantly affects employee behaviour. (Has anyone in an in-house position given this message and lived to tell the tale?) By the same token, there is ample evidence to show that increasing the power of supervisors increases both job satisfaction and performance among front-line employees.

WHO CAN EFFECT CHANGE?

All managers engage in activities that they intend to result in change, but that does not mean that employees will respond in a way that satisfies those intentions.

The relationship between a supervisor and his or her team should be seen as a subculture, one of many in every organization. To penetrate such sub-cultures with communication from 'above' or 'outside', a senior or middle-level manager needs to know how the people in that team approach organizational issues. The supervisor already knows.

Attention has to be paid, not to what team members say and do when they believe that they are expected to exhibit company-directed behaviours, but to what is said and done under real working conditions. Otherwise there is a danger that policies that would perhaps work under ideal conditions, will bear no relation to the real world of actual organizational behaviour.

The subjects under discussion also need to be relevant to, not remote from, the experience of the audience. Injecting a good deal more localization, listening, involving, and feedback and response can do a lot for the team briefing process, as can sharing its ownership and agenda.

WHO HAS THE SKILL?

But, having put that right, if the problem with the effectiveness of team briefing is seen to reside with the supervisors' communication skills – and everywhere you come across examples where such skills have not been transferred, but are assumed to be already part of the supervisor's equipment – then, eureka! It was an oversight. Team briefing will come good once training is provided.

The Larkins say not. Consider this:

> The least educated, most frustrated, most oppressed-feeling employees in the company are going to be gathered into a group where the least confident, least informed, least powerful member of management is going to give them a lot of statistics they don't want.

In other words, why should supervisors – whatever the degree of training provided – be better at giving public presentations than senior management? Especially when senior management frequently admit to being least comfortable and confident about their own skills in this department, even when they have received the best coaching money can buy?

Harvard professor Chris Argyris has observed that 'those members of the organization that many assume to be the best at learning are, in fact, not very good at it. I am talking about the well-educated, high powered, high commitment professionals who occupy key leadership positions in the modern corporation.' Makes you think.

Organizations might be lucky enough occasionally to find natural communicators among their supervisors (and, certainly, some women supervisors appear to have the necessary qualities), but in the main, is it realistic to expect front-line managers easily to become effective *formal* communicators, with all that that means in terms of facilitating, motivating, supporting, educating, influencing and enabling their teams?

If something isn't working, or is unlikely to work, why would you want more of it? A persistent chorus is in no doubt – scrap team briefings for the front-line.

Much better, they say, not to insist on a formal system, and to let supervisors communicate informally on a one-to-one basis. And give them something relevant and worth communicating – something that stands a chance of changing the behaviour of those for whom they are responsible.

It has been done. Some organizations have come to realize that if communication is to have any value, it should always bring about change or outputs.

Communication is not solely concerned with transferring data or information, or recording history. And it is certainly not about wielding power or corporate preening. For if those are the elements that go into team briefing, what's the point? What the board has to pull off in the next quarter has nothing to do with winning hearts and minds. That will not help the organization realize its potential or that of its people. It will not create the conditions under which people voluntarily release a greater contribution into the organization.

WILL IT ACTUALLY WORK?

Commentators are in general less clear on the practicalities of the alternative of running what might be for some organizations a large number of individual briefings. Perhaps the answer is to adopt the daily or impromptu 'huddles' of the Japanese motor industry and Asda, for example. They are not so far from the model proposed.

The next question is how do you feed what is relevant and worth communicating into a supervisor-centred system? The Larkins, for example, recommend a two-tier process.

Substantial changes should be communicated by setting up direct, two-way links between senior managers and supervisors, while traditional communication methods such as briefings, videos, newspaper should be confined to communicating with middle managers.

For all other communication purposes, middle managers should be pressured – and measured – to improve their links with supervisors, preferably through face-to-face contact.

The key to a system in which supervisors have the gatekeeper role is for the leadership to jack up the status of supervisors – to make it public that they have preferred communication supplier status, if you like. Such an approach reflects the view that management *is* communication, that its prime role is to support the front line, and that that means supporting those that the front line trusts.

To quote the Larkins again:

> We know employees are more satisfied with their supervisors when they believe those supervisors have power; and we know that employees who are satisfied with their supervisors think better of the entire company and do better work.

The next step is to involve supervisors in designing the communication process and content, and to involve them in decisions over which they and their teams genuinely do have control. Middle managers need not worry about losing power and status: most people do not want to take part in decisions affecting the whole company – just their workplace.

These recommendations are all very well – and there's no denying that a number of authoritative surveys continue to indicate that this is what employee customers want, or something close to it – but such a structure poses a number of challenges.

- It needs a high level of support from the top to establish the communication authority of supervisors, and this might prove difficult to sustain.
- It presupposes a high degree of discipline on the part of senior and middle managers, and supervisors, to stick by the rules. The only way of ensuring this would be to police the process by taking soundings at supervisor level and by bringing into line those managers identified as failing to involve supervisors in the way intended.
- It also requires a considerable act of faith on the part of leaders to believe that informal one-to-one briefings given by untrained supervisors would be capable of effecting the type of change they are looking for. But could any more be said of the old-style mass meeting or its modern equivalent, the video presentation?

In the light of all this, taking the plunge – not to say bungee jump – really depends on how much pain an organization is prepared to inflict on itself to make a communication breakthrough that might have only strategic value.

Another consideration is whether supervisors actually *want* to wear such a weighty communication mantle. It would certainly be a presumption to proceed without first soliciting their opinion.

BY-PASS COMMUNICATION: SUPPORT OR HINDRANCE?

So, if the message is communicate through supervisors, equally it is that the top should not seek to shorten the link even further by communicating directly with the front line – a by-pass operation many organizations resort to in the hope of solving their communication problems.

> The business leader who, in his attempts to reach employees, bypasses formal organizational and management channels is almost surely courting failure,

265

particularly if his message has to do with the organization and its work, for the most direct channel to employees is almost always through supervisors. All surveys, as well as common sense, show that employees are highly influenced in their attitudes and ability to absorb information by their immediate supervisors.

(George de Mare 1968)

George de Mare gave two reasons for taking that view.

One is that going direct is more symbolic than real, and employees have little love for symbols. It is simply not possible for leaders to give the responses that would ensure the credibility of the process. When they fail to materialize, the object of the exercise – to demonstrate that somehow a special relationship exists between the top and the bottom of the organization – is defeated.

The second reason is that going direct weakens the relationship between supervisors and their teams.

Nothing more undermines the supervisor's authority or arouses his resistance than leaving him out of the communication transmission line by using other channels for information which pertains to his functions.

Instead, de Mare recommends the following procedure:

1. Always inform supervisors first before attempting to reach employees.
2. Wherever possible, have material and messages pertaining to organization work or policy presented first through supervisors and through supervisors only.
3. Give supervisors the opportunity to comment on and appraise all material to be transmitted within their spheres.

DO WE EVEN NEED THE SUPERVISOR?

So, communicate through supervisors: don't go direct. It is not an isolated view. But, hold on. Not everybody agrees. Tom Peters for one.

Make no mistake, this self-management stuff means that there is no room – whatsoever – for the first-line supervisor as we have known him or her for the last 200 years.

And don't the Richard Bransons, Anita Roddicks and Bill Gates of this world transcend the rule? They are seen as instinctive direct communicators, and would appear to have a personal rapport with their staff. But they, too, run companies with well-structured communication processes. Whether formal or informal, and however much more creative and aligned, they are not so very different from those of other organizations.

The choices on the way to the glittering prize of whole company involvement, then, would seem to be these:

- trust your supervisors as key communicators since they have the trust of the front line

- trust your ability to communicate directly with the front line
- trust in the trickle-down effect of existing cascade systems, even with all their shortcomings.

A final thought. If people have most trust in their supervisors and believe what they tell them, what exactly are supervisors telling them now, if they are not the formally-recognized mainstay of the communication process? A survey would make interesting reading.

HOW TO FIND OUT MORE

Communicating for Leadership by George de Mare, Ronald Press (US), 1968

Work 2000 by John Stanworth and Celia Stanworth, Paul Chapman Publishing, 1991

'Subculture strife hinders productivity' by Shari Caudron, *Personnel Journal*, December 1992

Communications for Managers: a practical handbook edited by Jenny Davenport and Gordon Lipton, The Industrial Society, 1993

Are Managers Getting the Message? An IM report on communications in the flat organization by Aspen Business Communications, Institute of Management, 1993

'Speech therapy' by Lucie Carrington, *Personnel Today*, 12–25 October 1993

'The need to know organization' by Clare Hogg, *Human Resources*, Summer 1994

Communicating Change by T. J. Larkin and Sandar Larkin, McGraw-Hill, 1994

'On achieving excellence' by T. Peters, *Euromanagement*, TP Communications and The ITEM Group, September 1991

Communicating Corporate Change by Bill Quirke, McGraw-Hill, 1996

Part V
MEASURING SUCCESS

18 Why measure?

David Clutterbuck, *chairman, The ITEM Group*

*The pressure to develop and apply credible measures to internal commu-
nication activity is growing and emerges in successive studies among professional communicators as one of the issues highest on their agenda. This
'pressure to measure' arises from a number of sources, which this chapter
looks at in detail.*

Management guru Peter Drucker once famously observed 'You can't manage
what you can't measure.' The new demands for 'results' coming IC's way from
senior and line management could be interpreted as the surest sign that they
are beginning to take the area more seriously. But increased stimulus for
measurement activity relates to a range of factors.

Organizations generally more measurement-conscious

Business process re-engineering, benchmarking and quality standards have all
demanded measurement to provide vital input, both into continuous improvement and strategic refocusing/change programmes.

This in turn has led to widespread attempts to establish performance/
management competencies for individuals and functional groups, and to use
these as a measure of their contribution to the organization.

Competition for scarce resource

The recession of the late 1980s came on top of an explosion of international
competition over recent years, which in turn had generated the search for
world-class standards. Together, these factors have seen to it that the relative   *271*

size of the 'pot' for central support activity has grown smaller in most organizations, and those who access it more accountable.

Every central function has had to learn how to maintain and enhance its share of funds and other resources, by coming to terms with the need for continuous measurement and, in particular, the need to identify what measurements will provide (and be seen to provide) the greatest added value for the organization. For the developing IC function, therefore, learning how to manage the measurement process is not an option: it is an essential part of the professional portfolio.

Moreover, experience in the recession showed clearly that, even when IC can make a strong argument that this is the time to increase spending on communication rather than cut back, it has to fight hard to maintain its budgets and frequently fails to do so. The need to create a 'more provable' case is obvious.

On the other hand, developing an effective research and measurement capability related to the success of communication with internal audiences at various levels may well be an area where IC can offer services that are attractive to (and thereby attract funding from) other central functions. Figure 18.1 provides a few examples of areas where this could be the case.

Function/operation	Does the target group understand/accept:
Business development	• why the recent strategic shift (e.g. a change in competitor activity, product/technology, legislation, etc.) was necessary? • what they are supposed to be doing about it?
Finance (or Management Information Systems)	• why a new set of restraints or analysis (e.g. expenditure on land purchase, equipment, environmental issues, safe measures) is required? • how to put the relevant information together?
Marketing/New product	• why everyone (not just sales) should be involved in/get excited about the coming product/new concept development launch? • what to say about it – how it works, what the fascinating facts/chief benefits are?
IT/Manufacturing	• what the latest development can do to transform the organization's/their/their customer's working life or measurable performance output? • how to use it?
HR	• why this new bonus/pension benefit makes us the best employer in this field/location? • how to take it up?
PR	• why our decision to use X in making our product is socially acceptable? • how to find out/pass on more information?

272 **Figure 18.1   Offering services to other functions**

Demonstration of value added

IC must prove it can stand alongside the more mature disciplines in terms of achieving professional management standards generally, and measurement is a big part of doing that. As Robert Galvin put it: 'If you don't measure it, you're just practising.'

Walls full of awards from professional associations cut less ice than practical support for operational activities working towards business objectives, backed up by solid evidence of *the difference made*. Without the high credibility such evidence offers, it will be difficult, if not impossible, for IC to carve out, let alone retain, its independence, its budget and the perception that it has strategic relevance in the organization.

One of the quickest ways to gain credibility is to demonstrate that you have a sure handle on IC costs – even if it then takes longer to relate them to the real value created. For example the trend to reduce overheads and concentrate resources around core activities has made it essential to make sensible decisions on what to keep in-house and what to buy from external suppliers. That means understanding the real costs and impacts of staff functions' activities.

It is not, in fact, difficult to measure such costs: external consultancies who supply communication support services use cost/time measurement systems to identify where resources are used, so they can bill back or take decisions about the best way to improve margins on each job.

By contrast, the in-house situation is often highly obscure. Money spent on internal communication (by a range of functions) is not always 'visible' in the form of a budget, certainly not for in-house costs. Where there is a budget, it tends to be created and spent with relatively little detailed performance measurement. This is complicated by the detached attitude of some finance departments who determinedly make allocations on the basis of previous years no matter what.

But adopting the self-discipline of time-sheets and internal invoice control to establish a value for the time spent by IC staff and others can be rewarding. Detailed measurement will help you make (and *sell*) sensible decisions on what activities to carry out in-house and through subcontractors. It will also enable more accurate assessment of the cost-effectiveness of individual IC processes generally, and thereby to point to areas where unfocused communication activity is costing the organization dearly.

Controls and influence over communication processes

Who 'owns' the right to communicate with various internal audiences is an open question in most organizations. HR (including industrial relations), PR (corporate affairs etc.) and in some organizations, marketing, are long-running contenders. But the IT function frequently has a strong influence over the way communication develops, via its control of communications equipment and systems design capability. Line management has a clearer case than anyone but has rarely exercised the option – and even more rarely, until recently, in

273

any way more sophisticated than by creating a 'command and tell' environment.

Nowadays, the IC function is beginning – if it is well regarded within the organization – to assume responsibility for developing communication strategy and policy and for integrating the various communication systems and media. The keys to extending the ground thus far and further lie in strategic and business awareness allied to professional competence, and the ability to provide realistic and relevant measurements of communication effectiveness across the organization.

Above all, the IC function must find ways of maintaining access and listening to all sections of the organization. Good management contact at all levels is obviously vital but so too is the development and subsequent measurement of upward flows of communication. Without them, IC professionals deny themselves the feedback they need to carry their case; in short, they deny themselves the voice of their market.

THE IMPORTANCE OF DEVELOPING EFFECTIVE CHECKLISTS

The chapters that follow in this part of the Handbook explore a range of research and measurement possibilities. But measurement itself can be a costly and time-consuming business. So whatever method you plan to use, devise a checklist of key questions, like the ones that follow, to which you must always be able to provide adequate answers before racing ahead.

General

- Will the costs of acquiring and analysing the data (including inconvenience and loss of other opportunities) be heavily outweighed by the benefits?
- Will the research/measurement help us achieve our communication goal with substantially greater effect?
- Will it help us reduce costs significantly, without a corresponding fall in quality?
- Will it enhance the IC function's reputation?

Specific

- *Who will take responsibility for initiating change on the basis of this data once analysed?* Sometimes responsibility may be shared between individuals or departments. In such cases, you should have established with them how the responsibility should be shared and what mechanisms are needed to ensure you work together on fulfilling it.
- *Are we asking the right questions?* Have we covered all issues that actually concern people?
- *What level of performance is needed?* Is this a realistic requirement given the resources available to you?

- *Have we gained buy-in to using the results of the measurement?* Who else needs to be consulted – specific managers? the target audiences?
- *Who else apart from top management needs to know the outcome?* What and how much are you going to feed back to the people who provided the information? What promises should you make to these people? Have we defined a mechanism to report back to any wider audience that needs to know the results?
- *Is the measurement easily repeated to check on progress? How frequently?* Will a sample be acceptable? Is it going to compare apples with apples?
- *Have we clearly segmented our audience?* Blanket analysis often hides important data that could have been used to stimulate communication improvements.

HOW TO FIND OUT MORE

Marketing Research, Measurement and Method, 6th edition, by Donald Tull and Del I. Hawkins, Collins and Macmillan, 1992

The Audit of Communication Effectiveness by Mike Woodcock and Dave Francis, Gower, 1994

The Communicating Organisation by Michael Blakstad and Aldwyn Cooper, IPD, 1995

Managing Best Practice: the regular benchmark, employee communications, The Industrial Society, May 1994

19 What to measure

David Clutterbuck, *chairman, The ITEM Group* and
Mike Reed, *Clayton Reed Associates*

In measurement, what to measure *depends to a large extent on why you are doing it. This chapter will help you define clear objectives, set priorities and choose the right tools. It also talks about different 'levels' at which to measure, and how to distinguish 'hard' from 'soft' measures.*

A large UK manufacturing employer recently conducted an employee attitude survey. The consultants carrying out the survey had warned the top team that it had to be prepared to respond to and act on the concerns that would inevitably be raised. Sure enough, the results were far from the ringing endorsement of the management style and philosophy the top team had convinced itself to expect.

The top team's reaction was to attempt to suppress all the bad news. The 'results' were published with only the good news and a very watered down version of the bad news. Of course, people who attended the focus groups and who filled in questionnaires recognized that this was a distortion of their views. The top team buried the survey and did not implement any significant changes based on its conclusions. The only result of the exercise was an even more negative view of the company and the top team.

The moral of this story is that gathering data without a clear idea of how it will be used – along with a clear commitment that it *will* be used – is a dangerous strategy.

CHOOSING THE RIGHT TOOLS

The history of measurement in business is littered with examples of inappropriate selection of measures. Told they have to measure something, managers frequently select measurement criteria that are relatively simple for them to apply, or at best give them a practical basis for organizing the work of their function.

Such measures all too often distort the original purpose, from the internal or external customer's point of view. For example, training departments have traditionally reported the number of training days delivered as an indicator of efficiency and effort. But what the organization, and in particular the line managers who make up the internal customer base, actually want is a measure of effectiveness. In other words, what impact has the training had on the performance of the people who have attended courses and on the capabilities of the workforce as a whole?

IC managers have to be very careful not to fall into the same trap.

The head of one IC function proudly told senior managers that he had increased the number and frequency of core briefs issued on their behalf. Unfortunately, sending out pieces of paper has little to do with how often supervisors are prepared to pull their teams together. The further down the organization the brief went, the fewer actual briefings took place. Action was eventually taken to monitor whether line managers kept to their target number of team briefings each year, but still no account was taken of the quality of those briefings. The critical measure: 'to what proportion of the target audience is the message actually getting through?' was never asked.

ESTABLISHING PRIORITIES

Before embarking on any form of IC measurement, you need to establish priorities. Trying to measure everything isn't practical.

Priority measurements should be those that:

- relate directly to the core business objectives
- enable you to take specific action
- relate to outputs that matter to IC's key internal customers.

CHOOSING THE LEVEL OF MEASUREMENT

IC measurement can take place at one of several levels:

- message
- programme/campaign
- channel
- medium (including competency)
- environment.

Measurement at the message level

This level of measurement concerns how well key concepts are disseminated around the organization. Such concepts would include the vision and values, *277* or the general direction of the corporate strategy, or at an operational level, day-to-day information handling. Message measurement involves asking questions such as the following:

- was the message received?
- was it directed at the right audience?
- did people understand it?
- did they believe it?
- did it modify their opinions or behaviour?

Programme/campaign measures

These measures focus on the success of conveying a specific subset of messages, perhaps over time. Campaigns usually aim to gain commitment from the targeted audience to a specific business objective. Typical examples might be a customer care or service quality programme, a cost-reduction exercise, or an attempt to persuade people to join a voluntary scheme such as an Employee Share Ownership Programme.

They examine *process* from the following standpoints:

- which media were most effective in getting the messages across?
- success in integrating the various media
- relevance to the message
- quality of planning
- general cost-effectiveness.

They measure *outputs* in the form of defined changes in the level of people's understanding and/or behaviour. They involve questions such as:

- what percentage of people did we want to sign up to this programme?
- what percentage did so?
- is there a discernible pattern to those who did and those who didn't?
- did people buy into the special options designed for them?
- what were the top ten questions being asked on the campaign helpline?

Figure 19.1 provides a simpler, more memorable guide to the distinction between these two types of measurement.

Campaign processes	Campaign outputs
Efficiency of planning, timing and execution	Did anything change?
Media processes	**Media outputs**
Efficiency of each medium used	Effectiveness of each medium used

Figure 19.1   Processes and outputs

Channel measures

These measures examine what happens between two or more internal audiences, irrespective of the media used. They ask questions such as:

- how efficiently does each department or function communicate with its internal suppliers/customers?
- how well do the trust networks between different functions work?
- how efficiently do messages get through front-line supervisors to their teams?

Managing the channels is of great significance because these are the information arteries of the organization. Most organizations have very little information about what happens within specific channels, although they may have some data about the effectiveness of individual media.

Media measures

These measures are concerned with individual methods of reaching the target audiences. They aim to answer questions about the process such as:

- what do the recipients feel about each piece of media? (e.g. do they look forward to receiving it? do they find it interesting? relevant? useful? well presented? credible? value for money?)
- how often are team briefings actually held (compared with how often they are supposed to be held)?
- what proportion of the distribution was wasted/went to the wrong people?
- how much jargon and gobbledegook is there on average in our internal correspondence?

They also aim to answer questions about the outputs, such as:

- how effective is this medium (including, for example, line managers) in getting the message across?
- does the target audience have a greater understanding of the business priorities as a result of this communication?
- is the team briefing system helping to increase the quantity and quality of employee participation?
- how readable, understandable and friendly do customers find correspondence they receive from our organization?

When the medium for communication is a person rather than a 'vehicle', competence has many dimensions, from verbal and visual presentation to report writing; from reading body language to the effectiveness of appraisals or selection interviews. Most organizations have yet to come to terms with communication competency and what they could gain from it.

279

There is a significant opportunity here for the IC function to take an integrated approach. It would mean setting clear standards and developing and implementing viable measures to assess the progress of individuals, teams and the organization as a whole against those standards.

Resulting measurements would include:

- has communication training resulted in improved communication competence?
- are we experiencing fewer mistakes from communication breakdowns?
- are we seeing improved relationships between internal suppliers/customers?
- are we seeing improved relationships between the organization and its customers?

Environmental measures

These measures are concerned with the factors that affect how messages and media are received, independent of how well designed/competent they are. In other words, they look at the receptivity of the audience.

How well communication is received can be affected by factors such as the volume of change taking place within the organization. For example if people experiencing rapid, continuous change have not become acclimatized to it,

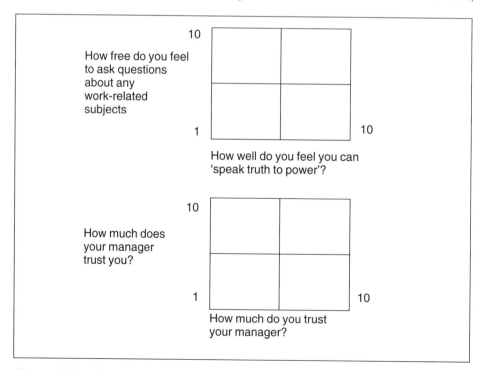

Figure 19.2   Communication climate surveys

they are likely to be resistant to news of more upheaval, attempting to shut it out of their consciousness and ignore the implications.

Receptivity may also be affected by general morale and motivation or by cultural factors. For example, supervisors giving performance appraisals to a team member need to be aware of how direct criticism will be regarded. In some cultures, it will be welcomed, in others resisted defensively and in others produce complete communication close-down. Figure 19.2 shows the kind of questions that can be used to conduct surveys in this area and can be correlated to indicate the climate for communication in an organization.

HARD AND SOFT MEASURES

For practical purposes, IC consultants tend to divide all such measurements into *hard* and *soft*. Hard measures provide quantifiable *performance* data. Soft measures put some statistical emphasis on *perception* data. Figure 19.3 gives an indication of how these measures can work in relation to output and processes.

Outputs	Changes in attitude, motivation	Changes in behaviour and understanding
Processes	Audience appreciation	Automatic audience feedback
	Soft	**Hard**

Figure 19.3   Soft and hard measures (outputs and processes)

Some examples of hard and soft data are shown in Figure 19.4.

Hard measures	Soft measures
% who receive a publication	% who say they are motivated by what they read
% who read a publication	% who believe it to be a credible and trustworthy source of information
% who know and understand the corporate vision and values	% of people who feel they can identify with the vision and values
Volume of usable suggestions/ suggestions contributed	Main reasons people say they do/don't
Average value of suggestions	% who feel their suggestions are listened to/valued
Average spend per internal customer	Degree to which customers feel they are receiving adequate, reliable communication
% of projects delivered on time	Internal customers' views of IC on service quality criteria
Number of informal briefing lunches run for top management	Value placed on them by participants

Figure 19.4   Examples of soft and hard measures

Hard measurements that tell a valuable story are far and away the most difficult to devise and, because of that, they hold the risk that managers will place too much reliance on them or misinterpret their significance.

For example top management may well conclude that an increasing IC spend per employee is a cost-control failing, when it may in reality be a rational and essential response to an increase in the pace of change. The IC function can in practice take the precaution of also measuring the relative pace of change, by adding up planned and contemplated change initiatives over the next 12, 24 and 36 months and applying an impact weighting to them.

Soft measurements often have a different, equally serious pitfall. They are easily influenced by external events. An employee attitude survey can be radically different in results, according to when it takes place for example. While most companies would avoid carrying out an extensive attitude survey during a series of delicate and bad-tempered salary negotiations, it is not unknown for organizations to do so at a time of combined bad profit figures and hefty salary increases for the board.

The prevailing economic climate can also have an impact on feelings and perceptions – people are likely to be less motivated, for example, if they know that the jobs market is depressed to the extent that they couldn't go elsewhere if they wanted to. Even the time of year may have an impact: people generally feel more upbeat looking forward to their summer holiday than when they come back from it!

In practice, a mixture of hard and soft measurements is usually needed to make a business case. What measures you choose will depend on the circumstances. However, the basic rule that should always apply is 'how relevant and rigorous would our internal customers regard this measure?'

20 Surveys

David Clutterbuck, *chairman, The ITEM Group* and
Mike Reed, *Clayton Reed Associates*

*Data collection methods suitable for IC use come in a variety of shapes,
sizes, cost and effectiveness. Selecting the most appropriate combination is
normally a matter of experience and will probably remain so, because the
variety of requirement is too large for simplistic rules. The remaining
chapters in this part of the Handbook cover most of them by looking at three
of the most common 'umbrellas' under which research and measurement
work is carried out in organizations, beginning here with an introduction to
the most basic, surveying.*

Surveying to collect facts or opinions appears to be an easy and rapid option
for collecting IC data, adaptable to almost any circumstance. That can be true,
but there are several caveats. Conducting research that is genuinely useful is
not something to be undertaken lightly, whichever means you choose. In the
case of surveys, simple questions tend inevitably to produce simple answers.
And even the 'simplest' of questions can be misinterpreted.

For example a US-owned multinational with a substantial UK subsidiary
introduced an appraisal system, which it attempted to implement internationally. The initial results appeared to indicate that employees in the UK were far
less motivated and ambitious than their US counterparts.

Radical changes in employment policy for the UK were discussed, until it
was pointed out that the language of the appraisal questionnaires was being
interpreted very differently by people from the two cultures. For example to
the question 'Do you feel challenged by your work?', US employees replied
enthusiastically yes, they did – meaning that they felt it gave them excitement
and interest. The British employees, however, assumed that the question
meant 'Do you find your work difficult?' and, of course, replied that they didn't!   *283*

Effective surveys take time to design and pilot. Badly constructed surveys can (and all too frequently do) reflect negatively on the function responsible for them – and IC can least afford to set a poor example in this regard.

Moreover, there is increasing resistance among internal customers to completing questionnaires, especially if they can perceive no direct benefit from doing so. 'Survey fatigue' is a real problem in companies with extensive service level agreements between departments. In one public sector enterprise in the middle of a service quality campaign, managers estimated that between 15 per cent and 20 per cent of their internal mail was surveys of one sort or another.

It is possible to offer some form of reward for taking part – gift tokens, bottles of wine, free entry into a draw for a much bigger prize like a balloon ride or a weekend away for two. This can work and is usually valued by participants, but some organizations believe offering rewards for participation runs counter to creating an ethos where everyone is expected to be involved in continuous improvement.

The most common use of surveys is the standard employee attitude survey, designed to test how a target audience feels about a range of subjects – from relationships at work to pieces of media, to the organization's performance on equal opportunities. If it is not possible to conduct a survey of your own, based solely on attitudes towards communication and its effectiveness, it would be a start to make sure the wider survey included a set of such questions.

PAPER-BASED SURVEYS

The standard survey medium is the paper questionnaire. It is relatively cheap to prepare and run. Standard questions and response levels are well known (contact organizations like The Industrial Society or the British Association of Communicators in Business for samples). And the use of simple questions wherever possible and the avoidance of too many open questions all make it relatively easy to analyse.

As a one-way communication, paper-based surveys have severe limitations in that you only get answers to the questions you ask. You can increase the flexibility and value of the written questionnaire by issuing it on computer disk or by e-mail, or even on the Internet, as an interactive medium that personalizes each questionnaire according to the user's answers, by drawing on a library of subsidiary questions. Trying to do this on paper would result in a very complex, user-hostile and bulky medium.

It is, of course, generally much easier to use interactive media for internal audiences than for external.

FACE-TO-FACE SURVEYS

Face-to-face survey work, including telephone surveys with individual respondents, can offer something of the best of both worlds. They can combine 'tick box' quantitative data with qualitative data from follow-up questions – though this would require a fairly high level of interviewer, with a good knowledge of the subject. Depending on sample size and number/complexity of questions, telephone surveys can also be quick and relatively cheap to carry out, using, for example, in-house reception or administrative staff during slack periods.

Figure 20.1 shows the results of a telephone survey carried out at home improvement retailer B&Q. Five questions were asked in all, three others relating to range modifications and a milestone in company success. The data were also broken down into head office and in-store staff, and by store type.

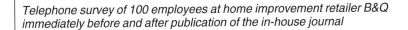

Telephone survey of 100 employees at home improvement retailer B&Q immediately before and after publication of the in-house journal

    Q1   People were given the name of the company's new buying philosophy and were asked what it was.

           A = correct, B = wrong, C = don't know

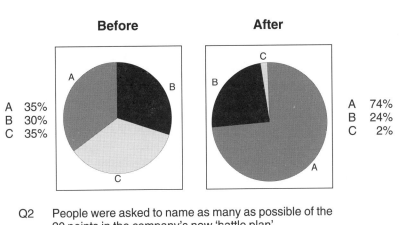

Before

A   35%
B   30%
C   35%

After

A   74%
B   24%
C   2%

    Q2   People were asked to name as many as possible of the 20 points in the company's new 'battle plan'.

           A = 16–20, B = 11–15, C = 5–10, D = 0–4

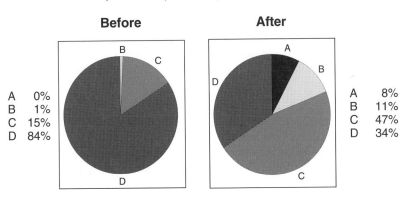

Before

A   0%
B   1%
C   15%
D   84%

After

A   8%
B   11%
C   47%
D   34%

Figure 20.1   Telephone survey results

Of course, the fact that people can recite beliefs, values or even the bulk of a 'battle plan' does not guarantee anything. A true measure of effectiveness is a measure of corresponding action. Considerable empirical research in the advertising world has explored the connection between advertising recall and corresponding shifts in attitude. Much can be learnt from such research and the relevant methods which, as far as we are aware, have not yet been applied in the internal communication field.

OBSERVATIONAL AND INFORMAL RESEARCH METHODS

Simple observation and informal research are underrated and often-overlooked mechanisms for gathering valuable information. So before you embark on a more expensive alternative, it is always worth considering what information your own eyes and ears can tell you about the effectiveness of communication in the organization.

For example do you need a reader survey to confirm that your internal newsletter is poorly read by staff, when a quick look at the shopfloor could easily tell you the same thing: piles of corporate newsletters have not been picked up or are clearly discarded unread. Moreover, an informal chat with one or two key people will probably reveal the main reasons why it is happening.

However, the representativeness of such informal research can easily be called into question, particularly if 'bad news' is reported. Senior managers are unlikely to be persuaded to abandon a communication method to which they have become accustomed, for example, on the basis of 'anecdotal' evidence. They may be even more disinclined to listen if the ineffectiveness appears to stem from a more deep-seated disquiet among the target audience, related to larger corporate issues – such conclusions arising even from controlled focus groups have been questioned.

The 'grapevine' too – often considered one of the most valuable sources of information about how internal audiences are thinking – can be difficult to tap into effectively, and therefore produce information that will convince managers.

With all informal research, careful preparation is required to ensure that your case is not open to the challenge that the views of 'the most vocal' respondents are over-represented.

FOCUS GROUPS

Focus groups provide more qualitative data but, depending on their structure, may not yield much in the way of quantitative results. Some research companies use focus groups to identify the key issues for a survey and provide anecdotal evidence; then design a quantitative survey based on what has been learned.

The facilitator role is vital to the effectiveness of focus group/workshop activity and requires a degree of professionalism if your results are to be relied on. In certain circumstances, for example, participants will speak more freely to an external facilitator than someone they see as part of the 'establishment'.

CONSULTATIVE PANELS

Basically a variation of focus groups, panels consist of semi-permanent groups of internal customers formed to give regular or occasional feedback on IC issues, plans and initiatives. While these are very useful, they should not automatically be taken as giving a representative view, especially as the independent perspective of the members will gradually erode as they become more familiar with each other and with the IC function and the restrictions it works under.

SOME GUIDING PRINCIPLES

Before you begin any formal survey work, whatever form it takes, you may find it useful to take on board the following principles. They are taken from a best practice statement being put together by the Human Resource Special Interest Group within the Market Research Society. The Group was formed as a direct result of the proliferation of opinion research among organizations' internal audiences.

- It is important for respondents to feel that any survey addresses the issues that are important to them, and not just those which are important to senior management.
- Care should be taken in the composition of focus groups as more junior staff may feel inhibited if senior employees are present.
- There must be senior management endorsement, and commitment of the management team who have the authority to make and implement decisions regarding the issues raised by the survey.
- Questionnaires should be piloted prior to the main survey.
- There should be communication of the survey prior to, and during the survey to encourage responses.
- The survey questionnaires should be accompanied by a covering letter from the chief executive or other senior manager. This letter reinforces that the process is a two-way communication, and outlines plans for feeding back results and actions that may follow.
- Time is set aside for employees to complete questions, or if questionnaires are to be returned direct to an external consultancy (which also reinforces confidentiality) at least two weeks are given to return the completed questionnaire.
- If a sample of employees is undertaken, sampling must be on a random basis.
- If sampling is the chosen methodology, the size of the sample must taken into account that small subgroups within the organization are adequately represented.

- Response rates are likely to vary between employees. Those who are more senior and have longer service are more likely to respond. If there is significant variance in response rates between different categories it may be necessary to weight the data during analysis.
- To alleviate concerns that respondents can be identified in small sub-groups, the number of demographics covered by the survey should be kept to a minimum.
- In accordance with the Market Research Society Code of Conduct any practitioner can guarantee to respondents that the employer will never see the original questionnaires.
- Adherence to strict anonymity also means that responses from groupings of staff should not be reported if they total less than 10 without the express consent of all those concerned.
- Clients of the research should not be allowed to sit in during group discussions.
- It is sensible to allow a year before conducting a follow-up survey.
- Commitments to feed back results must be honoured in full, to demonstrate that views have been listened to and action, where appropriate, has been taken.
- Group discussions following the survey can be valuable to consider the results of the survey and bring about a feeling of ownership of the results.

HOW TO FIND OUT MORE

Employee Attitude and Opinion Surveys, by Mike Walters, IPD, 1996

21 Audits

Mike Reed, *Clayton Reed Associates*

This chapter looks at communication audits, which integrate many of the data collection methods outlined in the previous chapter. A full audit is a structured and rigorous review of how an organization is currently communicating internally (and externally) and attempts to measure the effectiveness of the communication process.

Audits are becoming more popular as Internal Communication becomes more recognized as a strategic tool. In particular, the need to re-align the outputs of communication processes with corporate goals and values is leading more organizations to conclude that there is a lack of understanding about how their internal communication *really* works. Moreover, such in-depth analysis requires sizeable budgets, which means the validity of other, less formal research mechanisms is likely to be called into question by senior managers used to making decisions on the basis of verifiable information.

Should a communication audit be conducted in-house or by an external consultancy?

Experience suggests the answer is often to get help from outside. Not all organizations have the skilled resource needed (e.g. for facilitating focus groups) or if they have it, can afford to pull it all together at the right time.

More important, employees are very often suspicious about why a survey, let alone a complete audit, is being conducted: often they feel the need to be guarded in their responses. Managers in particular can have problems with the idea:

- fear of criticism
- research viewed as confirmation not exploratory

- lack of in-house research skills and resources
- inexperience in managing results.

Guarantees of confidentiality and of accurate reporting from an external source are often better received than similar promises from IC or HR personnel would be.

However, as when any IC work is contracted out, an in-house professional must be in a position to *manage* the process and ensure that the particular solution developed is right for the organization. Being a good buyer of IC services means being fully alert, certainly to the processes and principles involved, which is what this section of the Handbook attempts to cover. Some of the more technical aspects of data collection and analysis are named without explanation in what follows: for those interested, further reading is suggested at the end of this chapter. Either way – whether in-house or external resource is used – the audit manager needs to be aware that concerns can be alleviated if staff are well-informed about the audit's purpose, the reporting methods (e.g. the level of identity protection) and the expected use of results.

THE AUDIT PROCESS

A full audit is usually made up of eight distinct stages, as illustrated in Figure 21.1.

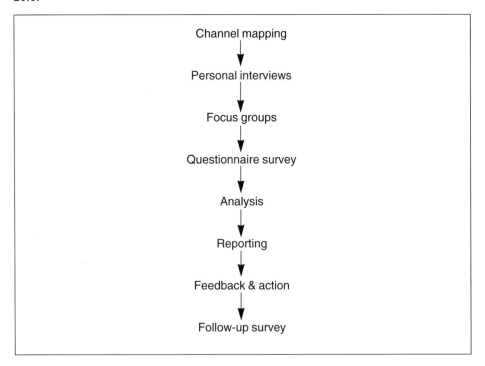

Figure 21.1   A full audit process

Channel mapping

If the communication process is to be utilized as a strategic tool, communication flows in all directions – down, up, horizontal, diagonal, internal–external – need to be mapped and their purposes properly understood. Each area of the organization needs to be examined: it is not unknown for one group of people to have an effective cascade briefing mechanism and multi-channelled upward and sideways communication at their disposal, while another group is relying on ineffective memos and irregular team briefings.

So before attempting to seek people's opinion, invest time in mapping which channels are currently open and in use. Then look at the media currently employed in them. This may sound obvious, but many people fail to put this basic building block in place – largely because of the general failure to distinguish between the channels or routes where communication should and could be taking place and the principal media being used.

Figure 21.2 can be used as a template for identifying where communication gaps may lie.

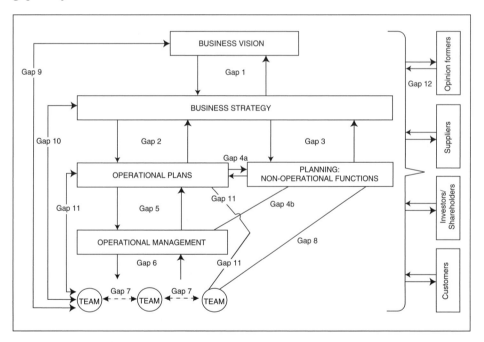

Figure 21.2   Where are the critical communication gaps?

Not only are regular media mapped during this stage, but the means by which different types of messages, day-to-day as well as those being exchanged via ongoing programmes and one-off campaigns, are travelling through the channels.

For each method of communication being used, the mapping process should put on record its:

- target recipient(s)
- avowed purpose
- corporate 'owner'
- cost
- speed of message delivery
- frequency.

Mapping media/processes involves creating a logic trail, detailing each activity that goes into delivering a communications output. For example, a logic trail for a traditional form of team briefing might look something like that illustrated in Figure 21.3.

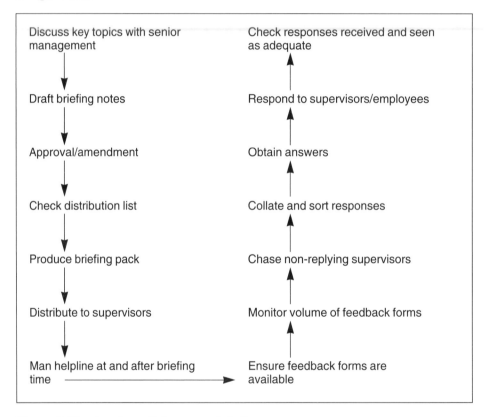

Figure 21.3   Logic trail for team briefing

Having drafted out what you *think* happens, check what really does happen, by trying out the diagram on people involved and by observing tasks as they are done. (See next section.)

Many improvements often take place simply from carrying out this analysis and observation alongside those involved. Each activity can be broken down into smaller tasks if you discover that it is a particular source of problems or wish to concentrate on it for any other reason.

Personal interviews

During this preliminary work it is worthwhile running a number of personal interviews with key people to establish what messages they are attempting to diffuse through the organization and what means they currently use to do so.

Such people would include:

- the senior team (as the strategic message makers)
- the heads of functions (as the policy implementers)
- media 'owners'
- selected line managers.

Focus groups

To determine whether potential gaps identified in the mapping process actually exist, if so why and the extent to which they present problems or lost opportunities, usually means carrying out an extensive and carefully designed survey.

So the next stage is to use focus groups to identify the principal communication issues involved. The danger of running surveys without this preliminary stage is that key questions and nuances can be overlooked. Once set up, the same focus groups can be used again later to permit potential solutions to be explored in depth.

Group participants should be of roughly the same grade/level and participation should be on a voluntary basis. A number of groups will be necessary to reflect adequately employee composition within an organization.

The output of the groups will be a number of hypotheses that can be tested during a quantitative survey.

Questionnaire survey

Qualitative findings give a 'feel' for how communication flows are currently travelling and how effective communication processes are. Only a quantitative survey can provide hard effectiveness data and measures.

Budgetary constraints typically govern research methodology and sample size. Self-completion questionnaires are the most common form of survey vehicle. Some companies prefer a 100 per cent census; others prefer random representative samples. Random samples are not without their problems – people who do not receive a questionnaire may feel neglected and worry why they have been omitted from the survey.

Appropriate segmentation must be built into any survey design. Management audiences in particular often have a view of communication vehicles that is distinct from the rest of the organization. The argument is often made, for example, that the more senior management dislikes an employee publication, the better the job it does in getting through to the bulk of the target audience. And how well the explanation of a relocation policy has been received would typically need to be measured across at least three audiences: *293*

- those directly affected
- their line managers
- the relocation administrators.

Professional questionnaire design employs a variety of scaling and rating techniques.

A *semantic-differential scale*, for example, can be used during a survey when researching the effectiveness of team briefings. Respondents are asked to read each set of phrases or adjectives and mark the cell that best reflects their views towards the briefing sessions (Figure 21.4).

Lively	☐	☐	☐	☐	☐	☐	☐	Dull
Helpful	☐	☐	☐	☐	☐	☐	☐	Unhelpful

Figure 21.4 Semantic-differential scale

A *Likert scale* requests respondents to indicate a degree of agreement or disagreement with a number of statements. Frequently employed in marketing research and employee attitude surveys, it is an ideal technique for use in audits. Figure 21.5 shows an example taken from a questionnaire developed for a large UK insurance company.

	strongly agree	**agree**	**neither agree nor disagree**	**disagree**	**strongly disagree**
I receive enough information to do my job.	☐	☐	☐	☐	☐
I have no means of expressing my views to management.	☐	☐	☐	☐	☐
My supervisor/manager has good communication skills.	☐	☐	☐	☐	☐
My supervisor/manager keeps me regularly informed of the company's progress	☐	☐	☐	☐	☐

 Figure 21.5 Likert scale

Analysis

Blanket analysis can hide important trends: along with careful survey design, professional analysis techniques may be needed to reveal important correlations. For example providing the number of responses is sufficiently high, cross-tabulation can uncover meaningful results between departments, divisions, countries or operating companies.

It is possible to carry out thorough analysis using frequency distributions, chi-square, non-parametric correlations and tests for significant differences (typically Mann–Whitney and Krusal–Wallis).

A growing body of opinion among professional researchers considers that univariate and bivariate analysis techniques (which analyse just one/two questions at a time) can fail to uncover important issues in internal opinion research. Multivariate analysis techniques such as factor and cluster analysis (which analyse three or more questions simultaneously) are increasingly employed.

Considerations surrounding respondent anonymity must be paramount during this stage.

Reporting

Few 'report back' situations are simply that. For a start, whoever is receiving the report will probably expect to hear not only conclusions but recommendations and, as someone aspiring to add to the debate at the strategic level, the audit manager will want to suggest a range of ideas for going forward.

The reporting stage is *the* opportunity, not simply to prove where the communication barriers and gaps exist, but to put together creative platforms that will feed through either directly into strategy/tactics or into further research. It is also your golden chance to gain understanding and commitment from senior champions (see Chapter 6).

A typical audit report contents list is shown in Figure 21.6.

Having decided how to structure the content of your report, it would be easy to forget that the process of reporting back is in itself a communication exercise – probably among the most important in the audit as a whole in terms of ensuring an effective outcome.

First, establish exactly who your audience is. In the case of a full audit, the report deserves to be presented at the highest executive level of the organization. It may also be useful to conduct advance runthroughs (either the whole or in part) with individuals. At every presentation stage, the needs, sensitivities and expectations of the audience must be taken into consideration – despite the fact that the information may in itself be considered 'factual' – otherwise the key messages may not get through, let alone stand any chance of being acted on.

Take care in choosing the presentation team: strike a balance between carrying technical, creative and political clout. The presentation and materials, including the tone, style and appearance of the report itself, should be *295*

An audit of internal communication prepared for Contact plc

Executive summary	**2**
Background and methodology	**3**
Channel mapping	5
Personal interviews	7
Focus groups	8
Questionnaire survey	9
Recommendations	**10**
Close the communication gaps	12
Develop a communication strategy	15
Continuous improvement – training	20
Implementation of best practice benchmarking (data sharing)	25
Recommendations for additional research	26
Follow-up survey timetable	27
Audit results	**28**
The channel map	29
Media/process logic trail	32
The communication gaps	34
Things we do well	37
New opportunities, as seen by:	
senior executives	45
other managers	47
everybody else	49
Summary of qualitative findings (focus groups)	53
Summary of quantitative findings (questionnaire)	58
Identification of best practice benchmarking indicators and partners	65

Figure 21.6 Audit report contents

designed for maximum impact, clearly. But before being tempted to use the full range of audiovisual devices available to you, that means establishing the presentation norms of the forum you will be addressing. Take any risks consciously, not from ignorance.

Feedback/action

Feeding back results and ensuring that action is not only taken, but seen to be taken, is critical to the audit process.

From the point of view of the participants, it is a matter of common courtesy, of showing respect for them and their contribution. By contrast, research without feedback can make people feel used, jeopardizing credibility and future cooperation. It should therefore be regarded as much as an obligation as an option.

But in any case, from the point of view of the IC function, it is another powerful opportunity to promote common understanding on critical issues, and to gain commitment to your plans for improvement, this time reaching wider and wider circles of influence.

Again the key is to be aware of particular audiences' needs at every turn. The level of detail required, and the means of communication will differ accordingly.

At one extreme, you may find yourself conducting what is in effect a personal training needs analysis with a particular manager or members of a functional group whose communication capability has been shown by the survey to need upgrading. At the other, it may be appropriate to create a special publication to publicize the findings and action points (in effect your communication strategy) to the organization as a whole.

In every case, you will want to point to the survey results as the basis for your actions – in other words, to show IC strategy to be customer-led.

Follow-up

The whole purpose of an audit is to identify immediate opportunities for improvement and, by providing a set of benchmarks, for continuous improvement in the future. Progress in individual areas can be measured along the way but it is also important to maintain a complete picture of what is happening and in particular, whether standards generally are improving or slipping.

Follow-up surveys – possibly mini-versions of the original but maintaining a core of key questions – would typically be carried out at yearly intervals (although some organizations are moving to even more frequent sampling). A reduced number of feedback groups would take place on a similar basis, using the same participants wherever possible. Again, some organizations have found it useful to turn successful focus groups into standing consultative committees which meet at more frequent intervals.

The outcome of this new research would prompt a further cycle of feedback, new targets and actions.

The channel 'map' you have created can be used as a source of advice when structural changes are proposed, as well as simply being updated and reviewed. If parts of the organizational structure change radically, mini-audits may become necessary in the areas affected. Eventually, as the organization evolves, it will become necessary to repeat the exercise as a whole.

How to find out more

Marketing research, measurement and method by D. S. Tull, D. I. Hawkins, 6th edition, Collier Macmillan Publishers, 1992

Market Research: a guide to planning, methodology and evaluation by Paul Hague and Peter Jackson, Kogan Page, March 1996

Marketing research by D. A. Aaker and G. S. Day, 4th edition, John Wiley & Sons, 1990

22 Benchmarking

David Clutterbuck, *chairman, The ITEM Group*

Best practice benchmarking involves comparing your activities with those of others – either another internal department or an external organization. It is a powerful technique for continuous improvement, increasingly applied across service as well as manufacturing activities. Internal communication is certainly as susceptible to benchmarking as any other business activity and can benefit as well as or better than most functions from benchmarking comparisons.

As a part of the planning process, best practice benchmarking enables the IC function to:

- 'borrow' other people's good practice in a systematic way
- demonstrate competence by comparison with other companies – or if the company is large enough, with other departments
- identify opportunities to improve the efficiency and effectiveness of internal communication processes
- quantify the gap between the effectiveness of its processes and those of 'best in class' IC functions.

What does it involve? Best practice benchmarking (BPB) is a series of planned activities aimed at:

- establishing the critical processes in an organization or function
- defining meaningful measurements for each element of those processes
- finding other organizations to compare against
- using the knowledge gained to make improvements in your own processes.

Comparisons are made at two levels – metric and process. Metric comparisons provide the quantifiable information (the what) that makes you question processes (the how).

For example a company that achieves a response rate of 60 per cent for an employee opinion survey might consider that to be quite good – until it finds out that another comparable company regularly achieves 85 per cent. This metric benchmark acts to unfreeze assumptions about performance, stimulating the IC manager to ask the critical question 'What is that they do and we don't, that makes that 25 per cent difference?'

Before you start to benchmark your processes, you have to gain a deep and clear understanding of them. See Chapters 19 and 21 on mapping processes for an example of how it can be done. Without this insight, it will be very difficult to make a meaningful comparison of the metric data, let alone understand how the other company's performance is achieved.

DEFINING MEANINGFUL MEASUREMENTS FOR EACH PROCESS ELEMENT

Most steps can be measured in some way. For example what percentage of supervisors send in their feedback forms within a week of their briefing? Or how quickly do you normally produce a briefing pack?

Measurements will generally relate to:

- cost
- quality
- time
- productivity
- impact (e.g. response rate or changes in perception).

Simply mapping and measuring the processes in this way will give you considerable insight into problem areas and enable you to set some priorities, both for things you can set about improving immediately and for activities where you suspect that external comparisons might show a significant performance gap.

You will obtain significant one-off benefits by instituting improvement plans based on the internal measurements. The greater benefits come, however, from comparing your processes and measurements with those of other companies.

Assuming they have mapped processes similar to your own, you can make very efficient use of time spent comparing with other companies. You will be able to identify precisely where they outperform you and by how much. You will also be able to pinpoint where their processes differ from yours and begin to assess the extent to which the process differences influence the performance differences.

The main difficulties lie in ensuring you are comparing like with like. For example can you compare cost per recipient when production costs vary on a non-linear basis according to volume? Can you compare reader responses for a publication aimed at pensioners with one for employees? At a metric level, probably not, because the two audiences have very different lifestyles, interests and amount of time to respond. However, there may be an opportunity for process comparisons – for example in how the two periodicals obtain and promote prizes, how they present and position readers' letters and so on.

The more you think about external comparability when you design your internal benchmarks, the more substantive the comparisons you will be able to make.

FINDING OTHER ORGANIZATIONS TO COMPARE AGAINST

In some ways, this is the easiest step of all. You can identify benchmarking partners through a variety of routes. Among the most common:

- IC networks you belong to
- trade federations for national/international comparators
- Chambers of Commerce or TECs for local comparators
- articles in the IC literature
- a targeted search by any of the top four or five IC consultancies
- via the Internal Communications Benchmarking Network (see below).

Before arranging any visits to other companies, it is best to filter them to identify those who really have something to offer. There are some key questions to ask.

- Has this organization already mapped and measured its IC processes?
- Is there any aspect of IC in which it is clearly a 'best in class' company?
- Are there sufficient similarities between their situation and yours to allow for meaningful comparison? You need to maintain a balance between organizations like yours, who will probably operate such similar processes that there is little radical to learn, and organizations very unlike yours, from whom you may be able to gain little by way of metric data, but much in terms of different approaches to process.
- Are they already familiar with the concept of best practice benchmarking, or will you have to educate them first?
- Are there likely to be any conflicts of interest?

A few telephone calls or faxes can usually establish the most likely candidates.

Where possible, try to exchange as much data before the benchmarking visit as possible. You need to spend the time on understanding the figures (How are they obtained? Are they really a meaningful comparison?) and exploring the other company's processes in detail. You need, at the end of the initial visit, to be fairly clear about what both sides could gain from the exercise.

Old hands at benchmarking extol the virtues of having a detailed list of questions to ask, of dividing responsibility for pursuing themes among the visit team, and of holding brief review meetings both immediately before the visit (to ensure everyone knows what they are to do) and immediately after, to capture the learning. It also pays to review the benchmarking process, with a view to applying continuous improvement there, too.

USING THE KNOWLEDGE GAINED

As the exemplar of good communications practice, it behoves the IC function to communicate its findings to key corporate audiences as soon as practical. Some changes will be relatively easy to implement within the current resources and authority of the department; others will need to be sold to senior management or to line manager customers. You may find you have a sufficiently interesting tale to tell to include a short story in the employee newspaper.

Applying the knowledge you have gained is one of the best tests of how well you have benchmarked. If you can't make any significant improvements you are either already world class (and who is going to believe that of themselves?) or you have not benchmarked effectively. The most common causes of the latter are inadequate measures or poor selection of benchmarking partners.

BENCHMARKING NETWORKS

A few companies, such as Lloyds Bank, have put together relatively informal benchmarking networks, usually quite small and relying mainly on broad process comparisons. Several new IC-specific networks have sprung up in response to recent growth in the industry, like the Employee Communications Association and ASPIC (Association for Strategic Planning in Internal Communications). These, plus seminars and conferences arranged by a variety of organizations, all provide opportunities for similar sharing of good practice on an informal basis (see Appendix to Chapter 16, p. 256). Figure 22.1 shows three types of benchmarking associations to which you can choose to belong, according to the kind of information you wish to use.

However, the most valuable benchmarking comes from a systematic gathering of metric and process data.

Several companies have recently come together to form the Internal Communications Benchmarking Network, coordinated by The ITEM Group,

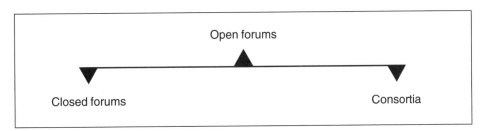

Figure 22.1   Three types of benchmarking associations

which will act as a clearing house for this kind of information. The idea is to collect metric data from participating companies and carry out research to map the critical processes that lie behind best in class performance.

TYPICAL CATEGORIES OF METRIC DATA

Three areas of internal communication activity seem most susceptible to metric measurement. These are:

- the structure and role of the IC function
- communication methods, such as team briefing
- management processes.

Figures 22.2, 22.3 and 22.4 will give you a series of starting points for thinking about this kind of measurement and whether you would find it valuable to share with others.

Communications strategy and planning

- frequency of strategic review
- frequency of planning review
- content of IC plans
- time invested in IC planning

Staffing, salaries, budget

- number of IC professionals per 100 employees
- IC spend as a percentage of total employment costs/total business overheads
- spend on internal vs external communications
- distribution of spend between salaries, continuous media and projects

Scope of responsibilities

- comparisons based on a list of key deliverables

Figure 22.2   Structure and role of the IC function

In general, there seems to be no difference between the Internal Communication function and any other staff function when it comes to benchmarking. As yet IC may be too new to have developed the wide spectrum of common processes that characterize some others, such as HR or IT for example. However, professionalization of the function is bringing such processes into existence, and with them the necessary common standards.

Employee periodicals

● number of periodicals to employee base
● editorial staffing and costs per page/1000 words of:
  – standard text
  – key message text
  – expert text
  (commissioning, writing, subbing and proofing)
● senior management input
● frequency of publication
● volume of reader feedback
● efficiency of distribution
● cost of distribution
● reader evaluation (what percentage read it, value it? frequency?)
● number of active correspondents per 100 employees

Team briefing

● frequency
● employee evaluation (what percentage value it, believe what they hear?)
● percentage that happen when they are supposed to
● volume of upward feedback

Suggestion schemes/speak up schemes

● number of useful/usable suggestions per employee
● average value of suggestions

Employee attitude surveys/communication surveys

● frequency
● scope
● number of questions
● percentage response to key questions
● cost
● percentage of employees who feel they receive sufficient information about the business
● percentage who feel they are listened to
● percentage of issues identified that lead to specific improvement action

Other media

● cost per minute of videos for employee communications (by category: high, medium and low visual impact)
● frequency of use of electronic mail, notice-boards and other media

Figure 22.3   Key communication methods

Measurement

- what processes the IC function measures

Large projects

- when IC budget agreed
- mean deviation from IC budget
- frequency of being asked to assist in communications aspects of large projects
- IC function input (strategic, tactical, implementation)
- whether measurement of communications impact included

Other face to face

- time spent by senior managers talking to target audience
- percentage of management time spent in meetings
- percentage of management time spent in appraisals

Figure 22.4   Management processes

Part VI
IC STRATEGY AT WORK

23 Andersen Consulting IC and recruitment: communicating efficiently, as well as effectively, with potential employees

Robert Greenshields *of Pauffley PRL*

Successful recruitment, to a large extent, is concerned with successful communication: some would argue the reverse is also true. This case study looks at the use of corporate branding and campaign management with a (would-be) employee audience. It shows how you can position an organization's profile as a whole with a large audience and, at the same time, target only certain individuals, gaining their interest against strong rival bids for attention.

The business of recruiting high-flying graduates has now become as competitive as any product market-place, with a range of leading employers competing to attract the best people from a limited pool of talent.

That may seem a surprising statement following the recent substantial growth in the number of university graduates in the UK. However, top employers generally set very high standards for academic results, extra-curricular achievements and personal qualities, which only a select few graduates can satisfy.

The challenge for employers trying to recruit from this group is to develop a career 'product' that not only meets the resourcing needs of the business but also satisfies the requirements of top graduates and is promoted in a way which makes it attractive.

As the world's leading business and technology consultancy, Andersen Consulting takes the planning and implementation of its graduate recruitment very seriously. Operating in a highly competitive and expanding business, its quality of service demands a regular input of outstanding talent.

Over recent years, the firm has established itself as a leading name in the minds of students at many campuses. This followed a major effort to establish a new corporate identity following its independence from Arthur Andersen, the accounting firm.

Evidence from focus group research regularly produces comments like 'Andersen Consulting is the best known recruiter on campus' and the numbers of applications received position the firm as one of the leading recruiters in the UK.

The problem is that attracting more applications is not a measure of success. More applications lead to extra work for recruiters in screening and interviewing. Inevitably it also leads to disappointment when unsuitable applications are rejected.

This latter point is not simply one of sensitivity. A complexity of recruitment marketing – particularly for a service business – is that many students are not only potential recruits, they are also potential future customers for the firm. Therefore, while ensuring that you are attracting the right people, in the right numbers, it is important to leave a positive image of your firm for others. Put simply, Andersen Consulting's problem was that its success in building awareness of its name meant it was attracting too many applications, many of which were unsuitable.

MARKET RESEARCH

As part of its regular review of recruitment marketing strategy, Andersen Consulting worked with communication agency Pauffley PRL to consider what action was needed. The first stage was to conduct research among target students to identify what they wanted from an employer and how they viewed the firm. Research was also conducted among recent recruits to the firm to identify what attracted them to Andersen Consulting.

The main attributes high-flying students wanted from an employer included predictable factors such as career prospects, salary and training. But they also included a number of softer factors:

- exclusivity/prestige
- variety/challenge
- chance to work with 'people like me'
- market leadership
- future growth potential.

These were all factors that Andersen Consulting believed it was well placed to deliver. However, the research indicated that this message was not getting through to the key target market as effectively as it might. For example:

- the high awareness of the firm's recruitment marketing led to the assumption that it was recruiting heavily and could not therefore be exclusive

- the work was widely seen as 'computer programming' and therefore not offering variety
- the firm's people were often perceived to be stereotypes and slightly arrogant – not 'people like me'
- the firm's market position was unclear but there was a feeling that it had been a success during the 1980s boom and its future attractiveness was not understood.

Based on this research – and on Andersen Consulting's own recruitment experience – the firm established the following brief for Pauffley PRL:

- reduce the quantity and improve the quality of graduate applicants
- position Andersen Consulting as a first-choice career option for high-flying graduates
- develop recruitment materials to communicate a highly distinctive working culture and environment.

ACTION TAKEN

The strategy to meet the above brief was developed taking into account previous experience and based on the research that had been undertaken. A key element was the creation of a new 'employer brand' for the firm, which positioned it as a highly selective employer of élite students rather than a hard sell, ever-present recruiter.

Establishing the employer brand involves all the different ways in which an employer presents itself to its market. This ranges from printed material and the way candidates are treated to the venues used for recruitment activity.

However, the two key elements of the campaign were the targeting strategy and the communication package.

TARGETING STRATEGY

As the target market was defined as the relatively small group of outstanding, high-flying students, it was essential to develop a strategy that focused on the best.

Targeting was based first on selecting universities according to their previous recruitment success records, existing level of awareness of Andersen Consulting and the suitability of students/courses.

The marketing campaign would then be tailored to suit local needs depending on these factors. For example at target campuses where the name was already well-known, the focus would move towards a more exclusive and selective approach.

On those key campuses where visibility was not so high, the marketing campaign would continue to build awareness without undermining the required image. Depending on the campus, this campaign would either be general or targeted on relevant departments.

In addition to the usual promotional activities such as brochures, presentations and careers fairs, a number of sponsorships were undertaken of carefully selected individual events and clubs on several campuses. Support activities such as summer placements and specialist courses were organized and promoted. In line with the targeting strategy, invitations to these could be issued on a pre-selected basis, rather than purely through open advertising.

COMMUNICATION

In developing the new employer brand for graduate recruits, the design, style and content of the communication material is an important factor.

In keeping with the desired brand, it was felt that the design solution had to be highly distinctive and exclusive.

First, a design style was developed using symbolic headlines based around the concept of the 'limited edition'. In general, the style avoided the use of striking colours or strongly-stated visual images on the cover. This, combined with brochures which were not the traditional A4 format, helped to position the Andersen Consulting material as distinct from the mainstream of graduate marketing material.

To preserve the exclusivity, the main brochure was not made widely available. Rather a distinctive pocket-sized trailer leaflet was produced for circulation through careers services, at presentations and at recruitment fairs. This combined facts about the firm with a flavour of the working environment and culture.

One of the key aims of the trailer leaflet was to encourage students to decide *before* applying whether they considered themselves likely to succeed in the selection process. This was done by clear definition of the requirements in terms of academic record and personal qualities, backed up by straight comments such as a quote from a new recruit saying – 'I don't have any illusions. I am expecting to work harder than I've ever worked before.'

The main brochure, which was available only to selected graduates, did not take a hard-sell line. Instead, it was designed to deliver some honest assessments about the demands of a career in consulting. Through a series of interviews, six individuals – four of whom did not even work for Andersen Consulting – provided their own unbiased assessments of the firm.

The brochure included an interview with a client stating 'you may have to sacrifice social plans sometimes – but look what you get in return' and a friend from university of a recent Andersen Consulting recruit saying of his friend: 'Even though there are aspects of his lifestyle that do appeal, I don't think I'd be happy in that environment' (Figure 23.1).

The aim of these statements is not to put everyone off applying – there are plenty of positive things to say about the firm. But the approach is one of honesty – stating what working at Andersen Consulting is really like and what recruits need to succeed. In summary, it is in the interests of both parties that people should apply only if they are sure that the firm is right for them.

In addition to the main brochures, a series of leaflets was produced to

Figure 23.1 Graduate recruitment brochure

support other activities such as vacation courses and business management workshops. A range of advertisements also appeared in the national and specialist press.

THE OUTCOME

The success of a graduate recruitment marketing campaign is highly tangible in that its effectiveness can be measured quickly in terms of the number of suitable applications and the rate of conversion to accepted offers.

This campaign was introduced fully in the 1994/95 recruitment season so the initial effects were only beginning to be measured at the time of going to press. However, in 1995 the indications were that the quality of applications was improving and that numbers were being controlled. Both the quality and numbers of recruits were highly satisfactory to Andersen Consulting.

A less tangible issue for recruitment marketers is the effect your activity is having on the people who don't apply. Employers always need to be concerned that if the message is wrong, they could be missing out on people who are highly suitable. This applies particularly when, as in this case, your campaign sets out to discourage some people from applying.

As far as the Andersen Consulting campaign is concerned, research was conducted among final year students and candidates who had recently decided to join the firm. This showed that the previous image was changing. Where the firm's people in the past were seen as stereotypes, they are now seen as a more diverse group of people who are more like 'one of us'. This applies particularly when graduates have met representatives of the firm at presentations or interviews, for example.

People tend to have very polarized views of the firm – they are either very attracted or definitely not. They recognize that they would be expected to work very hard but that the rewards are high. However, not everyone has a clear understanding of what the firm does and therefore they do not always appreciate the opportunities it can offer.

The lessons of this research are that the campaign is beginning to succeed in positioning the firm as a highly selective employer. However, the firm needs to ensure that the people being turned off are the ones it wants to discourage. The research also identified factors which can be promoted more strongly in the future.

CONCLUSION

Recruiting high quality graduates requires a thorough and up-to-date understanding of your target market. After all, unlike most other markets, the people in it change almost entirely every two or three years. It is also made up largely of 'first-time buyers'.

By understanding the market, not only can you tailor your career offer to ensure it appeals to the people you want, you can also develop the content and style of your promotional campaign to attract them.

In the future, this task will become even tougher as businesses become more global, as the education system changes and as employers continue to adapt their career offers to reflect changing work patterns.

24 Bass Taverns
Seize the day: winning senior management commitment

Anna Foster, *employee communications and quality manager*

It's something IC professionals are for ever saying: without backing from the top, you never get good communication in an organization. So how do you get that backing? And how do you make sure it goes further than fine words or good intentions? This case study shows how the IC team at Bass Taverns – the pub retailing division of Bass plc – seized on senior management's determination to push through a change programme, and turned it into an opportunity to integrate communication into the company's strategic and operational frameworks.

In January 1993, Bass Taverns began considering radical reorganization using Business Process Redesign (BPR). A project team of senior managers was set up to work towards implementation.

There were early indications that communications would have a significant role to play. The team saw results from The Cranfield School of Management's symposium of 65 BPR practitioners in 1993, which predicted that the hardest thing to change would be the company culture. This was underpinned by the results of research nearer home in 1994, among Bass Taverns' own top 150 managers, conducted by a market research group, and from its annual employee survey that same year.

Confronted with all these findings, the board realized that to achieve the radical changes in the company's operational processes it wanted, a change of culture, and therefore a comprehensive communications programme, would indeed be needed. This coincided with the appointment of an employee communications manager.

WERE WE JUST 'LUCKY'?

At that point, you could say senior commitment was in the bag, and Bass Taverns had what every communications professional dreams of: a board that has seen the light, as it were, and has been prepared to do something about it!

It is true that boards in general respond well to 'hard evidence' such as that provided by external and internal survey work. Certainly they are an extremely valuable starting point for getting senior managers on your side. But only a starting point. When an organization decides to 'change' itself, the primary need is for visible changes in behaviour at all levels of management, beginning with board members – and particularly in terms of communication styles and awareness. In how many organizations do all the good intentions falter right there?

There was also the very real danger that the new appointment would give senior managers the opportunity to abdicate their responsibilities and leave it all to the 'specialist'.

So, the point at which the stage seems set fair is more likely the point at which you have to start making your own luck.

It begins with recognizing the need to gain commitment, not just to communication in general terms, but to all aspects of a fully-developed communication strategy. We therefore developed one and, as you would expect, it made use of existing processes and tools:

- the company magazine – *Inn Touch* – would introduce a regular page covering various change projects as well as special features (Figure 24.1)
- a regular audio magazine would carry interviews with senior managers explaining the rationale behind change
- the core brief would include regular updates on change.

It also added new elements:

- change team roadshows for all corporate staff
- personal letters from the chairman and chief executive
- change focus groups
- video aimed at improving understanding of the cultural changes needed
- national conference for 1300 corporate and pub managers
- reorganization launch events for all 2700 pub managers
- briefing packs for 25 simultaneous senior management-led briefings on reorganization.

But the real key to the success of the programme lay not in the detail so much as in shaping it to gain senior management buy-in.

INSIDE:

■ **The New Retailing Initiative – the vital step forward – pages 2&3**

■ **Who's who – the new-look organisation – pages 4&5**

■ **The new structure – pages 6&7**

■ **What happens next? – page 8**

OCTOBER 3 1994: A REORGANISATION SPECIAL

SIGHTS ARE FIXED ON BEING THE BEST

A change in culture to create a company driven by the needs of its customers is shaping the future for Bass Taverns

ANNOUNCING radical changes to the Company's structure and ways of doing business, Chairman and Chief Executive Philip Bowman, said: "We have to focus on what our customers want, both now and in the future. Today's successful companies will be those that anticipate the needs of the customer of tomorrow."

The wide-sweeping changes announced include:-
● The structure for operations management through 22 Retail Directors and 145 Retail Business Managers
● The way the estate will operate in teams of around six pubs grouped in Community, Wet-led Destination or Food-led Destination segments
● Details of the operations support teams and locations
● Details on the structure of each corporate department and its role.

"We have to change our way of thinking and running the business to achieve our objective to be Britain's No 1 Pub Retailer," said Philip Bowman.

"We must achieve a culture which is customer-led rather than production-driven. This means having the market intelligence to predict trends to the year 2000 and beyond and to give customers what they want now and in the future. To achieve that, a root change is needed in Bass Taverns."

He explained why the publicised re-organisation had not gone ahead in June, as originally planned. "As the new Chief Executive I needed to take stock of the Business. To do this I needed to study the recommendations of the Business Process Redesign teams. I listened to a

Philip Bowman: we must be customer-led rather than production driven.

ion on our perceived strengths and weaknesses."

Philip Bowman said a commonly held view was that Cape Hill was a barrier to change rather than a force for change, hence the re-organisation and the appointment of three Operations roles on the Board, as opposed to one.

Board position of ... ctor – Food ... s the

ing closely with the pub business should be at the sharp end, to meet customers and be more attuned to their requirements.

The greater devolvement of control to Retail Directors brings with it greater accountability. "I'm all in favour of delegating authority but only if people are accountable for their own performance, profit and investment.

growing importance of food for Bass Taverns. "Catering will help drive the business forward and we will progress a chosen few branded food concepts. Opinion formers have told us for years that we have been slow on food. Now we can change that view."

The reduction of staff and the reorganisation of key departments ...

Appraise

"We will employ the best, train the best and pro-actively manage careers. We undertake to honestly and openly appraise people's performance and prospects."

The business will stand or fall on the success of its licensees and their retail staff. "We have to ensure we have the right people and incentivise and motivate them to succeed.

"We are all players in a team and we work together to achieve common goals," he added. This teamwork ...

"It is common-sense," stressed Philip Bowman. "We can pool best practices, share experiences and use the expertise we have amongst our pub managers much more effectively."

Expectations of Bass Taverns' performance have been increasing within the Bass Group and externally. "We need to focus on profit generation to meet these expectations. On average we operated 11 per cent fewer managed houses this year than last year. This trend cannot continue. We must improve the results of under-performing outlets rather than place them on the market for sale. In parallel, the acquisition and construction of destination outlets will be increased to speed the repositioning of our estate to meet customer requirements.

"Change will remain a way of life," said Philip Bowman. "We ... need to review ...

Figure 24.1 *Inn Touch*

WHAT MAKES A CONVINCING STRATEGY?

A well-made business case

We aligned our communication strategy's objectives directly with those of the business change plan and placed emphasis on achieving appropriate looked-for benefits in terms of changes in attitudes, behaviours, morale, effort, efficiencies and so on.

The strategy also emphasized strongly that when you impose a change situation on top of existing pressures in today's business climate, enabling people to communicate effectively becomes key – especially for managers.

Build tactics around facts wherever possible

Survey information continued to be used, this time as a basis for suggestions, for example employees' clearly-stated preference for face-to-face communication led to the inclusion of so many roadshows in the plan.

It's their responsibility but you can help

Any communication strategy must make it clear that employee communication is the principal responsibility of senior and line management. However, simply *having* an employee communication strategy, and having communications professionals to help implement it, will increase their chances of meeting this responsibility.

Parallel the business timetable

Our change communications timetable was drawn up alongside the known day-to-day business activities of the company, such as the budgeting period, start of the new financial year, copy dates for the company magazine, public holidays, etc. This helped managers visualize the whole process and anticipate heavy workloads and tight decision deadlines.

Give senior managers a leading part to play

Timing our detailed programme in with key business activities over the course of a year also allowed us to create plenty of opportunities for senior managers to show their commitment – not only to the BPR programme itself, but also to keeping everyone fully informed of the progress being made.

Sensible timing also helped us give our management team the right kind of support. In the case of the national conference, for example, the dress rehearsal was scheduled a full week before the actual event. The presenters felt that it was far better than leaving it to the day before. It allowed everyone the luxury of time to fine tune their presentation delivery. Interestingly enough, the autocue facility was made available for a couple of extra days. Nearly everyone made the time to take advantage of the extra practice this afforded.

Figure 24.2 shows the agenda for the conference and the telephone feedback audit questionnaire.

Make sure they have the right skills

The strategy emphasized the importance of training for all managers and allowed for its inclusion. We recognized that with increasing pressure on managers' time, communication – and in particular taking time out to learn *how* to communicate – is the one area often sacrificed or forgotten.

As for the senior managers, it soon became apparent that some were far more suited to delivering messages face to face than others. Additional presentation skills training was provided where it was felt it would be beneficial.

Show yourself to be proactive

To gain senior level support, communications activities are best directed towards anticipating what needs doing to *complement the aims* of the organization – rather than simply reacting to events or doing 'the obvious'. In putting a plan together, you can lead the way in discarding the old tired methods, and experiment with new ideas so the senior team becomes confident of always having a fresh and innovative communication strategy underpinning its business objectives.

Take people with you

In dealing with all our audiences, we endeavoured to explain the rationale behind each of our decisions as we went along.

BUILDING ON THE OPPORTUNITIES CHANGE BRINGS

Press for early decisions on timing, then keep managers informed

A key factor in the success of the change programme as a whole – as well as its communication – came from prompting the board into an early decision on when a full announcement on BPR would be made. And then communicating the date.

This made it possible to:

● plan events with some certainty
● illustrate to board members, via a regularly updated timetable, how their ongoing decisions would impact the timing of the process as a whole
● help the board make some of the less pleasant decisions, knowing that it must stick to an already-communicated date.

THE NEW RETAILING INITIATIVE

Wednesday, 29th March 1995
Tally Ho Sports & Conference Centre

AGENDA

2.15 p.m.	Welcome	Ian Payne
	The Need for Change	Ian Payne
	Development of the New Retailing Initiative	Ewan Harries
	How will it affect the LHMs & their Partners?	
	– Teamworking	Kieran Rabbitt
	– Empowerment	Simon Fitzgerald
	How does it affect the Retail staff?	
	– Succeeding with Customers	Tony Thwaites
	What support will the LHM receive?	Hugo Broadfoot
	The story so far . . .	Hugo Broadfoot
3.45 p.m.	Close	

(Coaches will depart promptly for returning
staff to Cape Hill & Crystal House)

'CHANGING THE WAY WE DO BUSINESS'

318   **Figure 24.2   Retailing initiative**

NEW RETAILING INITIATIVE
AREA 21 LAUNCH EVENT

Telephone Feedback Audit

1. **How did you find the length of the Launch event?**

    Too Long   Just Right   Too Short

2. **Following the presentations, do you have a better understanding of what the New Retailing Initiative is all about?**

    Much better   Slightly better   No

3. **Did you find the information as to why the NRI has been introduced useful? (Did it clarify the situation for you?)**

    Strongly Agree   Generally Agree   No

4. **Is the format and role of the LHMs teams clearer to you now?**

    Strongly Agree   Generally Agree   No

5. **Was the role of the Area Support Team clearly explained?**

    Strongly Agree   Generally Agree   No

6. **Do you have a clear understanding of what will happen next in terms of the NRI roll-out?**

    Strongly Agree   Generally Agree   No

7. **Did you feel that the information provided at the Launch was relevant to you?**

    Strongly Agree   Generally Agree   No

8. **Do you feel that anything was omitted from the Launch, that you would have found useful?**

    Yes (Allow for comments)   No

9. **How would you rate the overall Launch?**

    Excellent   Good   Fair   Poor

10. **What was the one question, if any, for you that was still unanswered at the end of the presentations?**

11. **General Comments (if any):**

Figure 24.2   concluded

Figure 24.3   Credit card

Establish policy, not just tactics

Creating the change strategy gave us the chance to lay down a policy that good communication should become a core measure of management ability at Bass Taverns and to have it built into managers' performance appraisals.

All managers have been issued with further confirmation of this, in the shape and size of a credit card, which highlights *Five things that every manager should do* (Figure 24.3).

1. *Communicate company goals and strategy* – so staff know what the company is trying to achieve and why, and how it plans to get there.
2. *Set objectives for your team* – so everyone knows what is expected of them.
3. *Formally review and appraise people* – so they know how they are doing.
4. *Hold regular team meetings* – so that people know how what they are doing fits together.
5. *Walk the job* – to keep in touch with what's happening on the ground.

Make the most of employee feedback

Effective feedback systems don't only make employees feel good. As feedback improves and the level of expectation grows, so senior management commitment to communication increases. That is the crucial combination which leads to communication becoming genuinely integrated into how the business operates.

WHAT HAPPENS NEXT?

We go back to the drawing board. We continue to manage our communications strategy no differently from the way other business managers would theirs. It must be subject to regular review in order to meet the new challenges facing the organization: what is right in today's environment may be grossly inadequate in tomorrow's.

We therefore:

- assess the progress we have made with communications over the past year
- evaluate what in general worked well and what didn't
- examine the feedback from specific communication exercises to assess if the delivery method was appropriate and timely, and whether its messages were relevant and understood
- review the potential impact of electronic communications and technology
- establish how we will keep everyone informed of the company's progress and reinforce the company culture in the year ahead.

As before, however, we will also consider how best to maintain management commitment to communication. The aim for any communications practitioner in this area can be simply expressed: that senior managers – indeed all managers – automatically consider the communication implications of a business decision as an integral part of making it, not as a sudden bolt-on at the end.

At Bass Taverns, we would not claim to have totally reached that point yet, but thanks to our change programme, we are on our way.

25 The Body Shop
Upward communication: choosing means, implementing it and measuring it

James Harkness, *head of internal communications*

Upward communication is not easy to achieve. Years of 'command and tell' culture in British business have left a strong stamp on managers and employees alike. But The Body Shop has attempted to break many UK business norms and this is one. While the company may have unique advantages – like a willing and well-regarded role model in Anita Roddick – the organization as a whole puts enormous effort into making employee involvement in communication a reality. This case study outlines some of what happens.

Communication has always been at the heart of what we do at The Body Shop. We encourage our staff to enter into dialogue with our customers – and if we truly believe our front-line people are the company's most important asset, then opening up communication channels with them is perhaps the first element of good service.

While that is a worthy sentiment, it is not easy to achieve in an international company. We have achieved tremendous growth as a business. From one shop in Brighton 20 years ago we now have almost 1400 shops in 45 countries and we trade in 24 languages. We continue to open a new shop, on average, every two and a half days. That scale of growth gives us additional challenges in maintaining our information channels and in creating supporting mechanisms that enable us to hear staff's suggestions and act on them across the globe.

This case study will focus on some of the mechanisms we use, how we implement them and how we monitor their success.

DIRECTOR-EMPLOYEE DIALOGUE

The business is rightly identified very strongly with Anita Roddick, its founder and chief executive, who opened the first shop and who continues to be the main driver for success in everything that we do.

Everybody wants to see her, whether it's the world's press, or staff in some remote shop. We realized early on that she couldn't be in all places at once and this led us to make regular video programmes to enable Anita to share with staff her vision on our values and products.

However, video is primarily a one-way information channel. What we needed was to get staff's views on the information they were receiving, their ideas for new products and how they believed we were achieving our mission. Quite simply what we wanted to achieve was direct communications between Anita and staff.

To start the process, Anita produced her own newsletter, *Gobsmack*, to let staff know what gets her adrenaline going. We also featured Anita, and other directors, on our regular video programmes and newsletters so that staff were familiar with the issues important to the company (Figure 25.1).

Figure 25.1 *Gobsmack*

This process started the flow of information and we supported it with a programme called Boardwalk which 'diarizes' directors to, as we call it, 'walk the talk'. In other words, we ensure that in their diaries, every month, there is a regular time when they visit different parts of the business to meet staff and find out at first hand what is important to them.

To generate feedback direct to directors we opened up a number of channels to ensure intimacy of these communications. Anita's personal fax number was provided to all staff and appears on every issue of *Gobsmack*. Staff can also e-mail her, or any other director, on any issue and are guaranteed a reply.

We also provide a series of special coloured envelopes for urgent communications with directors. Green is for issues that concern the environment and gold for staff to draw a director's attention to people they believe deserve special reward or recognition for 'going above and beyond the call of duty'.

Red envelopes are for those issues where staff have raised concerns or suggestions with either their managers or maybe a corporate department such as HR and where they feel they are not getting satisfaction. With a red envelope, they can address it to a director of their choice and the designated director is obliged to respond within 48 hours. The communication is strictly confidential between the addressee and the member of staff (Figure 25.2).

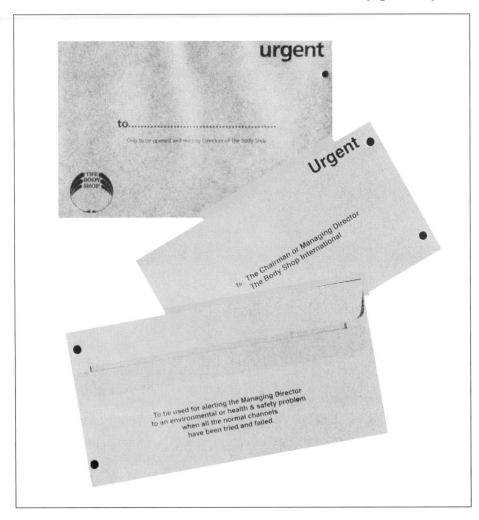

Figure 25.2   Envelopes for urgent communications with directors

INVOLVEMENT THROUGH IDEAS

While vertical communication is vital, we also want staff to speak up about issues that will improve the business. To capture these thoughts we use and actively promote our staff suggestion scheme – Ideas Boards. These exist throughout the company and are where staff are encouraged to provide ideas on how we can improve the way we work.

The ideas are collected every month by Corporate Communications and it is our responsibility to ensure that they are fielded to the most appropriate person and responded to both on the Ideas Boards and in *LA News* – our staff newspaper. As a feedback mechanism, it is very open: all the ideas and the responses are available for both staff and visitors to see.

This, I believe, is a practical demonstration of the openness of our communication and 'keeps managers on their toes' – if they say that 'an idea is currently being considered' staff soon see if they are considering it or not! (Figures 25.3 and 25.4)

Figure 25.3   Ideas Board

INVOLVEMENT IN COMMUNICATIONS VEHICLES

I also encourage people to speak up and contribute to our communications. Our staff newsletter is a contributions-driven vehicle and around 80 per cent of the copy arrives unsolicited for each issue every month. This helps ensure that we reflect staff views and that what the company needs to say is balanced by the audience's needs.

For our head office staff and people who work on our manufacturing and   *325*

Figure 25.4 *LA News*

warehouse sites in the UK we produce a monthly video programme called *The Pod*. To differentiate it from our other video programmes and to ensure that it reflects staff's views, we audition for a staff presenter each month, who contributes to the programme's content.

COMMUNICATOR NETWORK

An important part of our communication infrastructure is our Communicator network.

In every department we have a Communicator who is responsible for 'ensuring that communication happens in their area'. These people work with their managers to ensure that communication meetings take place on a regular basis in all departments. The Communicator plays an active role in these, ensuring that our campaigns and values feature as frequently on the agenda as production and efficiency performance indicators.

In our shops we have PROs (Public Relations Officers) and they perform a similar role, ensuring that communication happens both internally with staff and in the local community with the media and local organizations.

All these mechanisms are great for ensuring staff have both a process and an opportunity to speak out on a range of issues. But these regular channels need at times to be supplemented to meet special needs.

INVOLVING PEOPLE IN ISSUES AND CAMPAIGNS

326   Using one-off initiatives, I feel we can continue to motivate staff to speak out on our values and our campaigns. Our values and our campaigning activities are one of the most tangible ways in which The Body Shop differs from a more conventional company. We recognize and accept that you don't motivate staff to sell a moisture cream. What we do, however, is to ensure that our business is a force for social and environmental change and hence much more than a 9–5 job.

On a practical level, we do that by supporting campaigns targeting the millions of people passing through our shops. We use our shop windows to motivate people to take action on a range of issues.

Inside our shops and in our head office departments we use Action Stations where staff can sign a petition, write a letter to their MP, or simply get information on current campaigns. At times we also open up special telephone lines where staff can get additional advice or give their views.

We use our video *Soapbox* where staff can record a short video message on an issue they feel strongly about. The *Soapbox* is a powerful tool for me when I am trying to convey the emotion behind the message to senior managers.

NO BLAME CULTURE

One of the principal reasons our Speak Up strategy works is that we have a 'no blame' culture – so people are not afraid that they will be judged on the comments or ideas they give. I believe this is the key to obtaining staff participation in the first place.

To continue to achieve this degree of involvement requires the organization to communicate the results of the feedback, however unpleasant, and most importantly, to *act* on it.

ACTING ON CONTRIBUTIONS

From my own experience with other organizations I think too many of them are prepared to engage staff in dialogue without thinking through at the outset how the organization will respond. We continue to receive the volume of upward communication that we do because we act upon it. Staff, therefore, see it as being worthwhile.

Just as importantly, directors and senior managers are prepared to commit both the time and the energy to dealing with upward communication because it has clear benefits for the business and helps us achieve our mission.

1996 saw the publication of our *Social Statement* which has involved us talking with our key stakeholder groups in our first social audit. Although the *Social Statement* is already the result of considerable feedback from our staff, around 72 per cent of whom participated, the launch of this document will be for us the platform for further dialogue with staff on how we continue to integrate our values into everything that we do.

To be effective, the Speak Up strategy must be viewed as never-ending and integral to everything that we do.

26 The Boots Company Communicating financial information

Nicholas Wright, *head of employee communications*

The benefits of belonging to a large, well-established organization with a quality reputation like Boots are easily recognized. You might almost expect the ethos of such an organization to communicate itself to internal audiences. But Boots has never been fooled into such complacency. Particularly in the 1990s, with a third of the total workforce employed other than by the original Boots The Chemists store chain, the centre has been proactive in endeavouring to spread a unifying business philosophy throughout the group. Seen as critical to that process has been the reporting of financial information to employees, one of the most challenging of all internal communication tasks.

The Boots Company attaches real importance to communicating financial information to employees. Why? Because the group's central philosophy is *the creation of shareholder value*.

The fact is that The Boots Company is no longer just Boots The Chemists. In other words, Boots' general financial health – and therefore the creation of shareholder value – is, to a great extent, a function of the results of several individual businesses.

BTC is certainly still the largest business in the group, in both sales and profit terms. It employs more than 60 per cent of the workforce – over 50 000 people in over 1100 stores the length and breadth of the UK. But it is just one of nine strategic business units.

Other retail interests include Halfords and Boots Opticians. Then there is an over-the-counter healthcare business in Boots Healthcare International, which develops and markets well-known brands such as Strepsils, Optrex and Nurofen on a worldwide basis. Boots Properties manages a sizeable nationwide property portfolio. And a manufacturing operation, Boots Contract Manufacturing, supplies predominantly health and beauty products to customers, both within and outside the group.

Creating shareholder value is a process that Boots believes people at all levels, in all the businesses, can and should contribute to in a variety of ways. And it believes that fundamental to their ability to do so is the widespread sharing of performance information. Financial results in particular, through their influence on the share price and the amount that is paid out in dividends, have the clearest possible bearing – though not the only one – on shareholder value.

The communication objective is simply expressed: supply the right information, in a form that enables people to answer the question: 'How did we do?' The rather more difficult challenge is how to convey what may necessarily be complex data, on a subject with which many people may not feel at ease, and in which they may initially think themselves to have no interest.

And the challenge becomes even more interesting when it comes to communicating the corporate position. To be useful, financial information, more than most, has to be seen in its full context, but for most of our employees the need is to at least begin with the information closest and most relevant to them, and then maintain their interest while moving through to the 'big picture'. Figure 26.1 illustrates how this works in The Boots Company.

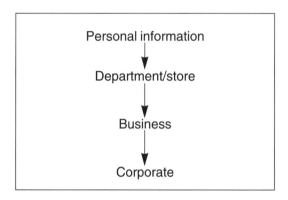

Figure 26.1   Moving through to the 'big picture'

WHERE WE STARTED FROM

The communication of results had always been important to The Boots Company. By the early 1990s, an annual report to staff was in place, along with an accompanying video and a general commitment to deliver.

In practice, particular problems were beginning to emerge:

- the importance of communicating financial results internally had become devalued through a continuing emphasis on their external communication
- the time taken for the results to reach employees was increasingly out of step with the immediacy expected and reported by the external media
- the process of communication was given less priority than the production of individual items relevant to the results
- little attempt was being made to segment the type of information being delivered or assess in any rigorous way the most appropriate means of delivery
- different approaches had been adopted each year in relation to specific items with no underlying rationale, leading to a lack of consistency and coherence.

In other words, financial information was being 'delivered' in a literal sense, but as a package it tended to be undifferentiated, poorly integrated and lacking in any sense of urgency.

To meet a general, and in theory undemanding objective – 'to deliver targeted communication in a suitable way to meet group and business needs' – change was needed.

THE APPROACH WE TOOK

We wanted to achieve incremental improvements rather than wholesale change for its own sake, but nevertheless to base our changes on research rather than tinkering in piecemeal fashion.

The only research of relevance was ten years old, having been conducted in 1982, and was primarily an assessment of the role of the company newspaper, though it also examined the annual report to staff. Although it was clear more recent research would be required, timing and logistical issues meant that this would not be possible before communication of the 1992 annual results.

A commitment was made to research immediately after the results communication process, as a starting point for subsequent years. But in that first year, we attempted only small changes to the process and the tools used. Relying on judgement and anecdotal evidence collected from a variety of sources, we identified areas that could be improved, including the elimination of wasteful duplication. Any changes made in this way would be used as a learning opportunity to provide consistent and cohesive building blocks for subsequent years.

At the same time, we recognized that certain of the issues relating to our concerns could not be resolved in one go and should be left alone at this stage: much of the work in future would concern attitudinal change and communication principles, rather than mechanics.

None the less, the rationale for the communication of financial results in that first year did exhibit some significant changes.

Employees were recognized not as a discrete and distinct group of people but part of 'an overall and overlapping communications audience'

They were identified not just as employees, but also customers, possibly members of pressure groups and certainly part of the local community. We recognized that they see and digest national and local media and that they talk to others outside work: family, friends and acquaintances. The communication of the results, therefore, needed to be framed to accord with the company's external communications strategy.

The audience was segmented and a service level based on speed of delivery was assigned to each element of the communication programme

This raised issues in relation to the robustness of the employee database (primarily used for personnel purposes rather than as a communication tool). Could we ensure that the 'ideal' audiences would be reached, let alone communicated to, either directly or through improved distribution systems?

The group centre's role as initiator of the results was clarified

It was aligned with the business philosophy as a whole in the context of the relationship between the businesses and the centre.

The then latest technology was harnessed

Fax transmission largely replaced mailings to improve speed and minimize duplication of effort.

Unnecessary duplication was assessed

The roles of all the existing communications involved were reviewed together, as components of a single process: the full news release and its notice-board version, the employee report, the employee newspaper, the annual report to staff video and the line management briefing structure (see Figure 26.2, p. 332).

We aimed for language that everyone could understand

The financial information was to be communicated in a style that was simple and succinct but not patronizing.

THE INITIAL COMMUNICATION PACKAGE

We divided the communication need into four elements.

1. Reporting the general results.
2. Providing information of relevance to employees' own workplace/ business area.

Method	Immediate	Within 1 hour	1–6 hours	6–12 hours	'Next day'	1–3 days	4–7 days	1–3 weeks	3 weeks +
			Results				Reflection		Review
Electronic mail									
Fax									
Internal mail									
External media – national – local									
Briefing packs									
Management conference									
Notice-boards									
Company publication									
Staff councils									
Local manager briefings									
Report and Accounts									
Report to staff									
Results video									

Figure 26.2 Techniques and timing sheet

3. Reviewing the previous year's performance.
4. Giving the outlook for the coming year.

1. Reporting the general results

News release

The full 17-page news release, which over the years had grown in complexity to meet the changing demands of the City, was distributed by fax and hand delivery to each of around 100 senior managers. This followed a commitment to communicate the results worldwide within an hour of their being released to the London Stock Exchange.

The release was also distributed, this time via the internal mail system, to a wider tranche of about 1000 managers as a basis for specific onward briefing.

A 'cut and paste' version of the full release was posted on all company noticeboards within 24 hours of the announcement, though this was normally achieved 'same day'. The full text of this version is given in the Appendix to this chapter.

Briefing pack

A briefing pack was distributed to the company's top 100 managers the next day, at an already well-established review meeting, where the chief executive and the finance director repeat the same presentation as that heard by City analysts and the media 24 hours earlier (see Figure 26.3, p. 334).

The pack contained:

- original copy of the news release
- scripts of the presentation
- hard copies of the slides plus contact details for sourcing OHP or slide packs
- other information, e.g. a front cover proof of the report to staff
- briefing notes.

Employee publications

The main employee company publication at that time, *The Boots Company News*, was rescheduled to ensure publication within two working days of the announcement. This allowed time to reflect on media reaction but recognized its role as a 'news' paper.

External media

Ostensibly there to deliver messages to external audiences, external media were recognized as having an important influence on internal perception. The principle of employees hearing the results first hand from the company is fine

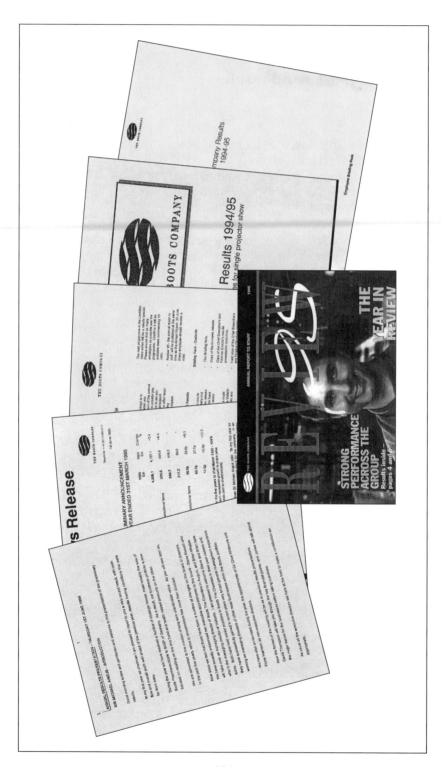

Figure 26.3   Employee briefing pack

in theory, but it ignores the realities of the communication process.

The problem is always most acute in Nottingham where the company is headquartered and where some 9000 of its 75 000 employees work. With local radio bulletins and a lunchtime edition of the evening paper, it was accepted at an early stage that for some staff these would be primary sources of information. Briefings with the local media were therefore made a priority to ensure messages being given internally and externally were consistent.

Staff councils

Staff councils provide a formal system for employees to express their views and to share information, knowledge and experience on business and employment matters. Within a week of the results announcement, the biannual combined central staff council was held.

Elected delegates, representing all companies within the group, attended a presentation on the results by the chief executive and finance director, followed by a question and answer session. The delegates received the full news release together with relevant press cuttings. Following the main meeting, the delegates broke up into individual business unit councils to discuss the results in more detail.

2. Providing information of relevance to employees' own workplace/business area

The key objective of the communication process was consistency of message. Alongside that, we also needed to cater for our recognition that employees are not one simple, discrete group. Accordingly, information needs would vary enormously between different parts of the company.

While the responsibility for the fast and succinct initial release of financial information clearly lay with the group's centre, local line management structures also had an all-important role to play.

Individual operating companies within the group took responsibility for communicating directly with their employees. It was decided that the group centre could not and should not attempt to second guess how best to get messages across within such widely differing business environments.

However, the group centre would provide a comprehensive set of tools, notes and guidelines. These were designed in a way that would facilitate face-to-face briefing generally, but allow for local flexibility.

With many meetings planned, additional briefing packs were produced and distributed, along with slides and scripts. A contact name and number were offered to help deal with additional requests, comments or concerns.

Just as important for the smooth running of local events was early communication to managers about revisions to the usual process – what they were and why they were needed. This was conveyed in a general way to senior managers and in more detail to the heads of personnel in each operating company.

3. Reviewing the previous year

It was decided to take an early opportunity to revitalize and re-establish the employee annual report as the best vehicle for the task of looking back over the past 12 months' performance, analysing trends, giving recognition and seeing what lessons had been learned.

Some general guidelines were agreed.

Objectives

The report's objectives were defined as follows:

- to convey quickly, easily and with impact, the progress of the company during the past financial year in financial, operational and human terms
- to convey company-wide values and philosophies clearly and explicitly
- to translate company values into information that an audience find relevant and accessible
- to communicate not only the historical perspective to the year but to provide an indication of future policy and practice.

Target audience

The target audience was defined as 'all employees', recognizing that a report of this kind was one of the few opportunities to present a consistent face to people at all levels across the group.

Nevertheless, and in a departure from the perceived wisdom of earlier years, this definition did not drive a belief that the report should try to be all things to all people – what I would call 'the lowest common denominator' trap, which typically satisfies no one. Therefore, bearing in mind that the group's senior managers already receive their financial information from a variety of sources, the brief stated explicitly that if the publication were to be steered in any way, it would be towards the 'majority' – primarily retail and factory-based employees, 75 per cent of whom are women.

Competition from other media

No other vehicle would compete with it in reviewing the year. The annual report video was discontinued as unnecessary duplication and the remit of the company newspaper confined to conveying news related to the results announcement and its aftermath.

It would not try to compete with other elements in the communication package. It would be properly integrated with the other methods used and would not overstretch itself in its ambitions.

Publication

It should be perceived as the employee's equivalent of the annual report to shareholders. Its publication was timed to coincide with this main report, some three weeks after the results.

Format

The report's format was considered very carefully. While the principle of an annual report to staff was well-established, reports had been produced in a variety of formats over the years. These had ranged from a four-page insert in the company newspaper to a much more formal 'annual report' style document (Figure 26.4).

Figure 26.4   Previous *Review* formats

We wanted to establish a fresh starting point, based on aligning the business need with the needs of the target audiences. We aimed to recognize that:

- we were communicating with an audience which, understandably, lacked familiarity with corporate finance: innovative graphics would be needed, along with appealing, jargon-free copy

- many people find difficulty in dealing with figures, which placed clarity and accuracy of presentation at a premium
- an employee report should actually feature employees.

A 'magazine' style format was agreed, based on the following rationale:

- an employee report mirroring the style of the annual report would be inaccessible and dry, as well as expensive to produce
- conversely a tabloid newspaper format, whilst accessible, is best suited to news reporting and immediacy, an area already being covered by the company newspaper following the results announcement
- it would be best to follow the 'popular' Sunday supplement/consumer magazine approach, being readable, accessible and yet reflective of the quality values that permeated the company.

The agreed format and style should become an established and consistent feature. While allowing for incremental improvement, the aim was to generate a feeling of anticipation and recognition about its appearance each year among employees.

On this basis, *Review '92* was produced and issued in June of that year (Figure 26.5).

4. Giving the outlook for the coming year

The reporting of financial information is essentially a historical exercise, but it is important to provide context that shows its relevance to 'future' performance – trends being set, for example, or anticipating the result of investments already made.

The need to look ahead to the future was not tackled explicitly in the initial communication package, but it was recognized as an element in already defined tools:

- an objective for the report to staff
- through the question and answer session at the combined central staff council and individual results meetings.

MEASURING SUCCESS

We commissioned an independent qualitative research study to follow the 1992 communications exercise. It had two main objectives:

- to evaluate the role and effectiveness of the complete package
- to provide an in-depth evaluation of one specific print medium – the annual report to staff.

The latter was particularly important. *Review '92*, being a radical departure

Figure 26.5 *Review '92*

from previous reports, had attracted some less than complimentary remarks from more senior levels in the company.

A series of individual and paired interviews were held with employees, lasting between 45 and 60 minutes. The sample was designed to reflect the diversity of the companies within the group, both in the UK and internationally, and to accord broadly with the general employee profile in terms of age, sex, status, etc.

The research exercise was an important and integral part of the process. It ensured that anecdotal comment about the communication package could be tested and that specific employee input could be used to help frame the package for subsequent years. The results were presented back to the company at director level.

Space does not permit a detailed feedback of these results from the exercise. Suffice to say that it was broadly positive. The following comments are taken from the qualitative research report.

> 'The clear indications are that the production of an annual results communication package by The Boots Company represents a mutually beneficial and worthwhile exercise.'
> '*Review '92* was preferred to the previous versions of the annual report to staff with the publication well positioned in terms of content and imagery.'
> 'The magazine format gives a higher quality, less disposable impression and should be retained.'
> 'The current content, approach and editorial style appear very effective and should be retained.'

Nevertheless there were areas of weakness, both in the package as a whole and in the report to staff. These were used as a platform for improvements in subsequent years. And independent employee research was carried out again in 1995, on a basis comparable to that used in 1992.

An equally important exercise, the second study has not only provided a mechanism for avoiding complacency, but refined and added substance to our views about future development and improvement. More specifically, we now have a full and accurate information base to draw on in responding to questions, comments or concerns relating to the communication process as a whole and its individual elements.

IMPROVING THE INITIAL PACKAGE

The following are some of the incremental improvements made since 1992.

Employee version of news release

A specific employee version of the full news release has been introduced. If anything the full release has grown more complex and thus a two-page edited version is produced for notice-boards and more general internal distribution, giving the top line figures and some general comment without any detailed interpretation.

New technology

The opportunities provided by new technology have been taken. In addition to fax, electronic mail and bulletin boards now support the distribution system, providing greater reliability and increased speed of delivery. The 'standard' results presentation is now available on disk, in addition to the more conventional approach using slides and OHP.

Video

Video has been re-introduced as a communications tool but to a different brief from that of the early 1990s. A quarterly magazine programme, *LiveWire*, now covers the results as an in-depth feature at the appropriate time. In this way, video from the group centre has become part of regular mainstream communication, not a one-off corporate vehicle.

Report to staff

The report to staff has carried improvements with each successive issue, while retaining the same title 'Review' and the same design template.
Improvements have centred on:

- presentation of the financial information
- greater representation of employees
- exposure of the wider senior management team, as well as the chief executive.

WHAT WE HAVE LEARNED

There are seven observations I would pass on to anyone attempting to communicate financial information to employees, particularly in a large and diverse company.

1. *It really is worth the effort.* Financial information is important: while not the only performance measure, it plays a significant part in the internal (and external) perception of the success (or otherwise) of a company.
2. *Do not produce communication material in isolation.* Recognize the role each item plays in the process as a whole and its particular advantages and disadvantages.
3. *Do not produce material that may alienate the majority employee audience.* No matter how warmly you are applauded by your peers or other senior members of the company, always analyse the audience as you would in any external marketing exercise and position the material accordingly.
4. *Develop trend data rather than just 'snapshots'.* Conduct research on a rigorous basis and at regular intervals.
5. *Ask the dumb questions about the financial data that others may be afraid to ask.* The answers will be illuminating and may be expressed in a much simpler way than that contained in more formal documents.
6. *Peer group recognition is useful.* Since 1992 the report to staff has won four awards, most notably being voted the best of its kind two years running by what is now the British Association of Communicators in Business. Meanwhile, *LiveWire* obtained a European Award of Excellence from the International Association of Business Communicators within

the first year of its launch. Such awards bring not only professional satisfaction, but beneficial internal PR.
7. *Finally, communicate your plans in advance to identified key people in the company.* These are people who will need to 'own' the information and whose support will be crucial to your success.

APPENDIX

THE BOOTS COMPANY

EMPLOYEE ANNOUNCEMENT

1st June 1995

PRELIMINARY ANNOUNCEMENT
FOR THE YEAR ENDED 31ST MARCH 1995

	1995 £m	1994 £m	Change %
* Turnover	4,308.1	4,167.1	+3.4
* Profit before tax before exceptional items	525.6	484.8	+8.4
* Profit before tax	849.7	416.3	–
* Net cash	517.2	69.0	–
* Earnings per share before exceptional items	36.0p	33.0p	+9.1
* Earnings per share	65.7p	27.7p	–
* Total dividend	17.0p	15.0p	+13.3

Total shareholder return for the five years to 31st March 1995 – 104%
(Total shareholder return represents growth in share price
plus dividends paid to shareholders)

Commenting on the results the chairman Sir Michael Angus said:

"In my first year as chairman, I am pleased to report to you a very sound result for the company. In an active year, we have undertaken the largest share repurchase in UK corporate history, and with the sale of Boots Pharmaceuticals rebalanced the business portfolio. Shareholder value has been more than doubled in the past five years.
Some of our retail businesses are trading in particularly competitive markets. However we have sufficient confidence in the underlying strengths of the total business to be sure of continuing to improve performance and shareholder returns."

Segmental information

Comparative figures have been restated to reflect changes in accounting policy and in presentation.

Turnover by business segment	Total 1995 £m	External 1995 £m	Total 1994 £m	External 1994 £m
Continuing Operations:				
Boots The Chemists	2,943.8	2,943.4	2,808.0	2,808.0
Halfords	377.9	377.1	357.0	356.1
Boots Opticians	119.1	119.1	102.1	102.1
Childrens World	104.8	104.8	84.1	84.1
A G Stanley	114.6	114.6	111.6	111.6
Share of Do It All	185.3	185.3	194.2	194.2
Boots Healthcare International	203.5	185.8	227.7	206.8
Boots Contract Manufacturing	216.0	31.8	208.8	30.5
Boots Properties (see below)	98.0	17.5	108.4	30.4
Sephora	–	–	24.5	24.5
	4,363.0	**4,079.4**	4,226.4	3,948.3
Discontinued Operation:				
Boots Pharmaceuticals	441.8	426.4	438.1	419.9
	4,804.8	**4,505.8**	4,664.5	4,368.2
Inter-segmental	(299.0)	–	(296.3)	–
	4,505.8	**4,505.8**	4,368.2	4,368.2
Analysed as:				
Group profit and loss account		**4,308.1**		4,167.1
Share of associated undertakings		**197.7**		201.1
		4,505.8		4,368.2

Turnover comprises sales to external customers (excluding VAT and other sales taxes) and rental income.

The group's associated undertakings during the year were the joint venture companies, Do It All and BHC Company. The group's interest in BHC Company was sold as part of the Boots Pharmaceuticals disposal on 31st March 1995.

Boots Properties' turnover includes development income of £5.6m (1994 £20.7m).

Profit by business segment	Before exceptional items 1995 £m	Total 1995 £m	Before exceptional items 1994 £m	Total 1994 £m
Continuing Operations:				
Boots The Chemists	349.7	349.7	323.9	323.9
Halfords	20.5	20.5	14.5	14.5
Boots Opticians	*8.3	11.1	6.7	6.7
Childrens World	.5	.5	(1.6)	(1.6)
A G Stanley	(8.5)	(8.5)	(1.2)	(1.2)
Share of Do It All	(6.3)	(6.3)	*(10.6)	(47.2)
Boots Healthcare International	9.8	9.8	21.3	21.3
Boots Contract Manufacturing	17.8	17.8	16.2	16.2
Boots Properties (see below)	66.8	66.8	67.1	67.1
Sephora	–	–	.2	.2
Group Costs	(24.8)	(24.8)	*(28.1)	(30.3)
	433.8	436.6	408.4	369.6
Discontinued Operation:				
Boots Pharmaceuticals	86.4	86.4	*79.5	44.5
Operating profit	520.2	523.0	487.9	414.1
Profit on disposal of fixed assets and businesses (net)	–	321.3	–	5.3
Net interest	5.4	5.4	(3.1)	(3.1)
Profit before tax	525.6	849.7	484.8	416.3

Boots Properties' result includes development profits of £1.7m (1994 £5.8m)

*Results stated before the following exceptional items:	1995 £m	1994 £m
Boots Opticians – VAT recoverable (following High Court judgement)	2.8	–
Share of Do It All – Restructuring costs	–	(36.6)
Group Costs – Privity of contract costs	–	(2.2)
Boots Pharmaceuticals – Manoplax write-off costs	–	(35.0)
Exceptional operating items	2.8	(73.8)

27 BP Chemicals
The role of IC in culture change management

John Bishop, *general manager, Communications Department*

In the early 1990s, employees of BP Chemicals were facing massive changes. They had already embraced one culture change, essential for survival in the chemical industry – continuous improvement with Total Quality Management. This case study picks up the story with another change about to begin as BP moved from a command and control organization to a flatter, more open style of management.

The booming profits of the late 1980s were giving way, in the cyclical chemicals business, to big losses in the early 1990s.

The emergence of a 'new' BP Chemicals in 1995 – substantially more productive (productivity up 50 per cent since 1990) and with sustainable profits – was the result of innovative changes in structure and processes. Uneconomic plants were closed, businesses were divested, working practices were revolutionized – staff became involved in the tough decision-making processes, and investments were made in new, modern plants in Europe and Asia Pacific. The slimmer, more resilient BP Chemicals had reduced staff numbers from 23 000 in 1990 to a number that is planned to be under 10 000 when the last of the major divestments is concluded at the end of 1995.

The building of the 'new' BP Chemicals makes a good story in itself. However, this case study will concentrate on the contribution made by the internal communication process to the creation of the 'new' BP Chemicals.

THE MEASUREMENT PROCESS BEGINS

As part of the move away from a command and control structure, BP began a process of listening to the views of staff. Measurements were taken through employee attitude surveys in 1989 and 1991 and they showed that although staff were by and large satisfied with employee publications, they were far from happy with internal communication in the company.

In 1989, only 20 per cent of BP employees felt they were well informed about management's plans and decisions. The same response rate – 20 per cent – was obtained to the same question in the 1991 employee attitude survey.

Arguably, this was progress, because BP had substantially raised the expectations of employees with a high profile culture change programme towards greater openness. The good news was that internal communication in BP Chemicals was no worse: the bad news was that it was no better.

The company recognizes that ratings on internal communication in employee attitude surveys can be adversely influenced by other factors and poor communication can mean that the method was effective, but the content was unwelcome.

THE WORK OF THE TASK FORCE

Of course, listening is only the first step. BP Chemicals started its response by setting up an Internal Communication task force – an international group of employees, including some communication professionals from all levels in the organization, led by a senior general manager. In good Quality style, their task was to identify the requirements for effective internal communication and make recommendations for improvement and implementation.

They consulted widely, met for long days in sunlit rooms throughout the summer of 1991, and concluded that BP Chemicals needed to improve internal communication, because staff who are both informed and listened to are more motivated and perform better ... and by 1991 BP Chemicals certainly needed to improve performance.

Satisfying or delighting the customer is an integral part of the Quality process and the task force used this concept to good effect in its recommendations – improving communication with 'the customer' or 'the audience' – in this case, each and every employee.

The task force was clear that effective communication was primarily about face-to-face communication – information flow, mutual understanding and listening ... supported by two-way feedback and above all by the right behaviours. Information had to be relevant to the audience and the method and style had to 'switch on' the audience. The task force underlined that good communication should occur up, down and across the organization. A *Communication Charter* was published that spoke of 'the right of every employee to expect, and the responsibility to promote, the highest standards of communication in an environment of teamwork, trust and mutual understanding'. The right to communicate has to be earned: without listening, there is no communication.

IMPLEMENTING THE CHANGES

The work of the task force was enthusiastically supported by the BP Chemicals

Executive Committee. The responsibility for implementing the changes with line management was given to a senior general manager, reporting directly to the chief executive officer.

And so began the long journey of implementing more effective internal communication, in support of performance improvement in BP Chemicals. The start of the process was a letter from the chief executive officer to each team leader, asking them:

- to use the existing team or work group structure to cascade messages – both ways – with active listening, starting with the findings of the task force
- at each team meeting, to ask teams how they could take ownership for the process and improve communication in their work area
- to seek a change in behaviour, particularly among line managers and team leaders, involving personal commitments and action plans to improve communication.

At many of BP Chemicals' locations, this process fitted quite naturally into the existing team briefing or Quality work group structure.

The BP Chemicals Executive Committee was the first to try the process at one of its monthly meetings. They discussed how they could improve internal communication and each of them wrote a personal action plan at the meeting. Examples of their actions were published to demonstrate the commitment from the top. They included smaller, more informal team meetings; regular walkabouts and town hall meetings (meetings of chief executives with groups of 30+ staff); and more visits to the BP Chemicals sites.

Overloaded management was pleading for no new initiatives and arguably none of this was new. Rather, it involved reinforcing practices that had become neglected in the drive for performance improvement, cascading messages up and down the existing work group structure, and line managers and team leaders taking ownership of the behaviour changes necessary to give the process credibility with employees.

Face-to-face communication was supported by:

- a special publication for all employees
- use of existing publications
- a slide pack for use by all teams
- changes to BP Chemicals training programmes and staff appraisal forms to reflect the new style of internal communication.

None of this was intended to be a substitute for face-to-face discussion between team leaders and staff, which was seen as the critical success factor.

A network of communicators was established, involving each location in BP Chemicals, to support line management's drive to improve internal communication.

Measurement and monitoring are axioms of the Quality process. Managers   *347* were given feedback on their performance by the use of upward appraisal. Best practice in internal communication was shared throughout the company and attempts were made to benchmark BP Chemicals' progress against that of other companies. Above all, a commitment was made to continue to measure progress through ongoing employee attitude surveys.

MEASURING AGAIN

In 1993, a third employee attitude survey was carried out and this showed a substantial improvement in satisfaction with internal communication. For the first time, the satisfied responses (40 per cent) outweighed the dissatisfied (26 per cent). The positive responses were much higher at management grades (60 per cent), with levels of satisfaction lower at non-management grades (37 per cent).

At last, there were signs of improvement in internal communication across the organization. The survey consultants, Sirota & Alper, provided benchmark comparisons with other companies. These showed that on a number of internal communication measures, BP Chemicals had climbed to above average, but was still some way from best-in-class – it has been difficult to identify best-in-class in internal communication, although various consultants advise that about 60 per cent satisfaction with internal communication may be achievable.

For the first time, staff were asked to rate the effectiveness of the communication processes. In confirmation of the findings of the task force, staff rated meetings with their boss and team briefings as the most effective, followed by e-mail, employee publications and town hall meetings, with videos rated as least effective. As far as internal communication was concerned, BP Chemicals was becoming a 'video-free zone'.

There were other important measurements of communication – related to how well staff understood strategy, goals and objectives, and their ability to relate what they did every day in their jobs with company goals and objectives. The answers were not encouraging. For example only 22 per cent of staff agreed that they had a good understanding of business goals and objectives. This was to become a priority for communications in the next two years, starting with a widespread communication of company strategy and leading on to a much better understanding of business objectives.

RESPONDING TO THE FEEDBACK

BP Chemicals was pleased to have doubled the level of satisfaction with internal communication to 40 per cent, but determined to keep trying. There was no wish for new initiatives, more programmes or more products. Rather, the aim was a steady improvement in face-to-face communication, encouraging managers and supervisors to learn the skills of good communication – in particular listening – and repeating the key messages time and again ... in the language of 'the audience'.

A number of processes were put in place to make internal communication easier for the hard-pressed (and still overloaded) managers and team leaders of BP Chemicals.

Materials for communication through teams and work groups

This material often took the form of e-mail for speed of communication, but included slide packs where a presentation was required. For example an e-mail communication of BP Chemicals' quarterly financial results from the chief executive officer was put in place. A widespread communication on BP Chemicals' performance in health, safety and the environment was put in place throughout the company – measurements through the employee attitude surveys show that this was appreciated by staff. These were regular, same-day internal communications about the many divestments, closures and investments as the 'new' BP Chemicals started to grow. It was important that staff heard about important changes from the company before they read about them in the newspapers. The role of line management was crucial in delivering these communications, actively supported by the network of communications professionals. For all communications, line management was encouraged to give messages a local context to ensure relevance to local staff.

Good practice in internal communication identified and shared

Five examples were chosen and publicized in a desktop publication (Figure 27.1):

- upward feedback in the USA
- internal communication workshops in Antwerp
- team briefing at Baglan Bay
- town hall meetings in the USA
- communication of BP Oil quarterly results.

This publication also described the many internal communication programmes and processes in use in BP Chemicals.

Communication awards introduced across BP Chemicals

These awards were designed to encourage and recognize good internal and external communication in the company. They were assessed by a mix of internal and external judges and were open not only to communications professionals, but also to staff and line managers. Although the competition was not restricted to internal communications and included entries from communications with all of BP Chemicals audiences, it is noteworthy that internal communications by staff have won the Gold Award in two of the three years of the competition.

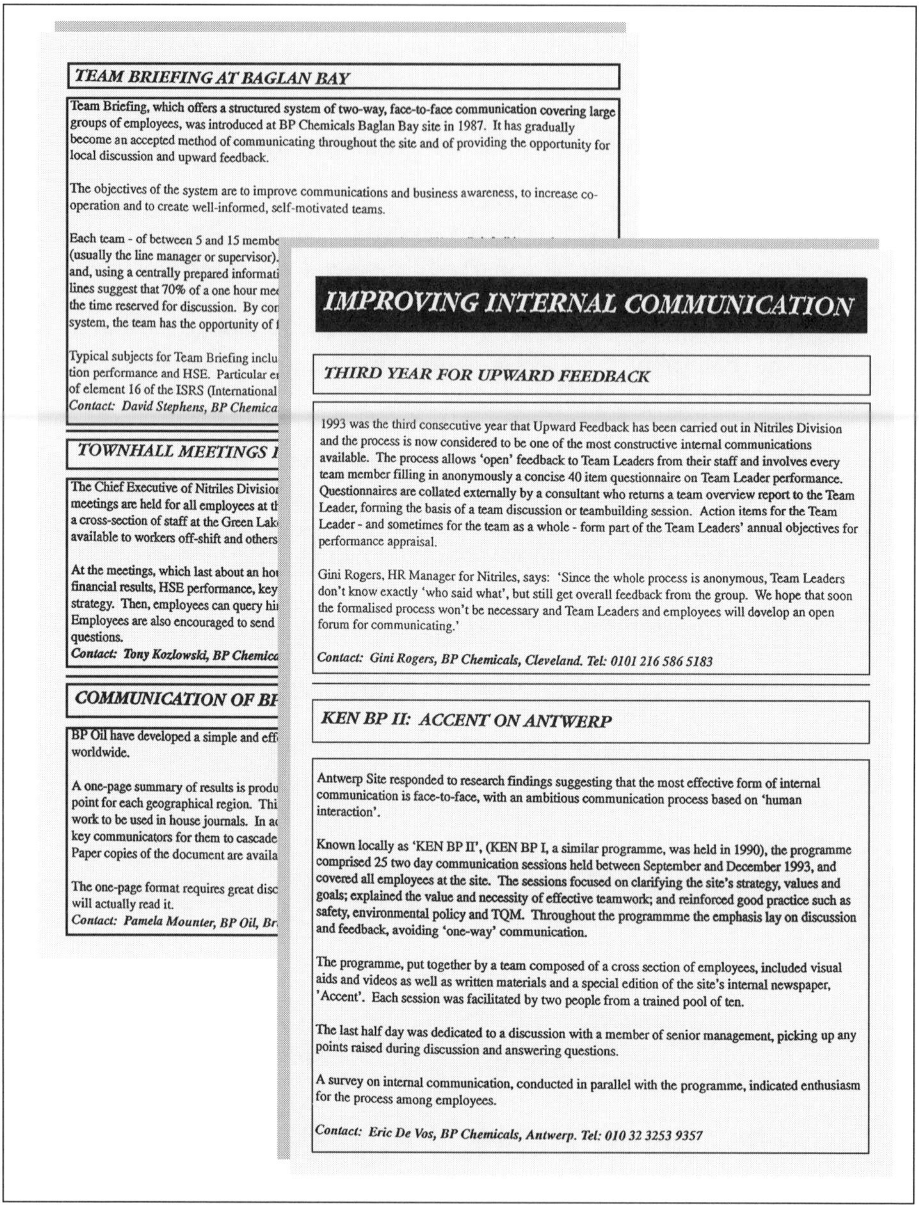

TEAM BRIEFING AT BAGLAN BAY

Team Briefing, which offers a structured system of two-way, face-to-face communication covering large groups of employees, was introduced at BP Chemicals Baglan Bay site in 1987. It has gradually become an accepted method of communicating throughout the site and of providing the opportunity for local discussion and upward feedback.

The objectives of the system are to improve communications and business awareness, to increase co-operation and to create well-informed, self-motivated teams.

Each team - of between 5 and 15 membe
(usually the line manager or supervisor).
and, using a centrally prepared informati
lines suggest that 70% of a one hour mee
the time reserved for discussion. By cor
system, the team has the opportunity of f

Typical subjects for Team Briefing inclu
tion performance and HSE. Particular e
of element 16 of the ISRS (International
Contact: David Stephens, BP Chemica

TOWNHALL MEETINGS I

The Chief Executive of Nitriles Divisio
meetings are held for all employees at th
a cross-section of staff at the Green Lak
available to workers off-shift and others

At the meetings, which last about an ho
financial results, HSE performance, key
strategy. Then, employees can query hi
Employees are also encouraged to send
questions.
Contact: Tony Kozlowski, BP Chemica

COMMUNICATION OF BP

BP Oil have developed a simple and eff
worldwide.

A one-page summary of results is produ
point for each geographical region. Thi
work to be used in house journals. In a
key communicators for them to cascade
Paper copies of the document are availa

The one-page format requires great disc
will actually read it.
Contact: Pamela Mounter, BP Oil, Br

IMPROVING INTERNAL COMMUNICATION

THIRD YEAR FOR UPWARD FEEDBACK

1993 was the third consecutive year that Upward Feedback has been carried out in Nitriles Division and the process is now considered to be one of the most constructive internal communications available. The process allows 'open' feedback to Team Leaders from their staff and involves every team member filling in anonymously a concise 40 item questionnaire on Team Leader performance. Questionnaires are collated externally by a consultant who returns a team overview report to the Team Leader, forming the basis of a team discussion or teambuilding session. Action items for the Team Leader - and sometimes for the team as a whole - form part of the Team Leaders' annual objectives for performance appraisal.

Gini Rogers, HR Manager for Nitriles, says: 'Since the whole process is anonymous, Team Leaders don't know exactly 'who said what', but still get overall feedback from the group. We hope that soon the formalised process won't be necessary and Team Leaders and employees will develop an open forum for communicating.'

Contact: Gini Rogers, BP Chemicals, Cleveland. Tel: 0101 216 586 5183

KEN BP II: ACCENT ON ANTWERP

Antwerp Site responded to research findings suggesting that the most effective form of internal communication is face-to-face, with an ambitious communication process based on 'human interaction'.

Known locally as 'KEN BP II', (KEN BP I, a similar programme, was held in 1990), the programme comprised 25 two day communication sessions held between September and December 1993, and covered all employees at the site. The sessions focused on clarifying the site's strategy, values and goals; explained the value and necessity of effective teamwork; and reinforced good practice such as safety, environmental policy and TQM. Throughout the programmme the emphasis lay on discussion and feedback, avoiding 'one-way' communication.

The programme, put together by a team composed of a cross section of employees, included visual aids and videos as well as written materials and a special edition of the site's internal newspaper, 'Accent'. Each session was facilitated by two people from a trained pool of ten.

The last half day was dedicated to a discussion with a member of senior management, picking up any points raised during discussion and answering questions.

A survey on internal communication, conducted in parallel with the programme, indicated enthusiasm for the process among employees.

Contact: Eric De Vos, BP Chemicals, Antwerp. Tel: 010 32 3253 9357

Figure 27.1 ***Improving Internal Communication***

Clarity of message

With so much going on and line managers still overburdened, there was a plea for clarity in the messages that needed to be repeated time and again. The five enduring messages for internal communication were identified as:

- strategy (including disciplined growth) and performance
- employee morale and motivation
- quality improvement, including integrated performance measures
- competitiveness of the European chemical industry
- health, safety and environmental performance.

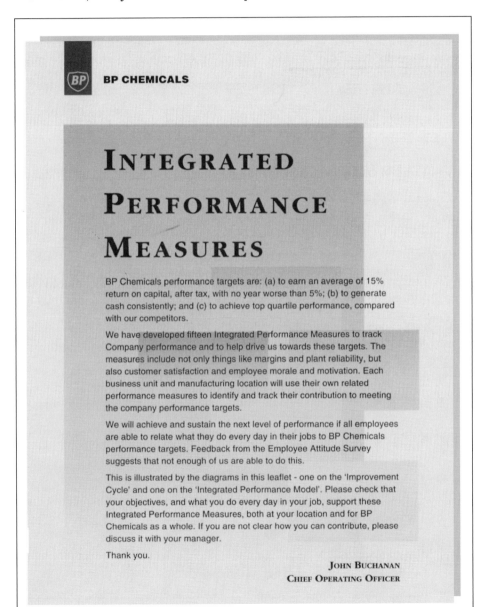

Figure 27.2 *Integrated Performance Measures* **booklet**

These enduring messages were produced using DTP and sent to line managers in a laminated format (they are 'enduring' after all).

Targeted internal communications about the performance of BP Chemicals to staff

Face-to-face communications, written materials and e-mails were used – all emphasizing the need for every member of staff to relate their objectives and what they do every day in their jobs to BP Chemicals' performance targets. Fifteen integrated performance measures were introduced throughout BP Chemicals, covering things as different as plant performance and employee morale and motivation. They were produced in a publication which was given to all staff through the now well-established cascade process in BP Chemicals (Figure 27.2).

WE NEVER STOP MEASURING

In 1995, a fourth employee attitude survey was carried out. It showed that general satisfaction with internal communication had increased further – from 40 per cent to 45 per cent (Figure 27.3). The increase was most apparent at management grades, but there was little change or even a small decline at non-management grades.

The emphasis placed on linking everyday jobs to business objectives was paying handsome dividends. In 1995, 57 per cent of staff agreed that they had a good understanding of business goals and objectives, compared with only 22 per cent in 1993.

In general, staff at BP Chemicals had given high ratings on performance

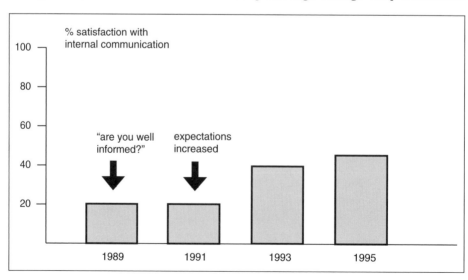

Figure 27.3   Employee Attitude Survey graph

issues, but this had been achieved at the expense of people issues. The BP Chemicals Executive Committee renewed its commitment to leadership in good internal communication by pledging to make personal time available for face-to-face communication, including:

- more recognition for good work
- listening to the concerns of employees
- informally walking around sites and offices to meet people.

Good internal communication in the 'new' BP Chemicals is seen as a journey not a destination. There will not be a last chapter to this case study – just a continuous process of measurement and improvement, as more and more staff enjoy and take responsibility for the highest standards of communication in an environment of teamwork, trust and mutual understanding.

28 Comet Group
Gaining credibility through measurement

Chris Carey, *internal communications manager*

Under pressure to help combat low morale and stem a tide of rumours about the company's future, Comet's fledgling IC department decided to measure the effectiveness of its campaign at each stage. In so doing, it gained the respect and support of senior management, which, with the crisis long past, continues to manifest itself in increased backing for IC, as well as greater access to and involvement in strategic planning.

Times were tough for electrical retailers throughout 1994. At Comet, a sharp decline in sales had led to a series of redundancies, followed by rumours of imminent store closures. And by early 1995, the company was about to announce a trading loss for the first time in its history.

Comet's top management team, well aware of how all this was affecting the workforce, was particularly concerned that the inevitable doom-laden reporting of the results by the national press would make things worse.

The IC department had recently been established. It had been set up to put in place a robust internal communication structure that would meet the needs of a business going through radical change. It was now tasked with creating opportunities to give the internal audience a more balanced view of the immediate situation. It was made clear, however, that at a time when every cost in the business was coming under the microscope, there would be no 'open purse' for IC to achieve its goal.

As elsewhere in the business, proof would be needed that the challenge was being tackled in the right way, and that the expense involved was paying dividends.

HOW DID WE BEGIN?

The main plank of our strategy was to run a special business briefing to coincide with the release of the annual results. Managers from all 232 stores and from head office would be brought together at a conference centre. There they would hear, direct from the top, where Comet had been going wrong and what was being done to restore the company's prospects.

Each manager would be asked to return to their teams and cascade the various messages onwards through the team briefing system. In addition, our internal newspaper, *Switched On*, would carry special stories reinforcing the messages.

Since it was clear that senior managers were at that time acutely aware of the role of IC, it was also decided to take the opportunity to gather information about the effectiveness of both these media. Measuring effectiveness in terms of this particular campaign would tend to suggest potential for effectiveness across a range of issues where a change of attitude or behaviour was required. If the results were good, it could only enhance the value placed on IC as a function, as well as the media being used.

DECIDING WHAT AND HOW TO MEASURE

We felt the most accessible and meaningful measure would be people's retention of the five key messages from the business briefing. The survey would cover a representative sample of 100 people from stores and from head office. To collect the data, we chose structured telephone interviewing: a quick turnaround was vital and we were keen to avoid taking people away from their primary responsibility of serving customers.

With resources at a premium, using suppliers for this task, or taking colleagues in HR away from their everyday duties to help, would have been difficult. Instead, we enlisted the help of one of our head office receptionists to carry out the measurement exercise. Her afternoons were relatively quiet, and she was able to carry out the telephone interviews and fulfil her normal duties at the same time.

PHASE ONE: DETERMINING THE SUCCESS OF THE BRIEFINGS

The main business briefing was held on a Wednesday: managers were given a Saturday deadline for briefing their teams. Phase one of the measurement exercise took place on Monday afternoon (Figure 28.1).

These are the questions we asked to determine retention of the five key messages.

1. What is the key theme of the new advertising campaign?
2. What new product ranges is Comet planning to stock this year?
3. How much extra investment is Comet going to make in training?
4. How many stores is Comet actually closing?

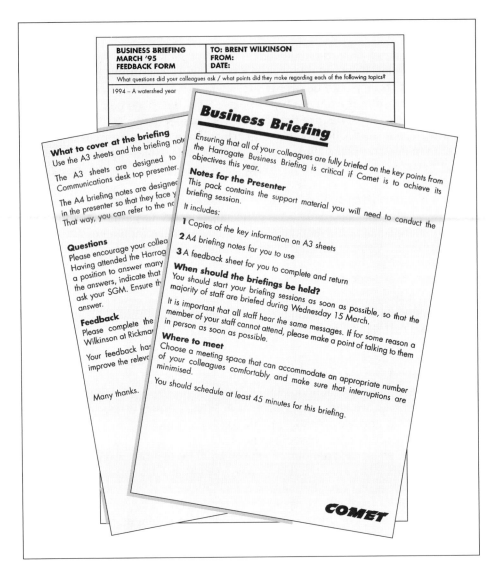

Figure 28.1 Business briefing

5. What are the two Key Performance Indicators for Comet as an organization this year? (If people were unsure about what exactly KPIs were, we defined them as goals or targets)

Interviews were conducted immediately after team briefings, and the results are presented in Figure 28.2.

The results gave us proof that the business briefing had successfully countered the rumours about store closures (Question 4). The results to

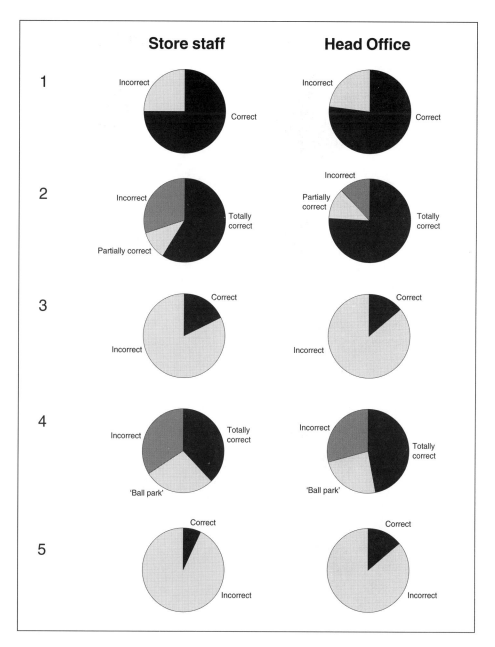

Figure 28.2   Effectiveness of team briefings

Questions 1 and 2 also showed that people were now aware of Comet's immediate battle plan, with high levels of understanding of the theme of the forthcoming advertising campaign and new product ranges.

Of course, outside factors will also have played a part – many stores were in   *357*

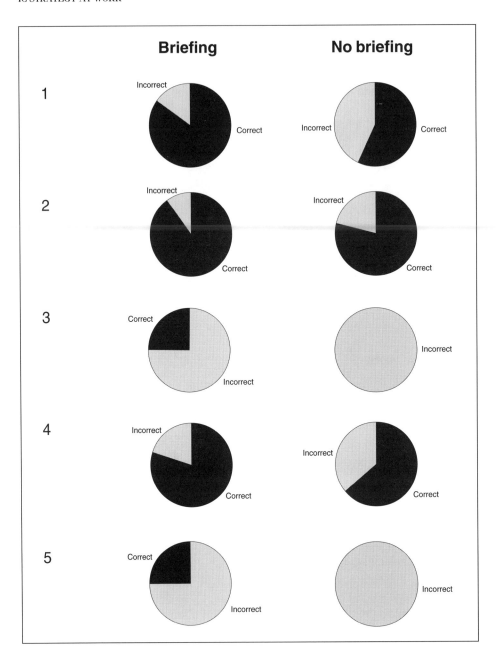

Figure 28.3   Incidence and effectiveness of head office briefings

the process of receiving point-of-sale material that shouted the theme of the advertising campaign loud and clear. There was no way we could run a control group to eliminate these kinds of outside influences.

Asking the obvious

On the surface, the results for head office staff were fairly encouraging. However, the grapevine told us that a number of managers at head office rarely carried out team briefings, assuming that their people already understood all key messages generated at the centre.

We wanted to take a more detailed look at the results as a way of challenging this assumption. So, we asked an additional 50 people at head office if they had received a briefing. We then proceeded to ask them our five questions to determine retention of the key messages.

The results are presented in Figure 28.3.

The results proved conclusively that the briefings, when delivered, were effective in head office, and gave us a good tool to use in persuading some of our less-committed head office colleagues of the importance of team briefings.

Confirming suspicions

Ostensibly the most disappointing result from phase one was the low level of retention of Comet's KPIs for the year. Although the results for this question were to improve significantly following publication of the internal newspaper, it confirmed our suspicion that people relate most easily to information about their local work area, and that the more strategic messages are harder to transmit.

PHASE TWO: DID THE NEWSPAPER HELP?

Switched On was distributed 10 days after the scheduled briefings. Interviews took place immediately after publication, involving a sample of 100 store staff. The results are presented in Figure 28.4.

Once again, we had evidence for the effectiveness of a particular medium in improving retention of key messages. In *Switched On*'s case, it was particularly clear in the results for Question 5, where the information given at the team briefing on KPIs was not reinforced in any way other than through the internal newspaper. The substantial improvement in employees' awareness of these two important business drivers, therefore, can fairly be put down to *Switched On* alone (Figure 28.5).

For the rest, we could by no means claim as direct an endorsement for the newspaper's contribution, but it is a reasonable assumption that *Switched On* did successfully reinforce the messages first communicated face to face in team briefings. It also justified our decision to tie the content of the newspaper closely to that of the team briefings.

MAKING THE MOST OF THE RESULTS

We looked for and were given an opportunity to present the results of the measurement exercise in person to the board of directors. It enabled us to

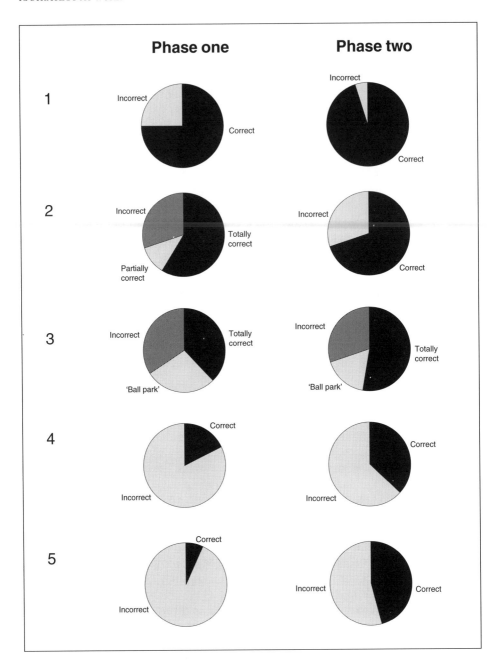

Figure 28.4   Effectiveness of staff newspaper

make a convincing case for the effectiveness of the campaign and the media. The results for retention of the two KPIs (Question 5) were critical because this message was communicated only through the briefing and the newspaper and could not have come from any other source.

Switched On

THE NEWSPAPER FOR COMET PEOPLE — **April 1995**

SWITCH ON TO INNOVATION – LATEST WINNERS – page 10

IDEAL HOME WIN page 12

RIVALS PAY 'THE PRICE'

'We will do it' says Chairman Eddie Styring

• *Chairman Eddie Styring at the Business Briefing in Harrogate.*

THE Comet Price will prove costly for the competition was the message relayed by managers at team briefings which took place at all Stores and Service Centres following last month's Business Briefing.

Staff heard how Comet's aggressive new advertising promises customers "You can't buy better" and marks a return to the company's traditional strength of offering unbeatable value for money.

And that value for money will be found especially in own-brands such as Goodmans and Blomberg and in the introduction of PCs to a selected number of stores.

To help staff convert this marketing support into increased sales, Comet is investing an extra £500,000 in training during the year.

STRATEGY

As well as announcing the company's plans for the coming year the Business Briefing was also designed to allay fears about the threat of store closures.

Chairman Eddie Styring arrived hot foot from announcing Comet's plans to the City and he had a very simple message for everyone.

"We've got the people, we've got the stores and we've now got a strategy which plays to our strengths. I know we will do it."

The conference also highlighted the two priorities for the business this coming year.

"Our key aims this year are very simple. We must return to profitability and increase our market share. Those are the performance indicators by which we will be judged," said Eddie.

BUSINESS BRIEFING SPECIAL REPORT – pages 4 & 9

STOP PRESS
Comet voted 'best' for Mobiles

MOBILE News magazine has voted Comet 'Best Multiple Retailer' in its annual awards. Andy Measham, Buying Controller for Electronics and Audio collected the award at a glittering ceremony held at a top London hotel. The judges praised Comet for its "commitment to training...and...serious approach to helping customers make the right choice". A full report will appear in the next edition of *Switched On.*

IMPORTANT INFORMATION FOR ALL COMET EMPLOYEES

SPECIAL 4 PAGE MORI PULLOUT

– starts page 5

IAN IS TOP OF THE FLEET
– page 3

Figure 28.5 *Switched On*

The internal communication department has since received strong backing from the board through increased resources and a much closer involvement in the strategic planning process.

The fact that Comet has successfully delivered against the promises originally made in the briefing process has also enhanced our credibility. The business is now well and truly back on track, with increases in market share and total sales paving the way to a return to profitability, and undoubtedly the IC function has played an important part. One of our key responsibilities has been to show how the business has been achieving its objectives, for example through a video that explained the new advertising campaign.

At a time when all functions are being asked to demonstrate their contribution, the measurement exercise allowed us not only to examine the effectiveness of what we had been doing but also to market our work internally. That in turn has helped us build a promising future for the function and for ourselves.

29 DO IT ALL
Using Team Listening® and coaching to change and maintain a company culture

Kim Fernihough, *formerly general manager, public relations*

Establishing a new culture after merger is something organizations rarely take time actively to manage, *let alone involve people in developing an approach. After a slow start, DO IT ALL took on both challenges squarely, and achieved a very positive result.*

Following the merger between WH Smith's DO IT ALL and Boots Payless in 1990, the company went through a period of great challenge and change.

Immediately afterwards and for about two years, fierce competitive pressure and a need to amalgamate the two businesses forced the company to make procedural needs a priority. Management focused on key operational issues such as store portfolio, supply chain, product range and information technology. People issues were therefore, wrongly, not high enough on the agenda.

Two years on, the company realized it had not developed its own culture. People in the stores and in head office continued to refer to themselves as 'Ex-Smiths' and 'Ex-Payless'. There was a need to establish the new DO IT ALL way of doing things.

In 1992, the Board of Directors met to discuss the issue. There was agreement on the need to develop a culture in which people could feel positive about change. They therefore decided that to provide an environment that would encourage participation and involvement in the business at every level – management and staff – would be a priority, and went on to formulate a 'culture paper' which set out the management style they wanted to adopt for the new organization.

HOW DO IT ALL CAME TO A SOLUTION AND WHY

No formal research was carried out, but senior management spent much time gaining an understanding of the current culture, through open and honest discussions with management and staff. This team debated the needs from their perspective and fed these through to the board.

The board appreciated that it would be the organization's people who would make any new direction work. It therefore set out to create opportunities for people, part-time and full-time, to contribute actively to the long-term future of the business.

There were three core requirements:

- *consistency* – the culture must permeate every area and every level of the business, starting with the board
- *skills* – management must develop the skills to solicit involvement and contributions from its teams
- *time* – in a busy retail environment, it is challenging to find the time to generate participation from staff: the board had to make it a priority so that the necessary time would be given to culture development.

IMPLEMENTING THE PROGRAMME

It was decided to develop a fully rounded, long-term programme that stores and head office would be exposed to equally, ensuring a cohesive and consistent approach. It centred on three elements:

- Team Listening
- formal launch of Team Listening through roadshows
- coaching skills.

Team Listening

DO IT ALL saw Team Listening as a programme of sessions encouraging staff to contribute their ideas and to share accountability for making improvements to their environments and the way they do things. Team Listening is not a new concept or one that is unique to DO IT ALL. But the company adapted the broad concept to work within its own environment and to meet its own needs.

A Team Listening brief is provided by head office offering a general outline for discussion. The brief is posted several days before the session, giving staff the opportunity to consider their own views and bring them to the meeting to share with the group. Managers are encouraged to approach the brief, and the sessions, in a style that works for their own team. Local issues are also highlighted by the manager to form an agenda for the session (Figure 29.1).

Importantly, Team Listening sessions are held outside normal trading hours and attendance is voluntary. Managers are given small budgets to provide refreshments and most hold sessions outside the store environment. Any

NG BRIEF TEAM LISTENING BRIEF TEAM LISTENING BRIEF

Barry Martin and Bob Wiffen are deeply involved in the development of the role of the "Customer Count Co-ordinators" and the first meeting has already taken place. Further information will follow soon.

EQUIPMENT AND MAINTENANCE PROJECT MANAGEMENT AND SHOP FITTING DEPARTMENT

The "Bucks" specialist equipment

prepared.

Please speak to your Store Manager who can provide you with details.

NEW RANGES

In last month's issue we launched two new exciting ranges in the Design Collection - Farmyard and Orange Blossom. March sees the introduction of another three designs - Kew, Academy and Bloomsbury. The first two are launched in the new DO IT ALL packaging with our special quality guarantee. All of our own brand designs have been produced for us to an agreed specification. This means that the textiles must pass through testing for wear and tear, light fastness to check that colour will resist fading when subjected to daylight and colour fastness during washing.

KEW is produced exclusively for DO IT ALL by Crown Wallcoverings and is a fresh floral design in lilac and cream.

ACADEMY from Fine Art, is a modern, dominant, masculine design in terracotta and jade.

BLOOMSBURY is a light patchwork floral design by Mary Quant.

The Product Management Team will be working with the Public Relations Department throughout the year to ensure that these products are promoted to our target female customers via women's press.

All of these designs will revitalise sales of the Design Collection area, which represents an important part of the new Decorating Department that will be introduced as more stores are refitted.

Don't forget to maintain stocks of all remaining designs - Phoenix continues to be the number one seller across the company.

AM LISTENING BRIEF TEAM LISTENING BRIEF TEAM LISTE

Team

LISTENING BRIEF

PROMOTIONS

A new and exciting approach to the presentation of projects in-store is currently being developed. This will be launched in SP1 with a Tiling Project, "Take a Look at Tiling".

ADVERTISING

Advertising for Easter is being developed. This will be featured in both press and on TV.

LOCAL STORE MARKETING

19 stores will receive support packages in the run up to Easter. These stores are particularly affected by competitor activity. The main thrust of activity will centre on the Bonus Card, with five consecutive Double Point weekends being run. These will be advertised via a mailed letter to all cardholders assigned to the 19 stores.

BONUS CARD

In addition to the Bonus Card support being given to the selected 19 stores, promotional activity will be run nationwide. The main objective of this is to start building traffic flow through stores in the run up to Easter. In addition we are also aiming to capitalise on the Easter Trading period by driving recruitment of new card holders in-store. A recruitment programme and supporting point-of-sale package will be launched in store during March.

We all need to refocus on Bonus Card Recruitment. Figures have now been published and are encouraging but even greater success can be attained. Congratulations to those at the top.

NEW STORE OPENINGS

A new support package for store relaunches and new store openings is also under development. This will be designed to communicate the DO IT ALL brand values of helpful accessible staff, easy to find products and breadth of range.

POINT-OF-SALE DEVELOPMENT EASTER/SPRING

Development of POS is ongoing to support the Easter and Spring campaign.

PRICE PROJECT

A major review of our current price projection across the store and how we can improve it is currently underway.

Initial POS concepts have been printed and approved, and we have been given the 'green light' to develop the design for a phased introduction from Easter onwards.

All elements of POS will be completely reviewed, right from the EPOS label to promotional material.

PROJECT FOCUS STORES

New graphics for the PROJECT FOCUS stores are being developed. Emphasis is being placed on creating inspiration within the decorating area. The objective is to introduce a complete 'new look' in Reading and Lichfield. Hyde, Kings Lynn and Chester refits will have some of the new ideas. They will be revisited at a later date to introduce the remainder of the scheme, which is still being designed and produced.

STORE PLANNING

Design work is to be implemented in Lichfield and Reading stores. Winnersh design work is now completed and work on-site has already commenced.

The Store Planning Team is now developing lower cost options of the new concept and adapting the design work to fit stores of differing shapes and sizes.

SPACE PLANNING AND ANALYSIS

The Space Census has been updated and issued to stores. In the first few days following its issue, over 30 were returned and the central footage records have been updated for these stores. These footage records support line control issue and the ABC ordering system, as well as the ongoing space analysis work being done within the department.

SPACE RE-BALANCING

Work has begun on the final six stores to undergo space re balancing, bringing the total to 54 stores.

Although this will conclude the space re-balancing exercise, a number of small works projects will be undertaken, continuing the improvements in stores.

RETAIL OPERATIONS

SALES DRIVE

The "Countdown to Easter" has been sent out to assist stores in planning their preparation for Easter, the DIY Retailers "Christmas"!

Figure 29.1   Team Listening brief

reluctant staff soon become interested in attending as they hear from their colleagues about what when on in the last session. The interest became infectious and now most staff attend.

Staff form Customer Action Teams to handle any larger issues brought out by the sessions, then report progress at the next session. They take responsibility for solving problems and making improvements. Any success that would benefit other stores or departments is shared through regular internal communication vehicles issued by the PR Department (Figure 29.2).

Figure 29.2   Customers count: links in the chain
Extract from manager's briefing pack handed out at a series of roadshows. It also contained larger posters with similar information for staff canteens

As Team Listening progressed, junior managers and staff were given the opportunity to hold sessions and to apply their creativity to make them interesting and fun for their colleagues. This also provided an opportunity for personal development and created ownership.

Formal launch of Team Listening

To establish this new way of doing things, DO IT ALL held a series of road-shows concerned with customer care, attended by managers across the business. The format was fun and, through team listening sessions held at the roadshows, concentrated on helping managers discover for themselves why customer service is important to the company's long-term future. Presentations outlined the intention to offer the best customer service in the retail industry and the attitude required for achieving it.

The theme for the roadshows, and the support material, was *DO IT ALL Together* – head office and stores together, departments together, store staff and management together and the whole business together. The theme in itself helped to create an environment of positive thinking and this was the start of establishing the new DO IT ALL culture.

Managers spent time at the roadshows deciding together how they would take these messages back to their teams. This was done very successfully because managers were excited about the opportunity put before them and they had the necessary support to make it happen.

Following the roadshows and Team Listening briefs, the progress resulting from the programme was communicated through a special monthly newsletter *Chain Mail* (Figure 29.3). Now, two years on, there is no longer a need for the special newsletter because Team Listening has become a natural part of the way that we work. News is still communicated through other regular vehicles, however.

Coaching skills

Managers must have the right skills to undertake Team Listening. They also need to have the confidence in their own managerial abilities to encourage their team to take ownership for solving issues that they themselves would have previously solved.

The coaching skills training started with the board, then extended to senior management and to store managers. Next, junior store managers and middle managers at head office experienced the training. This consists of a three-day programme, held externally, designed and managed by the DO IT ALL training department.

The training helps managers ask the right questions to enable their team to come up with their own answers and to solve issues with minimal guidance or involvement from management.

THE OUTCOME

Two years into Team Listening and coaching, there has been a dramatic shift in the way that DO IT ALL works. Even the most dogmatic of managers have adopted the approach and learned that the best way to improve is to put the accountability for improvement into the hands of their team. Trading results   *367*

MARCH 1994   **ISSUE 7**

HIGHER, HIGHER!
No, it's not another game show!

It is the impressive increase in the number of complimentary letters, which are currently pouring into stores and Head Office.

The postman, or should I say post-person, has delivered an incredible 42 customer complimentary letters during the past period.

And Down, Down, Down go service complaints! Over the last period there has been a 27% reduction in the number of service complaints. Impressive, I should say so! The Customer Charter is proving a real winner, so keep on doing what your doing and let's see complaints dwindle and compliments continue to fill the postman's sack!

Remain alert! Despite the upward trends in our standards of customer service, the

number of complaints in general, has risen by 10% over the last year.

COMPLAINTS

COMPLIMENTS

WE'LL ALWAYS TAKE IT BACK -
NO QUIBBLES

Our Promise gives you lots of opportunities to talk to customers. You can encourage them to buy. If they are wondering whether it will fit, if it will match or if they will like it when they get it home, you have the power to persuade them to make the purchase. After all, we provide the assurance that if they are ever unhappy with a product purchased from DO IT ALL, they can always bring it back.

One area where you and our Promise can have a great impact is when customers

actually do 'bring it back'. Simply taking the goods from them and either refunding their money or exchanging for another product is not enough. We have an excellent opportunity to emphasise that our customers enjoy risk free shopping at DO IT ALL. By smiling and saying 'No problem Sir/Madam, if you are not happy it is our policy to always take it back,' a once disgruntled and dissatisfied customer leaves the store happy, extremely pleased that they shopped at DO IT ALL and will almost certainly return.

**RISK
FREE
SHOPPING**

Figure 29.3   *Chain Mail*

Chain Mail featured customer service stories and individual staff successes. It also served as a starting point for Team Listening sessions.

Figure 29.4   Customers count: the chain reaction

for stores that regularly carry out Team Listening are typically better than stores which do not.

The programme has enabled DO IT ALL to implement its corporate strategy successfully, creating an environment that is positive and unique to the company. Staff and management at every level are no longer waiting for approval from their boss to make changes that they can implement themselves. They are making the necessary changes and are willing to try new approaches (Figure 29.4).

There is a new positive spirit – commitment to the business and loyalty to the company has never been so high or so obvious.

The success of the programme and the culture created has extended into the way that customers are treated, enabling DO IT ALL to make significant progress in its mission of becoming famous for customer service. The new culture gives DO IT ALL a competitive advantage because no competitor can approach customer service in the same way – they just do not have the right staff attitude to be serious about customer service and it would take them too long to develop it.

FIVE LESSONS LEARNED ALONG THE WAY

1. When times are tough, it's easy to slip back into the 'old' way of doing things. Success in Team Listening and culture development requires constant commitment and patience.
2. There is an absolute need to allocate significant resource to Team Listening. It is not just a 'buzz word' or a name for yet another new initiative. It is a way of doing things and it must permeate every area of the company and everything that it does.
3. Due to time pressures and a need to develop culture quickly, DO IT ALL launched team listening before coaching. By doing so, it encouraged the process of coaching before providing the necessary skills. There is no doubt that it has worked. However, DO IT ALL would have wished to complete coaching training before launching Team Listening.
4. DO IT ALL was fortunate to have commitment to Team Listening from the top. In this case, it was the board who initiated the culture change. Without this, progress would have been more laborious and the programme would have lost momentum before the results could begin to be seen.
5. With time, Team Listening becomes a natural part of management style. But in the beginning, there may be some reluctance to try the new approach. If this is understood and managers are supported along the way, they will discover for themselves how well it can work.

Note: Team Listening is a registered trade mark and copyright process of the Marketing and Communication Agency. Licensed for use in DO IT ALL

30 EMAP
Communicate the advantage: creating a benefits communication strategy
Nick Throp *of Sedgwick Noble Lowndes*

UK organizations between them spend millions of pounds on providing benefits to ensure that they have the right employees on board. Yet the absence of an effective communication strategy often means they fail to create the impact required or deserved. This case study examines how international media company EMAP, with the help of benefits specialists Sedgwick Noble Lowndes, has prioritized communication of its benefits package to help it stay ahead in the employment market-place.

Employee benefits come in many shapes and forms – pension schemes, employee share schemes, private medical insurance, life assurance, the list goes on. All of them should be there for the same purpose – to recruit, retain and motivate the people who work for the company.

But communicating the value of such benefits often poses problems for organizations.

Lack of a benefits-wide approach

The problems start with the fact that many companies have little or no idea of the value of the benefit package as perceived by existing or potential employees nor of the role that benefits play in how employees view the company.

Responsibility fragmented

Traditionally, another part of the difficulty has been that responsibility for employee benefits may lie in different areas of the organization. For example, the pension scheme may be the responsibility of the pensions manager and *371* finance director; the share scheme may be the responsibility of the company secretary; and Personnel or HR may control the private medical insurance.

Sporadic communication

In such circumstances, it is no surprise that companies rarely have an integrated communication strategy for benefits. Communication exercises tend to be ad hoc, run when there is a specific issue causing concern or when the company is planning to change an element of the package.

Complex material

Then there is the challenge of the subject matter, which is often complex. Explaining the concepts behind the company pension scheme, for example, can be a difficult task.

Low interest levels within the target audience

Communicating pensions – often the most expensive benefit provided by the company – is made even more challenging by the fact that the benefit they provide is long-term. The gap between the cost of the benefit and its enjoyment means it is regarded as being of very little interest, particularly by younger employees. That gap has to be filled by effective communication, if the company is to get value for money.

Emphasis on information rather than on communication

Many companies when faced by these challenges do not approach the subject as they would any other communication exercise. The temptation is to rely on requirements set by the government or professional bodies in providing a base level of information, often written in technically obscure language. The answer is not simply to disclose information but to explain, reassure and promote the benefit package.

HOW EMAP PLC TACKLED AND OVERCAME THE PROBLEMS

EMAP plc is a highly successful media company, active in the UK and Europe, employing around 7200 staff. Its principal activities are publishing magazines, providing business-to-business communications media, publishing and printing newspapers and operating radio stations. The group has been highly acquisitive and profits have risen from £13.5 million to £63.9 million during the last ten years.

EMAP's culture is centred on acknowledging the fact that the success of the organization is based on the efforts and creativity of its 350 operating units. EMAP plc has what it calls a 'cottage industry' approach to its business. There are no bureaucratic structures, no large head office resource whose cost has to be re-allocated to the profit-maker. Employees are young people in the main, in the late 20s/early 30s age group: they are mobile and entrepreneurial.

Benefit objectives

Despite – and to an extent because of – its employee profile and the scattered nature of its operations (there is no central HR function, for example) EMAP plc has looked closely at the role of benefits. It has been careful to match its benefit objectives with its corporate objectives:

- reflect the company's position as a leader in its market-place
- remain competitive in the employment market-place
- provide an affordable but attractive package for employees
- provide a link between employees and the group as well as their primary employer.

The logistical difficulties of conveying messages to so many people at so many sites spread through the UK, France, Germany and other European locations, also served to focus the company on how its benefits package is communicated.

Communication strategy

EMAP plc's small head office unit at Peterborough is not a conventional 'command and tell centre'. It sees itself as providing specialist support services to the operating units who make the group's profits. Within it is a dedicated benefits team, sponsored by Group Company Secretary Derek Walsmsley, consisting of a Group Benefits Manager, Ralph Turner, and a Benefits Co-ordinator, Andy Martin, with administrative support.

The team has adopted the specific role of:

- shaping the company's benefits strategy (including a communication strategy, which is seen as central to implementation)
- establishing and maintaining best practice
- responding to legislative changes.

In this way, the company overcomes two of the usual difficulties in one go – it has a benefits-wide approach and allocates clear responsibility for benefit communication.

Viewpoint employee attitude surveys

Involved in professional communication itself, EMAP plc recognized the importance of research. Employee attitude surveys, containing a section dedicated to employee benefits, were carried out in 1993 and repeated in 1995. Some of the key findings of the first survey are listed below:

- employees wanted the opportunity to join the pension scheme earlier
- cost was an issue for employees, with many unsure of how much the company contributed to benefits
- as employees in the media industry tend to move on quickly, the relevance of benefits needed to be re-enforced
- the level of awareness and understanding of employee benefits was limited.

Targeting audiences accurately

Many internal communication programmes simply target the largest audience (employees) as the primary audience. But the different roles people play in the organization and how they relate to each other are also significant. Interestingly, it sometimes seems more helpful to think of the audiences in terms of the role they play in the communication process rather than their job function.

To prioritize the tasks involved in communicating employee benefits, EMAP plc produced a matrix, matching tasks to target audience needs (Figure 30.1).

Task \ Audience	Existing members	New entrants	Management	Specialist areas	Staff representatives
Awareness	3	3	3	3	3
Information	2	2	3	3	3
Reassurance	3	2	2	1	3
Education	2	2	3	3	3
Control	1	1	3	3	1
Feedback	2	1	3	3	3
Action	3	2	1	3	1
	16	13	18	19	17

Key: 3 = highest priority; 2 = medium priority; 1 = weakest priority

Figure 30.1 Target audiences vs. communication task

Communication media

The company then produced a matrix of available media against their suitability for the communication task (Figure 30.2).

EMAP plc's employee-led approach, not only to the benefits it provides, but to media selection, mirrors how most businesses approach the task of selling to their customers. Based on the research findings, the media chosen

Task \ Media	Presentations	Video	Literature	Posters	Statements	Counselling	Helpline
Awareness	2	3	2	3	3	2	1
Information	2	2	3	1	3	2	1
Reassurance	3	1	2	1	3	3	3
Education	3	2	2	1	2	2	1
Control	2	3	3	2	3	2	2
Feedback	3	1	1	1	1	1	3
Action	2	1	2	2	2	3	1
	17	13	15	11	17	15	12

Key: 3 = most effective; 2 = moderately effective; 1 = least effective

Figure 30.2   Media vs. communication task

involve, wherever possible, some form of interactive communication – ideally, face to face. Much of the strategy consists of presentations, roadshows and a benefits help desk, dedicated to answering employee questions.

Broadcast media and printed material are used as a back-up, but to attract the interest of the primary audience – mostly professional producers of high quality consumer publications – their design has to be highly distinctive. The *Benefits* newsletter, for example, was produced in a magazine format. The use of novel images helps it take a strikingly different approach to the subject matter from that of most similarly-targeted publications (Figure 30.3).

Company branding

Many employee benefit schemes are run by third-party administrators – building societies for Save As You Earn Share Schemes, insurance companies for life assurance cover, health companies for private medical insurance. Sometimes this third party uses the communication material to brand itself rather than the company whose employee is receiving the benefit. In such cases the company is not getting value for money for the benefit it provides.

EMAP plc has taken the step of branding all of its benefits with the *Partners In EMAP* (or PIE) logo. This logo appears on all of the communication material, from *Benefits News* to benefit statements and a leaflet promoting the range of benefits to potential new employees (Figure 30.4).

THE RESULTS FOR EMAP PLC

In the latest (1995) Viewpoint employee attitude survey, the following perceptions of the benefits package were identified:

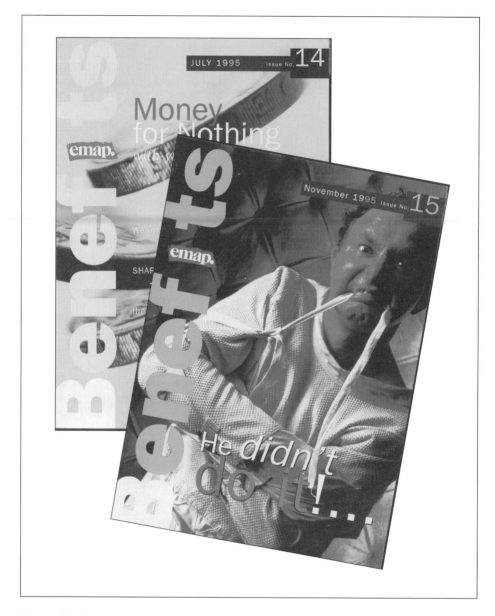

Figure 30.3 *Benefits News* - EMAP plc's employee benefits newsletter

- 80 per cent of employees felt encouraged to become shareholders through the employee share schemes
- 67 per cent of employees wanted more opportunities to take part in share schemes
- only 17 per cent of employees said they were less than satisfied with the benefit package as a whole

*Partners in
EMAP*

Figure 30.4   Partners in EMAP logo

- nearly 50 per cent of employees rated Flexiplan, the company's pension scheme, as good – a positive result for an audience of primarily young people.

As a mark of EMAP's success in this area, in competition with leading plcs in the UK, the company recently won the 1995 Pro-Share award for the best communication of an employee share scheme and best overall use of share schemes. More importantly, the take-up rates for the benefits, pensions and share schemes have increased significantly since the inception of a coordinated communication programme.

THE FUTURE – FLEXIBLE BENEFITS?

The concept of flexible benefits, where the company effectively gives employees a menu from which they can choose those benefits that most suit them, has been popular in the USA for some time but is now starting to develop in this country. EMAP plc is among the first companies in the UK to introduce such a scheme.

The motivation to introduce this system usually includes:

- the desire to control the cost of the benefits
- the provision of relevant benefits to the employee
- the communication of the total range and cost of benefits to the employee.

Because flexible benefits involve employees in choosing their own package (within the cost constraints affordable by the company), communication is even more important to their effective implementation.

EMAP plc is therefore truly setting communication at the heart of its benefit strategy. Other companies, equally eager to recruit and keep good employees, are likely to want to follow suit. When they do, designers of employee benefits packages – and particularly of the communication strategies that are integral to their success – will have to work harder and more intelligently than hitherto.   *377*

31 F.I. GROUP
Establishing workforce ownership

Joan Campbell, *marketing project coordinator*

This case study describes the communication programme surrounding the buy-out by the workforce of F.I. GROUP in 1991. It details the implementation and result of the offer together with the changes in strategies evolving from workforce share ownership.

In November 1991, shortly after the buy-out, F.I. GROUP chief executive Hilary Cropper told the workforce:

> You made it happen! At the roadshows I stated my own belief in FI and in my colleagues throughout the Group. I hoped you would all share my belief and enter into the spirit of a participative company through ownership and control. Your response has overwhelmingly confirmed my belief that we really can achieve our vision. We knew we already had the talent and enthusiasm – now we have the ownership in our hands.

FI is a leading information technology services and training organization. Customers of the Group are large organizations whose IT systems support UK, European and global operations. It is an independent UK company with, at the time of writing, a workforce of 1600 operating nationwide; it is a market leader through its MAINSTAY applications management services and has pioneered the partnership approach with organizations, seeking a strategic solution that offers substantial improvements in service and costs.

The company's turnover for 1994/95 was £61.7m (an increase of 196 per cent since the buy-out in 1991). Its customers include Barclays Bank, The Co-operative Bank, TSB, Granada UK Rental, Whitbread, Tesco, Dun & Bradstreet, Thames Water, the Department of Health and BT.

FI is unique in the scale by which it achieves flexibility in its workforce. Of its total workforce 609 are employees, the rest being associate suppliers. It operates from eight work centres spread across the country and has project teams working in numerous customer sites at any one time.

It follows that the expertise and commitment of its people are paramount to the Group's success. FI has always been, therefore, an open company that has placed workforce motivation high on its list of priorities. Against this background, in October 1991 FI established effective workforce control through a share offer that sold a block of shares belonging to the company's founder – Steve Shirley – directly to the workforce.

WHY THE BUY-OUT?

In 1990, strategically and emotionally the company wanted to remain independent but needed to find an exit route for Steve Shirley and to create an environment of greater freedom for expanding the business.

Original plans to float the company on the stock market had been abandoned, partly because of the recession and its impact on the company's track record but also because of the changing climate at the time making a public flotation of medium-sized companies unattractive.

A plan emerged to buy out Steve Shirley over a period of time and to take the first step through a share offer. This is aptly expressed by a quote at the time of the buy-out in 1991 from Shirley to all participants:

> Since founding the business of the Group nearly 30 years ago, I have been striving to bring about worker participation. In the early years it was profit sharing; later it was via the Shareholders' Trust. This now owns 23 per cent of the equity – very important if the company were threatened by take-over.
>
> But it has not been enough. I have come to realise that to enhance the Group's performance with the motivational thrust of workforce share ownership, people actually need to own shares directly. The concept is simple. It is for majority ownership to pass from me and my family substantially to you and your families.

Simple though the concept may have been, the execution was anything but. The appointment of Sir Peter Thompson as chairman provided valuable practical experience of employee share ownership (he had led the employee buy-out of National Freight Corporation) but FI was breaking new ground because its associate suppliers were not legally regarded as employees.

SCHEME DESIGN

Structure of the share offer

Since such a large part of FI's workforce are associate suppliers it was important to include them fully in the offer in addition to the employees. However, as far as the law is concerned they are members of the public.

This, together with the need to provide the founder with a premium price for ceding control of the business, whilst the shares were being offered at a fair *379* value, made the structure of the offer legally complex, resulting in a full prospectus. Two trusts were also established, an Employee Trust and a Non-employee Trust, which were involved in the purchase and resale of shares.

Employees were offered interest-free loans of up to £540 to buy shares.

Mechanisms for trading shares

An internal market was established, which operated two dealing days per year, the share price being set by an independent valuer. Only members of the workforce and other authorized purchasers could buy shares. When people left the company they could retain their shares, but when they sold them they could do so only through the internal market. The company articles were constructed to protect against unwanted shareholders.

Shares held by the workforce obtained a double vote in any poll on resolutions to amend the articles and on the appointment of directors. The double voting mechanism was achieved, without creating a separate class of shares, through the actions of the Employee and Non-employee Trusts which mirrored the workforce vote through Gold and Platinum shares.

THE ROLE OF THE SHAREHOLDERS' TRUST

The Shareholders' Trust is an FI employee benefit trust, set up originally by Steve Shirley to encourage members of the workforce to hold shares, and to represent the whole workforce whether they own shares or not. In 1995, it held 16.9 per cent of the equity, balloting the workforce before casting its votes. It actively supports workforce share ownership by being prepared to buy or sell shares to the workforce, within limits, to balance the demand. It also helps to monitor the company's progress towards participation and the attitude of the workforce to the company and to share ownership.

The Trust produces its own newsletter and supports charitable organizations by matching funds raised by the workforce and providing financial assistance for workforce social events. There are eight trustees, two of whom are elected employees and two elected associate suppliers.

THE RESULT OF THE OFFER

The offer was an overwhelming success, creating effective workforce control at one stroke. Over one-third of associate suppliers and 72 per cent of employees bought shares, raising a total of £1.25m. The distribution of shareholding and voting power before and after the offer is shown in Figure 31.1.

In March 1992 when 100 staff from Whitbread plc became FI employees under a Transfer of Undertaking, over 50 per cent of them bought shares within three weeks of the transfer. At the first dealing day following a similar transfer of staff from The Co-operative Bank to FI in 1994, 45 per cent bought shares.

FI shapes its remuneration policy towards performance-related pay with an

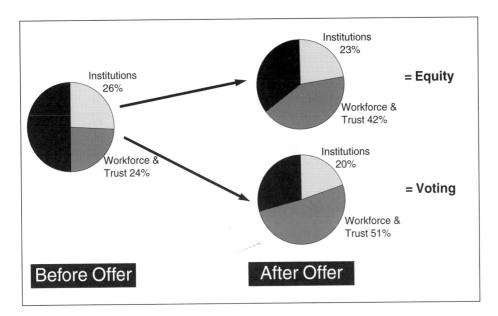

Figure 31.1   Distribution of shareholding and voting power before and after the buy-out offer

emphasis on increasing individual shareholdings through bonusing and profit share.

At the beginning of 1995 a trust called QUEST was established for the purpose of acquiring, holding and distributing shares to employees either directly or through profit-sharing schemes, playing, therefore, a vital role in the future development of workforce ownership within the company.

COMMUNICATIONS PROGRAMME

In a distributed organization, effective communications play a key role in the management of the company. The introduction of the share offer to a total workforce at that time of 1000 employees and associate suppliers working throughout the UK required a large integrated internal and external communications programme.

The programme was designed and developed by the in-house corporate marketing team in conjunction with the FI board. This allowed costs to be kept at a minimum with some specialized consultancy being bought in for the production of the company video, PR related to the financial press, and the design and production of corporate literature including the Prospectus, Annual Report and Annual Review.

Communication of the share offer was essentially in two phases: pre-prospectus and post-prospectus.

Pre-prospectus

The primary aim was to ensure there was sufficient support for the scheme, and then to communicate it in outline to prepare people for the offer later that year.

The board initially sought the commitment of the senior management group, and at the Top Team Conference in June 1991 communicated the vision of the new FI to the top 100 managers in the company. That conference resulted in a unanimous vote to support the vision and to communicate it down the line. An anonymous poll showed that this group of people was likely to invest up to three-quarters of a million pounds.

With this support the board communicated the vision through a series of roadshows to everyone in the company using a corporate video *Share in FI*.

Post-prospectus

Following the prospectus, the directors again went on the road to explain the details to the workforce and to answer any of their questions. A group of financial advisers joined this roadshow, and ultimately set up clinics around FI's UK offices to provide a financial helpline.

A series of press campaigns before, during and after the share offer were used to communicate key messages through the press to the company's customers as well as the workforce. This resulted in FI's biggest press campaign to date and was covered by most national, regional, business and computing press. This also led to the publication of numerous case studies on the Group. Corporate Communication notice-boards were sited in prominent positions in each office and work centre to stimulate interest and provide information and press and customer comments.

The roadshow and meeting programme was supported by written communications in the form of quarterly newsletters, monthly bulletins and full information packs on forthcoming events. All events were administered and coordinated centrally and great emphasis was placed on full participation at meetings and feedback and review for each event. All outstanding questions and concerns were fed up the line for resolution.

All communications material was subject to verification by the company's financial advisers throughout the programme.

MOVING ON BEYOND THE OFFER

Since 1991, the level of internal communication has not decreased and continues to be based on face-to-face meetings and two-way communication. As well as regular management briefings and twice yearly roadshows, Share Ownership employee and associate supplier handbooks have been produced.

FI's annual general meeting is a very important event in the calendar. The board takes the time to explain fully the progress of the company and the issues it faces. The AGM is held at the weekend and besides the serious business is organized as a family day out. Nearly 200 shareholders have attended each AGM for the last three years together with an additional 400 family members. Pre-share offer AGM attendance was around 40–70 shareholders.

MARKET RESEARCH

FI is committed to regular surveys of its workforce.

The first survey following the 1991 offer was commissioned in conjunction with the Shareholders' Trust in February 1992 and was carried out by The Industrial Society. The independent survey began with pilot face-to-face interviews across all sections of the company. Several focus groups met with Industrial Society representatives to discuss the key issues and to help frame the questionnaire. A full questionnaire was developed covering many issues including shareholding and the role of the Shareholders' Trust. The response rate was high: 74 per cent salaried staff and 53 per cent associate suppliers.

The response to questions in the 1992 survey, relating to why people bought shares, was mixed. The most important were a sense of loyalty to the company, a desire at that time to keep the company independent and a belief that achieving control would help to secure their jobs. A similar survey carried out at the end of 1994 showed greater emphasis on the accumulating value of the shares as a reason for investing.

MOTIVATION THE KEY

F.I. GROUP operates in a business sector where, perhaps more than most others, success depends on the consistent delivery of an excellent standard of service. To deliver that level of service requires not only a well-developed partnership with customers but also a partnership within the company with a workforce that is motivated and committed.

The success in establishing workforce ownership has been a critical factor in ensuring the continued motivation of the workforce aligned to the ongoing success of the business. This would not have been possible without the extensive communications programme throughout the campaign.

Since this case study was prepared, a proposal for the flotation of FI was presented through a nationwide roadshow to the workforce, who had collectively invested almost three million pounds in the company since the buyout. The proposal received overwhelming support and at the EGM held shortly afterwards, a resolution was passed by a 99.4 per cent vote from shareholders.

Following flotation in April 1996, new profit share and share option schemes were introduced to encourage and maintain workforce share ownership.

32 Glaxo Operations – Secondary Underpinning a major change programme

Liz Cochrane, *communications manager*

This case study covers a two-year period beginning in January 1994, during which Glaxo Operations – Secondary entered the throes of major change. Throughout this time, it was supported by a carefully-conceived communication strategy.

Before the merger of Glaxo and Wellcome in 1995, Glaxo Operations – Secondary was an operating company made up of two large pharmaceutical manufacturing and supply sites, Barnard Castle in County Durham and Ware in Hertfordshire, with a small head office at Stockley Park, Middlesex. It is now part of a larger operating company, Glaxo Wellcome Operations, which encompasses all of Glaxo Wellcome's manufacturing operations in the UK.

The pharmaceutical industry is undergoing unprecedented change as a result of healthcare reforms worldwide. The role of Glaxo Operations – Secondary was to manufacture and supply prescription medicines to its customers, Glaxo marketing companies across the world.

To support its customers in an increasingly demanding external environment, the company embarked on a major change programme, incorporating elements of business process re-engineering, and the introduction of MRPII – a disciplined business planning and product supply system. These changes, incorporated into the company's 1994 business plan, were essential if it was to achieve a set of challenging five-year goals. They would also demand the active support of the company's 3000 staff, requiring people to adopt new ways of working.

An effective communications strategy was essential to ensure that all staff understood:

- the reasons for change
- the company's strategies
- 'what it means for me'.

HOW WE ARRIVED AT A SOLUTION AND WHY

Assembling the right team

A communications strategy group was established to develop recommendations for ratification by the company Executive. Led by the communications manager, the group initially included the manager responsible for continuous improvement activities and the training and development managers for each site. Following adoption of the recommendations the group took an implementation remit and membership expanded to include other communications professionals from the sites, the head of corporate development and a product stream leader (responsible for one of the company's principal processes). A consultant from The Industrial Society also joined the group, to bring an external perspective and challenge, and to undertake regular ongoing research into the effectiveness of the approach.

Doing our homework

The group's first actions were to initiate research. We employed an independent consultancy to establish current perceptions and issues around communications.

Focus groups were made up of eight to ten staff, and used structured questions. Group members were selected on a 'random sample' basis, with each group comprising people representing a particular segment of the business – for example manufacturing and packaging operators, engineering staff, administrative staff (finance, personnel, etc.) and quality assurance staff. In tandem with this, a series of one-to-one interviews were held with members of the Executive Committee, to understand their expectations of what the strategy needed to deliver, and to define key messages.

Findings from the research identified a number of areas that needed to be taken into account when formulating the strategy, in particular:

- the Executive Committee was not seen as being committed to internal communications
- team managers concentrated on local issues when communicating with their teams, and tended not to reference 'the big picture'
- there was a lack of understanding of the complementary roles of different teams
- in some areas upward communications were poor, leading to 'information ceilings'
- a series of management forums during 1993 – designed to gain involvement in the development of the company's change programme – had

385

created some insecurity among other staff with concerns that there was a 'hidden agenda'
- most managers rated their own communications skills as 'good' – while saying that the skills of their colleagues needed to improve.

Understanding what the company required from the communications strategy in order to achieve its business goals led to the following principles being adopted:

- the need for wholesale involvement and commitment by staff to achieve the step change ahead: this meant developing an understanding of the 'big picture' – why change was required – and the company's plans for achieving its goals, linked to an understanding of the individual contribution required
- effective communication as a fundamental part of every manager's role
- the need for both effective two-way vertical communications and horizontal communication between teams
- the requirement for communications to prioritize customer needs.

HOW WE PUT THE STRATEGY TOGETHER

Providing a robust framework

The strategy built on and improved existing communication mechanisms, and introduced new elements.

The format of the bi-annual 'Cascade' was amended. A roadshow coinciding with the publication of the company's half- and full-year results, Cascade provided an overview of performance, progress against the company's strategies and key issues ahead. Cascades had previously been led by the managing director and members of the Executive, with a presentation followed by questions 'coaxed' from the floor. The revised format includes a shorter presentation, followed by attendees (all managers including first-line managers) breaking into discussion groups led by an executive committee member.

Having participated in Cascade, managers organized local Stage II Cascades for their areas, incorporating local performance and plans.

The success of the Cascade groups led the Executive to request the introduction of Interim Cascades held midway between each main Cascade. These are small, cross-functional discussion groups, and provide additional opportunities for exploring key issues and performance. Follow-up research revealed the following benefits of this approach:

- a deepening understanding of the 'big picture' by managers
- a turnaround in people's perception of the commitment of the Executive to communications
- direct feedback to the Executive
- a greater understanding of others' perspectives by all participants.

Communication Events

The principal new component in the framework was Communication Events. Held on a two-monthly basis (except during months where there was a Cascade) and covering 100 per cent of staff, these comprise small discussion groups made up of a diagonal slice across the organization, that is they are cross-functional and non-hierarchical.

The Events place emphasis on the external changes in the pharmaceutical industry, and the impact of these on customers and on specific elements of the company's business strategies, broken down into 'bite-sized chunks'. The aims include:

- breaking down barriers between different areas of the company
- communicating in an egalitarian way to build trust and common understanding and to symbolize the importance of everyone's contribution to the change process.

The Events also provide a direct, unfiltered feedback loop.

Each Event follows a two-stage process. On day one, Executive Committee members lead discussion groups for senior managers. On days two and three, those managers lead groups covering the whole organization. Leaders' notes are provided in advance (Figures 32.1 and 32.2).

Feedback and unanswered questions are recorded and sent to the communications department. In addition, a leaders' feedback session is organized after each event. Feedback is analysed, and a summary of key issues presented to the Executive which agrees subsequent actions. All questions are answered through a 'question and answer' document published following each Event.

The other component of the communications framework is team meetings. Held across the company, the format and style of these differ according to the needs of each area. Feedback from the Communications Events demonstrated that not all areas were holding team meetings on a regular basis, and a company standard was set, introducing a minimum requirement of one team meeting per month. Team meetings are mainly concerned with local performance and discussion of local issues. Managers were also asked to use the team meetings to discuss the local implications of Event topics. A monthly update on company performance against targets is made available for use in team meetings, with a recommendation that it is displayed on notice-boards.

Putting the competencies in place

The second, fundamental strand of the communications strategy was a programme to ensure a high level of communication competencies across the management group.

Led by the training and development managers, this programme involved defining a set of communication competencies, supported by positive and negative indicators for each. A computer-based training needs analysis   *387*

April '95 Communications Event

The Big Picture

This month's Event looks at the changes in the pharmaceutical industry: how these have affected our customers and how we need to respond to meet their needs and remain successful in the future.

The Event is based around a two-part video featuring interviews with customers and others outside Glaxo Wellcome Operations, and an interview with Ian McInnes. The interview with Ian also covers other areas in which staff have expressed ongoing interest.

Your role is to help your group to pull out the key messages from the interviews, and to ensure they are understood. The leaders' notes have been designed to help this process.

It is likely that the video will prompt a number of questions from staff (particularly around the impact of the Glaxo Wellcome merger). This is a healthy part of the change process. It is important that people have the opportunity to ask questions – and receive a reply – to minimise the potential negative impact of uncertainty and to build trust.

Please answer questions where you can and capture those where you were not confident of the reply on the question forms.

To help you answer the questions

Please ensure that you are familiar with the content of the video.

If there are areas where you would like additional information, contact the Communications Department (please allow sufficient time for a response to be obtained), or ask at the Stage 1 Event – which will include a showing of the video.

Please familiarise yourself with the relevant sections of the Q&A document issued by Group Public Affairs re Glaxo Wellcome. If you do not have a copy of this document, please contact the Communications Department.

Following the positive response to the interactive element of last month's Event, an optional interactive section has been included this month. Please take a judgement on whether to use this, based on your delivery style and the time you will need to answer the number of questions likely to come from your group.

Dec '95 Communications Event

The Way Ahead

Please find script enclosed, also a copy of the business plan.

The objectives for this session are to:

1 introduce the Glaxo Wellcome Operations business plan

2 build understanding of what 'to be the supplier of choice' means

3 communicate the most recent new product pipeline update (in response to staff feedback)

4 gather views on achieving the 'people' breakthrough objective in the business plan

5 gather feedback from all groups on what people want to hear about: this will be an input to the Glaxo Wellcome Operations Communications Strategy.

Please note: it is very important that the feedback gathered on achieving the 'people' breakthrough objective and on future communication content is fed back in a form which is readily understandable to the group who will subsequently use this data. Please arrange for the feedback to be typed or e-mailed and sent to the Communications Department, Ware, by Friday 8 December (ie no flipcharts, please!).

Please ensure the following

1 **Feedback on 'people' objective and on communications are typed on separate headed sheets/separate e-mails.**

2 **Feedback is returned in a form which can be easily understood by someone who was not present at the session.**

3 **Each feedback sheet is headed with the date, time and location of the session, together with your name and extension number.**

Many thanks for your help.

Figure 32.2 'The Way Ahead' – leaders' notes

389

program was developed, involving 360° feedback on an individual's communication skills – from team colleagues, peers, direct reports and managers. An open learning programme was also developed, with modules relating to each main competency. Workshops were made available for areas where role-playing formed an essential part of competency development.

WHAT WE LEARNED FROM IMPLEMENTATION

The progress of the strategy as a whole was monitored on a regular basis by the strategy group, which adopted a continuous improvement approach throughout. Monitoring mechanisms included ongoing analysis of the feedback from the integral feedback loops, together with focus groups conducted on a six-monthly basis by The Industrial Society.

Establishing a new and different communication mechanism is tough, and a number of valuable lessons have been learned during the implementation process.

1. *Effective discussion groups require a leader with a high level of facilitation skills* – particularly in diagonal slice groups, where some group members may have more expertise in the area under discussion than the leader. Significant effort has gone into identifying the most competent Communications Event leaders, as this has been the factor that has most coloured participants' views of the Events. The difference having a good facilitator can make is illustrated by the somewhat unguarded and now infamous remark from one leader that the buzz he got from the Events was 'better than sex'! Particularly in the early days, some group members voted with their feet – missing their scheduled session in order to attend one where word of mouth had it that a leader was particularly good.

2. *Be aware of people's 'comfort zones'.* Initially, it was planned to mix Event group members, and leaders, on a regular basis. Feedback from all concerned quickly demonstrated that this would not make sense. Effective dialogue between group members grew where group members remained constant, and where they were led by the same (good quality) leader. Leaders also expressed a strong preference for keeping groups together, allowing them to build a rapport with group members.

3. *Making information relevant and interesting is also vital.* Following a 'false start' – where feedback showed the subject matter was seen as boring – an interactive approach was quickly adopted, incorporating group exercises and learning games related to the topic. Successful use has been made of low budget videos, featuring, for example, staff interviewing key customers, to understand their needs, and a city analyst, to get his views on the pressures of the industry. In September 1995, the format for the Events changed from being totally cross-functional to being product stream based, i.e. groups made up of a mix of manufacturing and packaging staff for a particular product type plus staff from support areas. This

allows leaders to provide more pertinent local examples to illustrate the topic.

4. *The discussion group format, providing a direct feedback loop, ensures that key issues can be captured and addressed* – but also significantly increases expectations that actions will follow points raised. An improvement programme is currently underway to provide additional breakdown of feedback and direct it immediately to the point where action can best be taken.

5. *The organizational implications of arranging cross-functional (or product stream) groups are enormous, and have at times dominated perceptions of the Events.* Though attendance at each Event has averaged 70–80 per cent, with the remainder attending follow-up sessions, it has proved difficult to achieve total stability in groups. A significant portion of one administrator's role, at both main sites, is now dedicated to supporting the Events and Cascades.

HOW WELL DID THE STRATEGY SUCCEED?

The focus groups conducted by The Industrial Society indicate a high level of awareness of key messages about the need for change and the company's plans. This is underlined by a strong desire from staff for additional detail on performance and on progress against strategies. Set against this is the fact that Events are not always consistently followed up by every manager in team meetings, meaning that some operators find it difficult to see the relevance of Events for them. This issue is currently being addressed.

The Cascades are universally popular, and are seen as meeting their objectives.

In general, people have also found the Events useful, with the majority (except for some operators) saying that they would attend the sessions even if they were voluntary – with the proviso that they be well led. A number of staff like the cross-functional nature of the Events, with the opportunity to break barriers and broaden horizons. Others would prefer the information to be given by a local senior manager. This links strongly with the communication skills of the local manager.

The communication competency package has not been as well used as anticipated. This is mainly because of business circumstances – the demands of the change programme overlaid by the local implications of Glaxo's merger with Wellcome. As this is a vital component of the strategy, the package is currently being reviewed for effectiveness prior to a re-launch across Glaxo Wellcome Operations as part of the communications strategy for the integrated company.

LOOKING TO THE FUTURE

The approach described above has been central to managing the immediate – and pressing – communication needs facing the organization over the initial two-year period.

The longer-term strategy is to move towards a higher level of integrated communication processes, led by line managers, while retaining the benefits of breaking down barriers, ensuring strong upward feedback, and maintaining the visibility and accessibility of the top team.

This strategy will be achieved by a combination of effective use of the competency package, implementation of a people strategy developed by the HR function, and ongoing monitoring and adaptation of the existing framework, so that it evolves to the desired end state.

33 IBM
How the original Speak Up! system works

Lyn Cannings, *UK Speak Up! coordinator*

IBM's much-admired and rigorously-administered Speak Up! programme is now over 35 years old and has been used as a patent for similar systems in many other organizations. Employees write anonymously to experienced coordinators who forward the information to the right person in the company, and track response through a formal procedure – normally expected to take under ten days. Points deemed to be of sufficient public interest are given publicity.

The Speak Up! programme is only one of several upward communication mechanisms open to IBM employees. It is there to complement the main route, through the employee's manager, along with appraisal and counselling, an open door programme for approaching senior managers, and opinion surveys.

Speak Up! is now in place worldwide with active programmes in most countries. It facilitates two-way, written communication on any company-related topic. The programme can be used to ask questions, make comments or voice complaints about any aspect of IBM's business operations.

One of its most important features is that the identity of the writer is protected. The identity is known only by the programme's coordinator, except in the case of a Speak Up! interview when it may be passed to an interviewer, but only with the writer's agreement. This right to anonymity is strictly observed and respected, up to and including the highest levels of corporate management.

THE COORDINATOR'S MAIN RESPONSIBILITIES

Appropriate reporting and analysis

Meaningful analyses help to highlight significant trends in the use of the programme, which in turn enable management to judge what that reveals about the impact of company policies and practices, and about employee attitudes and concerns in general.

Facilitating the process

Coordinators assess the urgency of a Speak Up! and determine the method of handling it. They contact the appropriate manager and collaborate in preparing replies, including editing, revising, correcting and refining the quality of the response. They also expedite the response time and ensure appropriate executive sign-off.

Assessment

All aspects of the complaint are assessed with the employee so that the relevant manager can be provided with any useful additional information not included in the Speak Up! At the same time, coordinators are expected to use their judgement to ensure anonymity is maintained. They also help managers determine the suitability of a Speak Up! for publication.

ACCEPTING SPEAK UP!S

The programme is open only to IBM employees, not to members of an employee's family, or to retired, contract or temporary personnel. If, when the coordinator checks up, they are found not to be on the payroll, their Speak Up! is returned and they are told why. However, coordinators may feel some other action is appropriate. If the subject is of significant importance, they will pass the concern raised on to the relevant department but no formal response will be prepared.

All Speak Up!s are re-typed by the coordinator, as a further protection of the writer's identity and because the text is distributed softcopy via the internal mail system (NOSS) to the respondent. Coordinators use their judgement to edit the Speak Up!, if necessary, for example to correct grammatical errors or delete any identifying information. From then on, the letter is referred to in all correspondence only by its allocated number.

If the Speak Up! has been signed by more than one person, the coordinator checks each signatory identity to ensure each is a current IBM employee. Each individual is given a copy of the answer. Speak Up!s signed by more than one employee are seen as 'multisignature' and may be considered 'sensitive'.

If the Speak Up! is unsigned, it is not processed. Depending on the significance of the issues or concerns raised, however, the appropriate manager

Figure 33.1   Speak Up! form and envelope

would be informed and a response prepared and kept on file. If the coordinator is approached subsequently by the writer of an unsigned Speak Up! and is satisfied that the renewed contact is indeed from the original writer, they may release the reply – providing it was received no more than three months earlier. If renewed contact is made after that time, the originator of the reply is asked to review the answer before it is released.

Habitual writers of Speak Up!s are not dissuaded from using the programme unless they are abusing it. No special separate record, statistical or otherwise, is kept of the correspondence of such employees.

When a Speak Up! letter inadvertently reveals the writer's identity, which can happen in smaller countries, departments or locations, coordinators may offer to assist in rewriting the letter to avoid exposure.

If the writer has copied the Speak Up! to others and signed it, they are advised that the usual degree of anonymity cannot be maintained. The answer would, in any case, be addressed to the writer only.

RECORDING THE SPEAK UP!

A number is allocated to each Speak Up! as soon as it has been accepted: the use of any other form of code for Speak Up! letters or their writers is not allowed.

An acknowledgement is sent immediately to the writer, giving the number and advising that all further correspondence will reference that number. The acknowledgement stresses that the confidentiality of the programme is as much the responsibility of the writer as of the coordinator.

The number is recorded in three places:

- on the Speak Up! letter
- on the bottom of the letter where the personal information is recorded
- in the Speak Up! log book.

The writer's personal information is then separated from the letter and locked in a safe place known only to the coordinator and a deputy. If the original letter was handwritten this too is locked away.

Each coordinator keeps a record of the Speak Up!s received, typically including:

- Speak Up! number
- subject
- date the letter was received
- to whom it was sent for reply and when
- date the reply was received
- date the reply was sent to the writer
- the response time
- whether the Speak Up! was signed, unsigned, or multisignature
- whether it was published internally
- whether it resulted in or contributed to any action
- any follow-up action required
- the date of interview if appropriate.

ROUTING SPEAK UP!S

Answers are regarded as company answers and not as the personal view of an individual manager. Therefore, though coordinators select the manager they consider most appropriate to respond to the writer's remarks, in most cases either the head of the function concerned, or a senior manager, signs the reply.

If Speak Up! writers specify a particular manager, department or function to which they would like the letter addressed, those wishes are respected where possible. The manager concerned is told that the letter is being sent at the writer's request.

If coordinators consider it appropriate to send a letter to more than one manager, each is given the name or names of the others.

Speak Up!s should in general be answered within a maximum of ten working days. Managers are reminded in the coordinator's cover letter that a prompt reply is necessary. If one has not been received after five working days, the coordinator contacts the manager to establish the cause and tries to obtain a commitment to an anticipated reply date.

Part of the coordinators' responsibility is to ensure that writers are kept aware of the current status of their Speak Up! at all times. They are informed immediately of any delay, given reasons for the delay and told when an answer is expected. Coordinators also inform their own manager about out-of-line situations.

HANDLING REPLIES

If coordinators are not satisfied that the reply addresses clearly ALL the points in the Speak Up!, clarification is requested on the outstanding issues. If necessary, the writer is informed of any delay.

When the reply is acceptable, it is returned to the writer with a request to complete a questionnaire and return it to the coordinator (Figure 33.2). The questionnaire is then used to monitor the satisfaction of the writer with the programme.

INVOLVING SENIOR MANAGEMENT

Senior managers are actively encouraged to become involved in the programme for three reasons:

- it is an opportunity to reconsider the policy, practice or procedure that is the subject of the Speak Up!
- it guarantees the validity of the reply
- more generally, it keeps them informed of employees' current concerns and can alert them to potentially serious situations.

FORWARDING THE REPLY

The Speak Up! reply is sent to the writer and the appropriate entries made in the Speak Up! log book. Wherever possible, an original signed reply is sent and a copy retained on file.

```
Speak Up! No:                        Return by:  ASAP

Respondent:                          Subject:

To ensure the programme's continued success, please complete
the following questionnaire and return it to the address shown
overleaf.

1.  How satisfied are you with the reply?

    (  ) Very satisfied
    (  ) Satisfied
    (  ) Neither satisfied nor dissatisfied
    (  ) Dissatisfied
    (  ) Very dissatisfied

2.  If you are unhappy with your reply, please indicate the
    reason.

    (  ) Reply did not answer my question
    (  ) Reply not clear
    (  ) Do not agree with policy
    (  ) Reply took too long
    (  ) Other *..........................................
         ...................................................

3.  How satisfied are you that your Speak Up! was given careful
    review by management?

    (  ) Very satisfied
    (  ) Satisfied
    (  ) Neither satisfied nor dissatisfied
    (  ) Dissatisfied
    (  ) Very dissatisfied

4.  Do you believe that management will take action as a
    result of your Speak Up!

    (  ) Action will be taken immediately
    (  ) Action will be taken soon
    (  ) No action will be taken
    (  ) N/A

5.  Will you use the Speak Up! programme again?

    (  ) Yes, definitely
    (  ) Yes, probably
    (  ) No, probably not
    (  ) No, definitely not (please state reason/s) ........
         ...................................................

* If you require a further reply, please complete a new Speak
Up! form quoting the number shown at the top of this page and
stating that it is a follow up.

        INSERT IN A WINDOW ENVELOPE OR FOLD, STAPLE AND MAIL TO
                        ADDRESS OVERLEAF
```

Figure 33.2   Speak Up! questionnaire

speak up !

To: _____ Date _____

The attached Speak Up! _____ is sent for reply by you or your deputy. Please return it to me by _____

If you consider the Speak Up! does not fall in your area, please notify me by telephone within 24 hours, indicating who you feel should answer it.

It would be helpful if you would keep the following points in mind when preparing a Speak Up! answer:

• Tell the employee as frankly as possible what he or she wants to know.

• Avoid legalistic or technical explanations and references.

• Write simply and clearly.

• Give up-to-date, accurate information.

• Tell not only what the company is doing, but how and why.

• Don't be reluctant to admit mistakes.

Finally, if you do not wish to see your reply published, please indicate why not:

_____

_____

_____

_____

_____

_____

_____

Figure 33.3   Speak Up! check-list

The Speak Up! check-list (Figure 33.3) is designed to help the manager to produce a good reply. If it is necessary to modify the original reply, changes are made only with the full agreement of its originator.

Speak Up! reply letters are not addressed personally to the writer. This information appears only on the envelope, which is sent to the writer's home address whenever possible.

Coordinators must be reasonably sure that the writer will be satisfied with the reply. The time taken to reply should always suggest that management has seriously considered the writer's comments and, even though the reply may be disappointing to the writer, they should be satisfied that careful and sufficient thought has been given to the problem and that management's reasoning is acceptable.

Managers other than the reply's originator can be made aware of the Speak Up! correspondence if the coordinator believes it necessary.

THE SPEAK UP! ANSWER

A good Speak Up! reply is a constructive reaction to an idea or problem. It answers all the questions raised; it is direct and helpful, not evasive or defensive. It should be brief, clear and well organized.

34 Kent County Council
Faith, hope and measurement: measuring the effects of communication

Judith Trafford, *MIPR, publicity manager*

Finding ways to prove IC's success is never easy. But what happens in the public sector where there is no such thing as a bottom line? Kent County Council's case study examines two cases where an objective demonstrably in the organization's interest – in one case the very survival of the council under local government reorganization – became the marker for achievement.

There are those in the public sector, as in the private sector, who still believe communicating with staff is a luxury. That's why when times are hard this can be where the first cuts come. Of course it should be the last place to make cuts. Hard times and change scenarios – and there are plenty of both everywhere in the 1990s – need plenty of good communication if organizations are to survive and prosper. The one way to convince the sceptics is to prove that employee communication works, by measuring the benefits – though because of some of the difficulties involved and the cost too, I myself recommend a mixed approach of faith, hope and measurement.

At Kent County Council we are not slaves to measurement, but we do believe in it. Measurement makes life easier. It can offer you several desirable qualities.

- *Confirmation* You had faith – you knew you were doing the right thing, but isn't it good to be able to prove it? And, if your measurement shows poor results, at least you've got a sound basis for adjustment and improvement.
- *Credibility* It gives what you do a more professional edge. It gives you the confidence to build on your success. You can be more assertive in promoting your ideas and gaining support for them.

- *Clout* This can mean influence, funds, promotion, fame, glory. It helps put employee communications where it belongs – on the agenda at the top table.

So measurement is good, but what are we measuring? We need to define the bottom line.

In the private sector, this usually means profit – how much money did making widgets make for your shareholders? I know that communicators in the private sector find it difficult to make the link between their contribution and that 'ultimate' bottom line. But it has to be even more difficult for those of us working in the public sector who neither manufacture widgets nor make a profit.

None the less we try, and I believe with two of our recent internal communication programmes we succeeded, albeit that the two had very different 'bottom lines' and we therefore measured their success in different ways.

PROGRAMME 1: MAKING CONNECTIONS

Making Connections was based on the premise that:

> better informed staff = higher morale/motivation = better services = more satisfied customers.

Its target audience was middle managers – the people who inform and influence those who actually deliver the services. The managers are also the people on whom directors rely for feedback from the front line.

The programme came about because, at a time of complex challenges and continual change in local government, two departments concerned with communication – Human Resources and Public Relations – were each keen to address the manager audience.

They came together with distinct motives:

- *The 'soft' HR motive* – as a responsible and caring employer we wish to inform, involve and develop our managers.
- *The 'hard' PR motive* – our own staff are a very cost-effective means of getting messages out to the public.

There was initial conflict. To get the balance right between individuals' needs for personal development and the organization's need for better informed managers, compromises had to be made. For example, coming from PR, I wanted a corporate agenda for discussion groups, while our personnel people wanted more freedom for the groups to decide their own agenda. But Making Connections did get off the ground – and this is how it worked.

- 80 managers at a time came together for a whole day.
- The chief executive presented a corporate overview of the big issues, inviting questions.

- Two other directors 'chaired' the complete day, showing top level commitment.
- Managers were in mixed groups of eight – typically a social worker, highways engineer, accountant, headteacher, marketing manager, etc.
- Groups worked on current topics and made short presentations.
- Each group had to make their own arrangements to meet for another four half-days to work on a topic or project of their choice – some met in offices, other in pubs. One group even met on a cross-Channel ferry.
- Groups reported back to another 80-strong meeting, making presentations about their project and/or experiences of Making Connections.
- Group work was fed into the organization via directors who were each assigned an issues heading, such as communications or competitive tendering. Some, but not all of this work has altered the way we do things.

The Making Connections brand was created and used for all activities associated with the programme (Figure 34.1). Such distinctive branding is essential for recognition in a paper – intense organization.

The whole programme took more than a year – the costs in terms of materials were modest, but astronomical in terms of management time. Did it succeed and how did we measure that success?

In the early stages, measurement took the form of feedback. Delegates told us what they did and didn't like – we were able to adjust as we went along. Almost without exception, managers valued the links they made with people from other specialisms and departments and the wider view this gave them of Kent County Council. Recent research has shown that managers definitely want more of this lateral communication. They were also, through their group work, able to contribute to changing the organization. Being involved in doing something is always better than having it done to you!

Measuring whether managers and their own staff became better informed as a result of Making Connections, and whether this had a direct impact on quality of services, is probably in the 'mission impossible' category in measurement terms. But by referring back to our bottom-line aim – customer satisfaction – we had the chance to offer real proof. Kent County Council's annual consumer monitoring survey showed us at the top of MORI's local government customer care satisfaction lists. Faced with that evidence, not even the most sceptical could say we could have achieved it with ill-informed, unmotivated staff.

PROGRAMME 2: LOCAL GOVERNMENT REVIEW

The second programme's objective was a good deal more serious (at least for us) – the survival of Kent County Council. Its premise was that:

better informed staff = better informed public = more support = the survival of Kent County Council.

Figure 34.1   Making Connections letterhead

At the beginning of 1994 we fully expected to be abolished. Central government had decided that unitary or do-it-all local authorities would do a better job in country areas than the current system of two tiers. In Kent, for example, there is the one county council and 14 district councils. The Local Government Commission was set up and the expectation was that all 15 of these councils would be abolished, to be replaced by about seven unitary councils.

404   Our first staff newsletter appeared as long ago as May 1991, on the basis that

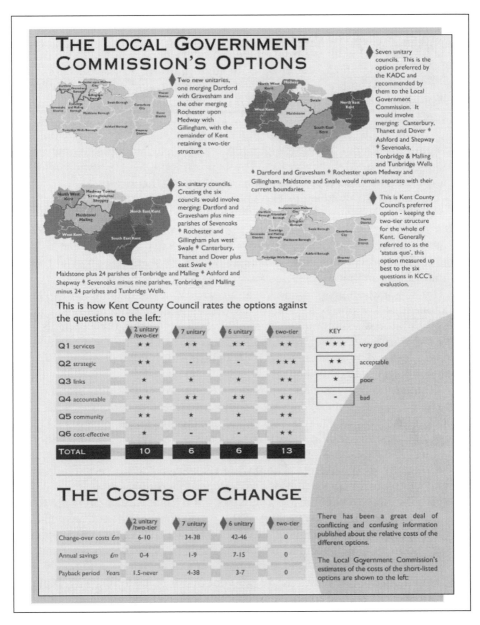

THE LOCAL GOVERNMENT COMMISSION'S OPTIONS

Two new unitaries, one merging Dartford with Gravesham and the other merging Rochester upon Medway with Gillingham, with the remainder of Kent retaining a two-tier structure.

Seven unitary councils. This is the option preferred by the KADC and recommended by them to the Local Government Commission. It would involve merging: Canterbury, Thanet and Dover ✦ Ashford and Shepway ✦ Sevenoaks, Tonbridge & Malling and Tunbridge Wells

✦ Dartford and Gravesham ✦ Rochester upon Medway and Gillingham. Maidstone and Swale would remain separate with their current boundaries.

Six unitary councils. Creating the six councils would involve merging: Dartford and Gravesham plus nine parishes of Sevenoaks ✦ Rochester and Gillingham plus west Swale ✦ Canterbury, Thanet and Dover plus east Swale ✦ Maidstone plus 24 parishes of Tonbridge and Malling ✦ Ashford and Shepway ✦ Sevenoaks minus nine parishes, Tonbridge and Malling minus 24 parishes and Tunbridge Wells.

This is Kent County Council's preferred option - keeping the two-tier structure for the whole of Kent. Generally referred to as the 'status quo', this option measured up best to the six questions in KCC's evaluation.

This is how Kent County Council rates the options against the questions to the left:

	2 unitary /two-tier	7 unitary	6 unitary	two-tier	KEY	
Q1 services	★ ★	★ ★	★ ★	★ ★	★ ★ ★	very good
Q2 strategic	★ ★	-	-	★ ★ ★	★ ★	acceptable
Q3 links	★	★	★	★ ★	★	poor
Q4 accountable	★ ★	★ ★	★ ★	★ ★	-	bad
Q5 community	★ ★	★ ★	★	★ ★		
Q6 cost-effective	★	-	-	★ ★		
TOTAL	10	6	6	13		

THE COSTS OF CHANGE

	2 unitary /two-tier	7 unitary	6 unitary	two-tier	
Change-over costs £m	6-10	34-38	42-46	0	
Annual savings £m	0-4	1-9	7-15	0	
Payback period Years	1.5-never	4-38	3-7	0	

There has been a great deal of conflicting and confusing information published about the relative costs of the different options.

The Local Government Commission's estimates of the costs of the short-listed options are shown to the left.

Figure 34.2 Extract from Local Goverment Review staff newsletter, June 1994

the least we could do was keep all staff at every level informed. We recognized from the start that we couldn't tell them what they actually wanted to know – such as would they still have a job, would there be career opportunities with new unitary councils or could they join the rising-fifties, early-retirement club and take their money and run? The best we could do was keep them up to date and let them know that we were banging on doors to get information about and influence decisions on staff issues.

Obviously, the staff were interested in every aspect of the case. But local people – whose views would be critically important to the decision-making process since the Local Government Commission had promised to listen to them – greeted the prospect of the Local Government Review with a yawn. We therefore took a conscious decision to treat staff as an information conduit to the wider public, so that when public opinion was sought they would have some level of understanding. Figure 34.2 shows one example of how we went about this in the staff newsletter. Thus our strategy for staff was twofold – to inform them and use them as a means of informing the wider public.

As the time drew near for the Local Government Commission to come to Kent, we stepped up communication with all our audiences. We were by this time going it alone: attempts to present a united front with Kent's district councils had broken down. The media became a battleground – even so we had to avoid a campaigning style, not least because we are not allowed to spend public money in that way.

The information programme began in earnest at the beginning of 1994, with staff seen as just one of a range of important audiences. Kent County Council believes internal communication should sit firmly within the Public Relations or Corporate Communication function, and that to treat internal communication as a stand-alone discipline is to belittle the contribution staff make to corporate reputation and influence.

Although targeted at different audiences, the messages and branding were consistent throughout. We wanted a fully integrated programme, with instant recognition, and no mixed messages. During 1994, we published 12 staff newsletters; two public information leaflets, delivered door-to-door; the various formal submissions to the Commission; and, of course, a vast quantity of personally written letters. There were also face-to-face meetings – from high level one-to-ones to presentations to community groups.

If staff wanted to become local activists – and there was no pressure to do so – they were given plenty of material to take to their residents' association or whatever. A Local Government Review office was set up as a focal point for information and advice and its telephone number was widely advertised.

E-mail was used often to get announcements of decisions out quickly. But as we would only reach 4000 (just 10 per cent of our staff) in this way, it played a supportive rather than a leading role.

Our commitment to staff was that we would inform them faster than the grapevine. It is a worthy objective at any time, but particularly so in the midst of acrimony between councils and a local press that, as one would expect, often went for sensational headlines rather than balanced debate.

The speed of our communication was demonstrated to best effect in June when, following submissions from all the councils, the Local Government Commission announced its draft recommendations, upon which it would consult all residents of Kent. We had an inkling of what was about to be announced and prepared a four-page newsletter. Before the announcement, copy was written and checked, and maps with a variety of boundaries prepared. DTP operators and printers were on standby.

Within minutes of the announcement final figures and maps were slotted in and a few hours later, as senior managers gathered at County Hall to hear the news at first hand from the chief executive, the first copies were ready for them to take away. Meanwhile, a carefully prepared distribution network was sending 30 000 newsletters to staff across the county.

Speed was important because the draft recommendations were not what we wanted – even though they represented a substantial achievement. Keeping the status quo (and therefore Kent County Council) had moved from being a non-starter to being one of the four options the Commission considered viable for Kent – but it was not its preferred option.

Thus the new priority of the newsletters was to make sure that when people received the Commission's own leaflet through their letterboxes, listing its preferred and other options, they ticked the right box. We couldn't and wouldn't tell our staff which box to tick, but we hoped that by keeping them fully informed they, and through them their friends and families, would reach the right conclusions. They did.

How well did we do with local people?

Of the people who responded to the Commission's questionnaire, 67 per cent said they wanted no change. This consultation was not a referendum, but the Local Government Commission had promised to listen to the views of the people and, in the face of this evidence, recommended *in October 1994* no change for Kent. We had succeeded. The fact that the government didn't like the recommendation, that the Commissioner resigned and four districts of Kent are being reviewed again at the time of going to press is another story.

Obviously we cannot isolate the role that internal communication played, amidst all the other activities, in our survival, but there is no doubt in anybody's mind that well-informed staff had made a significant contribution, knowing as we do through our consumer monitoring programme, how closely being well informed is linked to being satisfied and supportive.

How well did we do with staff?

As for the other part of our strategy, to keep staff well informed, we have a more accurate measure – our Sounding Board.

Every few months we call together about 12 people from different departments, particularly those who work away from headquarters, for example from a social services area office or a far-flung library.

We have a two-hour lunchtime session during which they report what they and their colleagues know about the big issues, how they found out and whether they felt they were kept properly informed.

The Sounding Board has highlighted serious communication problems on other issues, but staff consistently reported that they felt well informed about   *407* the Local Government Review and confident that KCC was doing its best to protect their interests.

How well did we do in general?

We clearly did succeed in bottom-line terms. The measurement of our success is that we will continue to exist – at least 10/14ths of us will and we are, at time of going to press, still fighting for the other 4/14ths.

Yes, measurement is important and gives you confirmation, credibility and clout. And lack of funds for state-of-the-art measurement techniques is no good reason for not communicating. There are other useful ways, if not as scientific, of measuring the success of internal communications. There's also faith in your own instincts and professional skills – and the hope that you are probably, after all, right in what you are doing.

35 Rover
Providing a framework for improving communication skills

Stuart Bayliss, *director, Alexander Consulting Group Communication Practice*

In less than four years, from 1988 to 1992, Rover leapt from being a disappointing (even ridiculed) manufacturer to one recognized for world-class technology and quality and for its innovative human resource practices. This rapid change – true in reality, not just in perception terms – resulted from a planned strategy, a key element of which was a complete restructuring of the company's approach to internal communication.

Today, Rover regards the development of a 'people strategy' as an integral and disciplined part of business planning. Plans, policies and processes relating to people are not seen as 'soft' issues – or, indeed, solely as 'personnel' issues. Management teams at all levels up to the main board initiate, plan and implement people-related actions. And, as with all other business disciplines, people interventions are underpinned by strategic planning and accountability – a key word in Rover's emerging success culture. As a result, people programmes at Rover now have measurable goals and performance is measured. Benchmarking has become routine, part of the company's all-embracing 'total quality' or 'continuous improvement' philosophy.

TARGETING INTERNAL COMMUNICATION

Internal communication was identified in 1988 as a significant improvement area within the people strategy (see Figure 35.1) and in 1989 the company began work with The Alexander Consulting Group. Over the next four years, Rover created and embarked on a strategy which would:

- establish benchmarks and performance improvement goals through an internal communication audit (1989)

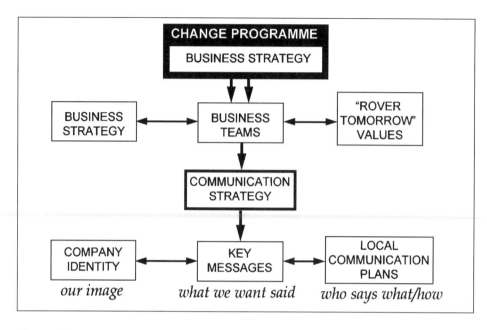

Figure 35.1   Communication strategy overview, July 1991

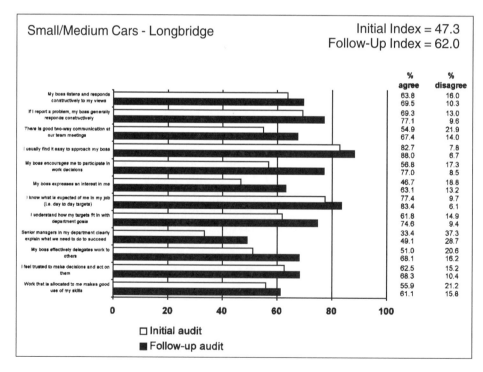

Figure 35.2   Devcom communication programme: example of follow-up audit results, 1992

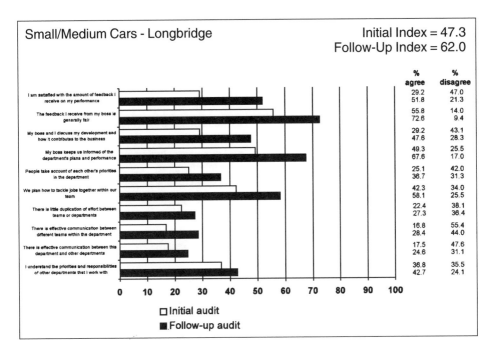

Figure 35.3 Devcom communication programme: example of follow-up audit results, 1992

- devolve ownership, design and implement robust communication strategies to management teams at all levels of the organization (1990)
- develop a high performance communication skills programme, from the bottom up, using audit benchmarks (1991 onwards) (see Figures 35.2 and 35.3)
- measure performance, track improvement trends and assist local management with their continuous communication improvement processes (1992 onwards).

PROVIDING THE RIGHT ENVIRONMENT

Armed with facts from the communication audit, it became possible to help management teams understand the communication needs in their areas, and to identify them as essential components in achieving their own business goals. That quickly led to the teams producing their own communication strategies.

It also led to their recognizing the existence of a quantifiable need to improve communication skills and behaviours. And, from 1991 onwards, it was production managers and engineers who were calling for communication skills/training programmes (see Figure 35.4). This 'demand-led' – not 'force-fed' – response to training needs created the right environment to achieve real and measurable improvement.

411

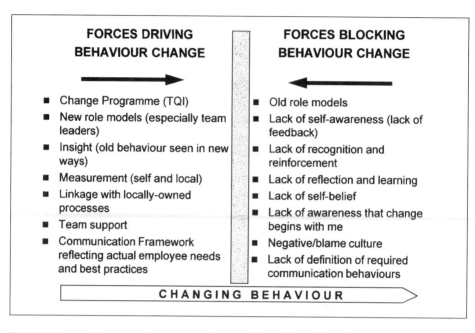

FORCES DRIVING BEHAVIOUR CHANGE →	FORCES BLOCKING BEHAVIOUR CHANGE ←
■ Change Programme (TQI)	■ Old role models
■ New role models (especially team leaders)	■ Lack of self-awareness (lack of feedback)
■ Insight (old behaviour seen in new ways)	■ Lack of recognition and reinforcement
■ Measurement (self and local)	■ Lack of reflection and learning
■ Linkage with locally-owned processes	■ Lack of self-belief
■ Team support	■ Lack of awareness that change begins with me
■ Communication Framework reflecting actual employee needs and best practices	■ Negative/blame culture
	■ Lack of definition of required communication behaviours

CHANGING BEHAVIOUR ⟩

Figure 35.4   Devcom: forces driving and blocking behaviour change

WHY A SKILLS PROGRAMME WAS NEEDED

In employee surveys the communication skills associated with face-to-face, routine interactions at work are always identified as a key weakness. The trouble is, research also shows that little progress has been made in the last two decades.

Why is this? Not for lack of effort or investment – many companies have responded to surveys by introducing formal mechanisms such as team briefings, and endless top-down campaigns. But the fact is, these sorts of programmes never can succeed in reshaping communication behaviour – the root cause of the problem.

It all boils down to one simple question: 'Why should any employee who receives poor communication from managers and colleagues most hours of the working day and week, suddenly be expected to support, positively and enthusiastically, the weekly briefing or other formal communication channels?'. It simply isn't common sense. And the basis of Rover's 'high performance communication' *is* common sense – getting the basics right.

Figure 35.5 provides a breakdown of the complete learning process.

How Rover's programme works

A core train-the-trainer programme, designed using detailed data from the audit, is made available to management teams. They vote on whether or not to

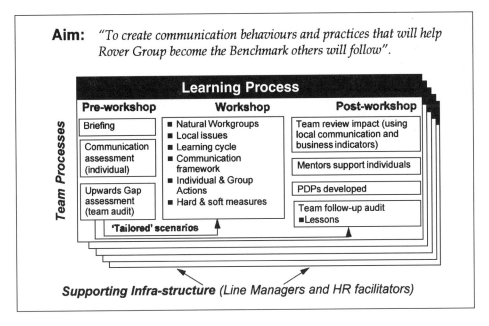

Figure 35.5   Devcom: concept overview

'buy' it. Nothing is mandatory: if they don't like it, they don't have to buy it. It is the communication team's job to explain and encourage buy-in.

If a team votes for the programme, the first stage is for consultants, working with the managers involved, to tailor the course content to include issues that are live locally.

Volunteers from any level are then trained, having first been assessed for suitability for training others. They then pass on what they have learned to mixed groups of employees in a monitored process.

At Rover's Longbridge plant, a large, complex site, it took six months to cover 1000 senior operators, team leaders and junior middle managers. Each unit sets up its own benchmarks against which improvements are measured.

The training itself concerns communication 'basics' in five key areas:

- job-related
- performance feedback
- attitude and behaviour
- group skills
- inter-group cooperation.

The training begins by examining apparently straightforward (though over-looked) routines such as job coaching, checking understanding and agreeing standards. It then turns to more difficult, one-to-one skills such as communi-cating with good and bad performers, listening and responding, and career counselling.

The course then moves on to group skills. Again using audit data as a guide, the training concentrates on breaking down barriers within *and* between groups. The latter is a difficult area: we know of no survey in recent years where employees were more than 30–40 per cent positive about lateral communications.

The training produces practical outputs (solutions) as well as improvements in skills. Participants tackle real problems. The approach has been described by one manager as 'the basics of minute-by-minute communication'.

HOW IS IT WORKING OUT?

The strategies surrounding improved communication at Rover were built to be robust rather than showy. Accountability remains vital – there is a strong belief that 'what gets measured, gets done'. Surveys of performance, employee opinions and internal communication have been carried out: all show significant gains. More important still, processes have been put in place to ensure that these are not temporary but incremental gains.

36 SmithKline Beecham Communication strategy for acquisition and integration

Toby Maloney, *vice-president and director of internal communication and services*

In October 1994, the IC function at SmithKline Beecham was asked to develop a communication programme for a major acquisition. Its first step was to take a critical look at what the organization had done in the past when confronted with similar challenges. This case study takes you through ten lessons it learned and acted on.

We are fortunate at SmithKline Beecham. Our senior management has always looked to the internal communication function as a strategic resource when planning, developing and implementing organizational change.

We started by reviewing our efforts at the time of the merger of SmithKline and Beecham in 1989 to identify key learning points and opportunities for improvement. Although the process of reviewing one's earlier efforts requires a thick skin and a true belief in continuous improvement, we felt it was an excellent way to develop a more effective strategy.

So what did we learn and how did we improve our efforts to communicate complex information to a global audience of 54 000 employees?

1. Review your previous efforts and look outside to see how other companies dealt with similar challenges before launching new initiatives

We learned many valuable lessons from work that we had done at the time of the merger of SmithKline and Beecham in 1989. In hindsight, some of them should have been obvious but they weren't. At a time of dramatic change, the symbols and language that you use to communicate take on immense importance. In 1989, we were merging two companies that had their headquarters in the UK and the USA. Do you use American or English spelling and style in your communications? How do you treat symbols that have great meaning for your audiences? Do you communicate directly to all employees or do you use a cascade system? Do you create a centrally-produced newsletter or is there a better way to deliver timely information? These are just a few of the myriad questions that we were better able to answer because we spent the time reviewing our previous efforts and truly learned from some of our earlier mistakes.

We also used outside consultants and research from our trade associations (including IABC among others) to determine how other best practice companies were handling some of these challenges.

2. Make sure you have a clear understanding of what you're attempting to achieve and that you have a strong link to senior management

One of the most important elements of our success was that we had a strong link with senior management and an effective system of sharing information between the communication team and the senior management team that was leading the integration effort. We also developed a clear picture of our charter, objectives and deliverables.

At a time of enormous, rapid change, there was a reliable process for sharing information between the two teams and an ability to adapt the role of the communication team as necessary, which at times seemed to be an almost daily occurrence. Easy access to decision-makers made our task much easier. We had two key 'champions' at the senior level who gave us strong support.

3. Put the right team together and you're halfway there

Putting the right team together is never easy, but it's the way to go. By forming a special team that cuts across the organization, you are most likely to be able to get a range of cross-discipline skills necessary for success.

As a team leader attempting to manage workloads, priorities and egos against tight deadlines, you will need Solomon-like wisdom in putting a team together, but the pay-off is enormous. Make sure that you have basic skills, including project management, information systems, writing skills, etc., covered for smoother sailing. Demonstrated ability to work on a team is another important skill that isn't always easy to find.

Elicit all the counsel you can at this stage. We took full advantage of tapping into a team of experts from existing staff and outside specialists. In addition, we used secondees from other parts of the company who were an essential part of the team's success. Don't be afraid to ask for the resources you need to get the job done.

4. Make sure your flow of information is continuous and that there is a vehicle for two-way communication

By looking back to earlier efforts, we were able to avoid making some of the same mistakes twice. Specifically, we learned the importance of generating a continuous flow of information, so we attempted to build a communication process built on a cascade of information.

At the time of the earlier merger, there were periods when we didn't communicate anything and as a result employees filled in the blanks themselves. Long periods without any information provide fertile breeding grounds for rumours, so we regularly communicated with employees and created an ongoing information stream. The Integration Update bulletins shown in Figure 36.1 were an important part of this effort. We also established an Open Line that enabled employees to flag concerns and rumours and to identify issues that we could address in our various communication vehicles.

5. Build on existing systems and cultural expectations

In SmithKline Beecham, the lowly bulletin system is a highly-effective communication tool that employees look to for information. Aware of the impact of this system, we built much of our global communication on this solid foundation, but with an improvement.

We created special *Integration News* bulletin paper to help alert readers to this 'special' news that might have a substantial impact on the company and on them. More important than this step, however, was our decision to use a cascade system for all important news. We identified nearly 600 key managers worldwide who received Cascade Packs that included advance bulletins, organizational charts and Q&As that would help them answer questions about the many changes taking place. All of these materials were distributed 24 hours prior to releasing the bulletins for the all-employee audience.

This approach solved the problem of line managers knowing no more than their employees and gave them an excellent opportunity to provide context for the changes that were occurring.

6. Establish specific measures to monitor your success

We quickly established four key performance indicators (timeliness, credibility, consistency and planning) and measures of success that we used throughout the process to determine the impact of our efforts.

Our measures of success were very specific and included a turnaround time for approvals from our senior management of 24 hours. Although we didn't always meet our goal, we had a clear standard that we were working toward. We also set a goal that all of our managers around the world would receive briefings within five days of a decision or event. Again, the important learning was to establish clearly objectives against which we would be judged. A popular saying at our company is 'If you're not keeping score, you're just practising', and we attempted to keep score for every key element of our work.

417

Figure 36.1 *Integration Update* **bulletins**

7. Selecting the appropriate medium is an important part of successful message delivery

418   In addition to the global bulletin system, we evaluated all potential ways of communicating to determine how we could best ensure that our messages would reach the targeted audiences in the most effective way.

We analysed the products available to us and evaluated their key features, when to use them and the type of message that they are best suited for. Cascade Briefings, which we used extensively, had the advantage of empowering line managers to answer questions and made them a participant rather than just an observer of the changes that were taking place. The Cascade Briefings included a full information package and allowed greater detail to be given to the managers. They also allowed individual managers to deliver messages in their particular style before bulletins were posted for all employees. We also considered how existing management publications and dedicated newsletters could be used to deliver our messages.

8.   Don't be afraid to try innovative approaches

In the past when special communication needs arose, we would produce special newsletters centrally to cover the issues in more depth. The end product was a solid, informative publication but if often took so long that we were delivering old news.

This time we relied more heavily on a combination of electronic mail delivery of cascade kits and locally-produced newsletters that followed a centrally-developed template. The end result was a much higher level of local ownership, accurate translations and a much faster turnaround time. The locally-produced approach for newsletters was adopted with some trepidation as we had no idea what the response would be on a global basis. By the end of the project we had more than 30 newsletters in multiple languages that followed the standard template but included local context and positioning.

9.   Continue to reinforce your key messages

From the outset, we had a clear strategic message that we wanted employees to understand and that our chief executive was repeating throughout the organization at every opportunity. We were making these organizational changes to ensure that we were creating a world-class customer-driven company, that we were aligning our cost-structure to the competitive environment and that our emphasis was on developing pioneer products and services.

In addition to working these messages into our communication effort, we made a determined attempt to show that the integration effort was a planned process and that open, timely communication was a hallmark of this process.

10.   Use daily meetings to build your core team's effectiveness

Throughout the process, our core team met almost every morning to share information, review priorities and balance the workload. An almost immediate outgrowth of this daily meeting was the establishment of a team spirit that was at the core of our success. We truly were able to move far beyond merely meet-   *419* ing our objectives to working as a team where spontaneous problem-solving and true teamwork became the norm.

The use of the daily meeting has now evolved to become a fundamental part of our routine operations.

37 WH Smith Retail
Employee-generated TV ... or is it? A practical guide to running a video magazine

Angela Newman, WOW TV/Bright Ideas coordinator

The magazine format – whether in print or on screen – remains one of the most flexible and motivating available to the IC professional. Making it more interactive, to reflect and support the greater involvement being sought by almost all organizations, is among the biggest challenges being faced by forward-thinking producer/editors. This case study on WH Smith's Wow TV not only gives an insight into every aspect of handling a video magazine, but assesses whether genuine employee involvement is possible.

Why did we start WOW TV? Because we had a gap – a motivation gap. Bridge it through involvement, communication and just plain fun, we thought, and we could improve the working environment and build towards the business need for enthusiastic and happy staff. And I do believe that motivation, while hard to measure, is being increased by WOW TV (Figure 37.1).

We also had barriers – geographical barriers. WH Smith Retail is spread over some 450 sites; most are retail branches, four are head office buildings. What happens in Bognor Regis may go unseen in Gateshead. What happens in a branch may not be understood at head office and vice versa: there was a divide.

Certainly, our long-running communications weren't hitting the right spot. Neither *Intercoms*, a group-wide newspaper detailing products and promotions, nor other paper-based methods were bringing the retail business alive or opening the doors to two-way communication, giving the opportunity for everyone to be involved.

Yet that was the very thing we wanted: to involve everyone in a regular communication, updating them on the latest developments and issues of interest. We also wanted to produce something that could be honest and fun and

Figure 37.1   Another edition of WOW TV at the production studio

balanced. From the smallest WH Smith branch to the most recent book award, we needed to bring people together, regardless of location or position, with a means of communication accessible to all.

We decided on a magazine in video form and today WOW TV is generally seen as a valuable resource. It is well liked by most – probably because it is an investment for everyone.

WHAT ARE THE ISSUES?

First and foremost: the cost

Video is not a cheap option – but you are paying for its effectiveness. Each edition can cost £15–20k. But don't reel from the horror of this – you are investing in time, professional editing, directing, two days of filming with an experienced crew, to name but a few. When divided among our personnel, the cost per person, per edition is approximately £1, and well worth it for the impact.

Different corporate video production companies will give alternative amounts of film days/edit times. We find two days sufficient to film everything we need for a 15-minute video.

Part of the cost is the facility to play videos. All our branches and head office sites already had access to video-playing equipment: the transition was not needed. Obviously, the initial cost is heightened if video-recorders have to be purchased.

Outside resources

Resources also include coordination. When we began, we simply moved from one edition to the next – though using the same video company, in our case Jacaranda, each time. We learned through experience. After 12 editions, we took stock of what was happening. We decided a contract was needed for consistency and value. And a permanent resource, in the form of a coordinator, for practicality and commitment. Dedication was necessary to make the most of our investment.

Over time we have built a good relationship with the production company. With the creation of a contract, Jacaranda's Caroline Gray has been permanently assigned to produce/direct WOW TV and forward planning is made all the easier through this commitment.

We now have a bank of film days – for one edition we may need only one, for another three. The bottom line is that we allocate 12 film days in total for six editions. This works well. That said, I would recommend that the ad hoc basis is good to start with, while a contract has the all-round long-term benefits necessary for consistency and a fuller understanding. The production company needs to understand your business to make a successful magazine: they don't just edit, they create a programme from the basic stories; they build a picture from your plan. Figure 37.2 shows contents lists for two past editions of the video magazine.

The in-house resource

Our personnel department could not give the much-needed time to WOW TV as busy schedules were already being juggled. Therefore I was seconded in on a year's contract from a branch.

Why me? I represent our majority of personnel from the branch front of the business. Why a secondee? After a year, someone else can take over, giving a new look to WOW TV and keeping the video fresh and alive.

This works for us and has proved successful. Necessarily I have another personnel function, namely administering the staff suggestion scheme. The balance is probably 40/60 in favour of the latter. WOW has bursts of activity and then lulls (mainly during distribution) but it did require a new position in personnel. Tagging it to someone's current responsibilities does a disservice to the financial investment a video demands.

All my video 'know-how' was learned on the job. How to coordinate is all down to internal PR and communication. It's a question of enthusiasm balanced with realism. You need to know everything that is happening in your business and liaise with key people (internal and external) to draw up a schedule of features.

WOW TV 4

INTRODUCTION

INTERVIEW WITH THE NEW CHAIRMAN

WAREHOUSE: day in the life of a skip (carries products from warehouse to branches)

COMPETITION: special leaflet going in a skip, branch to receive it gets a prize

TRAINING: inside look at a training course at our training centre Milton Hill, Abingdon

MIND BOGGLING BOOKS: presentation of children's book award.
Interview/chat with Andy & Tony CBBC

VICTORIA ISLAND BRANCH: chat with manager about station trading.
Staff and customer comments

WH SMITH CHARITY OF THE YEAR FEATURE

BRITT EKLAND: book signing

VIDEOS: D-Day video

TRADING PERFORMANCE UPDATE

WOW HOTLINE PHONE NUMBER

WOW TV 12

INTRODUCTION

VIDEO: latest clips

DID YOU KNOW? . . . short interesting fact about WH Smith

MULTIMEDIA: visit Microsoft

NATIONAL LOTTERY: public views.
Interviews with coordinators at WH Smith

EPOS III: new till system: staff and trainer views

DID YOU KNOW? . . . another interesting fact

GIFT VOUCHERS AND BOOK TOKENS: feature

HOW DO THEY DO THAT?: behind the scenes at EMI CD factory

COMPETITION: call WOW Hotline with the answer

Figure 37.2   Programme contents of two editions of WOW TV

You need to organize delivery of the tapes – we do this via our internal mail – and WOW TV is returned once watched to be recycled. There is an edition every six weeks, which is planned into the branch weekly training sessions and head office meetings.

BUT IS WOW TV TWO-WAY?

When I took on the role of coordinator I contacted everyone I could think of. I wrote to all the key head office departments and put features in the in-house magazines. I hoped to involve everyone: let them tell me what's happening and what they want on WOW TV. In addition, we have a WOW TV Hotline answerphone for comments and suggestions.

I formed my plan for the year's editions around the response and, to be honest, 95 per cent came from head office managers detailing key dates and promotions. A couple of branches invited us to visit ... but not much else. A request for presenters on WOW TV produced a huge response from the 'young and the beautiful'. I clearly wasn't touching our core personnel (no personal affront intended).

As the year passed, branches and individuals did begin to send in footage. Invitations to branches often have to be turned down – distance being of the essence on a two single-day film schedule. There has to be a reason for visiting a branch to film, for example a new promotion, but this limits us to the big and the beautiful.

We tend to trail our initiatives in our high profile shops:

Reading: *The Fun Zone*
Holborn Circus: *Project Enliven*
Brent Cross: *Computerized customer order processing*

We therefore tend to go to the same sort of shops. So I went for the phrase 'If we can't come to you you can come to us'. This inspired two or three branches to send in footage.

EMPLOYEE-GENERATED? STILL NOT QUITE

We have all the intentions to be employee-generated but haven't quite hit the balance. I therefore encourage shop personnel to get involved. For example we ask staff what they think of new initiatives when we visit branches. But then we are accused of 'scripting' people. Of course, we never tell anyone to make a positive comment, but put a camera under someone's nose in the knowledge that the footage will be seen by everyone at WH Smith Retail ... what do you expect? What they really think, what they think we are asking them to say, who knows?

We're also accused of the opposite – that we're looking out for negative comment. It's usually because most initiatives improve an outdated system and therefore comments are often positive at that early stage. Later, problems become more apparent and people are in a position to evaluate. Then the recommendations come forward for further change.

We recently filmed staff using our new EPOS till system. 'It's brilliant' was the phrase ... and it is, compared to before. Who can argue? It's only later that suggestions begin to come in via the suggestion scheme. We don't look for problems, we don't want to depress ... we try to get honesty. We should try harder.

SO, WHO OWNS WOW TV?

The answer to the question is still everyone, but this is hard to convey. This is where communication comes in ... if we choose to do a marketing feature, we make it an insight into a new product – not a training feature on how to sell it. Editorial ownership lies with me and a suggestion for WOW is not a guarantee of exposure. WOW is a magazine and should be treated as such. Getting people to recognize this is not so easy.

On taking up my role I led discussion groups across the company to discuss and measure the success of WOW TV. We aim to follow this up with regular feedback forms and increased use of the Hotline. Misguidedly, it appears that 'WOW TV' has become the generic term for any internal training video made (though realistically the balance is probably 80/20 in favour of those who see it as a magazine rather than a training tool). Then again, we had a comment that it was 'communication to the masses'. Employee-generated TV ... well, er ... not exactly. It all underlines the fact that while the intention is still commendable, there is a lot of work to be done.

WHAT AM I GOING TO DO ABOUT IT?

WOW TV is close to people's hearts but can't please everyone. Therefore it must have 'something for everyone' in each edition not 'everything for someone'. I find this is the best way to approach it without chasing round in circles to fulfil an impossibility.

Planning is going to take an even bigger role, with meetings a month before filming to draw up the contents of the next programme, ideally more than one edition in advance. The schedule for 1995/96 is set out in Figure 37.3. Fitting WOW to key points in our retailing year will give it a defined business purpose. A video programme must stay in people's minds and consistency is the key.

Edition	Shoot week commencing	Promotional material required w/c	Postroom Greenbridge	In branch/ head office	Shown w/c
14	05/06/95	12/06/95	19/06/95	22/06/95	26/06/95
15	17/07/95	24/07/95	03/08/95	07/08/95	14/08/95
16	28/08/95	04/09/95	18/09/95	20/09/95	25/09/95
17	09/10/95	16/10/95	30/10/95	01/11/95	06/11/95
18	13/11/95	20/11/95	04/12/95	06/12/95	11/12/95
19	08/01/96	15/01/96	29/01/96	31/01/96	05/02/96
20	26/02/96	04/03/96	18/03/96	20/03/96	25/03/96
21	15/04/96	23/04/96	06/05/96	08/05/96	13/05/96

Figure 37.3   WOW TV schedule 1995/6

Regular marked sections, such as 'introduction' or 'products' help greatly, but ultimately there needs to be flexibility to keep the video fresh and exciting.

Work will continue in close contact with the production company, one of the main benefits of a long-term business relationship. However, we should not rest on our laurels. Always be aware of what others have to offer. We recently looked at satellite business television – a new concept in broadcasting but returned to our video format with renewed conviction that we had the best option for our needs. Video is flexible. It can be shown at any time, in any branch, if standard training times are not convenient, or taken home to watch.

The key is to know your business, know what you want from the communication and shop around.

Then you need to market it. We have T-shirts printed with our logo which are sometimes popular. I have just introduced a WOW Hotline poster to give the phone number a higher profile and to encourage more employee involvement. We will soon see a new feature – *Branch Diary* – put into action, with branches/head office departments being given a camcorder for a month and filming their own feature. This will be followed through with an invitation to the edit suite.

WE ARE ON OUR WAY TO EMPLOYEE-GENERATED TV!

I firmly believe that employee-generated TV can happen, but it will be within constraints. We are retailers, not TV personalities. Individuals can give up only so much time to take part in WOW TV – travelling and filming involve time and money. There has to be a point to it all. If we don't learn from it then it becomes a series of 'jollies' – dabbling in the camcorder hobby. It is not like a school magazine. WOW TV isn't a vehicle for learning journalistic skills. That's not what WH Smith's is about. WOW TV is concerned with communication, motivation and keeping us up to date and in touch. And helping every individual to feel part of the whole. Employee involvement in WOW TV is part of that, but it is a professionally-made means of communication, not jollification. If we learn from it, it's worth it.

Asked for conclusion, I'd say employee-generated TV is about achieving a balance, not a complete liberalization. It's an idealistic concept that has to fit into a working environment where actions must be justified and budget holders are accountable. There is no room for the frivolous in employee-generated TV, but plenty of room for fun.

38 Unigate Dairies
Supporting first-line managers in a change environment

Roy Johnson *of PACE Ltd*

Hit by demographic changes in its traditional doorstep market-place, Unigate Dairies Limited decided to turn its milk delivery employees into a network of franchisees. It saw quickly that a critical factor for success would be the attitudes and behaviours of its sales managers – especially how they would handle communication with their former team members, now semi-independent and regarded by the business as customers.

To help these managers adjust to the new situation, Unigate Dairies worked with the Oxfordshire-based consultancy PACE, specialists in applying Neuro Linguistic Programming techniques to improve people's performance potential.

That doorstep delivery of milk is a much-loved British institution was confirmed by the outcry which followed an EC suggestion that it should be stopped. But while a European Directive may not bring about its demise, fierce price competition and changes in buying patterns have resulted in a decline in doorstep sales in recent years.

Among those facing up to that challenge in the 1990s has been Unigate Dairies Limited, the liquid milk producing division of Unigate plc. Unigate Dairies employs about 4500 people, and is one of the best known milk suppliers in the south of England. Its doorstep operation supplies around 1.3 million households most days of the week, delivering milk and a range of other high quality products.

Determined to halt the decline in doorstep sales, Unigate decided on franchising as a way of motivating staff afresh, by spreading a greater sense of involvement in the business. The plan was to move to an 80 per cent fully franchised business over a period of four years.

Until the switch, Unigate's sales managers had each run an operation servicing between 25 and 40 milk rounds. They spent most of their time handling logistics, their management style based on the philosophy that 'whatever else happens, the milk must go out'.

In the new environment, by contrast, their job would be to motivate a group of quasi-independent businesspeople – to help them set goals, plan and sell effectively. In other words, they would have to learn to become leaders rather than controllers.

REVELATIONS AT THE RESEARCH STAGE

Initial research led to the identification of eight competencies that would be needed by managers in the new setting:

- goal-directed behaviour
- proactivity
- efficiency orientation
- influencing skills
- positive regard
- timeliness
- adaptability
- performance observation.

Unigate's own employee development staff worked closely with PACE to verify these competencies and to design a training programme that would deliver the results required.

The process began with interviews with the sales managers individually and in groups. Some were able to achieve high scores on the competencies immediately; others had lower scores at this stage. When the differences between the two groups were analysed, it seemed the most effective managers were able to articulate a vision of where their home delivery centre was going in the future.

Interestingly from the Neuro Linguistic Programming (NLP) point of view, the two managers who came out top in this area would always look up and to the right in order to describe the visual picture they had of their depot in the future... 'This will be here, that will be there' etc. They could describe in detail what they were seeing in their mind's eye, having compared it with the present and judged whether progression to the vision was viable. Indeed, it turned out, they would carry on this internal exercise when at home, driving the car or whatever, and then use their supervisors and front-line people as sounding boards for their theories.

Those without this ability responded in one of two ways. Some looked straight down into their own feeling (yes – down and to the right) and responded along the lines of 'You can't possibly have a long-term view in this business – we're concerned with managing day to day events'. Others had an incomplete vision: they could see the picture of the future but had no means of checking within themselves that this was right.

429

At the end of the verification and assessment process therefore, a ninth competency for managers was added – *breadth of vision.*

CREATING A PROGRAMME

The next step was to pull together this group of apparently disparate competencies into a development programme. The key lay in recognizing that what was required was a change in attitudes and behaviour rather than conceptual skills; moreover that the managers were practical people, unused to an academic environment, who would respond best to examples that would be relevant to their jobs.

Phase one was designed to provide 'a watershed event' that would mark the transition from one mode of behaviour to another. It emerged as a four-day induction programme, which started with a surprise outdoor activity – 'Expect the unexpected' – in which teams had to navigate their way through an obstacle course in the New Forest. The object was to stimulate people to re-think some of their beliefs before tackling the technical aspects of the move to franchising. It also encouraged managers to begin to exercise some of the competencies.

Four phases of competency training followed, spaced out over a couple of months.

- Developing vision   1.5 days
- Vision to action   2 days
- Negotiating for success   1.5 days
- Creating change through people   1.5 days

NLP techniques of understanding verbal and non-verbal behaviour were a key to the goals and levels of success in all modules.

Developing vision

This phase of the programme began by helping managers form a clear picture of how their sales areas might develop over the next two years (literally by drawing pictures: many of these creations were taken back to the depots and pinned on walls to stimulate interest among teams). They went on to learn how to plan ways to involve and communicate to their people, using them to help refine the vision, and to develop short-term goals that would introduce change step by step. Finally, they pictured potential problems and thought through and specified necessary contingency plans.

Vision to action

The 'vision to action' phase helped managers develop plans that would balance risk and return and gave them an up-to-date appreciation of performance and progress towards their long-term goals. They learned to decide priorities

---

5. LEADERSHIP

Leader	Manager
Innovates	Administers
Focus on people*	Focus on systems and structure
Inspires trust	Relies on controls
Long term view	Short term view

(from Warren Bennis)

We would add:-

Creates vision	Devises operating plan
Proactive	Reactive

Exercise 7: Leader and manager

Outcome: Understanding aspects of the Franchise Manager's job.

Consider to what extent a Franchise Manager will need to operate as a leader, and/or as a manager, and which parts of the job fall into each category

....
....
....
....
....
....

* Focus on people means being aware of their <u>personal goals.</u> It means knowing why they want to be franchisees and what they hope to GAIN from it. Establishing these goals can be time consuming at first. It needs a <u>proactive</u> LEADER. But once established, your ability to INFLUENCE will be greater.

Figure 38.1　Leadership sheet

systematically, to delegate authority to others and in doing so, to manage their time effectively.

Negotiating for success

This phase trained managers in methods of negotiation where both parties have the opportunity of achieving their goals and satisfying their interests. It　*431* gave them the skills to read commitment, confidence, understanding and agreement in the non-verbal behaviours of others. It showed them how to build a success path for individuals by agreeing achievable goals and taking supportive action – though in the case of consistently low performers, escalating to strong action if cooperation was not returned. Figure 38.1 (see page 431) gives an idea of some of the materials used in this phase.

Exercise 5: Influencing Styles 1

Outcome: To identify your current and most used influencing style.

For each question, tick the choice that most accurately describes your activities. Make one choice only for each question. ("Usually", "Often", "Sometimes" or "Seldom").

	Usually	Often	Some times	Seldom
1. I supervise subordinates closely in order to get better work from them.				
2. I believe that since I carry the ultimate responsibility, subordinates must accept my decisions.				
3. I establish controls to ensure that subordinates are getting the job done.				
4. I show subordinates my goals and objectives and sell them on the merit of my plans.				
5. I support spontaneous but unauthorised decisions made by subordinates.				
6. I make sure that subordinates' major workload is planned for them.				
7. I check with subordinates frequently to see whether they need help.				
8. I push my people to meet schedules if necessary.				
9. I step in as soon as anything indicates that the job is slipping.				
10. I hold frequent meetings to keep in touch with what is going on.				

©: Unigate/PACE (Performance & Communication Enterprises) Ltd. 1990
Franchise Managers Training Programme
24

Figure 38.2   Exercise sheet: influencing style

Creating change through people

The emphasis of this phase was on the process of introducing and managing a change. It explored managers' own responses to change as a first step to facilitating others and developed skills needed for working on change with groups and with individuals. It offered ways to develop rapport by matching other people's values, to manage feelings (the manager's own and other peoples') during times of change, and to communicate changes that the manager wants to make, both up and down the line. Figure 38.2 (see page 432) provides an example of an exercise on influencing style

One of the tasks of the sales manager is to meet the prospective franchisee's partner to explain and discuss the impact of the change on the family. Role-playing possible discussions and their outcomes provided an enjoyable way of getting issues across.

Two more phases of competency training were added later. 'Successful business reviews' was designed to demonstrate appraisal and coaching skills when it became clear that the regular monthly business review between manager and franchisee was emerging as a central plank in the management process.

The second addition – 'Managing the conversion' – was built around a model of best practice resulting from a case study of managers who were most successful in converting managed milk round staff into franchisees. Now managers can evaluate their own performance against the model before, during and after the programme and as a result form action plans in the form of SMART (Specific, Measurable, Attainable, Relevant, Trackable) goals that are followed through and supported on an individual basis.

The complete training period was designed to last three months, with each module building on results and experience resulting from the one before and from 'hands on' experience in the depot. All modules were run away from the work environment so people could relax and concentrate without distraction. Case studies, video feedback, mini-lectures and project work all form part of the training process. The use of role plays was critical, allowing managers to experiment and rehearse new skills in a safe environment. The *Franchise Manager's Handbook* provided programme notes and a users' guide (Figure 38.3).

As a whole, the programme was designed to draw on managers' wits, abilities, strengths and existing skills – as well as adding new ones. The object was to encourage each person to change by becoming more aware of their strengths and to develop confidence in using these strengths more effectively.

WHAT WAS THE OUTCOME?

The results of the programme speak for themselves. By the second year of the programme, the decline in annual doorstep milk sales had been significantly arrested. Sales of other goods had increased between 25 and 50 per cent.

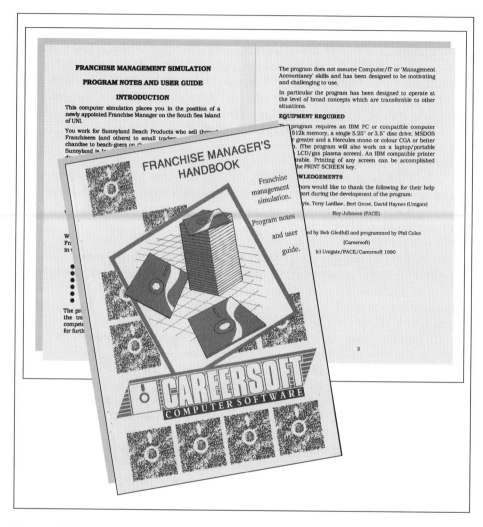

Figure 38.3   *Franchise Manager's Handbook*

Regular customer surveys indicated an improvement in the daily services. And a turnover of 5 per cent of franchisees compared favourably with that of 35 per cent for managed sales staff. Among the sales managers themselves, turnover was down to 4 per cent. Moreover, costs were effectively reduced through a lowering of the ratio of support to operational staff to 1.3 to 1. Indeed, Unigate publicly attributed the improved profitability of the company in part to the changes in attitude and behaviour of this key group of managers within the business. And finally, the programme modules have since been broadened and redesigned to be used as generic management training modules elsewhere in Unigate plc.

434   Terry Mills, Unigate's Employment Development Manager, describes the

winning of a National Training Award in 1993 for the programme as an 'added bonus' to achievements on the ground. 'We wanted to equip our sales managers with the skills to recruit franchisees who show potential and calibre, and then to educate, guide and motivate them at every stage of their development,' says Terry, 'helping them through the challenging transition from employed to self-employed and ultimately, to handling the demands of this difficult market-place.'

Index